Maida Heatter's
Book of
Great Desserts

MAIDA HEATTER'S

BOOK
OF GREAT
DESSERTS

Drawings by Toni Evins

ALFRED A. KNOPF   NEW YORK   1982

Some of these recipes have been printed in *The
New York Times*, the Miami *Herald*, the Miami Beach
Sun, Craig Claiborne's Journal, and *Woman's Day*.
Chocolate Mousse Heatter (p. 339) originally appeared in
House & Garden. Mildred Knopf's Orange Puff Cake
(page 107) is from *The Perfect Hostess Cookbook*, by
Mildred O. Knopf. Reprinted with permission of
Alfred A. Knopf, Inc.

Library of Congress Cataloging in Publication Data

Heatter, Maida.   Book of great desserts.

1. Desserts.   I. Title.
TX773.H35   1974   641.8'6   73–20764
ISBN 0–394–49111–4

Manufactured in the United States of America
Published October 15, 1975
Reprinted Seven Times
Ninth Printing, March 1982

Contents

List of Illustrations

Acknowledgments

People often ask me how I started to cook, and I'm startled. It was so natural, part of life. That was because of my mother, a most unusual woman. She could do almost anything and did everything well. She was a great cook and true gourmet. Every meal was an occasion . . . the menu planned with care, the table set beautifully and arranged with an artist's eye. Whether or not she had help, she did most of the cooking herself because she loved it. And she imparted that love to me. We were very close and there was hardly a day that we didn't talk, either in person or on the telephone, usually about food. For me, life's problems seem less important and easier to cope with while trussing a chicken, chopping onions, kneading a yeast dough, or icing a cake. And all seems well to me when popovers and soufflés rise to magnificent heights. My mother taught me that cooking is an act of love—and a beautiful, mountainous escape.

My mother taught me my philosophy of cooking; but for an endless supply of tropical, Southern, and native recipes—many of which have become my favorites and are included in this collection—I am deeply grateful to my mother-in-law, Mrs. Thelma Langford of Jacksonville, Florida.

And finally, I want to thank my husband, Ralph Daniels, for his help in making this book possible. During the years I worked on these recipes, I was generally in a world of my own. I was not much company and could take very little time for us to go places and do things. Physically I was stuck in the kitchen and mentally I was preoccupied with the recipes. If he had not been so patient and tolerant, if he had demanded more of my time and attention, if he had not encouraged me all the way, I could never have finished this book.

Introduction

This is not intended to be a complete book of every dessert recipe. Most of these are desserts that I prepared daily for many years. They were for my husband's restaurant, but I made them in my kitchen at home and Ralph transported them twice a day. You will find that the number of servings indicated will provide large portions—because that is what the customers wanted. And since it was important to have desserts that would remain fresh so that they would still be good at dinner if they weren't all eaten at lunch, there is an abundance of recipes that can be made ahead of time. I hope you won't be disappointed if you look for something (such as a fruit pie for instance) and find that it is not included, but that is probably the reason.

I kept a daily chart of the number of portions of each dessert sold at the restaurant each day, and just as a matter of interest Raspberry-Strawberry Bavarian was always the leader. Chocolate Mousse Heatter came in second, and Black-and-White Cheesecake and Queen Mother's Cake tied for third.

I have cooked and tested every one of the recipes in this book over and over so that they are worked out perfectly. But in order for these recipes to work for you as they do for me, it is of the utmost importance that you follow every direction exactly. Many instructions might seem trivial, arbitrary, or unimportant, but there really is a practical reason for everything.

If a recipe says to line a cookie sheet with aluminum foil, it is not because I am a fuddy-duddy and care about keeping cookie sheets clean. The foil is essential to keep the cookies from sticking. In some recipes, such as Oatmeal Wafers or Benne Seed Wafers, you would encounter disaster without the foil. With it, if you are like me, you will squeal with joy at the ease, fun, and satisfying excitement of peeling the foil from the smooth, shiny backs of the cookies.

If a recipe includes directions to refrigerate for at least 10 hours or longer (see Flan), it is because the custard would collapse if it were served sooner. With adequate baking and chilling time it will hold its shape like a smooth cheesecake, and serving it (to say nothing of eating it) will be a sensuous thrill.

If Pecan Buttercrunch is not allowed to stand for the specified time after it comes out of the oven, it will ooze when you try to cut it into portions. And if the Brownies are cut too soon they will squash.

I could go on and on, but please, take my word for it. Read the recipes carefully and follow them exactly.

I wish you good luck with this book. I have had pleasure, satisfaction, moments of pride, and even some of sheer ecstasy with these recipes. And I wish you the same.

Maida Heatter

Maida Heatter's
Book of
Great Desserts

Ingredients

BUTTER

Whenever butter is called for it means sweet butter; if you use salted butter, adjust the salt if it is called for in the recipe.

To Clarify Butter

Clarified butter may be used for buttering pans and is good for frying crêpes or pancakes; it lessens the chances of sticking and is less likely to burn. It will keep indefinitely in the refrigerator.

To make a large amount: Place any amount of cut-up sweet butter in a saucepan, preferably a wide, shallow one rather than a deep, narrow one, and large enough to allow the butter to bubble up. Cook without stirring over medium heat. Turn down the heat and let it cook slowly for about 5 minutes. With a large spoon, carefully skim the foam off the top. Do not disturb the milky substance in the bottom. Let the butter cool for 5 minutes or so and then, very gently, pour the clear butter off the top and discard the milky residue.

To make a small amount (¼ to ½ pound): The following is Craig Claiborne's method. Place the cut-up butter in a heatproof glass measuring cup (a 1-cup size for ¼ pound of butter; the 2-cup size for ½ pound of butter) in a 250-degree oven until the butter is melted. Skim off the foam. Carefully pour the clarified butter off the top and discard the milky residue.

When clarified, butter loses one-fourth of its original volume.

To Cream Butter

The butter may be cut up and softened slightly at room temperature before using, but do not allow it to soften completely or to become oily. Do not heat it or melt it. "Cream the butter" means to beat it, or work it, until it is soft enough to mix smoothly with other ingredients. This may be done with an electric mixer, with the back of a wooden spoon, or with your fingertips or bare hand. In most of these recipes the butter is creamed first, then the sugar is added and the creaming is continued until the ingredients are thoroughly mixed.

CHOCOLATE

Kinds of Chocolate

UNSWEETENED CHOCOLATE, also called baking chocolate or bitter chocolate (packed in 8-ounce packages of eight 1-ounce squares), is made by both Baker and Hershey.

SWEET, SEMISWEET, BITTERSWEET, and EXTRA-BITTERSWEET are generally interchangeable in cooking and baking, depending on your taste and on the availability of chocolates. Among the brands available are:

> Baker's German's Sweet (4-ounce bar)
> Maillard's Eagle Sweet (8-ounce bar)
> Hershey's Special Dark (packaged in bars of
>   1.2, 3.5, and 8 ounces). In local food stores this is
>   in the candy department.
> Baker's Semisweet, also known as "Dot" (8-ounce
>   package of 1-ounce squares)
> Nestlé's semisweet (6-ounce bar). This is in
>   the candy department of local food stores.
> Tobler Tradition (a bittersweet chocolate) and
>   Tobler Extra-Bittersweet, from Switzerland
>   (3-ounce bar)
> Lindt Excellence (bittersweet), and Lindt Extra-
>   Bittersweet, from Switzerland (3-ounce bar)
> Suchard Bittra (bittersweet) from Switzerland
>   (3-ounce bar)

There are many others available in different areas: Ghiradelli chocolate from San Francisco, Zaanland from Holland, and in France there is a great Nestlé chocolate called Chocolat Fondant.

SEMISWEET CHOCOLATE MORSELS, CHIPS, or BITS (6-ounce or 1-cup package, and 12-ounce or 2-cup package) are made by Nestlé, Baker, and Hershey. I seldom use them in cooking or baking (although many people do with excellent results), except for making one of the greatest cookies of all, Toll House Cookies. The recipe for those cookies is printed on the package of Nestlé's Chocolate Morsels.

MILK CHOCOLATE. I have never used milk chocolate in cooking or baking.

PREMELTED (or NO-MELT) CHOCOLATE (8-ounce package of eight 1-ounce plastic packets). I never use this semiliquid, unsweetened chocolate product, although many people do and are completely satisfied. It is not really chocolate; it is cocoa and hydrogenated vegetable oil. It may be substituted ounce for ounce in recipes. If it is too stiff to press out of the packet, hold it under running hot water to soften.

COMMERCIAL CHOCOLATES. There are many marvelous chocolates, unfortunately only available from wholesale bakery supply stores in 10-pound bars. They are used in commercial baking, generally by just cutting up and melting a portion, and then using it as is to ice cookies and petits fours. I have best results with Stollwerk's Royal York Coating Chocolate #2246, or Wilbur's #37 Darkcote Confectionery Coating. I cut it into large pieces, wrap them individually, and store at room temperature. I use it for making chocolate curls with a swivel-bladed vegetable peeler, Chocolate Cones (page 408), Mushroom Meringues (page 221), and Chocolate Cigarettes (page 411), which are long, thin, chocolate curls.

COCOA. Any unsweetened cocoa may be used in baking and cooking, but I prefer Dutch process. It has nothing to do with Holland or the Dutch—it has been treated with alkali to neutralize the natural acids. It is darker than other cocoa and, to my taste, has a richer and better flavor. I use Droste.

LINDT THINS (5-ounce box). These are 1½-inch square, paper-thin pieces of semisweet or milk chocolate. They are meant for eating as a candy, but are great for decorating. Any desserts that have been prepared in individual portions and topped with whipped cream, or any of the pies or icebox desserts that have been topped with whipped cream, may be decorated with some of the squares, standing them upright or on an angle in the whipped cream. Lindt Thins are available at most specialty food or candy stores.

To Melt Chocolate

When melting chocolate with no other ingredient, it is imperative that the container in which you are melting it be absolutely dry. Even the merest drop of moisture will cause the chocolate to "tighten." (If it should "tighten," stir in 1 tablespoon of homogenized vegetable shortening for each 3 ounces of chocolate.) Melt it over hot, but not boiling water. The reason for this is that boiling water might bubble up and get into the chocolate. It may also be melted in a shallow, heatproof cup in a low— about 175-degree—oven.

Chocolate should melt slowly, never over direct heat—it burns easily. To be sure chocolate doesn't get overheated and burn, it is always advisable to remove it from over the hot water before it is completely melted and then stir it until it is entirely melted and smooth.

COFFEE

Instant coffee in a recipe means dry—powdered, chunks, or granules.

Instant coffee powder will dissolve more easily than chunks or granules. If you happen to have one of the other two on hand, it is easy to powder it yourself. Whirl some in the blender, then strain it and return the coarse part to the blender until it is all powdered. I use Spice Islands instant coffee because it is powdered. It is available at specialty food stores.

CREAM

Light Cream

Light cream is not "half-and-half." Light cream generally has 20% butterfat; half-and-half has about 12% and, incidentally, while on the subject, homogenized milk has about 3½% and heavy cream 40%.

To Whip Cream

Heavy cream may be whipped with an electric mixer, a rotary beater, or a large, balloon-type wire whisk (the same kind as described for beating egg whites (page 8). It will whip more easily and give better results if the cream, bowl, and beaters are cold. The bowl should be metal (but not copper), as that gets and stays colder. Place the bowl and beaters in the refrigerator or the freezer until just before using them. If the room is very warm, the bowl in which you are whipping the cream should be placed in a larger bowl of ice and water.

Do not overbeat or the cream will lose its smooth texture; if you beat even more it will turn into butter. (See recipe below.) If you use an electric beater, a handy safeguard is to stop beating before the cream is completely whipped and then finish the job with a wire whisk. This allows less chance for overbeating.

It is best not to whip cream too far ahead of time. However, if you do, cover and refrigerate it and then check it before serving. It will probably have separated slightly and the bottom will be watery. But it may be reincorporated easily by mixing very briefly—a wire whisk is best.

To Make Butter

To make quick, homemade butter (delicious and such fun), beat 1 pint of heavy cream at high speed until the liquid begins to separate. Then reduce the speed to prevent the cream from spattering, and continue to beat until the butter separates from the milk. Pour through a strainer and then return the solid part to the mixing bowl. Add ice water, about as much as there was buttermilk, and mix at lowest speed (it will splash) to wash the butter. Drain again, then mix again with fresh ice water. Drain this, too, then stir the butter briefly in the strainer to remove any trapped milk. You may want to add a scant ¼ teaspoon of salt, as this quick, homemade butter tastes a bit flat without it.

One pint of cream will make ½ pound (1 cup) of butter, but you can use this same process with as much cream as you want. Pack the butter into a crock or any covered container, or roll it in wax paper and shape it into a roll or block.

EGGS

Size

These recipes are all based on the use of eggs graded extra-large or jumbo, unless otherwise indicated. Using slightly smaller eggs (large or medium) will not materially affect the results, except where specifically noted in certain recipes. But if you use eggs graded small, add one or two extra for every four or five called for in the recipe.

To Open Eggs

If directions call for adding whole eggs one at a time, they may all be opened ahead of time into one container and then poured into the other ingredients, approximately one at a time. Do not open eggs directly into the batter—you wouldn't know if a piece of shell had been included.

To Separate Eggs

A new bride, when faced with the direction "separate eggs," placed them carefully on the table about 4 inches apart, and wondered how far they should be from each other.

Eggs separate more safely when they are cold.

Place three small bowls in front of you, one for the whites and one for the yolks. The third one might not be needed, but if you should break the yolk when opening an egg, just drop the whole thing into the third bowl and save it for some other use.

When cracking the shell it is important not to use too much pressure or you will break the yolk at the same time.

There are many gadgets available for separating the yolks from the whites. The most common is cup shaped with small openings in the bottom. The egg is cracked over the form set on a small bowl—the yolk stays in the top section and the white runs through the holes. Some cooks can do the same thing by opening the egg directly onto the palm of a hand and letting the white run through their fingers into a bowl while the yolk remains in their hand.

The most popular method is to tap the side of the egg firmly on the edge of a bowl to crack the shell. Then, holding the egg in both hands, separate the two halves of the shell, letting some of the white run out into a bowl. Now pour the yolk back and forth from one half of the shell to the other, letting all of the white run out. Drop the yolk into the second bowl.

As each egg is separated the white should be transferred to another container, because if you drop all of the whites into one container there is a chance that the last egg might have a broken yolk, which could spoil all of the whites. Generally, a bit of yolk or shell can be removed with an empty half shell.

To Freeze Egg Whites

Leftover egg whites may be kept covered in the refrigerator for a few days or they may be frozen. I prefer to freeze them individually in ovenproof glass custard cups. When they are frozen, run hot water over the back of the cups (or place the cups in shallow hot water) until the frozen white falls out. Then wrap them individually in small freezer bags. To thaw, remove the number you want, transfer them to a cup or bowl, and let them stand at room temperature or place them in a very slightly warm oven. One cup of egg whites is made up of the whites of 6 extra-large or jumbo eggs, 8 large ones, or 10 medium.

Frozen egg whites are handy to have for recipes such as the Mushroom Meringues (page 221) or the filling for Black Velvet (page 275).

To Beat Egg Whites

Egg whites may be beaten with an electric mixer, a rotary egg beater, or a large balloon-type wire whisk. Both the bowl and beater must be perfectly clean and dry. Just a bit of oil or grease will prevent the whites from inflating properly.

If you use an electric mixer or a rotary beater, be careful not to use a bowl that is too large or the whites will be too shallow to get the full benefit of the beater's action. Also, if you use an electric hand mixer or rotary beater, keep moving it around in the bowl. If you use a mixer on a stand, use a rubber spatula frequently to push the whites from the sides of the bowl into the center.

If you use a wire whisk, use one that is at least 4 inches wide at the top and that has many thin wires instead of fewer heavy ones, and beat in an unlined copper bowl, if you have one. (You may use glass, china, or stainless steel, but do not beat egg whites in aluminum or plastic.) To prepare the copper bowl, it should be treated before using as follows: Put 1 or 2 teaspoons of salt in the bowl and rub thoroughly with half a lemon, mixing the lemon juice into the salt. Rinse with hot water (no soap) and dry.

Do not beat egg whites ahead of time. They must be folded in immediately after they are beaten. If it is a cake that you are making, it must then be placed in the oven right away.

Do not overbeat the whites or they will become dry and you won't be able to fold them in without losing the air you have beaten in. Beat only until they hold a shape or a point—"stiff but not dry."

FLOUR

With only one or two exceptions these recipes call for *sifted* flour. This means that it should be sifted immediately before it is measured. If the flour is not sifted, or if it is sifted long before it is to be used, it packs down and 1 cup is liable to contain a few spoonfuls more than 1 cup of flour sifted immediately before measuring. If you have one, use a triple sifter; otherwise sift the flour twice. Sift onto a piece of paper, sifting a bit more than you will need. Use a metal measuring cup. Spoon the sifted flour lightly into the cup. Do not shake the cup or pack or press the flour down; just scrape any excess off the top with a metal spatula or any flat-sided implement. It is not necessary to wash a flour sifter, just shake it out firmly and store in a plastic bag or a dust-free closet.

SUGAR

When sugar is called for in these recipes, unless it is qualified it means granulated white sugar.

Sugar should be measured in the same metal cups as those recommended for flour. If granulated sugar is lumpy it should be strained before it is used. Brown sugar and confectioners sugar are best strained also. (Hard lumps in brown sugar will not disappear in mixing or baking.) Unlike flour, though, sugars may all be strained ahead of time and you may do several pounds at once. Use a very large strainer set over a large bowl and press the sugar through with your fingertips.

Confectioners Sugar

I would rather strain than sift it. Maybe it is easier or maybe it is just habit. However, when I open a box I work it through a large strainer set over a bowl and use my fingertips to press the sugar through the strainer. Then transfer it for storage.

To sprinkle confectioners sugar over a cake or cookies, use a small strainer. This makes it very easy to control the amount and placement of the sugar.

Vanilla Sugar

To make vanilla sugar, fill a covered jar (about 1-quart size) with confectioners sugar and bury 1 or 2 split vanilla beans in it. Cover tightly, and let stand for at least a few days before using. As the sugar is used it may be replaced. The vanilla beans will continue to flavor the sugar for several months. Vanilla sugar adds a lovely flavor when strained over cakes and cookies.

NUTS

Over 2 ounces, I've given weights as well as measure for nuts; if measure only is given, weight is under 2 ounces.

To Store

All nuts should be stored in the freezer or refrigerator. Always bring them to room temperature before using, and smell them and taste them—rancid nuts would ruin a whole cake or an entire batch of cookies.

To Blanch

To blanch almonds: Cover almonds with boiling water. Let them stand until the water is cool enough to touch. Pick out the almonds one at a time, and squeeze each one between thumb and forefinger to squirt off the skin. As each one is skinned, place it on a towel to dry. Then spread the almonds in a single layer in a shallow baking pan and bake in a 200-degree oven for half an hour or so until they are dry. Do not let them brown. If the almonds are to be split or sliced or slivered, cut them one at a time immediately after removing the skin. Bake to dry as above. Sliced almonds are those that have been cut into very thin slices. Slivered almonds are the fatter, oblong, "julienne" shaped pieces.

To blanch hazelnuts: Spread the hazelnuts on a baking sheet and bake at 350 degrees for 15 minutes or until the skins parch and begin to flake off. Then, working with a few at a time, rub them in a coarse towel. Most of the skin will come off. Pick out the nuts and discard the skins. Don't worry about the few little bits of skin that may remain.

To blanch pistachio nuts: In a small saucepan bring a few inches of water to a boil. Drop the nuts (no more than ¼ to ½ cup of them at a time, as the skin is difficult to remove after the nuts have cooled) into the boiling water and let them boil for only a few seconds. They will lose their color if boiled for too long. Remove one nut and pinch the skin off with your fingers. If it slides off easily, immediately drain them all and turn them out onto a paper towel. While they are still warm pinch off the skins. Now they may be either slivered with a small paring knife or chopped into pieces that are coarse or almost as fine as a powder.

To Decorate with Pistachios

Chopped green pistachio nuts are an attractive and elegant topping when sprinkled lightly on whipped cream or cake icings (before the icing is dry).

Buy shelled, unsalted green pistachios. These are not readily available, but specialty nut shops and wholesale nut dealers carry them as do both Paprikas Weiss and H. Roth & Son mentioned below.

The nuts are green or yellow-green with reddish-purple skin. It is not essential to remove the skin, as the nuts may be chopped skin and all and the color won't be disturbing. However, the skin can be removed (see above) if you want a more elegant product and have the time to do it.

After the nuts have been blanched and skinned, some chefs heat the nuts in a moderate oven to crisp them. If you are a perfectionist you might want to do so, but be very careful not to leave them in too long or they may lose their color.

To Grind Nuts

When the instructions say "ground" it means that the nuts should be reduced to a powder, the consistency of coarse flour. Chopped nuts are much less fine and are left in visible pieces.

Ground nuts are available in some specialty food stores in large cities. But to grind your own you may use a blender, although the nuts may clump together and form oily lumps. If so, unless the recipe says that they do not have to be strained, with your fingertips force them through a large strainer set over a bowl to aerate them into a powdery condition. Any pieces too large to go through the strainer should be stirred back into the nuts.

Nut grinders give better results than a blender. A food processor does an excellent job but be careful not to overdo it and make nut-butter. I recommend the kind that screws onto the side of a table. The nuts go into the top and come out through the side when the handle is turned. These are generally available in Hungarian-type food stores. In New York they are available (by mail, too) from Paprikas Weiss, 1546 Second Avenue, New York, New York 10028, or H. Roth & Son, 1577 First Avenue, New York, New York 10028.

CURRANTS

Occasionally, currants have hard seeds. Taste them, and if they do, do not use for baking. Pick them over to remove any stems. Currants might be gritty, some more than others, and should be washed thoroughly. Soak them in warm water for at least 10 minutes, stirring occasionally, then shake them in a strainer under running water for several minutes. Drain and dry them thoroughly between paper towels.

DATES AND RAISINS

Raisins and dates must be fresh and soft—baking will not soften them. They may be softened by soaking them in hot water for about five minutes. Dates and raisins should be stored in the refrigerator or freezer.

ORANGE AND LEMON RIND

When grating orange or lemon rind, if your grater has different-shaped openings, it is best to grate the rind on the side with the small, round openings, rather than the diamond-shaped ones.

One teaspoon of prepared dried lemon peel is equal to the freshly grated peel of 1 medium-size lemon. One tablespoon of prepared dried orange peel is equal to the freshly grated peel of 1 medium-size orange.

Equipment

BAIN MARIE

If, when baking custards, puddings, some cheesecakes, or other dishes in a large pan of hot water (bain marie), the large pan is made of aluminum, the hot water will discolor it. To prevent this, add ½ teaspoon cream of tartar for each quart of water. Just drop it in; no need to stir.

The water in a bain marie should never boil. Check it occasionally and, if necessary, reduce the oven temperature and drop one or two ice cubes into the water to stop the boiling.

DOUBLE BOILER

Some directions call for a double boiler, perhaps a larger or smaller one than you have. If necessary, you can create a double boiler by placing the ingredients in a heatproof bowl over a saucepan of shallow hot water. The bowl should be wide enough so that its rim rests on the rim of the saucepan and the bowl is supported above the water.

ELECTRIC MIXERS

I use an electric mixer on a stand, the type that comes with two different size bowls. Mine is a Sunbeam. However, these recipes may be followed with other equipment. My mother loved her Kitchen Aid mixer, the type with only one bowl. Many people have excellent results with an electric hand mixer. Susan, my mother's cook for 35 years, beat egg whites with a tree branch, in spite of a fantastically well-equipped kitchen. In the country she picked a fresh one as she needed it; in the city she always washed it carefully and put it away.

If you have an electric mixer, I recommend that you buy one or two extra sets of beaters. If you do much baking and dessert-making, you will find that it will save washing time and make the work much easier. An additional set of mixer bowls is also nice to have. Extra beaters and bowls are available wherever mixers are sold.

Because I use an electric mixer on a stand, I have given directions for beating times based on this type of mixer; a hand-held mixer will take longer. If you are not using a mixer on a stand, when directions call for "small bowl of electric mixer" use a bowl with a 7-cup capacity. When directions are for "large bowl of electric mixer" use one with a 4-quart capacity.

Some of these recipes would be too much without any mixer. Others, especially many of the cookies, may be made using your bare hands for creaming and mixing. Don't be afraid to use your hands.

MEASUREMENTS

To Measure Heat: Oven Thermometer

Success in baking depends on many things. One of the most important is correct oven temperature. Most gas and electric companies are helpful in checking your oven temperature for you. I also suggest that you buy an oven thermometer, preferably a mercury thermometer, but any is better than none. Hardware stores sell them.

Measuring Cups

Glass or plastic measuring cups with the measurements marked on the sides and the 1-cup line below the top are only for measuring liquids. With the cup at eye level, fill carefully to exactly the line indicated. To measure dry ingredients, use the metal cups that come in sets of four: ¼ cup, ⅓ cup, ½ cup, and 1 cup. Fill to 'overflowing and then scrape off the extra with a metal spatula, a dough scraper, or the flat side of a large knife.

Measuring Spoons

Standard measuring spoons must be used for correct measurements. They are sold in sets of four: ¼ teaspoon, ½ teaspoon, 1 teaspoon, and 1 tablespoon. When being used for dry ingredients, fill to overflowing and then scrape off the excess with a small metal spatula or the flat side of a knife.

PASTRY BAGS

The best pastry bags are those made of canvas and coated on one side only with plastic. The small opening generally has to be cut a bit larger to allow the metal tubes to fit. It is easier to work with a bag that is too large rather than one that is too small.

PASTRY BRUSHES

There are different types of pastry brushes. Use a good one, or the bristles will come out while you are using it. Generally, the flat brush with bristles about ¾ inch long is practical and does a good job. Sometimes I use an artists' watercolor brush in a large size; it is softer and there are times when I prefer it.

RUBBER SPATULAS

Rubber spatulas are almost indispensable—not plastic; they are not flexible enough. Use rubber spatulas for folding, for some stirring, for scraping bowls, pots, etc. I suggest that you have several. They are made in three sizes, of which I find "medium" the most useful and most generally available. I have very little, if any, use for the smallest, which is called a bottle scraper. The largest is hard to find, unfortunately, as it is marvelous for folding large amounts of whipped cream or beaten egg whites. I buy the large size at restaurant supply stores.

TURNTABLE

When icing a cake it is easier to get a smooth, professional look if you work on a turntable. The cake is turned while the spatula smoothing the icing is held still. A Lazy Susan is a good substitute if you don't have a turntable. Turntables are available at specialty kitchen shops and at bakery or restaurant supply stores. In my experience, bakery or restaurant supply stores do not object to selling individual items to nonprofessionals.

Procedures

BEFORE YOU BAKE:
CHECK LIST

1. Read the recipe completely. Make sure that you have everything you will need, especially the correct size baking pan.
2. Remove butter, cream cheese, eggs from the refrigerator.
3. Adjust oven racks and preheat oven.
4. Prepare the pan according to directions.
5. Grind or chop nuts.
6. Sift flour (and other dry ingredients) onto a large piece of paper.
7. Open eggs (separate them if necessary).
8. Measure all the other ingredients and organize them into the order called for in the recipe.

CAKES

To Prepare the Cake Pan

I use butter, which I spread on with a crumpled piece of wax paper.

If directions call for lining the pan, use wax paper, aluminum foil, or baking pan liner paper (also called "cooking parchment") that has been treated with silicone on both sides to prevent sticking. It comes in sheets or in rolls like wax paper and is available in specialty kitchen shops or in some large hardware stores. It may also be ordered by mail from Maid of Scandinavia Company, 3245 Raleigh Avenue, Minneapolis, Minnesota 55416, or Colonial Garden Kitchens, 270 West Merrick Road, Valley Stream, Long Island, New York 11582.

Place the pan, right side up, on the paper and trace around it. If it is a tube pan, stick the pencil into the tube and trace the opening. Cut the paper with scissors. After you have cut the opening for the tube, cut short lines radiating from the tube hole about ½ inch deep and ¼ inch apart to insure a smooth fit. If you do much baking, cut several pieces of paper at once and keep a supply on hand.

For most recipes (but not all) I prefer to coat the buttered pan with bread crumbs rather than flour. Put a few spoonfuls of crumbs (or flour, when specified) into the prepared pan. Holding the pan over a piece of paper, tilt it in all directions. Tap the pan and shake it back and forth until it is completely coated. Invert the pan over the paper and shake out the excess crumbs or flour. It should be a thin, even coating.

Naturally use unseasoned bread crumbs, which all food stores carry. Or make your own by removing the crust from white bread and drying it in a low oven (225 degrees) until it is completely dry and crisp. Then break it up coarsely and whirl it, a little at a time, in the blender. If necessary, strain the bread crumbs through a coarse strainer and return any chunks to the blender. Store bread crumbs in a screw-top jar.

Timing

The minute you put the cake into the oven set a timer, if you have one. But even if you do, write down the time that it should be finished. Good insurance.

It is important not to overbake cakes, or they become dry. There are several ways to test for doneness, but the tests vary with different cakes. (All of these recipes indicate which test or tests to use.) Some cakes will come slightly away from the sides of the pan when done, the top of others will spring back when touched lightly with your fingertip, while still others must be tested with a cake tester. Cake testers are available in hardware stores and kitchen-equipment shops. A cake tester is a 6-inch piece of thin wire with a ring at the top for ease in handling, or for hanging. The wire should be inserted gently straight down into the middle of the cake, going all the way to the pan. Withdraw it gently. If it comes out clean, the cake is done. If some moist batter clings to the tester, the cake needs to be baked longer. Test in two or three places to be sure.

To Freeze Cakes

All of the cakes in this book may be frozen before icing (individual layers should be wrapped separately or they will stick together), and most of them can also be frozen after, except where indicated in individual recipes. (For instance, Seven-Minute Icing doesn't freeze.) Iced cakes should be frozen unwrapped and then, when firm, they should be wrapped airtight—plastic wrap is best for this.

If you freeze a cake on a plate and then want to remove it from the plate to wrap it, there should be wax paper between the cake and the plate or else they will stick together.

Having frozen every freezable recipe in this collection, I find that contrary to general opinion it is better to thaw iced cakes before removing the wrapping. They sweat while thawing. If they have been unwrapped the moisture collects on the cake. If they have not been unwrapped, the moisture collects on the outside of the wrapping.

Even if the cakes are not iced, I prefer to allow all cakes to thaw before unwrapping.

To Prepare the Cake Plate

When you are ready to ice a cake, begin by tearing off 10 inches of wax paper. Fold it crossways into four parts, then cut through the folds with a knife, making four 10 × 3-inch strips. Place them in a square on the cake plate to protect it. As soon as the cake is iced remove the paper, pulling each strip out by a narrow end and leaving the cake plate clean.

FOLDING

Ingredients are folded together rather than mixed when it is necessary to retain air that has been beaten into one or both of the mixtures. If one of the mixtures is heavy, first actually stir in a bit of the lighter mixture. Then, with a rubber spatula or with your bare hand (or occasionally on lowest speed of an electric mixer), gradually fold the remaining light mixture into the heavier mixture as follows:

Place part of the light mixture on top.

With a rubber spatula: Rounded side down, cut down through the center to the bottom, then toward you against the bottom of the bowl, then up against the side, and finally out over the top, bringing the heavier ingredients from the bottom over the top. Rotate the bowl slightly with your other hand. Repeat cutting with the rounded side down, rotating the bowl a bit after completing each cut. Continue only until both mixtures are combined. Try to make every motion count—do not handle any more than necessary.

With your bare hand: First of all, use a large enough bowl. Keep the fingers of your right hand spread slightly apart. With the side of your hand

cut down through the middle of the mixture, toward you across the bottom, up against the side of the bowl, and then out over the top, folding the ingredients from the bottom to the top. With your left hand rotate the bowl slightly and continue to repeat the process until ingredients are combined. Do not handle any more than necessary. With your left hand wipe the ingredients off your right hand.

With an electric mixer: I do not recommend an electric mixer for folding beaten egg whites or whipped cream. However, flour may be folded into a well-beaten egg-and-sugar mixture with an electric mixer if you are careful not to overmix. Use lowest speed and with a rubber spatula constantly push the ingredients from the sides of the bowl toward the center, mixing only until the flour is incorporated.

USING INGREDIENTS

To Bring Ingredients to Room Temperature

In individual recipes I have indicated the very few times I actually bring ingredients to room temperature before using. Otherwise they may be used right out of the refrigerator. If butter is too hard, cut it into small pieces and let it stand only until it may be worked with.

To Add Dry Ingredients Alternately with Liquid

Always begin and end with dry ingredients. The procedure is generally add about one-third of the dry ingredients, half of the liquid, then a third of the dry, the rest of the liquid, and finally the last third of the dry.

Use the lowest speed on an electric mixer for this. After each addition mix only until smooth. If your mixer is the type that allows for a rubber spatula to be used while it is in motion, help the blending along with the rubber spatula to scrape around the sides of the bowl. If the mixer does not allow room, or if it is the hand-held kind, stop it frequently and scrape the bowl with the spatula.

Tortes

LINZER TORTE

DOBOSH TORTE

CHOCOLATE MOUSSE TORTE

QUEEN MOTHER'S CAKE

TRUFFLES TORTE

HELEN McCULLY'S FRENCH
  CHOCOLATE TORTE

CHOCOLATE APPLESAUCE
  TORTE WITH KUMQUATS

SMALL WALNUT TORTE (*Hungarian*)

SWEDISH ALMOND TORTE

ROYAL VIENNESE WALNUT TORTE

MOCHA PECAN TORTE (*Mexican*)

ROYAL NORWEGIAN MACAROON
  TORTE

CARROT-NUT TORTE

The difference between a torte and a cake is not clear. Experts differ in their definitions. Basically torte or torta is a European word meaning cake, and, as many European cakes are made without flour, a torte is often defined as a cake without flour. (Ground nuts or bread crumbs generally take the place of the flour.)

But it's all very complicated, especially as many classic torte recipes do call for flour. For instance, Dobosh Torte and Sacher Torte both do. (Incidentally, Sacher Torte is not included in this collection of recipes because, if you want a dense chocolate cake, I think that Queen Mother's Cake is so much better. To further complicate the subject, Queen Mother's Cake, although it is called a cake, is included in the torte section because it has *no* flour.) And many classic desserts called tortes are really neither cakes nor tortes. Linzer Torte, for example, is really a tart or a European pie.

Therefore, the recipes in this section are here for one of two reasons: either they are classically called tortes, or they are made without, or almost without, flour.

And a final fillip—Chocolate Mousse Torte, which is included here because it is made without flour, is really a kind of pie.

O.K.?

Linzer Torte

2 9-INCH
TORTES,
EACH
8 PORTIONS

CRUST

3 cups sifted all-purpose flour
2 teaspoons cinnamon
½ teaspoon powdered cloves
¼ teaspoon salt
10 ounces (1¼ cups) butter, cut up
1⅔ cups sugar
1 pound (4½ cups) walnuts, finely ground
(See page 11. For this recipe they do not
have to be strained.)
1 egg plus 1 egg yolk
Finely grated rind of 1 large lemon (or 2 small)

Put flour, cinnamon, cloves, and salt in a large mixing bowl. With a pastry blender cut in the butter until the mixture resembles coarse crumbs. Stir in the sugar and walnuts. Mix the egg and egg yolk slightly and add along with the lemon rind. Work the dough with your hands a bit, and then turn it out onto a large board or smooth surface and squeeze it between your fingers until it holds together. Now "break off" the dough as follows: Form it into a slightly flattened ball. Start at the further end of the dough and, using the heel of your hand, push off small pieces (about 2 tablespoons), pushing it against the work surface and pushing away from you. Continue pushing off, or breaking, until it has all been broken off. Re-form the dough and "break" it off one more time.

Adjust rack one-third up from bottom of oven. Preheat oven to 400 degrees.

Butter two 9-inch round layer-cake pans, preferably pans with removable bottoms. (See Note.) Line the bottom with paper. Butter the paper. (If you use baking pan liner paper, butter the pans to hold the paper in place, but it is not necessary to butter the paper.)

Divide the dough in half, and then in half again. Place one of the quarters in each pan. Press it into place with your fingers. (If the dough is sticky dip your fingers in flour as necessary.) Press evenly and firmly over the bottoms of the pans and about 1¼ to 1½ inches up on the sides. Don't worry about making a smooth or level edge on the sides. That will be filled in later.

Bake these shells for about 15 minutes or until they barely begin to color.

While the shells are baking roll the remaining dough between two large pieces of wax paper to about ¼- to ⅜-inch thickness. Leave both pieces of wax paper on the dough. Slip a cookie sheet under it and place in the freezer for 10 to 15 minutes (or a little longer in the refrigerator) until the dough is well chilled.

Meanwhile, remove baked shells from the oven. Reduce oven temperature to 350 degrees and raise the rack to one-third of the way from the top of the oven.

FILLING

¼ cup of fine, dry bread crumbs
24 ounces (2 cups) seedless raspberry jam

Sprinkle about 2 tablespoons of the bread crumbs evenly over the bottom of each shell.

Stir the jam until it is soft and spread 1 cup in each shell. Set filled shells aside.

Remove the dough from the freezer (or refrigerator) and from the cookie sheet. Place it on a large board. Remove the top piece of wax paper. Use a small, sharp knife and cut the dough, cutting through the bottom wax paper at the same time, into strips ½ to ¾ inch wide. Lift each strip by the wax paper ends. Starting in the middle of the torte, flip one strip over the top of the jam. Peel off the wax paper. Cut the ends of the dough by pressing them on the sides of the pan. Place the strips ½ to ¾ inch apart, crisscrossing them to make a lattice top. Use the leftover pieces of dough to fill in the empty spaces between the strips around the edges. (The unbaked strips and the baked rim will blend together.) Press the outer edge with your fingertips or a spatula to level it. Score the rim with a fork.

TOPPING

1 egg yolk
1 teaspoon water
5 ounces (1 cup) slivered almonds
    (slivered almonds are the oblong,
    "julienne" shaped pieces)

Make a glaze by mixing egg yolk and water. Brush it all over pastry strips and border. Sprinkle ½ cup almonds evenly over each torte. Bake for 1 hour or so until crust and almonds are well browned.

Remove from oven. Cool in pans on racks. When removing tortes from pans, if the sides stick release them carefully with a small, sharp knife. The sides are crisp and heavy handling will crack them. However, if you have used a loose-bottomed pan you will probably be able to release the sides by gently pushing the bottom up.

In order to remove the tortes without losing the loose almonds on top, cover torte with clear wrap or foil. Place cake rack on top. Invert. Remove pan and paper lining. Place cake plate or rack over the torte. Invert again, right side up, and remove clear wrap or foil. Let stand overnight before serving.

OPTIONAL: *Sprinkle tops generously with confectioners sugar through a fine strainer.*

NOTE: *This recipe will make one large Linzer Torte in an 11- or 12-inch shallow pan, or a large quiche pan with fluted sides and removable bottom. I've made it in a variety of unconventional forms and pans. In any event, it must be made in a shallow pan, and the bottom must be lined with paper or the torte will stick to the pan.*

Dobosh Torte

12 PORTIONS

Patience is the name of the game.

7 eggs, separated, plus 3 egg yolks
1 pound (3½ cups) confectioners sugar
¾ cup sifted all-purpose flour
1 tablespoon lemon juice
⅛ teaspoon salt

To prepare for baking seven cake layers (the usual number): Tear off seven pieces of aluminum foil, or baking pan liner paper (see Note 1), each about 11 inches long. Spread softened butter lightly over a 10-inch square area in the center of each piece of foil or paper. Sprinkle with flour. Shake and tilt the foil or paper to make sure the buttered area is thoroughly floured and shake off any excess. On the floured area trace a 9-inch circle. (Use any 9-inch circular object as a pattern: the bottom of a 9-inch springform pan, an inverted 9-inch cake tin, or a 9-inch pot cover.) Repeat with remaining pieces of foil or paper. Set aside.

Place rack in the center of the oven and preheat to 450 degrees.

In the large bowl of an electric mixer at high speed, beat the 10 egg yolks for a few minutes until they are pale lemon-colored. Reduce speed and gradually add sugar. Increase speed to high again and beat for 5 minutes until very thick. Reduce speed and gradually add the flour, then again increase it to high and beat for 5 minutes more (mixture will be almost stiff), scraping the bowl occasionally with a rubber spatula. Mix in the lemon juice and remove from mixer. (The mixture will be very thick —use your fingers to get it all off the beaters.)

Beat the 7 egg whites with the salt until they hold a point—stiff, but not dry. Since the yolk mixture is very thick, actually stir a few spoonfuls of the whites in to lighten it a bit. Then fold in a few large spoonfuls three or four times until the mixture lightens.

Gently fold in the remaining whites.

Although a Dobosh Torte is generally seven layers high, I pride myself on the number and thinness of my layers. If you only make seven layers, that's perfectly all right—trying for more is one of my own personal hang-ups. With a large serving spoon, place two or three large spoonfuls of the batter on one of the pieces of prepared foil or paper. Using the back of the spoon, spread the batter thin, slowly rotating the paper with your left hand as you spread the batter with your right hand. Make it thin but do not leave any holes in it. A ¼-inch thickness should give you seven layers. Do not make the edges too thin. Follow the lines closely, but don't worry—the edges may be trimmed later.

Slide a cookie sheet under the foil or paper and bake for 5 to 7 minutes or until the top is golden brown with dark brown spots. If the layers are thicker than mine are, they will take longer to bake. If they are not baked long enough they will stick to the foil or paper. Repeat with remaining layers. If you bake more than one layer at a time, rotate the position of the pans during baking to insure even browning.

When a layer is baked and out of the oven, lift the corners of the foil or paper and invert onto a rack. Peel off the paper and immediately invert the layer onto another rack to cool, right side up. (Letting the layer cool upside down will make it stick to the rack.) When you run out of racks, layers may cool on smooth toweling that has been dusted with confectioners sugar. When you run out of room, cooled layers may be stacked if you sprinkle the tops lightly with confectioners sugar and place wax paper between them.

Cooled layers may be trimmed to even the edges. Working on a board, place an 8½-inch or 9-inch pot cover or cake pan on the layer. Cut around with a small sharp knife or trace with the knife and then cut with scissors.

Prepare the following:

FILLING AND ICING
FOR DOBOSH TORTE

½ pound semisweet or bittersweet chocolate
½ pound (1 cup) butter
1 teaspoon vanilla extract
3 egg yolks
2 tablespoons confectioners sugar

Melt the chocolate in the top of a small double boiler over hot water on moderate heat. Remove from heat, stir until smooth, and set aside to cool completely.

In small bowl of electric mixer cream the butter. Add vanilla and egg yolks and beat well. Add sugar and cooled chocolate. Beat until thoroughly mixed, scraping the bowl with a rubber spatula.

Place four strips of wax paper around the outer edges of a cake plate. Place one cake layer on the plate and with a long, narrow metal spatula spread with a thin layer of the chocolate filling. If you have made more than seven layers, the filling must be spread *very* thin, in order to have enough for all. Place another layer on top, adjusting it carefully so that the edges are lined up evenly. Continue icing the layers, stacking them as evenly as possible.

Spread the remaining chocolate smoothly around the sides first and then over the top.

Remove wax paper strips by pulling each one out by a narrow end (see page 18) and refrigerate cake for at least several hours to set the icing. Store in refrigerator and serve cold.

NOTES: 1. *If you use baking pan liner paper it must be buttered and floured for this recipe or the layers will stick to it.*

2. *This is a very firm cake; use a sharp, heavy knife for serving.*

3. *Dobosh Torte may be made a day ahead, or it may be frozen.*

4. *Dobosh Torte is traditionally made with a layer of caramelized sugar on top. I prefer it this way with icing on top—it is easier to prepare, easier to serve, easier to eat, and, to my taste, more delicious.*

Chocolate Mousse Torte

Of the many recipes that were born in my kitchen, this was one of the most exciting because it became The New York Times's *1972 Dessert of the Year.*

6 TO 8 PORTIONS

8 ounces (8 squares) semisweet chocolate
1 tablespoon instant coffee
¼ cup boiling water
8 eggs, separated
⅔ cup sugar
1 teaspoon vanilla extract
⅛ teaspoon salt

Adjust rack to center of oven. Preheat oven to 350 degrees. Butter a 9-inch round ovenproof glass pie plate. Dust it with fine, dry bread crumbs. Set aside.

Place chocolate in the top of a small double boiler over hot water. Dissolve the coffee in the boiling water and pour it over the chocolate. Cover and let stand over low heat, stirring occasionally with a small wire whisk until the chocolate is almost melted. Remove chocolate from heat and continue to stir until smooth. Set aside to cool slightly.

In the small bowl of an electric mixer beat the yolks at high speed for about 5 minutes, until they are pale lemon-colored and thickened. Gradually add the sugar and continue to beat at high speed for 5 minutes more until very thick. Add the vanilla and chocolate, beating slowly and scraping the bowl with a rubber spatula until blended.

Remove from mixer. In the large bowl of electric mixer beat the whites with the salt until stiff but not dry. Gradually, in two or three small additions, fold half of the whites into the chocolate (do not be too thorough) and then fold the chocolate into the remaining whites, folding only until no whites show. Handling as little as possible, gently remove and set aside about 4 cups of the mousse. Turn the balance into the pie plate; it will barely reach the top. Very gently spread level and place in oven to bake.

Cover reserved mousse and refrigerate.

When mousse has baked 25 minutes turn off the heat. Leave it in the oven for 5 minutes more. Then remove from oven and cool on a rack. (Mousse will rise during baking and then, while cooling, it will settle in the center, leaving a high rim.)

When *completely* cool, remove reserved mousse from refrigerator.

until it is completely coated. Invert the pan over the paper and shake out the excess crumbs or flour. It should be a thin, even coating.

Naturally use unseasoned bread crumbs, which all food stores carry. Or make your own by removing the crust from white bread and drying it in a low oven (225 degrees) until it is completely dry and crisp. Then break it up coarsely and whirl it, a little at a time, in the blender. If necessary, strain the bread crumbs through a coarse strainer and return any chunks to the blender. Store bread crumbs in a screw-top jar.

Timing

The minute you put the cake into the oven set a timer, if you have one. But even if you do, write down the time that it should be finished. Good insurance.

It is important not to overbake cakes, or they become dry. There are several ways to test for doneness, but the tests vary with different cakes. (All of these recipes indicate which test or tests to use.) Some cakes will come slightly away from the sides of the pan when done, the top of others will spring back when touched lightly with your fingertip, while still others must be tested with a cake tester. Cake testers are available in hardware stores and kitchen-equipment shops. A cake tester is a 6-inch piece of thin wire with a ring at the top for ease in handling, or for hanging. The wire should be inserted gently straight down into the middle of the cake, going all the way to the pan. Withdraw it gently. If it comes out clean, the cake is done. If some moist batter clings to the tester, the cake needs to be baked longer. Test in two or three places to be sure.

To Freeze Cakes

All of the cakes in this book may be frozen before icing (individual layers should be wrapped separately or they will stick together), and most of them can also be frozen after, except where indicated in individual recipes. (For instance, Seven-Minute Icing doesn't freeze.) Iced cakes should be frozen unwrapped and then, when firm, they should be wrapped airtight— plastic wrap is best for this.

If you freeze a cake on a plate and then want to remove it from the plate to wrap it, there should be wax paper between the cake and the plate or else they will stick together.

Having frozen every freezable recipe in this collection, I find that contrary to general opinion it is better to thaw iced cakes before removing the wrapping. They sweat while thawing. If they have been unwrapped the moisture collects on the cake. If they have not been unwrapped, the moisture collects on the outside of the wrapping.

Even if the cakes are not iced, I prefer to allow all cakes to thaw before unwrapping.

To Prepare the Cake Plate

When you are ready to ice a cake, begin by tearing off 10 inches of wax paper. Fold it crossways into four parts, then cut through the folds with a knife, making four 10 × 3-inch strips. Place them in a square on the cake plate to protect it. As soon as the cake is iced remove the paper, pulling each strip out by a narrow end and leaving the cake plate clean.

FOLDING

Ingredients are folded together rather than mixed when it is necessary to retain air that has been beaten into one or both of the mixtures. If one of the mixtures is heavy, first actually stir in a bit of the lighter mixture. Then, with a rubber spatula or with your bare hand (or occasionally on lowest speed of an electric mixer), gradually fold the remaining light mixture into the heavier mixture as follows:

Place part of the light mixture on top.

With a rubber spatula: Rounded side down, cut down through the center to the bottom, then toward you against the bottom of the bowl, then up against the side, and finally out over the top, bringing the heavier ingredients from the bottom over the top. Rotate the bowl slightly with your other hand. Repeat cutting with the rounded side down, rotating the bowl a bit after completing each cut. Continue only until both mixtures are combined. Try to make every motion count—do not handle any more than necessary.

With your bare hand: First of all, use a large enough bowl. Keep the fingers of your right hand spread slightly apart. With the side of your hand cut down through the middle of the mixture, toward you across the bottom, up against the side of the bowl, and then out over the top, folding the ingredients from the bottom to the top. With your left hand rotate the bowl slightly and continue to repeat the process until ingredients are combined. Do not handle any more than necessary. With your left hand wipe the ingredients off your right hand.

With an electric mixer: I do not recommend an electric mixer for folding beaten egg whites or whipped cream. However, flour may be folded into a well-beaten egg-and-sugar mixture with an electric mixer if you are careful not to overmix. Use lowest speed and with a rubber spatula constantly push the ingredients from the sides of the bowl toward the center, mixing only until the flour is incorporated.

USING INGREDIENTS

To Bring Ingredients to Room Temperature

In individual recipes I have indicated the very few times I actually bring ingredients to room temperature before using. Otherwise they may be used right out of the refrigerator. If butter is too hard, cut it into small pieces, and let it stand only until it may be worked with.

To Add Dry Ingredients Alternately with Liquid

Always begin and end with dry ingredients. The procedure is generally to add about one-third of the dry ingredients, half of the liquid, the second third of the dry, the rest of the liquid, and finally the last third of the dry.

Use the lowest speed on an electric mixer for this. After each addition mix only until smooth. If your mixer is the type that allows for a rubber spatula to be used while it is in motion, help the blending along by using the rubber spatula to scrape around the sides of the bowl. If the mixer does not allow room, or if it is the hand-held kind, stop it frequently and scrape the bowl with the spatula.

Tortes

LINZER TORTE

DOBOSH TORTE

CHOCOLATE MOUSSE TORTE

QUEEN MOTHER'S CAKE

TRUFFLES TORTE

HELEN McCULLY'S FRENCH
  CHOCOLATE TORTE

CHOCOLATE APPLESAUCE
  TORTE WITH KUMQUATS

SMALL WALNUT TORTE (*Hungarian*)

SWEDISH ALMOND TORTE

ROYAL VIENNESE WALNUT TORTE

MOCHA PECAN TORTE (*Mexican*)

ROYAL NORWEGIAN MACAROON
  TORTE

CARROT-NUT TORTE

The difference between a torte and a cake is not clear. Experts differ in their definitions. Basically torte or torta is a European word meaning cake, and, as many European cakes are made without flour, a torte is often defined as a cake without flour. (Ground nuts or bread crumbs generally take the place of the flour.)

But it's all very complicated, especially as many classic torte recipes do call for flour. For instance, Dobosh Torte and Sacher Torte both do. (Incidentally, Sacher Torte is not included in this collection of recipes because, if you want a dense chocolate cake, I think that Queen Mother's Cake is so much better. To further complicate the subject, Queen Mother's Cake, although it is called a cake, is included in the torte section because it has *no* flour.) And many classic desserts called tortes are really neither cakes nor tortes. Linzer Torte, for example, is really a tart or a European pie.

Therefore, the recipes in this section are here for one of two reasons: either they are classically called tortes, or they are made without, or almost without, flour.

And a final fillip—Chocolate Mousse Torte, which is included here because it is made without flour, is really a kind of pie.

O.K.?

Linzer Torte

2 9-INCH
TORTES,
EACH
8 PORTIONS

CRUST

3 cups sifted all-purpose flour
2 teaspoons cinnamon
½ teaspoon powdered cloves
¼ teaspoon salt
10 ounces (1¼ cups) butter, cut up
1⅔ cups sugar
1 pound (4½ cups) walnuts, finely ground
(See page 11. For this recipe they do not
have to be strained.)
1 egg plus 1 egg yolk
Finely grated rind of 1 large lemon (or 2 small)

Put flour, cinnamon, cloves, and salt in a large mixing bowl. With a pastry blender cut in the butter until the mixture resembles coarse crumbs. Stir in the sugar and walnuts. Mix the egg and egg yolk slightly and add along with the lemon rind. Work the dough with your hands a bit, and then turn it out onto a large board or smooth surface and squeeze it between your fingers until it holds together. Now "break off" the dough as follows: Form it into a slightly flattened ball. Start at the further end of the dough and, using the heel of your hand, push off small pieces (about 2 tablespoons), pushing it against the work surface and pushing away from you. Continue pushing off, or breaking, until it has all been broken off. Re-form the dough and "break" it off one more time.

Adjust rack one-third up from bottom of oven. Preheat oven to 400 degrees.

Butter two 9-inch round layer-cake pans, preferably pans with re-movable bottoms. (See Note.) Line the bottom with paper. Butter the paper. (If you use baking pan liner paper, butter the pans to hold the paper in place, but it is not necessary to butter the paper.)

Divide the dough in half, and then in half again. Place one of the quarters in each pan. Press it into place with your fingers. (If the dough is sticky dip your fingers in flour as necessary.) Press evenly and firmly over the bottoms of the pans and about 1¼ to 1½ inches up on the sides. Don't worry about making a smooth or level edge on the sides. That will be filled in later.

Bake these shells for about 15 minutes or until they barely begin to color.

While the shells are baking roll the remaining dough between two large pieces of wax paper to about ¼- to ⅜-inch thickness. Leave both pieces of wax paper on the dough. Slip a cookie sheet under it and place in the freezer for 10 to 15 minutes (or a little longer in the refrigerator) until the dough is well chilled.

Meanwhile, remove baked shells from the oven. Reduce oven temperature to 350 degrees and raise the rack to one-third of the way from the top of the oven.

FILLING

¼ cup of fine, dry bread crumbs
24 ounces (2 cups) seedless raspberry jam

Sprinkle about 2 tablespoons of the bread crumbs evenly over the bottom of each shell.

Stir the jam until it is soft and spread 1 cup in each shell. Set filled shells aside.

Remove the dough from the freezer (or refrigerator) and from the cookie sheet. Place it on a large board. Remove the top piece of wax paper. Use a small, sharp knife and cut the dough, cutting through the bottom wax paper at the same time, into strips ½ to ¾ inch wide. Lift each strip by the wax paper ends. Starting in the middle of the torte, flip one strip over the top of the jam. Peel off the wax paper. Cut the ends of the dough by pressing them on the sides of the pan. Place the strips ½ to ¾ inch apart, crisscrossing them to make a lattice top. Use the leftover pieces of dough to fill in the empty spaces between the strips around the edges. (The unbaked strips and the baked rim will blend together.) Press the outer edge with your fingertips or a spatula to level it. Score the rim with a fork.

TOPPING

1 egg yolk
1 teaspoon water
5 ounces (1 cup) slivered almonds
(slivered almonds are the oblong,
"julienne" shaped pieces)

Make a glaze by mixing egg yolk and water. Brush it all over pastry strips and border. Sprinkle ½ cup almonds evenly over each torte. Bake for 1 hour or so until crust and almonds are well browned.

Remove from oven. Cool in pans on racks. When removing tortes from pans, if the sides stick release them carefully with a small, sharp knife. The sides are crisp and heavy handling will crack them. However, if you have used a loose-bottomed pan you will probably be able to release the sides by gently pushing the bottom up.

In order to remove the tortes without losing the loose almonds on top, cover torte with clear wrap or foil. Place cake rack on top. Invert. Remove pan and paper lining. Place cake plate or rack over the torte. Invert again, right side up, and remove clear wrap or foil. Let stand overnight before serving.

OPTIONAL: *Sprinkle tops generously with confectioners sugar through a fine strainer.*

NOTE: *This recipe will make one large Linzer Torte in an 11- or 12-inch shallow pan, or a large quiche pan with fluted sides and removable bottom. I've made it in a variety of unconventional forms and pans. In any event, it must be made in a shallow pan, and the bottom must be lined with paper or the torte will stick to the pan.*

Dobosh Torte

12 PORTIONS

Patience is the name of the game.

7 eggs, separated, plus 3 egg yolks
1 pound (3½ cups) confectioners sugar
¾ cup sifted all-purpose flour
1 tablespoon lemon juice
⅛ teaspoon salt

To prepare for baking seven cake layers (the usual number): Tear off seven pieces of aluminum foil, or baking pan liner paper (see Note 1), each about 11 inches long. Spread softened butter lightly over a 10-inch square area in the center of each piece of foil or paper. Sprinkle with flour. Shake and tilt the foil or paper to make sure the buttered area is thoroughly floured and shake off any excess. On the floured area trace a 9-inch circle. (Use any 9-inch circular object as a pattern: the bottom of a 9-inch spring-form pan, an inverted 9-inch cake tin, or a 9-inch pot cover.) Repeat with remaining pieces of foil or paper. Set aside.

Place rack in the center of the oven and preheat to 450 degrees.

In the large bowl of an electric mixer at high speed, beat the 10 egg yolks for a few minutes until they are pale lemon-colored. Reduce speed and gradually add sugar. Increase speed to high again and beat for 5 minutes until very thick. Reduce speed and gradually add the flour, then again increase it to high and beat for 5 minutes more (mixture will be almost stiff), scraping the bowl occasionally with a rubber spatula. Mix in the lemon juice and remove from mixer. (The mixture will be very thick —use your fingers to get it all off the beaters.)

Beat the 7 egg whites with the salt until they hold a point—stiff, but not dry. Since the yolk mixture is very thick, actually stir a few spoonfuls of the whites in to lighten it a bit. Then fold in a few large spoonfuls three or four times until the mixture lightens.

Gently fold in the remaining whites.

Although a Dobosh Torte is generally seven layers high, I pride myself on the number and thinness of my layers. If you only make seven layers, that's perfectly all right—trying for more is one of my own personal hang-ups. With a large serving spoon, place two or three large spoonfuls of the batter on one of the pieces of prepared foil or paper. Using the back of the spoon, spread the batter thin, slowly rotating the paper with your left hand as you spread the batter with your right hand. Make it thin but do not leave any holes in it. A ¼-inch thickness should give you seven layers. Do not make the edges too thin. Follow the lines closely, but don't worry—the edges may be trimmed later.

Slide a cookie sheet under the foil or paper and bake for 5 to 7 minutes or until the top is golden brown with dark brown spots. If the layers are thicker than mine are, they will take longer to bake. If they are not baked long enough they will stick to the foil or paper. Repeat with remaining layers. If you bake more than one layer at a time, rotate the position of the pans during baking to insure even browning.

When a layer is baked and out of the oven, lift the corners of the foil or paper and invert onto a rack. Peel off the paper and immediately invert the layer onto another rack to cool, right side up. (Letting the layer cool upside down will make it stick to the rack.) When you run out of racks, layers may cool on smooth toweling that has been dusted with confectioners sugar. When you run out of room, cooled layers may be stacked if you sprinkle the tops lightly with confectioners sugar and place wax paper between them.

Cooled layers may be trimmed to even the edges. Working on a board, place an 8½-inch or 9-inch pot cover or cake pan on the layer. Cut around with a small sharp knife or trace with the knife and then cut with scissors.

Prepare the following:

FILLING AND ICING
FOR DOBOSH TORTE

½ pound semisweet or bittersweet chocolate
½ pound (1 cup) butter
1 teaspoon vanilla extract
3 egg yolks
2 tablespoons confectioners sugar

Melt the chocolate in the top of a small double boiler over hot water on moderate heat. Remove from heat, stir until smooth, and set aside to cool completely.

In small bowl of electric mixer cream the butter. Add vanilla and egg yolks and beat well. Add sugar and cooled chocolate. Beat until thoroughly mixed, scraping the bowl with a rubber spatula.

Place four strips of wax paper around the outer edges of a cake plate. Place one cake layer on the plate and with a long, narrow metal spatula spread with a thin layer of the chocolate filling. If you have made more than seven layers, the filling must be spread *very* thin, in order to have enough for all. Place another layer on top, adjusting it carefully so that the edges are lined up evenly. Continue icing the layers, stacking them as evenly as possible.

Spread the remaining chocolate smoothly around the sides first and then over the top.

Remove wax paper strips by pulling each one out by a narrow end (see page 18) and refrigerate cake for at least several hours to set the icing. Store in refrigerator and serve cold.

NOTES: 1. *If you use baking pan liner paper it must be buttered and floured for this recipe or the layers will stick to it.*

2. *This is a very firm cake; use a sharp, heavy knife for serving.*

3. *Dobosh Torte may be made a day ahead, or it may be frozen.*

4. *Dobosh Torte is traditionally made with a layer of caramelized sugar on top. I prefer it this way with icing on top—it is easier to prepare, easier to serve, easier to eat, and, to my taste, more delicious.*

Chocolate Mousse Torte

Of the many recipes that were born in my kitchen, this was one of the most exciting because it became The New York Times's *1972* Dessert of the Year.

6 TO 8 PORTIONS

8 ounces (8 squares) semisweet chocolate
1 tablespoon instant coffee
¼ cup boiling water
8 eggs, separated
⅔ cup sugar
1 teaspoon vanilla extract
⅛ teaspoon salt

Adjust rack to center of oven. Preheat oven to 350 degrees. Butter a 9-inch round ovenproof glass pie plate. Dust it with fine, dry bread crumbs. Set aside.

Place chocolate in the top of a small double boiler over hot water. Dissolve the coffee in the boiling water and pour it over the chocolate. Cover and let stand over low heat, stirring occasionally with a small wire whisk until the chocolate is almost melted. Remove chocolate from heat and continue to stir until smooth. Set aside to cool slightly.

In the small bowl of an electric mixer beat the yolks at high speed for about 5 minutes, until they are pale lemon-colored and thickened. Gradually add the sugar and continue to beat at high speed for 5 minutes more until very thick. Add the vanilla and chocolate, beating slowly and scraping the bowl with a rubber spatula until blended.

Remove from mixer. In the large bowl of electric mixer beat the whites with the salt until stiff but not dry. Gradually, in two or three small additions, fold half of the whites into the chocolate (do not be too thorough) and then fold the chocolate into the remaining whites, folding only until no whites show. Handling as little as possible, gently remove and set aside about 4 cups of the mousse. Turn the balance into the pie plate; it will barely reach the top. Very gently spread level and place in oven to bake.

Cover reserved mousse and refrigerate.

When mousse has baked 25 minutes turn off the heat. Leave it in the oven for 5 minutes more. Then remove from oven and cool on a rack. (Mousse will rise during baking and then, while cooling, it will settle in the center, leaving a high rim.)

When *completely* cool, remove reserved mousse from refrigerator.

Handling as little as possible, place the refrigerated mousse in the center of the shell of baked mousse. Mound it slightly higher in the center, but be careful to handle as little as possible or it will lose the air beaten into it.

Refrigerate for at least 2 to 3 hours.

TOPPING

1½ cups heavy cream
1½ teaspoons vanilla extract
⅓ cup confectioners sugar

In a chilled bowl with chilled beaters, whip above ingredients until they hold a definite shape. Spread over the unbaked part of the mousse, excluding the rim. Refrigerate.

OPTIONAL: *Coarsely grate some semisweet chocolate over the top.*

NOTES: 1. *An alternate and very attractive way of applying the whipped cream: Use a pastry bag fitted with a medium star tube and, as Jean Hewitt did when she prepared this torte to be photographed for* The New York Times, *form a lattice pattern over the top of the pie and a border around the edge.*

2. *Place the pie plate on a folded napkin (on a platter or cake plate) to hold the plate steady when serving.*

Queen Mother's Cake

12 PORTIONS

Jan Smeterlin, the eminent pianist, picked up this recipe on a concert tour in Austria. He loves to cook, and when he baked this to serve to the Queen Mother of England, she asked for the recipe and then served it frequently at her royal parties. If there could be only one cake in the whole world, this would be my choice.

6 ounces sweet or semisweet chocolate,
    coarsely cut or broken
    (I prefer Maillard Eagle Sweet.)
6 ounces (¾ cup) butter
¾ cup sugar
6 eggs, separated
6 ounces (1¼ cups) almonds, finely ground
    (See page 11.)
⅛ teaspoon salt

Adjust rack to one-third up from the bottom of the oven. Preheat oven to 375 degrees. Butter a 9 × 2½- or 3-inch spring-form pan and line the bottom with wax paper or baking pan liner paper. Butter the paper and dust all over it lightly with fine, dry bread crumbs.

Melt chocolate in the top of a small double boiler over hot water on low heat. Remove from heat and set aside to cool slightly.

In the small bowl of an electric mixer cream the butter. Add sugar and beat at moderately high speed for 2 to 3 minutes. Add yolks one at a time, beating until each addition is thoroughly incorporated.

Beat in the chocolate and then, on lowest speed, gradually beat in the almonds, scraping the bowl with a rubber spatula as necessary to keep mixture smooth. Transfer to a large mixing bowl.

In the large bowl of an electric mixer beat the salt with the whites until they hold a definite shape, or are stiff but not dry. Stir a large spoonful of the whites into the chocolate and then, in three additions, fold in the balance. Turn into pan. If necessary, level top by rotating pan briskly from side to side.

Bake for 20 minutes at 375 degrees. Reduce oven temperature to 350 degrees and bake for an additional 50 minutes. (Total baking time is 1 hour and 10 minutes.) Do not overbake. Cake should remain soft and moist in the center.

Wet and slightly wring out a folded towel and place it on a smooth surface. Remove spring form from oven and place it directly on the wet towel. Let stand 20 minutes. Remove sides of spring form. Place a rack over the cake and carefully invert. Remove bottom of form and paper lining. Cover with another rack and invert again to cool right side up. The cake will be about 1¾ inches high. If the top is uneven cut it level with a long thin knife.

When the cake is completely cool, place four strips of wax paper around the edges of a cake plate. Gently transfer the cake to the plate, bottom up. Handle with care. Chilling the cake will make it easier to handle, but then it must be room temperature when it is iced. If the cake is iced when cold the icing will be dull. Prepare the following:

ICING FOR QUEEN MOTHER'S CAKE

½ cup heavy cream
2 teaspoons instant coffee
8 ounces sweet or semisweet chocolate,
coarsely cut or broken
(I prefer Maillard Eagle Sweet.)

Scald the cream in a medium-size heavy saucepan over moderate heat until it begins to form small bubbles around the edge or a skin on top. Still over heat, add instant coffee and stir briskly with a small wire whisk until dissolved. Add chocolate. After 1 minute remove from heat and stir with wire whisk until chocolate is melted and mixture is smooth. Transfer to a small bowl or place the bottom of the saucepan in cold water to stop the cooking.

Let mixture stand at room temperature for 15 minutes or more, stirring occasionally until it reaches room temperature. Stir (do not beat) and pour all over the top of the cake. Use a long narrow metal spatula to smooth the top, letting a bit of the icing run down the sides. Use a small metal spatula to smooth the sides. After about 5 minutes remove the wax paper strips, pulling each one out by a narrow end (see page 18) before the icing hardens.

NOTES: 1. *The cake may rise and crack unevenly during baking—O.K. It will level almost completely while cooling.*

2. *If you have a turntable or a Lazy Susan, use it when icing the cake. (See page 15.)*

Truffles Torte

10 PORTIONS

4 ounces (4 squares) semisweet chocolate
2 ounces (2 squares) unsweetened chocolate
3 tablespoons sifted all-purpose flour
7 ounces (2 cups) pecans, finely ground
  (See page 11.)
6 ounces (¾ cup) butter
¾ cup sugar
5 eggs, separated
Pinch of salt

Adjust rack to center of oven. Preheat oven to 350 degrees. Butter a 9 × 2- or 3-inch spring-form pan. Dust it all over lightly with fine, dry bread crumbs.

Melt both chocolates in top of double boiler over hot water on moderate heat. Set aside to cool slightly. Stir the flour into the pecans. Set aside.

In the small bowl of an electric mixer cream the butter. Add sugar and beat at moderately high speed for 1 to 2 minutes. Add yolks one at a time, beating well after each. On low speed add the chocolate and then gradually add the nuts, scraping the bowl with a rubber spatula as necessary to keep mixture smooth. Transfer to a large mixing bowl.

Beat whites with the salt until they hold a point, stiff but not dry. The chocolate mixture will be quite stiff. First, stir two or three spoonfuls of the whites in to lighten it a bit. Then in three or four additions, small at first, gently fold in the balance of the whites. Turn into pan. Level top by rotating pan briskly back and forth.

Bake for 1 hour. Remove from oven. The cake will be 1¾ inches high. Cool in pan on a rack for about 15 minutes. Remove sides of pan and then cover with a rack and invert. Remove bottom of pan. Cover with another rack and invert again to cool completely, right side up.

While cake is baking or cooling, make the truffles, or they may be made ahead of time and kept at room temperature for a day or frozen for a longer time.

TRUFFLES

3 ounces (3 squares) semisweet chocolate
2 tablespoons butter (at room temperature)
1 egg yolk
optional: 1 teaspoon light or dark rum,
    or Cognac
Unsweetened cocoa

In top of small double boiler set over hot water on moderate heat, melt the chocolate. Remove chocolate from heat. With a small wire whisk beat in the butter, then the yolk, and the optional rum or Cognac. Beat until smooth. Let stand, stirring occasionally, until mixture thickens slightly. (It may be stirred very briefly over ice water.) Drop in ten mounds on wax paper. Let stand for about half an hour to an hour until firm enough to handle.

Strain some cocoa onto a piece of wax paper. Have another piece of wax paper ready for the finished truffles. Coat your hands lightly with cocoa. Roll each truffle into an uneven ball. Roll it around in the cocoa. Place it on the wax paper. Continue to cocoa your hands as necessary. (If necessary, reroll truffles in cocoa before placing them on the cake.)

Place four strips of wax paper around the edges of a cake plate. Gently transfer the cake to the plate, bottom up.

ICING

6 ounces (6 squares) semisweet chocolate
¼ pound (½ cup) butter
1 egg yolk
1 tablespoon light or dark rum, or Cognac

Melt chocolate in top of double boiler over hot water on moderate heat. Set aside to cool.

In the small bowl of an electric mixer cream the butter. Beat in the cooled chocolate, yolk, and rum or Cognac. Beat briefly at high speed until a bit lighter in color. Smooth over top and sides of cake. Place truffles evenly around top of cake, one to a portion. Remove wax paper strips by pulling each one out by a narrow end. (See page 18.)

Helen McCully's French Chocolate Torte

6 PORTIONS

This divine cake, small and chic, is a specialty of my good friend Helen McCully, the food editor of House Beautiful.

4 ounces (4 squares) semisweet chocolate
¼ pound (½ cup) butter
⅔ cup sugar
3 eggs
¼ cup fine, dry bread crumbs
5 ounces (1 cup) almonds,
  finely ground
  (See page 11. For this recipe
  the nuts need not be strained.)
Finely grated rind of 1 large orange

Adjust rack to center of oven and preheat oven to 375 degrees. Butter an 8-inch round layer-cake pan. Line the bottom with paper. Butter the paper. Dust all over with fine, dry bread crumbs. (These are in addition to those called for in the list of ingredients.)

In the top of a small double boiler over hot water on moderate heat, melt the chocolate. Remove pan from heat and set aside to cool slightly.

Meanwhile, in the small bowl of an electric mixer, cream the butter. Gradually add the sugar and beat at moderately high speed for a few minutes. Beat in the eggs one at a time, beating well after each and scraping the bowl with a rubber spatula as necessary to keep mixture blended. It will look curdled—O.K. On lowest speed add the chocolate, bread crumbs, and almonds, beating only until smooth. Remove from mixer and stir in orange rind.

Turn into prepared pan. Spread the top level. Bake in preheated oven for 25 minutes. The center of the cake will be soft and moist and will not seem thoroughly baked; this is correct.

Remove from oven and cool in pan on a rack for about 30 minutes. With a small, sharp knife cut around edge of cake to release. Place rack over cake and invert. Remove pan and paper. Let stand until completely cool. The cake will be soft. Either let it stand for a few hours or refrigerate it briefly until firm.

Place four strips of wax paper around the edges of a cake plate. The cake is very fragile; with a wide metal spatula transfer it to the plate, bottom up. Brush away any loose crumbs.

GLAZE

2 ounces (2 squares) unsweetened chocolate
2 ounces (2 squares) semisweet chocolate
2 ounces (¼ cup) butter
2 teaspoons honey
optional: ¼ cup toasted, slivered almonds
   (see Note), or 6 pieces of chocolate-
   covered candied orange rind

Place both chocolates, butter, and honey in the top of a small double boiler over hot water on moderate heat. Cook, stirring occasionally, until melted and smooth. Remove from heat.

Replace the water in the bottom of the double boiler with ice water, deep enough to touch the upper section. Place glaze over ice water and stir briefly and constantly only until it cools and barely begins to thicken very slightly. Watch it carefully so that it doesn't harden.

Pour over top of cake. With a long, narrow metal spatula spread it smoothly over the top, letting some run down on the sides a bit. With a small, narrow metal spatula smooth the sides. Remove the wax paper, gently pulling each piece out by a narrow end. (See page 18.)

OPTIONAL: *Before the glaze hardens, garland the rim of the cake with toasted, slivered almonds, placing them close together, or with 6 pieces of chocolate-covered orange rind (1 on each portion).*

NOTE: *"Slivered" almonds are those cut in squarish oblongs, or "julienne." To toast them, bake in a small shallow pan in the center of a preheated 350-degree oven. Shake pan occasionally until nuts are lightly browned, about 7 to 8 minutes.*

Chocolate Applesauce Torte with Kumquats

10 PORTIONS

1 cup fine, dry bread crumbs
1½ teaspoons double-acting baking powder
6 eggs, separated
1 cup sugar
2 tablespoons unsweetened cocoa
½ cup applesauce
Finely grated rind of 1 large orange
⅛ teaspoon salt

Adjust two oven racks to divide the oven into equal thirds. Preheat oven to 350 degrees. Butter three round 9-inch layer-cake pans, and dust all over lightly with fine, dry bread crumbs. (These are in addition to those called for in the recipe.) Set aside.

Place bread crumbs in a small bowl. Through a fine strainer add the baking powder. Stir well to mix and set aside.

In small bowl of electric mixer beat the egg yolks for 1 minute. Gradually add the sugar and beat at high speed for 5 minutes until thick. On lowest speed add the cocoa and the applesauce. Then add the bread crumbs, scraping the bowl with a rubber spatula and beating only until smooth. Remove from mixer. Stir in orange rind. Set aside.

In large bowl of electric mixer beat the egg whites with the salt until the whites hold a definite shape, stiff but not dry. Fold about one-third of the whites into the cocoa mixture and then fold the cocoa mixture gently into the remaining whites until no whites show.

Turn into prepared pans. Tilt pans gently to level batter. Bake 18 to 20 minutes or until tops spring back when lightly touched and layers begin to come away from sides of pans.

Remove from oven and let stand for about 3 minutes. Cover each pan with a rack and invert. Let stand for a minute or so until layers fall out of pans. If layers are stuck to the sides anywhere, release them with a small knife. Remove pans. Cover each layer with another rack and invert again to finish cooling, right side up. Layers will be thin, about ¾ inch.

Place four strips of wax paper around the edges of a cake plate. Place one layer of cake on plate.

Prepare the following:

KUMQUAT CREAM

1 10-ounce jar preserved kumquats
¼ cup brandy, or dark rum
3 cups heavy cream
⅔ cup confectioners sugar
1 tablespoon vanilla extract

Thoroughly drain the kumquats in a strainer set over a bowl. Mix ¼ cup of the drained kumquat syrup with the brandy or rum and set aside.

On a board, with a small, sharp knife, cut the kumquats roughly into quarters. Carefully remove the pits. Chop the kumquats into small dice, about ⅛ inch. Set aside.

In a chilled bowl with chilled beaters, whip the cream with the sugar and vanilla until it holds a shape and is firm enough to be used as filling and icing.

Brush one-third of the kumquat and brandy or rum syrup over the first layer of cake. Spread with a thick layer of the whipped cream. Sprinkle with one-third of the kumquats. Cover with the second layer of cake; brush second layer with syrup, spread with whipped cream, sprinkle with kumquats. Top with third layer and remaining syrup. Spread the remaining whipped cream over the sides and top. Sprinkle remaining kumquats evenly over the top. Remove wax paper strips by pulling each one out by a narrow end. (See page 18.)

Refrigerate for several hours before serving for flavors to blend. Serve very cold.

OPTIONAL: *Some of the whipped cream may be reserved to be piped on the finished cake, using a pastry bag and a star tube, and piping the cream in a ruffle (after removing the wax paper) around the base and the rim.*

NOTE: *In the absence of kumquats you might use ¼ to ½ cup of Grand Marnier for brushing the cake layers and either use the whipped cream alone or top it with coarsely cut walnuts or pecans.*

Small Walnut Torte

(Hungarian)

6 TO 8 PORTIONS

5 ounces (1¼ cups) walnuts, finely ground
(See page 11.)
3 tablespoons cornstarch
½ teaspoon double-acting baking powder
4 eggs, separated
½ cup sugar
1 tablespoon lemon juice
⅛ teaspoon salt

Adjust rack to center of oven. Preheat oven to 350 degrees. Butter two 8-inch round layer-cake pans. Line the bottom with paper. Butter the paper and dust lightly with fine, dry bread crumbs.

Place walnuts in a medium bowl. Through a fine strainer, add the cornstarch and baking powder. With a fork, stir until completely mixed. Set aside.

In the small bowl of an electric mixer at high speed beat the yolks and sugar for 10 minutes until very thick. On low speed, add the lemon juice and the nut mixture. Remove from mixer.

Beat egg whites with the salt until stiff but not dry. The yolk mixture will be very stiff. In order to lighten it a bit, actually stir in two to three spoonfuls of the beaten whites. Then gradually, in four or five additions, fold in the balance of the whites.

Divide the mixture between the prepared pans (layers will be thin). Spread gently to level. Bake 25 to 30 minutes or until tops spring back when lightly touched and cakes come away from sides of pans. Remove from oven and let stand for 2 or 3 minutes.

If necessary, cut around the sides to release. Cover each layer with a rack and invert. Remove pans and papers. Cover with racks and invert again to cool completely right side up. Prepare Bittersweet Chocolate Icing.

BITTERSWEET CHOCOLATE ICING

6 ounces semisweet, bittersweet,
or extra-bittersweet chocolate
¼ pound (½ cup) butter
1 egg

Break up chocolate in top of small double boiler. Place over hot water on moderate heat to melt. Remove from hot water and set aside to cool to tepid. In small bowl of electric mixer, cream the butter. Beat in the egg. (Mixture will not be smooth.) Add the chocolate and beat, scraping the bowl with a rubber spatula, until very smooth and slightly lightened in color.

Place four strips of wax paper around the edges of a cake plate. Place one layer on the plate, upside down. With a long, narrow metal spatula, cover with about one-third of the icing. Place second layer on, right side up. Cover top and sides smoothly with the remaining icing, spreading with a small metal spatula around the sides.

Remove wax paper strips by pulling each one out by a narrow end. (See page 18.) Refrigerate. Serve cold.

OPTIONAL: *Some of the icing may be reserved and used with a pastry bag and a star tube to decorate the torte, or the top and/or sides of the torte may be covered with chopped walnuts. Or place 6 to 8 large walnut halves around the top.*

Swedish Almond Torte

10 PORTIONS

PASTRY

1⅔ cups sifted all-purpose flour
1¼ teaspoons double-acting baking powder
¼ cup sugar
¼ pound (½ cup) cold butter,
     cut into 6 pieces
1 egg

Butter a round cake pan measuring 9 × 1½ to 1¾ inches. Line the bottom with paper and butter the paper.

Sift together flour and baking powder into a bowl. Stir in the sugar. With a pastry blender cut in the butter until the mixture resembles coarse crumbs. Stir egg slightly with a fork and, using the fork, stir it into the flour mixture. Turn it onto a board or smooth surface and knead slightly until it holds together. "Break" the dough by pushing off small amounts of the dough (about 2 tablespoons) with the heel of your hand, pressing each piece against the working surface and pushing away from you. Continue until all the dough has been pushed off. Re-form the dough and push it off, or "break" it, again. Form the dough into a ball. Flatten slightly.

Place dough between two sheets of wax paper. With a rolling pin roll gently, working from the center out, in all directions. Roll into a circle 11½ to 12 inches in diameter. Work quickly or the dough will become sticky. (If that should happen, chill it a bit.)

Remove top piece of wax paper. Invert dough into the cake tin, dropping it carefully into place. Remove remaining wax paper. Press the dough firmly into place against the bottom and sides. If it is sticky, flour your fingertips. Cut off any excess and use it to patch any low or empty spots. Cut dough even with top of cake pan. Set aside.

FILLING

¼ cup nuts (any kind), finely ground
    (see page 11),
        or fine, dry bread crumbs
1 cup fruit preserves, jam, or jelly
    (thick and seedless)

Sprinkle nuts or bread crumbs evenly over pastry. Stir preserves to soften slightly. Drop the preserves in small mounds, close together, over the ground nuts or bread crumbs, and with the back of a teaspoon spread evenly. Refrigerate while preparing the topping.

Adjust oven rack one-third of the way up from the bottom. Pre-heat oven to 325 degrees.

TOPPING

5 ounces (1 cup) blanched almonds
¼ pound (½ cup) butter
1 cup confectioners sugar
½ teaspoon almond extract
2 eggs
Finely grated rind of 1 lemon

Grind almonds in a nut grinder or blender. For this recipe they do not have to be strained. Set aside. In small bowl of electric mixer cream the butter. Add sugar and beat until smooth. Add almond extract and 1 egg. Beat until smooth, scraping bowl with a rubber spatula as necessary to keep mixture smooth. On lowest speed gradually add the ground almonds and then the remaining egg. Beat until smooth. Remove from mixer. Stir in lemon rind. Spread this topping evenly over filling. Pastry shell should extend slightly above topping.

Bake 1 hour and 20 minutes or until top is well browned. Remove from oven and place on a rack to cool completely. (While cooling, the torte will sink a bit in the center.) Cover with a rack and invert. Remove pan and paper. Cover with another rack and invert again, leaving torte right side up.

Strain confectioners sugar generously over the top or prepare the following glaze:

GLAZE

½ cup confectioners sugar
1 scant tablespoon lemon juice
1 teaspoon tasteless salad oil
   (such as safflower or corn oil)
optional: Toasted, sliced almonds

Place the sugar, lemon juice, and salad oil in a small bowl. With a rubber spatula mix until completely smooth. Glaze should be the consistency of thick cream sauce. If necessary, adjust with additional sugar or lemon juice.

Pour the glaze over the topping, and with a pastry brush spread a thin coating of it over the topping only, not the crust. If glaze settles heavily in the center well of the torte, remove excess with the brush.

While the glaze is still wet it may be sprinkled with a few spoonfuls of the optional toasted, sliced almonds.

Let torte stand at least 3 to 4 hours or overnight before serving.

Royal Viennese Walnut Torte

12 TO 16
PORTIONS

¼ cup strained, unsweetened cocoa
  (preferably Dutch process)
1 pound (4½ cups) walnuts, finely ground
  (See page 11.)
12 eggs, separated
2 cups sugar
¼ teaspoon salt

The three layers for this torte should not be baked too high or too low in the oven or they will burn. Adjust two racks to divide the oven in equal thirds. Preheat oven to 350 degrees. Butter three 9-inch round layer-cake pans (not the kind with loose bottoms). Line the bottoms with paper. Butter the paper. Dust all over lightly with fine, dry bread crumbs.

Add the cocoa to the walnuts and, with a fork, stir to mix. Set aside.

In the small bowl of an electric mixer, at high speed, beat the yolks about 3 minutes until thick and pale lemon-colored. Reduce the speed and gradually add the sugar. Increase the speed to high again and continue to beat for 5 minutes more, until very thick. Remove from mixer and transfer to a very large bowl.

In the large bowl of an electric mixer (with clean beaters) beat the egg whites and the salt until stiff but not dry. Remove from mixer. Fold half of the nut mixture into the yolks and then, in the following order, fold in one-third of the whites, the remaining half of the nut mixture, half of the remaining whites, and then the balance of the whites.

Divide the batter among the prepared pans. Spread tops level.

Bake 45 to 50 minutes or until tops spring back when lightly touched and layers come slightly away from the sides of the pans. (During baking the layers will rise and then sink—O.K.)

Remove pans from oven. Cover with racks and invert but *do not remove pans until they are cool enough to handle.* If necessary, cut around edges to release, invert, remove pans and papers, cover with racks, and invert again to finish cooling right side up.

Prepare the following Coffee Buttercream for filling and icing:

COFFEE BUTTERCREAM

6 egg yolks
½ cup sugar
3 tablespoons instant coffee
½ cup boiling water
1 pound (2 cups) butter
1 teaspoon vanilla extract
3 tablespoons dark rum, or Cognac
optional: ¼ cup additional rum, or Cognac,
    or crème de cacao

Place yolks in top of small double boiler. Beat a little, just to blend, with a small wire whisk. Gradually stir in the sugar. Dissolve instant coffee in boiling water. Very gradually whisk the coffee into the yolk mixture. Place over hot water on moderate heat. *Water must not touch top of double boiler and it must not boil,* or the mixture will curdle. Cook over moderately low heat, stirring and scraping pot constantly with a rubber spatula, for about 10 to 15 minutes until mixture thickens to a soft custard consistency, about 170 to 175 degrees on a candy thermometer. Remove from heat. Place the custard mixture over ice water. Stir occasionally until mixture is cool.

Beat butter in small bowl of electric mixer to cream it slightly. Very gradually add the custard mixture, the vanilla, and the 3 tablespoons rum or Cognac and beat until smooth. (If necessary, refrigerate mixture to firm it, and then beat again.)

Place four strips of wax paper around the edges of a cake plate. Place the first layer on the plate right side up. Optional, additional rum, Cognac, or crème de cacao may be sprinkled over each layer before spreading with the buttercream. (The filling must be spread thin or you won't have enough to cover the top and sides.) Continue stacking layers (right side up) and buttercream. Cover the sides and then the top with the buttercream, spreading it smoothly.

If you wish, reserve some of the buttercream and with a pastry bag fitted with a small star tube, form a ruffled border on the top rim of the cake and another around the base.

Remove wax paper strips, sliding each one out by a narrow end. (See page 18.) Refrigerate and serve cold.

OPTIONAL: *Decorate top with 12 walnut halves and, if you wish, coat the sides with rather finely chopped walnuts, applying them with the palm of your hand and your fingers before removing the wax paper strips.*

Mocha Pecan Torte
(Mexican)

10 PORTIONS

3 tablespoons sifted all-purpose flour
1 teaspoon double-acting baking powder
12 ounces (3½ cups) pecans, finely ground
(See page 11.)
6 eggs, separated
2 tablespoons instant coffee
1½ cups sugar
⅛ teaspoon salt

Adjust rack to the center of the oven. Preheat oven to 350 degrees. Butter two 9-inch layer-cake pans. Line the bottoms with wax paper. Butter the paper and dust with fine, dry bread crumbs.

Sift or strain flour and baking powder over the pecans. Stir to mix thoroughly and set aside.

In the small bowl of an electric mixer beat egg yolks at high speed for about 3 minutes until pale lemon-colored. Reduce speed while gradually adding instant coffee and sugar. Increase speed to high again and beat for 5 minutes until very thick. Remove from mixer and set aside.

In large bowl of electric mixer (with clean beaters) beat egg whites with the salt until stiff but not dry. In three additions, fold about three-quarters of the whites into the yolks. Pour the yolks over the balance of the whites and fold together—don't be too thorough. Pour all of the egg mixture over the nut mixture and fold gently until blended.

Divide batter into prepared pans. Level tops with spatula. Bake 35 to 40 minutes or until tops spring back when lightly touched, and layers barely begin to come away from sides of pans.

Invert onto racks, but do not remove cake pans. Let cool for about 10 minutes. Then, if necessary, cut around cakes to release, cover with racks and invert, remove pans and papers, cover with racks, and invert again to finish cooling right side up.

FILLING AND ICING FOR MOCHA PECAN TORTE

3 ounces (6 tablespoons) butter
4 ounces (4 squares) unsweetened chocolate
1 tablespoon plus 1 teaspoon instant coffee
2 cups confectioners sugar
⅓ cup milk
2 eggs
1 teaspoon vanilla extract
optional: Crème de cacao, Kahlúa, or Cognac

Place butter and chocolate in top of small double boiler over hot water on moderate heat. Stir until melted. Add instant coffee and stir to dissolve. Remove from heat and set aside to cool.

In a small mixer bowl, mix sugar, milk, eggs, and vanilla. Place in a larger bowl half filled with ice and cold water. Add cooled chocolate and beat at high speed for 3 to 4 minutes, scraping bowl occasionally with a rubber spatula until mixture becomes fluffy and light in color and the consistency of whipped butter—stiff enough to hold its shape.

Place four strips of wax paper around edge of cake plate. Place first layer upside down. If you wish, brush with optional crème de cacao, Kahlúa, or Cognac. Spread with filling about ½ inch thick. Cover with top layer, right side up. Again, brush with optional liqueur. Spread icing smoothly over top and sides of cake. Cut carefully between bottom of cake and wax paper strips, and then remove wax paper by pulling each strip out by a narrow end. (See page 18.)

Refrigerate for 2 to 3 hours or more before serving.

OPTIONAL: *Reserve a bit of the icing to use with a pastry bag fitted with a small star tube and form a border around the upper rim and another around the base of the cake. Or with the bag and star tube form ten rosettes around the top of the cake and place a large pecan half upright in each.*

NOTE: *If you have a turntable or Lazy Susan to work on, the icing may be spread smooth. If not, it might be easier to fluff it in irregular peaks with a spatula or the back of a spoon.*

Royal Norwegian Macaroon Torte

12 OR MORE
PORTIONS

PASTRY

2 cups sifted all-purpose flour

2 teaspoons double-acting baking powder

¼ teaspoon salt

½ cup sugar

½ pound (1 cup) butter

1 egg

Finely grated rind of 1 large lemon

Sift together flour, baking powder, and salt into a large bowl. Stir in the sugar. With a pastry blender, cut in the butter until mixture resembles coarse crumbs. With a fork, beat the egg lightly just to mix and stir it in along with lemon rind. Turn out onto a large board or smooth surface. Squeeze between your hands two or three times and then knead briefly with the heel of your hand only until the mixture holds together and leaves the board clean. Divide the dough in half and wrap one half in wax paper. Flatten slightly and refrigerate.

Place the other half in the center of an unbuttered 9-inch square cake pan. With floured fingertips press it out to cover the bottom and to rise 1 inch up the sides of the pan. Place in freezer or refrigerator while you prepare filling.

Adjust rack one-quarter up from bottom of oven. Preheat oven to 375 degrees.

FILLING

½ pound (1⅔ cups) blanched almonds,
   finely ground (See page 11.
   For this recipe they do not have
   to be strained.)

2 cups confectioners sugar

1 egg white

¼ cup light rum

¼ teaspoon almond extract

3 drops green food coloring

½ cup thick apricot preserves

In large bowl of electric mixer, on low speed, mix almonds, sugar, egg white, rum, almond extract, and green food coloring, scraping the bowl with a rubber spatula and beating until smooth.

Remove pastry shell from freezer or refrigerator. Stir the preserves slightly to soften and spread over the pastry, leaving ½-inch border around the edge of the pan.

Drop the filling over the preserves by small spoonfuls. The spoonfuls should touch each other and ought to cover the bottom and touch the sides of the crust. But it is all right if a bit of the preserves or bottom crust show through in a few spots.

Remove remaining half of pastry from refrigerator. Working quickly, roll between two pieces of wax paper into a 9-inch square. Remove top piece of paper. Using another 9-inch square pan over the rolled pastry, or a 9-inch square of wax paper as a pattern, cut uneven edges. Save trimmings to fill in where needed. If dough has become sticky, chill it briefly in the freezer.

Invert over filled torte and ease it gently into place. Remove wax paper. If necessary, trim the edges with a small, sharp knife, pressing the pastry trimmings into any gaps.

Bake 1 hour and 10 minutes or until top is well-browned and torte begins to come away from sides of pan. Cool to room temperature in cake pan on a rack.

With a small, firm, sharp knife cut around edges to release. Cover with a rack or cookie sheet and invert. Remove pan. Cover with another rack or cookie sheet and invert again, leaving torte right side up.

The torte must be refrigerated or placed briefly in the freezer until it is well chilled before it can be cut. Transfer to a cutting board.

With a very sharp, long, thin knife cut into oblongs, thin slices, or small squares. Serve at room temperature.

NOTE: *This rich pastry, if cut into small pieces, may be served on a tray of petits fours.*

Carrot-Nut Torte

8 PORTIONS

Finely grated rind of 1 large lemon
3 tablespoons lemon juice
1 cup very finely grated carrots, tightly packed
    (about 3 medium-size carrots) See Note 1.
6 ounces (1¼ cups) almonds, finely ground
    (See page 11. For this recipe
    they do not have to be strained.)
¾ cup fine, dry bread crumbs
¼ teaspoon mace
1 teaspoon double-acting baking powder
6 eggs, separated
1¼ cups sugar
⅛ teaspoon salt

Adjust rack one-third up from the bottom of the oven. Preheat oven to 350 degrees. Butter an 8-inch spring-form pan. Line the bottom with paper. Butter the paper and dust it all over with fine, dry bread crumbs (in addition to those called for in the recipe).

Mix lemon rind and juice and set aside. Place grated carrots and almonds in a large bowl and stir or toss with your fingers to mix thoroughly. Place bread crumbs in a small bowl and, through a fine strainer, add mace and baking powder. Stir to mix. Add to the carrot-almond mixture and, with a rubber spatula, mix thoroughly. Set aside.

In small bowl of electric mixer at high speed, beat the yolks about 3 minutes until they are pale lemon-colored. Reduce the speed and gradually add the sugar. Increase speed to high again and beat for 5 minutes more until very thick. Remove from mixer and stir in rind and juice. Add to carrot mixture and mix thoroughly with a rubber spatula.

Beat egg whites with the salt until they are stiff but not dry. In three or four additions (small at first) fold them into the carrot mixture. (When folding, grated carrots will collect on edge of rubber spatula. To remove them, reverse the spatula frequently, first folding with the curved edge down, and then with the straight edge down.) Fold only until no whites show.

Turn into prepared pan. If necessary, shake pan gently to level batter. Bake 1 hour and 5 minutes or until a cake tester comes out dry and the top springs back when lightly touched. Cool torte in pan on a rack for about 20 minutes.

With a sharp knife, pressing firmly against the sides of the pan, cut around the sides to release—do not use a sawing motion. Remove sides of pan. Cover torte with a rack, invert, and remove bottom of pan and paper. Cover with another rack and invert again to finish cooling right side up.

Place four strips of wax paper around the edges of a cake plate and gently transfer the torte, bottom side up. Prepare glaze.

GLAZE

1¾ cups confectioners sugar
1 tablespoon lemon juice
1 to 2 tablespoons boiling water

In a small bowl, stir ingredients very thoroughly to mix well, adjusting amount of liquid or sugar to make a mixture about the consistency of thick cream sauce. If it is too thin it will run. Pour it on the torte and with a long, narrow metal spatula smooth it over the top only. If a bit runs down the sides leave it that way, do not spread. Remove wax paper strips, pulling each one out by a narrow end. Let stand several hours or overnight for the glaze to set.

OPTIONAL: *Before the glaze sets, decorate the rim with lightly toasted whole almonds, or 8 whole glazed red cherries; or place one or more (depending on their size) marzipan carrots on top.*

NOTES: 1. *There is no need to peel the carrots. Just wash them and grate on a grater with small, round—not diamond-shaped—openings.*

2. *Do not freeze this torte after glazing it—the glaze becomes wet after thawing.*

Chocolate Cakes and Layer Cak

Chocolate Cake Squares

(Grandma Hermalin's)

9 PORTIONS

1 cup sifted all-purpose flour
1 teaspoon baking soda
½ teaspoon double-acting baking powder
⅛ teaspoon salt
¼ pound (½ cup) butter
1 teaspoon vanilla extract
1 cup sugar
1 egg
½ cup powdered, unsweetened cocoa
½ cup milk
1 tablespoon instant coffee
½ cup boiling water

Adjust oven rack one-third up from the bottom of the oven. Preheat oven to 350 degrees. Butter a 9-inch square cake pan and dust the bottom only, very lightly, with fine, dry bread crumbs.

Sift together flour, baking soda, baking powder, and salt. Set aside.

In small bowl of electric mixer cream the butter. Add vanilla and sugar and beat for a minute or two. Beat in the egg. On lowest speed, add the cocoa. Then, in this order, gradually add one-half of the milk, one-half of the dry ingredients, remaining milk, and remaining dry ingredients, scraping bowl frequently with a rubber spatula all during mixing. Mix only until smooth after each addition.

Dissolve the instant coffee in the boiling water. While it is still hot, add it very gradually on lowest speed to the chocolate mixture. Beat only until smooth. Batter will be thin. Turn it into the prepared pan.

Bake 40 minutes or until top springs back when lightly touched. Cool in pan on a rack for about 10 minutes. Cover with a rack and invert. Remove pan. Cover with another rack and invert again to finish cooling right side up. Prepare the following icing:

ICING

4 ounces (4 squares) semisweet chocolate
  (See Note.)
2 ounces (¼ cup) butter, cut in 4 pieces

In the top of a small double boiler over hot water on moderate heat, melt the chocolate. Remove top of double boiler. With a small wire whisk beat in the butter, one piece at a time, beating until each piece is thoroughly incorporated before adding the next.

This icing may be used immediately, or, if it is too thin, place the pan into ice water and stir constantly until icing thickens very slightly, but watch it closely to see that it doesn't harden. It should still be fluid when used.

Pour it over the cake and smooth with a long, narrow metal spatula.

NOTE: *If you like bittersweet chocolate, substitute 1 ounce of unsweetened chocolate for 1 ounce of the semisweet chocolate.*

Chocolate Cake Squares

(*Lydia Pinkham's*)

Lydia Pinkham was best known for her cure-all vegetable compound and her many activities in all the women's rights movements of her time. But first and last she was a good old-fashioned cook and housekeeper. Her recipe for chocolate cake does not contain any of her patent medicine.

9 PORTIONS

¼ pound (½ cup) butter
1 teaspoon vanilla extract
1 cup sugar
¼ teaspoon salt
1 egg
2 tablespoons powdered, unsweetened cocoa
1 teaspoon baking soda
1 cup buttermilk
1½ cups sifted all-purpose flour

Adjust rack to center of oven. Preheat oven to 350 degrees. Butter an 8- or 9-inch square pan and dust the bottom only with fine, dry bread crumbs.

In small bowl of electric mixer cream the butter. Add vanilla, sugar, and salt and beat for a minute or two. Beat in the egg, scraping bowl with a rubber spatula as necessary until smoothly blended. On lowest speed beat in the cocoa.

In a small bowl stir the baking soda into the buttermilk to dissolve and then gradually beat it into the batter. The mixture will look curdled—

O.K. On lowest speed, gradually add the flour, scraping the bowl with the rubber spatula and beating only until smooth.

Turn into prepared pan. Smooth the top and run the batter up on the sides a bit, leaving it slightly lower in the center.

Bake 40 minutes or until top springs back when lightly touched and cake begins to come away from sides of the pan. Remove from oven and cool in pan for about 5 minutes. Cover with a rack and invert. Remove pan. Cover with another rack and invert again to finish cooling right side up. Prepare the following icing:

ICING

6 ounces (6 squares) semisweet chocolate
   (or Tobler or Lindt Extra-Bittersweet)
3 tablespoons butter
1 egg plus 1 egg yolk

In the top of a small double boiler over hot water on moderate heat, melt the chocolate. Transfer melted chocolate to small bowl of electric mixer. Cool slightly for a minute or two. Add butter, egg, and yolk and beat on slow speed only until smooth, thick, and shiny. Do not overbeat. It should stay dark; additional beating will lighten the color.

Turn all the icing onto the top of the cake and with a long, narrow metal spatula spread over the top only (not the sides). Then, with the tip of a small spoon, pull it up in small peaks, making even rows that completely cover the top of the cake.

Fudge Cake with Fudge

12 TO 16
PORTIONS

4 ounces (4 squares) unsweetened chocolate
½ cup hot water
1¾ cups sugar
2 cups sifted cake flour
1 teaspoon baking soda
¼ teaspoon salt
¼ pound (½ cup) butter
1 teaspoon vanilla extract
3 eggs
⅔ cup milk

Adjust racks to divide oven in thirds. Preheat oven to 350 degrees. Butter two 9-inch square cake pans.

Place chocolate and hot water in top of small double boiler over hot water on moderate heat. Cook, stirring occasionally, until chocolate is melted and mixture is smooth. Mix in ½ cup of the sugar (reserve remaining 1¼ cups) and continue to cook 2 minutes longer, stirring with a rubber spatula to keep mixture smooth. Remove top of double boiler and set aside.

Sift together flour, baking soda, and salt. Set aside. In large bowl of electric mixer cream the butter. Add vanilla and reserved 1¼ cups sugar and beat for about a minute or two. Scrape the bowl with a rubber spatula as necessary to keep mixture smooth. Beat in eggs one at a time, beating until thoroughly incorporated after each addition. On lowest speed alternately add sifted dry ingredients in three additions and milk in two additions, scraping the bowl with the spatula as necessary and beating only until smooth after each addition. Add the chocolate mixture (don't worry if it is still warm) and beat only until smooth.

Divide evenly between prepared pans. Tilt pans gently to level batter. Bake 30 to 40 minutes or until the tops spring back when lightly touched and cakes come away from sides of pans.

Cool cakes in pans for 5 minutes. Cover with racks or cookie sheets and invert. Remove pans. Cover with racks and invert again to cool right sides up.

Place the bottom layer upside down on a platter or board. Prepare the following fudge for filling and icing:

FUDGE

3 cups sugar
1 cup milk

56

Pinch of salt
3 tablespoons light corn syrup
4 ounces (4 squares) unsweetened chocolate,
    coarsely cut
⅓ cup (5⅓ tablespoons) butter
2 teaspoons vanilla extract

Place sugar, milk, salt, corn syrup, and chocolate over moderate heat in a heavy saucepan with at least a 3-quart capacity. (See Note 1.) Bring slowly to the boil, stirring occasionally with a wooden spoon or spatula until the sugar is dissolved and the chocolate is melted. Insert a candy thermometer in the saucepan and let the syrup boil until the temperature reaches 232 degrees (or until the syrup forms a very soft ball in cold water).

Immediately, in order to stop the cooking, transfer to a large mixing bowl. Cut the butter into small pieces and add. Replace the thermometer and let mixture stand without stirring until the temperature drops to 110 degrees. (This might take as long as 1 hour.)

Add the vanilla. With a heavy wooden spatula stir and beat for 3 to 5 minutes until this heavy mixture thickens a bit more. Do not wait too long. You are making fudge; it will harden quickly and it must be spread before it hardens. Work very quickly—spread about half the fudge roughly on the bottom layer, cover with top layer placed right side up so that both flat sides meet in the center, and spread fudge on top. Do not try to spread it on the sides, but just let some of it run down unevenly.

NOTES: 1. *If the saucepan is too small, the syrup will boil over.*

2. *If the fudge icing becomes too thick and stiff, add boiling water, a few drops at a time, to soften it to the right consistency.*

3. *To make Fudge Squares, ice the layers separately and do not stack them on top of each other.*

4. *Serve as is, or à la mode with ice cream, or all the way—with a bowl of ice cream, a bowl of whipped cream, and a bowl of walnut halves.*

Walnut Fudge Pie à la Mode with Hot Fudge Sauce

Although this is called a pie, it does not have a crust. It is a dense chocolate cake, almost like Brownies baked in a pie plate.

2 ounces (2 squares) unsweetened chocolate
¼ pound (½ cup) butter
1 teaspoon vanilla extract
1 cup sugar
2 eggs, separated
2 tablespoons hot water
⅓ cup sifted all-purpose flour
½ cup walnuts, cut in medium-size pieces
Pinch of salt

6 TO 8 PORTIONS

Adjust rack to center of oven. Preheat oven to 350 degrees. Line a 9-inch ovenproof glass pie plate with a large piece of aluminum foil. (See directions for crumb crust, page 284, for lining a pie plate with aluminum foil.) Brush the foil well with soft or melted butter.

In the top of a small double boiler over hot water melt the chocolate. Remove from heat and set aside.

In small bowl of electric mixer cream the butter. Add the vanilla and sugar and beat for a minute or two. Beat in the egg yolks and then the chocolate. When smooth add the hot water and then the flour, scraping bowl with a rubber spatula as necessary and beating only until smooth. Remove from mixer and stir in the walnuts.

Beat the whites with the salt until they hold a peak, stiff but not dry, and fold them into the chocolate mixture. Turn into pie plate and spread the top level.

Bake 35 minutes. During baking the cake will rise and then sink—correctly. The top will have formed a crust but it will be soft inside. Cool in the plate on a rack. When *completely* cool, let stand for about ½ to 1 hour to become firm and then cover with a cookie sheet or a rack and invert. Remove pie plate and aluminum foil. Replace pie plate over pie and invert again.

Just before serving place scoops of ice cream on the top of the pie; or place a ring of whipped cream (1 cup heavy cream beaten with ¼ cup confectioners sugar and 1 scant teaspoon vanilla) around the edge and fill the center with ice cream.

With this, pass Hot Fudge Sauce (page 399), or any other chocolate sauce.

Palm Beach Chocolate Layer Cake

3 ounces (3 squares) unsweetened chocolate
2 cups sifted cake flour
1 teaspoon baking soda
½ pound (1 cup) butter
1 teaspoon vanilla extract
1 pound (2¼ cups, firmly packed)
    dark brown sugar
2 eggs
1 cup boiling water

10 PORTIONS

Adjust rack to center of oven. Preheat oven to 375 degrees. Butter two round 9-inch layer-cake pans and dust all over lightly with fine, dry bread crumbs. Set aside.

Melt chocolate over hot water, then set aside to cool. Sift together flour and baking soda and set aside.

In large bowl of electric mixer cream the butter. Add vanilla. Gradually add the sugar and beat for a minute or two, scraping the bowl with a rubber spatula as necessary. Beat in the eggs and then the melted chocolate. Beat until smooth. On lowest speed alternately add the sifted dry ingredients in three additions and the boiling water, very gradually at first, in two additions, scraping the bowl as necessary with the rubber spatula.

Divide into prepared pans. Bake 30 minutes or until cakes come away from sides of pans and tops spring back when lightly touched.

Cool in pans on racks for about 5 minutes. Cover with racks and invert. Remove pans. Cover with racks and invert again to finish cooling right side up.

When cool, place one layer upside down on a cake plate protected with four strips of wax paper. Prepare the following:

PALM BEACH CHOCOLATE FILLING AND ICING

4½ ounces (4½ squares) unsweetened chocolate
3 ounces (¾ stick) butter
1 pound (3½ cups, packed) confectioners sugar
2 eggs
1 tablespoon hot water
1 teaspoon vanilla extract

In a small, heavy saucepan over low heat, melt the chocolate and butter. Transfer to large bowl of electric mixer. Add all remaining ingredients at once. Starting at low speed and gradually increasing to high, beat until smooth, scraping bowl as necessary with a rubber spatula.

Use immediately, as icing forms a crust very quickly. Work quickly. Spread about one third over bottom layer. Cover with top layer, placed right side up so that both flat sides meet in the center. Pour remainder of icing over the top and quickly spread it on the top and sides of the cake.

Remove wax paper strips by pulling each one out by a narrow end. (See page 18.)

Palm Beach Chocolate Tube Cake

8 TO 10 PORTIONS

2 cups sifted cake flour
1 teaspoon double-acting baking powder
3 ounces (3 squares) unsweetened chocolate
¼ pound (½ cup) butter
1 cup boiling water
2 cups sugar
1 teaspoon vanilla extract
2 eggs, separated
1 teaspoon baking soda
½ cup sour cream
Pinch of salt

Adjust rack one-third up from bottom of oven. Preheat oven to 350 degrees. Butter a 9-inch tube pan. Line the bottom with paper and butter the paper. Dust very lightly with fine, dry bread crumbs. Set aside.

Sift together flour and baking powder and set aside.

Combine chocolate, butter, and boiling water in a small saucepan over moderate heat. Stir until chocolate and butter are melted. Transfer to large bowl of electric mixer.

Beat sugar and vanilla into warm chocolate mixture. Beat in egg yolks, scraping bowl with rubber spatula to keep mixture smooth.

In a small bowl stir the baking soda into the sour cream and beat it into the chocolate mixture. On lowest speed add the sifted dry ingredients, scraping bowl with the rubber spatula and beating only until smooth. Remove from mixer.

Beat egg whites with salt until they hold a point or are stiff but not dry. Fold a few large spoonfuls of the chocolate mixture into the whites, and then fold the whites into the remaining chocolate mixture.

The batter will be thin. Pour it into prepared pan. Bake for 1 hour or until a cake tester comes out dry and top springs back when lightly touched.

Cool cake in pan on a rack for about 5 minutes. Cover with a rack and invert. Remove pan and paper. Cover with a rack and invert again to finish cooling right side up.

Place cooled cake right side up on a cake plate protected with four strips of wax paper. Prepare the following:

ICING

8 ounces (8 squares) semisweet chocolate
¾ cup sour cream, at room temperature
　(See Note.)
1 egg

Melt chocolate in top of small double boiler over hot water on moderate heat. Transfer to small bowl of electric mixer. Immediately beat in sour cream and egg, scraping the bowl with rubber spatula and beating until smooth.

If mixture is too thin or too soft, let it stand at room temperature for about 10 minutes, stirring occasionally, until very slightly thickened.

Reserve a few tablespoons of the icing and pour the balance over the top of the cake. Spread it over the top and sides.

Apply the reserved icing with a pastry bag fitted with a large star tube, forming 8 to 10 large rosettes on top of the cake; or, with a large spoon, drop 8 to 10 egg-shaped mounds.

Remove wax paper by pulling each strip by a narrow end. (See page 18.)

NOTE: *If the sour cream is too cold, it will set the icing too quickly; it may be softened over hot water and then beaten again until smooth.*

Sour Cream Chocolate Layer Cake

12 PORTIONS

3 ounces (3 squares) unsweetened
    chocolate
½ cup boiling water
2 cups sifted cake flour
1½ teaspoons double-acting
    baking powder
1 teaspoon baking soda
¼ teaspoon salt
6 ounces (¾ cup) butter
2 teaspoons vanilla extract
1 cup granulated sugar
⅔ cup light brown sugar, firmly packed
3 eggs
1 cup sour cream

Adjust rack to center of oven and preheat oven to 375 degrees. Butter two 9-inch round layer-cake pans and dust both lightly with fine, dry bread crumbs.

In a small, heavy saucepan over low heat melt the chocolate with the boiling water. Stir occasionally with a small wire whisk until smooth. Set aside to cool.

Meanwhile, sift together flour, baking powder, baking soda, and salt. Set aside.

In large bowl of electric mixer cream the butter. Add vanilla, granulated sugar, and light brown sugar and beat well, scraping the bowl with a rubber spatula as necessary to keep mixture smooth. Beat in eggs one at a time, beating well after each.

Stir sour cream and cooled chocolate together until smooth and add to batter, beating only until mixed.

On lowest speed, add the sifted dry ingredients, continuing to scrape the bowl with a rubber spatula. Beat only until smooth.

Turn into prepared pans. With rubber spatula spread tops smooth and then run the batter up on the sides a bit, leaving the batter slightly lower in the centers.

Bake 35 minutes or until tops spring back when lightly touched and layers come away from sides of pans.

Cool in pans for about 5 minutes. Place racks over the cakes and invert. Remove pans. Cover with racks and invert again to cool right side up.

Prepare the following:

cut around the sides to release—do not use a sawing motion. Remove sides of pan. Cover torte with a rack, invert, and remove bottom of pan and paper. Cover with another rack and invert again to finish cooling right side up.

Place four strips of wax paper around the edges of a cake plate and gently transfer the torte, bottom side up. Prepare glaze.

GLAZE

1¾ cups confectioners sugar
1 tablespoon lemon juice
1 to 2 tablespoons boiling water

In a small bowl, stir ingredients very thoroughly to mix well, adjusting amount of liquid or sugar to make a mixture about the consistency of thick cream sauce. If it is too thin it will run. Pour it on the torte and with a long, narrow metal spatula smooth it over the top only. If a bit runs down the sides leave it that way, do not spread. Remove wax paper strips, pulling each one out by a narrow end. Let stand several hours or overnight for the glaze to set.

OPTIONAL: *Before the glaze sets, decorate the rim with lightly toasted whole almonds, or 8 whole glazed red cherries; or place one or more (depending on their size) marzipan carrots on top.*

NOTES: 1. *There is no need to peel the carrots. Just wash them and grate on a grater with small, round—not diamond-shaped—openings.*

2. *Do not freeze this torte after glazing it—the glaze becomes wet after thawing.*

Chocolate Cakes and Layer Cakes

CHOCOLATE CAKE SQUARES
(*Grandma Hermalin's*)

CHOCOLATE CAKE SQUARES
(*Lydia Pinkham's*)

FUDGE CAKE WITH FUDGE

WALNUT FUDGE PIE A LA MODE
WITH HOT FUDGE SAUCE

PALM BEACH CHOCOLATE LAYER
CAKE

PALM BEACH CHOCOLATE TUBE
CAKE

SOUR CREAM CHOCOLATE LAYER
CAKE

DEVIL'S FOOD CAKE

MONTANA MOUNTAIN CAKE

RUM CREAM LAYER CAKE

RUM CHOCOLATE LAYER CAKE

COCONUT LAYER CAKE

Chocolate Cake Squares

(Grandma Hermalin's)

9 PORTIONS

1 cup sifted all-purpose flour
1 teaspoon baking soda
½ teaspoon double-acting baking powder
⅛ teaspoon salt
¼ pound (½ cup) butter
1 teaspoon vanilla extract
1 cup sugar
1 egg
½ cup powdered, unsweetened cocoa
½ cup milk
1 tablespoon instant coffee
½ cup boiling water

Adjust oven rack one-third up from the bottom of the oven. Preheat oven to 350 degrees. Butter a 9-inch square cake pan and dust the bottom only, very lightly, with fine, dry bread crumbs.

Sift together flour, baking soda, baking powder, and salt. Set aside.

In small bowl of electric mixer cream the butter. Add vanilla and sugar and beat for a minute or two. Beat in the egg. On lowest speed, add the cocoa. Then, in this order, gradually add one-half of the milk, one-half of the dry ingredients, remaining milk, and remaining dry ingredients, scraping bowl frequently with a rubber spatula all during mixing. Mix only until smooth after each addition.

Dissolve the instant coffee in the boiling water. While it is still hot, add it very gradually on lowest speed to the chocolate mixture. Beat only until smooth. Batter will be thin. Turn it into the prepared pan.

Bake 40 minutes or until top springs back when lightly touched. Cool in pan on a rack for about 10 minutes. Cover with a rack and invert. Remove pan. Cover with another rack and invert again to finish cooling right side up. Prepare the following icing:

ICING

4 ounces (4 squares) semisweet chocolate
(See Note.)
2 ounces (¼ cup) butter, cut in 4 pieces

In the top of a small double boiler over hot water on moderate heat, melt the chocolate. Remove top of double boiler. With a small wire whisk beat in the butter, one piece at a time, beating until each piece is thoroughly incorporated before adding the next.

This icing may be used immediately, or, if it is too thin, place the pan into ice water and stir constantly until icing thickens very slightly, but watch it closely to see that it doesn't harden. It should still be fluid when used.

Pour it over the cake and smooth with a long, narrow metal spatula.

NOTE: *If you like bittersweet chocolate, substitute 1 ounce of unsweetened chocolate for 1 ounce of the semisweet chocolate.*

Chocolate Cake Squares
(Lydia Pinkham's)

Lydia Pinkham was best known for her cure-all vegetable compound and her many activities in all the women's rights movements of her time. But first and last she was a good old-fashioned cook and housekeeper. Her recipe for chocolate cake does not contain any of her patent medicine.

9 PORTIONS

¼ pound (½ cup) butter
1 teaspoon vanilla extract
1 cup sugar
¼ teaspoon salt
1 egg
2 tablespoons powdered, unsweetened cocoa
1 teaspoon baking soda
1 cup buttermilk
1½ cups sifted all-purpose flour

Adjust rack to center of oven. Preheat oven to 350 degrees. Butter an 8- or 9-inch square pan and dust the bottom only with fine, dry bread crumbs.

In small bowl of electric mixer cream the butter. Add vanilla, sugar, and salt and beat for a minute or two. Beat in the egg, scraping bowl with a rubber spatula as necessary until smoothly blended. On lowest speed beat in the cocoa.

In a small bowl stir the baking soda into the buttermilk to dissolve and then gradually beat it into the batter. The mixture will look curdled—

O.K. On lowest speed, gradually add the flour, scraping the bowl with the rubber spatula and beating only until smooth.

Turn into prepared pan. Smooth the top and run the batter up on the sides a bit, leaving it slightly lower in the center.

Bake 40 minutes or until top springs back when lightly touched and cake begins to come away from sides of the pan. Remove from oven and cool in pan for about 5 minutes. Cover with a rack and invert. Remove pan. Cover with another rack and invert again to finish cooling right side up. Prepare the following icing:

ICING

6 ounces (6 squares) semisweet chocolate
      (or Tobler or Lindt Extra-Bittersweet)
3 tablespoons butter
1 egg plus 1 egg yolk

In the top of a small double boiler over hot water on moderate heat, melt the chocolate. Transfer melted chocolate to small bowl of electric mixer. Cool slightly for a minute or two. Add butter, egg, and yolk and beat on slow speed only until smooth, thick, and shiny. Do not overbeat. It should stay dark; additional beating will lighten the color.

Turn all the icing onto the top of the cake and with a long, narrow metal spatula spread over the top only (not the sides). Then, with the tip of a small spoon, pull it up in small peaks, making even rows that completely cover the top of the cake.

Fudge Cake with Fudge

12 TO 16 PORTIONS

4 ounces (4 squares) unsweetened chocolate
½ cup hot water
1¾ cups sugar
2 cups sifted cake flour
1 teaspoon baking soda
¼ teaspoon salt
¼ pound (½ cup) butter
1 teaspoon vanilla extract
3 eggs
⅔ cup milk

Adjust racks to divide oven in thirds. Preheat oven to 350 degrees. Butter two 9-inch square cake pans.

Place chocolate and hot water in top of small double boiler over hot water on moderate heat. Cook, stirring occasionally, until chocolate is melted and mixture is smooth. Mix in ½ cup of the sugar (reserve remaining 1¼ cups) and continue to cook 2 minutes longer, stirring with a rubber spatula to keep mixture smooth. Remove top of double boiler and set aside.

Sift together flour, baking soda, and salt. Set aside. In large bowl of electric mixer cream the butter. Add vanilla and reserved 1¼ cups sugar and beat for about a minute or two. Scrape the bowl with a rubber spatula as necessary to keep mixture smooth. Beat in eggs one at a time, beating until thoroughly incorporated after each addition. On lowest speed alternately add sifted dry ingredients in three additions and milk in two additions, scraping the bowl with the spatula as necessary and beating only until smooth after each addition. Add the chocolate mixture (don't worry if it is still warm) and beat only until smooth.

Divide evenly between prepared pans. Tilt pans gently to level batter. Bake 30 to 40 minutes or until the tops spring back when lightly touched and cakes come away from sides of pans.

Cool cakes in pans for 5 minutes. Cover with racks or cookie sheets and invert. Remove pans. Cover with racks and invert again to cool right sides up.

Place the bottom layer upside down on a platter or board. Prepare the following fudge for filling and icing:

FUDGE

3 cups sugar
1 cup milk

Pinch of salt
3 tablespoons light corn syrup
4 ounces (4 squares) unsweetened chocolate,
    coarsely cut
⅓ cup (5⅓ tablespoons) butter
2 teaspoons vanilla extract

Place sugar, milk, salt, corn syrup, and chocolate over moderate heat in a heavy saucepan with at least a 3-quart capacity. (See Note 1.) Bring slowly to the boil, stirring occasionally with a wooden spoon or spatula until the sugar is dissolved and the chocolate is melted. Insert a candy thermometer in the saucepan and let the syrup boil until the temperature reaches 232 degrees (or until the syrup forms a very soft ball in cold water).

Immediately, in order to stop the cooking, transfer to a large mixing bowl. Cut the butter into small pieces and add. Replace the thermometer and let mixture stand without stirring until the temperature drops to 110 degrees. (This might take as long as 1 hour.)

Add the vanilla. With a heavy wooden spatula stir and beat for 3 to 5 minutes until this heavy mixture thickens a bit more. Do not wait too long. You are making fudge; it will harden quickly and it must be spread before it hardens. Work very quickly—spread about half the fudge roughly on the bottom layer, cover with top layer placed right side up so that both flat sides meet in the center, and spread fudge on top. Do not try to spread it on the sides, but just let some of it run down unevenly.

NOTES: 1. *If the saucepan is too small, the syrup will boil over.*

2. *If the fudge icing becomes too thick and stiff, add boiling water, a few drops at a time, to soften it to the right consistency.*

3. *To make Fudge Squares, ice the layers separately and do not stack them on top of each other.*

4. *Serve as is, or à la mode with ice cream, or all the way—with a bowl of ice cream, a bowl of whipped cream, and a bowl of walnut halves.*

Walnut Fudge Pie à la Mode with Hot Fudge Sauce

6 TO 8 PORTIONS

Although this is called a pie, it does not have a crust. It is a dense chocolate cake, almost like Brownies baked in a pie plate.

2 ounces (2 squares) unsweetened chocolate
¼ pound (½ cup) butter
1 teaspoon vanilla extract
1 cup sugar
2 eggs, separated
2 tablespoons hot water
⅓ cup sifted all-purpose flour
½ cup walnuts, cut in medium-size pieces
Pinch of salt

Adjust rack to center of oven. Preheat oven to 350 degrees. Line a 9-inch ovenproof glass pie plate with a large piece of aluminum foil. (See directions for crumb crust, page 284, for lining a pie plate with aluminum foil.) Brush the foil well with soft or melted butter.

In the top of a small double boiler over hot water melt the chocolate. Remove from heat and set aside.

In small bowl of electric mixer cream the butter. Add the vanilla and sugar and beat for a minute or two. Beat in the egg yolks and then the chocolate. When smooth add the hot water and then the flour, scraping bowl with a rubber spatula as necessary and beating only until smooth. Remove from mixer and stir in the walnuts.

Beat the whites with the salt until they hold a peak, stiff but not dry, and fold them into the chocolate mixture. Turn into pie plate and spread the top level.

Bake 35 minutes. During baking the cake will rise and then sink—correctly. The top will have formed a crust but it will be soft inside. Cool in the plate on a rack. When *completely* cool, let stand for about ½ to 1 hour to become firm and then cover with a cookie sheet or a rack and invert. Remove pie plate and aluminum foil. Replace pie plate over pie and invert again.

Just before serving place scoops of ice cream on the top of the pie; or place a ring of whipped cream (1 cup heavy cream beaten with ¼ cup confectioners sugar and 1 scant teaspoon vanilla) around the edge and fill the center with ice cream.

With this, pass Hot Fudge Sauce (page 399), or any other chocolate sauce.

Palm Beach Chocolate Layer Cake

10 PORTIONS

3 ounces (3 squares) unsweetened chocolate
2 cups sifted cake flour
1 teaspoon baking soda
½ pound (1 cup) butter
1 teaspoon vanilla extract
1 pound (2¼ cups, firmly packed) dark brown sugar
2 eggs
1 cup boiling water

Adjust rack to center of oven. Preheat oven to 375 degrees. Butter two round 9-inch layer-cake pans and dust all over lightly with fine, dry bread crumbs. Set aside.

Melt chocolate over hot water, then set aside to cool. Sift together flour and baking soda and set aside.

In large bowl of electric mixer cream the butter. Add vanilla. Gradually add the sugar and beat for a minute or two, scraping the bowl with a rubber spatula as necessary. Beat in the eggs and then the melted chocolate. Beat until smooth. On lowest speed alternately add the sifted dry ingredients in three additions and the boiling water, very gradually at first, in two additions, scraping the bowl as necessary with the rubber spatula.

Divide into prepared pans. Bake 30 minutes or until cakes come away from sides of pans and tops spring back when lightly touched.

Cool in pans on racks for about 5 minutes. Cover with racks and invert. Remove pans. Cover with racks and invert again to finish cooling right side up.

When cool, place one layer upside down on a cake plate protected with four strips of wax paper. Prepare the following:

PALM BEACH CHOCOLATE FILLING AND ICING

4½ ounces (4½ squares) unsweetened
  chocolate
3 ounces (¾ stick) butter
1 pound (3½ cups, packed)
  confectioners sugar
2 eggs
1 tablespoon hot water
1 teaspoon vanilla extract

In a small, heavy saucepan over low heat, melt the chocolate and butter. Transfer to large bowl of electric mixer. Add all remaining ingredients at once. Starting at low speed and gradually increasing to high, beat until smooth, scraping bowl as necessary with a rubber spatula.

Use immediately, as icing forms a crust very quickly. Work quickly. Spread about one third over bottom layer. Cover with top layer, placed right side up so that both flat sides meet in the center. Pour remainder of icing over the top and quickly spread it on the top and sides of the cake.

Remove wax paper strips by pulling each one out by a narrow end. (See page 18.)

Palm Beach Chocolate Tube Cake

8 TO 10 PORTIONS

2 cups sifted cake flour
1 teaspoon double-acting baking powder
3 ounces (3 squares) unsweetened chocolate
¼ pound (½ cup) butter
1 cup boiling water
2 cups sugar
1 teaspoon vanilla extract
2 eggs, separated
1 teaspoon baking soda
½ cup sour cream
Pinch of salt

Adjust rack one-third up from bottom of oven. Preheat oven to 350 degrees. Butter a 9-inch tube pan. Line the bottom with paper and butter the paper. Dust very lightly with fine, dry bread crumbs. Set aside.

Sift together flour and baking powder and set aside.

Combine chocolate, butter, and boiling water in a small saucepan over moderate heat. Stir until chocolate and butter are melted. Transfer to large bowl of electric mixer.

Beat sugar and vanilla into warm chocolate mixture. Beat in egg yolks, scraping bowl with rubber spatula to keep mixture smooth.

In a small bowl stir the baking soda into the sour cream and beat it into the chocolate mixture. On lowest speed add the sifted dry ingredients, scraping bowl with the rubber spatula and beating only until smooth. Remove from mixer.

Beat egg whites with salt until they hold a point or are stiff but not dry. Fold a few large spoonfuls of the chocolate mixture into the whites, and then fold the whites into the remaining chocolate mixture.

The batter will be thin. Pour it into prepared pan. Bake for 1 hour or until a cake tester comes out dry and top springs back when lightly touched.

Cool cake in pan on a rack for about 5 minutes. Cover with a rack and invert. Remove pan and paper. Cover with a rack and invert again to finish cooling right side up.

Place cooled cake right side up on a cake plate protected with four strips of wax paper. Prepare the following:

ICING

8 ounces (8 squares) semisweet chocolate
¾ cup sour cream, at room temperature
  (See Note.)
1 egg

Melt chocolate in top of small double boiler over hot water on moderate heat. Transfer to small bowl of electric mixer. Immediately beat in sour cream and egg, scraping the bowl with rubber spatula and beating until smooth.

If mixture is too thin or too soft, let it stand at room temperature for about 10 minutes, stirring occasionally, until very slightly thickened.

Reserve a few tablespoons of the icing and pour the balance over the top of the cake. Spread it over the top and sides.

Apply the reserved icing with a pastry bag fitted with a large star tube, forming 8 to 10 large rosettes on top of the cake; or, with a large spoon, drop 8 to 10 egg-shaped mounds.

Remove wax paper by pulling each strip by a narrow end. (See page 18.)

NOTE: *If the sour cream is too cold, it will set the icing too quickly; it may be softened over hot water and then beaten again until smooth.*

Sour Cream Chocolate Layer Cake

12 PORTIONS

3 ounces (3 squares) unsweetened
   chocolate
½ cup boiling water
2 cups sifted cake flour
1½ teaspoons double-acting
   baking powder
1 teaspoon baking soda
¼ teaspoon salt
6 ounces (¾ cup) butter
2 teaspoons vanilla extract
1 cup granulated sugar
⅔ cup light brown sugar, firmly packed
3 eggs
1 cup sour cream

Adjust rack to center of oven and preheat oven to 375 degrees. Butter two 9-inch round layer-cake pans and dust both lightly with fine, dry bread crumbs.

In a small, heavy saucepan over low heat melt the chocolate with the boiling water. Stir occasionally with a small wire whisk until smooth. Set aside to cool.

Meanwhile, sift together flour, baking powder, baking soda, and salt. Set aside.

In large bowl of electric mixer cream the butter. Add vanilla, granulated sugar, and light brown sugar and beat well, scraping the bowl with a rubber spatula as necessary to keep mixture smooth. Beat in eggs one at a time, beating well after each.

Stir sour cream and cooled chocolate together until smooth and add to batter, beating only until mixed.

On lowest speed, add the sifted dry ingredients, continuing to scrape the bowl with a rubber spatula. Beat only until smooth.

Turn into prepared pans. With rubber spatula spread tops smooth and then run the batter up on the sides a bit, leaving the batter slightly lower in the centers.

Bake 35 minutes or until tops spring back when lightly touched and layers come away from sides of pans.

Cool in pans for about 5 minutes. Place racks over the cakes and invert. Remove pans. Cover with racks and invert again to cool right side up.

Prepare the following:

FILLING AND ICING

3 ounces (3 squares) unsweetened chocolate
2 tablespoons butter
¾ cup sour cream
1 teaspoon vanilla extract
¼ teaspoon salt
1 pound (3½ cups, packed)
  unsifted confectioners sugar

In top of small double boiler over hot water on low heat, melt chocolate and butter. Stir until smooth and remove from heat to cool completely.

In small bowl of electric mixer at low speed, beat sour cream, vanilla, and salt just to mix. Gradually beat in the sugar, scraping the bowl with a rubber spatula. When smooth, add cooled melted chocolate and beat at high speed for about ½ minute until very smooth.

Place four strips of wax paper around the edges of a cake plate to protect it while icing cake. Place one layer on the plate upside down. Spread with filling. Cover with second layer, right side up so that both bottom sides meet in the center. Cover the sides and then the top with remaining filling and icing, smoothing it with a long, narrow, metal spatula; then, if you wish, use the back of a teaspoon to form swirls and peaks all over the sides and top.

Remove wax paper by pulling each strip by a narrow end. (See page 18.)

Devil's Food Cake

*A high, three-layer black cake
with fluffy Seven-Minute Icing.*

8 TO 10
PORTIONS

3 ounces (3 squares) unsweetened chocolate
2½ cups sifted cake flour
2 teaspoons baking soda
½ teaspoon salt
¼ pound (½ cup) butter
2 teaspoons vanilla extract
2½ cups dark brown sugar, firmly packed
3 eggs
½ cup buttermilk
1 cup boiling water

Adjust rack to center of oven. Preheat oven to 375 degrees. Butter three round 8-inch layer-cake pans. Dust bottoms with fine, dry bread crumbs.

Melt chocolate in top of small double boiler over hot water on moderate heat. Set aside. Sift together flour, baking soda, and salt. Set aside. In large bowl of electric mixer cream the butter. Add vanilla and sugar and beat for a minute or two. Beat in eggs one at a time, scraping the bowl with a rubber spatula as necessary to keep mixture blended. Continue to beat for 1 to 2 minutes after the last egg has been added. Beat in melted chocolate. On lowest speed add half of the sifted dry ingredients, then the buttermilk, and then the other half of the dry ingredients, scraping the bowl as necessary with the rubber spatula and beating only until smooth after each addition. Gradually beat in the boiling water.

Batter will be thin. Divide it among the prepared pans.

Bake for 25 minutes or until tops spring back when lightly touched and cakes come away from sides of pans.

Cool cakes in pans for about 5 minutes. Cover with racks or cookie sheets and invert. Remove pans. Cover with racks and invert again to finish cooling right side up.

When layers have cooled completely, use a long, thin, sharp knife to cut off any rises in the tops, making them level.

Place the bottom layer on a cake plate protected with four strips of wax paper around the outer edge. Prepare the following icing:

7-MINUTE ICING

4 egg whites
1½ cups sugar

¼ cup plus 1 tablespoon cold water
1 teaspoon cream of tartar
⅛ teaspoon salt
1½ teaspoons vanilla extract

Mix everything except the vanilla in the top of a large double boiler; it must have at least an 8- to 10-cup capacity. Place over hot water on moderate heat. Beat with electric mixer at high speed for about 5 minutes until mixture stands in peaks when beaters are withdrawn. Immediately, in order to stop the cooking, transfer mixture to large bowl of electric mixer. Add vanilla. Beat at high speed until mixture is smooth and stiff. Use immediately.

Stack and frost each layer, then cover sides and top of cake, pulling the icing up in irregular peaks, if you wish.

Remove wax paper strips, pulling each one out by a narrow end. (See page 18.)

NOTE: *Seven-Minute Icing does not freeze well. It is best to ice the cake the day it is to be served.*

Montana Mountain Cake

10 PORTIONS

A high three-layer chocolate cake filled and iced with Caramel Coffee Seven-Minute Icing.

3 ounces (3 squares) unsweetened chocolate
3 cups sifted cake flour
1½ teaspoons baking soda
½ teaspoon salt
6 ounces (¾ cup) butter
1½ teaspoons vanilla extract
2¼ cups sugar
3 eggs
1½ cups ice water

For 8-inch pans adjust rack to center of oven. For 9-inch pans adjust two racks to divide oven in thirds. Preheat oven to 375 degrees. Butter three 8- or 9-inch round layer-cake pans and dust them lightly with fine, dry bread crumbs.

Melt the chocolate in top of small double boiler over hot water on moderate heat. Set aside. Sift together flour, baking soda, and salt and set aside. In large bowl of electric mixer cream the butter. Add vanilla and sugar and beat for a minute or two. Beat in eggs one at a time, scraping the bowl with a rubber spatula as necessary to keep the mixture well blended. Continue to beat for 2 to 3 minutes. Beat in the chocolate. On lowest speed alternately add sifted dry ingredients in three additions and ice water in two additions, continuing to scrape the bowl as necessary with the spatula and beating only until smooth after each addition.

Divide batter into prepared pans. Spread tops level and then push the batter up on the sides a bit so that the centers are slightly lower.

Bake 25 to 30 minutes or until tops spring back when lightly touched and cakes begin to come away from the sides of the pans.

Cool in pans for about 5 minutes. Cover with racks or cookie sheets and invert. Remove pans. Cover with racks and invert again to finish cooling right side up.

Place four strips of wax paper around the edges of a cake plate. Place one layer on the plate, right side up. Prepare the following icing:

CARAMEL COFFEE 7-MINUTE ICING

Follow recipe for Seven-Minute Icing (page 64) with the following changes: Substitute 1½ cups light brown sugar (or 1 cup dark brown sugar and ½ cup granulated white sugar) for all-white sugar. Use strong coffee in place of the water (about 1 tablespoon instant coffee dissolved in ¼ cup plus 1 tablespoon hot water).

With a long, narrow, metal spatula spread icing over the layer. Place second layer on right side up. Spread with icing. Top with third layer, also right side up. Spread icing on sides and top.

With the spatula or with the back of a spoon, quickly pull the icing up in definite peaks all over the cake.

Remove wax paper strips by pulling each one out by a narrow end. (See page 18.)

NOTES: 1. *If you have used 8-inch pans, the finished cake will be about 6 to 7 inches high—startling! You will need large plates for serving.*

2. *Seven-Minute Icing does not freeze well. It is best to ice the cake the day you are going to serve it.*

Rum Cream Layer Cake

12 PORTIONS

Four light, white layers, generously brushed with rum, filled with rum-flavored whipped cream, covered with chocolate. An heirloom recipe.

2 cups sifted cake flour
2 teaspoons double-acting baking powder
¼ teaspoon baking soda
¼ teaspoon salt
½ cup orange juice (Before squeezing juice, grate and reserve rind of 1 orange to use below.)
3 tablespoons light rum
¼ pound (½ cup) butter
¼ teaspoon almond extract
½ teaspoon vanilla extract
1 cup sugar
2 eggs, separated

Adjust rack to center of oven. Preheat oven to 350 degrees. Butter two round 9-inch layer-cake pans, line the bottoms with paper, butter and flour the lined pans and set aside.

Sift together flour, baking powder, baking soda, and salt. Set aside. Combine orange juice and rum and set aside.

In large bowl of electric mixer, cream the butter. Add almond and vanilla extracts, and ¾ cup of the sugar (reserve remaining ¼ cup). Beat for a few minutes until creamy. Add egg yolks. Beat well, scraping bowl with a rubber spatula as necessary to keep mixture smooth. On lowest speed alternately add sifted dry ingredients in three additions, and orange juice-rum mixture in two additions, scraping bowl with the rubber spatula and beating only until smooth after each addition. Remove from mixer and stir in orange rind.

In small bowl of electric mixer, on high speed, beat whites (with clean beaters) until they increase in volume and thicken slightly. Gradually add reserved ¼ cup of sugar and continue to beat until they hold a definite shape—stiff, not dry. Fold into orange mixture.

Turn batter into prepared pans. With a rubber spatula, spread tops level and then run batter up on sides of pans a bit, making layers slightly lower in the centers.

Bake 20 to 23 minutes or until tops spring back when lightly touched and cakes come away from sides of pans. Remove from oven and cool in pans for 2 to 3 minutes. If necessary, cut around sides to release. Cover each layer with a rack, invert, remove pan and paper, cover with another rack and invert again to finish cooling right side up.

When completely cool, with a long, thin, sharp knife cut each layer in half, making four thin layers. The baked layers will each be about 1 inch high, so that when you cut them you will end up with four ½-inch layers.

RUM CREAM FILLING

1 tablespoon (1 envelope) unflavored gelatin
3 tablespoons cold water
1 cup light rum
3 cups heavy cream
¾ cup confectioners sugar
1 teaspoon vanilla extract

Sprinkle the gelatin over the water in a small, heatproof cup. Let stand 5 minutes. Stir in ¼ cup of the rum (reserve remaining ¾ cup). Place cup in shallow hot water (about halfway up the side of the cup) in a small saucepan or skillet over low heat until gelatin is dissolved. Remove from heat and set aside.

In large bowl of electric mixer, with bowl and beaters chilled, at high speed beat the cream, sugar, vanilla, and ¼ cup of the rum (reserve remaining ½ cup rum to brush on layers) until the cream barely starts to thicken. Quickly stir one or two spoonfuls of the partially whipped cream into the gelatin, and then add the gelatin all at once to the cream and continue to beat until firm enough to be used as a filling. (Be careful not to overbeat.) Remove from mixer.

The two bottom cake layers should be placed upside down and the two top layers right side up, so that both original undersides meet in the center. Place the bottom layer on a cake plate protected with four strips of aluminum foil. (See Note 1.) Brush with 2 tablespoons of the reserved ½ cup rum. Spread with one-third of the filling. Continue with remaining layers, rum, and filling. If any filling extends out beyond the layers, it should be scraped off.

Chill cake 1 to 2 hours (or more if you wish) in refrigerator, or about ½ hour in freezer, until cream filling is set.

Prepare the following icing:

CHOCOLATE ICING

4 ounces (4 squares) unsweetened chocolate
1 cup confectioners sugar
2 tablespoons hot water
2 eggs
3 ounces (6 tablespoons) butter,
    cut in 4 pieces

Melt chocolate in top of small double boiler over hot water on moderate heat. Transfer to small bowl of electric mixer. Immediately add sugar, water, and eggs. Beat at moderately high speed until smooth, scraping bowl with a rubber spatula as necessary to keep mixture smooth. Beat in butter, one piece at a time, beating until smooth after each addition.

Pour over top of cake. Work quickly before chilled cake makes icing set. With a long, narrow metal spatula spread smooth, letting it run down the sides, then smooth the sides. Remove the foil strips, gently pulling each one out by a narrow end. (See page 18.)

Refrigerate the cake at least 1 hour before serving. But it may stand, refrigerated, overnight.

OPTIONAL: *With a long, thin knife, mark the top into 12 portions. Place a Chocolate Cone (see directions, page 408), lying on its side, open end out, on each portion. Or eliminate Chocolate Cones and, before removing the foil, press chopped walnuts generously into the sides of the chocolate (not the top). Or place 1 large walnut half on each portion.*

NOTES: 1. *Because the layers will be brushed with rum, they will be quite wet and would wet wax paper, which might tear when being removed; aluminum foil will not tear.*

    2. *When filling the layers, if the weight of the cake presses the filling beyond the edge of the cake, spread the filling and chill it briefly in the freezer or refrigerator before covering it with the next layer of cake.*

Rum Chocolate Layer Cake

8 TO 10 PORTIONS

Four thin layers of fine-grained sponge cake, brushed with rum and layered with chocolate buttercream. The layers, a classic recipe for Hot Milk Sponge Cake, lend themselves to any of your own creations.

1½ cups sifted cake flour
1½ teaspoons double-acting baking powder
¼ teaspoon salt
3 eggs
1½ cups sugar
¾ cup milk
⅓ cup (5⅓ tablespoons) butter
1 teaspoon vanilla extract

Adjust rack to center of oven. Preheat oven to 375 degrees. Butter two round 8-inch layer pans. Line the bottoms with paper. Butter the paper and dust lightly with flour.

Sift together flour, baking powder, and salt. Set aside. In small bowl of electric mixer at high speed, beat eggs until they are light lemon-colored. Reduce speed and gradually add sugar. Increase speed again and continue to beat for 5 minutes until the mixture forms a heavy ribbon when beaters are lifted.

Meanwhile, place milk and butter in a small saucepan over low-medium heat. It is best to have the milk and butter getting hot while you are beating the eggs. Otherwise the beaten eggs have to stand and wait too long. The milk should be quite hot by the time the eggs are beaten so that it doesn't take too long then to bring it to a boil.

After beating eggs for 5 minutes, beat in vanilla and transfer to large bowl of mixer. On low speed add the sifted dry ingredients, scraping the bowl with a rubber spatula as necessary and beating only until smooth.

Bring the milk and butter to a boil and, at low speed, gradually beat into the batter, scraping bowl with spatula. As soon as mixture is smooth turn it into prepared pans. Batter will be thin. Bake 30 to 35 minutes or until layers begin to come away from sides of pans and tops spring back when lightly touched.

Remove from oven. Let stand for a few minutes. If necessary, cut around edges to release. Cover each layer with a rack and invert. Remove pans and papers. Cover with racks and invert again to cool right side up.

When completely cool, using a long, thin, sharp knife, slice each

1-inch layer in half, making four ½-inch layers. Prepare the following buttercream:

RUM CHOCOLATE BUTTERCREAM

12 ounces semisweet chocolate
     (morsels, squares, or Tobler Tradition
     or Extra-Bittersweet)
½ pound (1 cup) butter
1 teaspoon instant coffee
3 egg yolks, jumbo or extra-large
     (or 4 medium)
½ cup light rum (to be brushed
     on cooled layers)

In the top of a small double boiler over hot water on moderate heat, melt the chocolate. When partially melted remove from heat and stir until completely melted and smooth. Set aside to cool.

In small bowl of electric mixer cream the butter and coffee. Add yolks individually, beating well after each. Beat in the cooled chocolate, beating until smooth and slightly lightened in color.

Place four strips of aluminum foil (see Note 1) around the edges of a cake plate. (The two bottom layers should be placed upside down and the two top layers right side up so that the two cake bottoms meet in the center.) Place one layer on the plate. Brush bottom layer with about 2 tablespoons of the rum. (Reserve remaining rum.)

Spread the buttercream rather thinly over the first layer. Continue with the remaining layers, brushing both sides of each layer with rum and then spreading the tops with buttercream. Reserve about ¾ cup buttercream to ice the top and sides. Then spread the reserved buttercream over the sides and finally over the top. Remove aluminum foil strips, pulling each one gently by a narrow end. (See page 18.)

Refrigerate for 1 or 2 hours to set the buttercream (or overnight if you wish), but remove from refrigerator 15 to 20 minutes before serving.

NOTES: 1. *Because the layers will be generously brushed with rum, they will be quite wet and would wet wax paper, which might tear when being removed; aluminum foil will not tear.*

2. *If you wish, reserve some of the icing to decorate the cake, using a pastry bag and a star tube.*

Coconut Layer Cake

10 PORTIONS

2½ cups sifted cake flour
1 tablespoon double-acting baking powder
¼ teaspoon salt
¼ pound (½ cup) butter
1 teaspoon vanilla extract
1½ cups sugar
2 eggs
1 cup milk
Finely grated rind of 1 large orange
  (or 2 small)
A few spoonfuls of melted and strained
  apricot preserves
8–10 ounces (3–4 cups) grated coconut
  (See Note 1.)

Adjust rack to center of oven. Preheat oven to 375 degrees. Butter two 9-inch round layer-cake pans. Line the bottoms with paper. Butter the paper and dust all over lightly with flour. Set aside.

Sift together flour, baking powder, and salt and set aside.

In large bowl of electric mixer, cream the butter. Add the vanilla and sugar and beat for a few minutes. Add the eggs and beat until smooth. On lowest speed add the dry ingredients in three additions—alternately with the milk in two additions—scraping the bowl with a rubber spatula as necessary and beating only until smooth after each addition. Remove from mixer and stir in orange rind.

Divide batter into prepared pans. Tilt and shake pans gently to level batter. Bake 25 to 30 minutes or until cakes come away from sides of pans and tops spring back when lightly touched.

Remove from oven. Let stand about 5 minutes. Cover with racks or cookie sheets and invert. Remove pans and papers. Cover with racks and invert again to cool right side up.

When layers have cooled completely, place four strips of wax paper around a cake plate and place one layer on the plate, upside down. Spread with a thin layer of smooth preserves, reserving some for second layer. Prepare following icing:

FLUFFY WHITE ICING
(A different 7-Minute Icing)

4 egg whites
¼ cup light corn syrup

2 tablespoons water
2½ cups confectioners sugar
Pinch of salt
1 teaspoon vanilla extract
¼ teaspoon almond extract

Mix all ingredients except vanilla and almond extracts in the top of a large double boiler; it must have at least an 8- to 10-cup capacity. Place over hot water on moderate heat. Beat with an electric mixer at high speed for 5 to 6 minutes until mixture stands in peaks when beaters are lifted.

Immediately, in order to stop the cooking, transfer to large bowl of electric mixer. Add vanilla and almond extracts and beat at high speed for about 5 minutes more, scraping sides and bottom of bowl almost continuously with a rubber spatula, until mixture is smooth and very thick. Use immediately.

Spread one-third of the icing on the bottom layer. Sprinkle with one-third of the coconut.

Put on second layer, right side up, so that the two cake bottoms meet in the middle. Spread the top with remaining apricot preserves. Use another third of the icing around the sides and then the remaining third on the top. Quickly spread with a long, narrow metal spatula to smooth the top and sides.

With the palm of your hand, press another third of the coconut onto the sides and sprinkle the remaining coconut evenly over the top.

Remove the wax paper strips, pulling each one out by a narrow end. (See page 18.)

NOTES: 1. *Fresh coconut, freshly grated, is a rare treat. If possible, use it. (It is available in some frozen food departments.) Fresh coconut is moist. If you use canned coconut, use the moist type and the most finely shredded.*

2. *When serving, dip knife in hot water before making each cut to prevent the icing from sticking to the knife.*

3. *This icing does not freeze well. It is best to ice the cake the day it is to be served.*

Coffee Cakes, Nut Cakes, Fruit Cakes, and Cakes Made with Fruit

BUDAPEST COFFEE CAKE

SOUTHERN NUT CAKE

TEXAS FRUIT CAKE

CREOLE CHRISTMAS CAKE

TOASTED ALMOND BUTTER CAKE

DANISH LOAF CAKE

COFFEE WALNUT LOAF

CARROT LOAF

CREOLE APPLESAUCE CAKE
  WITH RUM OR BRANDY

DATE-NUT CAKE SQUARES

TRINIDAD TORTE

PUMPKIN CAKE

BLUEBERRY CRUMB CAKE

PRUNE-PECAN CAKE

BANANA-NUT CAKE

PEACHES-AND-CREAM RUM CAKE

WALNUT-PEACH KUCHEN

APPLE KUCHEN

Budapest Coffee Cake

12 PORTIONS

NUT FILLING

¾ cup dark brown sugar, firmly packed
1 tablespoon cinnamon
1 tablespoon powdered, unsweetened cocoa
2–3 tablespoons currants or raisins,
    coarsely chopped (See page 12.)
3½ ounces (1 cup) walnuts, finely cut

In a small bowl stir brown sugar, cinnamon, and cocoa to mix thoroughly. Stir in the currants or raisins and then the walnuts, and set aside.

CAKE BATTER

3 cups sifted all-purpose flour
1½ teaspoons double-acting baking powder
1½ teaspoons baking soda
½ teaspoon salt
6 ounces (¾ cup) butter
2 teaspoons vanilla extract
1½ cups sugar
3 eggs
2 cups sour cream

Adjust rack one-third up from the bottom of the oven. Preheat oven to 375 degrees. Butter a 10-inch (12- to 14-cup capacity) Bundt pan. (This is best baked in a Bundt pan, but a tube pan of similar size may be substituted.) Even if the pan is Teflon, it should be buttered for this recipe.

Sift together flour, baking powder, baking soda, and salt. Set aside. In large bowl of electric mixer cream the butter. Add vanilla and sugar and beat for a minute or two. And eggs individually, beating until thoroughly incorporated after each. Scrape bowl with a rubber spatula as necessary to keep mixture smooth, and beat at high speed for a minute or so until mixture is light and creamy.

On lowest speed alternately add dry ingredients in three additions and sour cream in two additions, continuing to scrape the bowl as necessary with the rubber spatula and beating only until smooth after each addition.

Spread a thin layer of the batter in the bottom of the pan. Sprinkle very generously with about one-third of the nut filling. Continue making layers, four of the batter and three of the filling. The top layer should be batter. It will take a bit of patience to spread the batter thin. It will be easier if the batter is placed on by many small spoonfuls and then spread with the back of the spoon, instead of just being dropped on in two or three large amounts.

Bake 50 to 60 minutes or until cake tester comes out dry and the top feels firm and springy. If the cake was baked in a tube pan rather than a Bundt pan it will take longer to bake. Be sure it is done. Remove from oven. Leave cake in pan for 5 minutes, no longer. The cake should be hot when glaze is applied.

Meanwhile, prepare glaze.

GLAZE

2 cups confectioners sugar
1 teaspoon vanilla extract
2–3 tablespoons hot milk

In a small bowl, with a rubber spatula, mix sugar with vanilla and about 2 tablespoons of the hot milk. Very gradually add more milk, just a bit at a time, using only enough to make a semifluid mixture about as thick as thick cream sauce.

Cover cake with a rack and invert over a large piece of wax paper or aluminum foil. Remove pan, leaving cake upside down. Immediately pour on the glaze—just pour it on quickly, don't spread it or work over it—and let it run down the sides unevenly.

When the glaze has set, use a small cookie sheet as a spatula to transfer cake to cake plate. Serve the cake while still slightly warm or after it has cooled completely.

Southern Nut Cake

This large cake is almost solid nuts, with just enough batter to hold them together— dramatic, delicious, extravagant.

16 OR MORE
GENEROUS PORTIONS,
EACH 2 OR 3
THIN SLICES

1 pound (4½ cups) walnuts
1 pound (4½ cups) pecans
3½ cups sifted all-purpose flour
2 teaspoons double-acting baking powder
½ teaspoon mace
¼ teaspoon salt
¾ cup milk

¼ cup brandy or bourbon
¾ pound (1½ cups) butter
2 cups sugar
6 eggs
optional: 3 or 4 tablespoons additional brandy
or bourbon

Adjust oven rack one-third of the way up from the bottom of the oven. Preheat oven to 325 degrees. Butter a 10 × 4-inch tube pan. Line the bottom with paper. Butter the paper and dust all over lightly with fine, dry bread crumbs. Or, if you use a 10-inch nonstick tube pan, either line the bottom of the pan with baking pan liner paper (unbuttered), or line it with wax paper and butter the wax paper.

Break or cut the nuts into large pieces. They should *not* be finely chopped. Place the nuts in your largest mixing bowl, 6- to 8-quart capacity. If you don't have a very large mixing bowl, use a saucepan or roasting pan instead.

Sift together flour, baking powder, mace, and salt. Set aside. Combine the milk and ¼ cup brandy or bourbon and set aside.

In large bowl of electric mixer, cream the butter. Add sugar and beat for a few minutes, scraping the bowl as necessary with a rubber spatula. On moderate speed, add eggs one at a time, beating until thoroughly incorporated after each and scraping the bowl with the rubber spatula as necessary to keep everything well mixed. Increase speed and beat for about 3 minutes until very light and fluffy. Mixture might look curdled at this point—O.K.

On lowest speed alternately add the sifted dry ingredients in three additions and the milk mixture in two, scraping the bowl as necessary with the spatula and beating only until smooth after each addition. Pour the batter over the nuts. Stir with a large wooden spatula or large wooden spoon until the nuts are all coated with the batter. Turn into pan. Spread the top level.

Bake for 1¾ hours or until a cake tester comes out dry. Remove from oven and place cake pan on a rack. Sprinkle or brush optional brandy or bourbon over top of hot cake. Let cake cool in pan for about 20 minutes.

Cover cake with a rack and invert to remove pan and paper. Cover with another rack and carefully invert again to cool. Let cake stand overnight before cutting. Cut with a very sharp knife into thin slices.

Texas Fruit Cake

This cake is so thick with fruit and nuts it is almost a confection. Recipe may be multiplied by any number provided you have a very large container for mixing it in. In place of a large bowl use a roasting pan or a dish pan.

12 SLICES

8 ounces (1 cup) pitted dates, left whole
1 cup candied cherries, tightly packed
    and left whole
1 cup (4–5 slices) candied pineapple,
    each slice cut in 8–10 wedges
½ cup sifted all-purpose flour
8 ounces (2½ cups) mixed walnut
    and pecan halves, left whole
½ teaspoon double-acting baking powder
¼ teaspoon salt
2 eggs, separated
½ cup sugar
½ teaspoon vanilla extract
2 tablespoons bourbon

Adjust oven rack one-third of the way up from the bottom. Preheat oven to 325 degrees. Butter a 9 × 5 × 3-inch loaf pan. Then cut two strips of aluminum foil to line the pan, one for the length and one for the width. Put them into place carefully; the foil should remain smooth. Brush with melted butter and dust lightly with fine, dry bread crumbs. Set aside.

Pick over the dates carefully to see that there are no pits or stems left in them. Rinse the cherries quickly in cold water and dry them thoroughly between paper towels.

Place the dates, cherries, and pineapple in a large mixing bowl. Add 2 tablespoons of the flour and toss with your fingers to separate and coat each piece of fruit thoroughly. Add the nuts and toss again. Set aside.

Sift the remaining flour with the baking powder and salt and set aside.

In small bowl of electric mixer at high speed beat the egg yolks and sugar for about 3 minutes until light. Reduce the speed to low and add the vanilla, bourbon, and then the sifted dry ingredients, scraping the bowl with a rubber spatula, and beating only until smooth.

Beat the egg whites until they hold a firm shape, or are stiff but not dry. Fold the egg whites into the egg yolk mixture.

Pour the batter over the prepared fruit and nuts. With your hand, fold together, and then, with your hand, transfer to prepared pan. With your fingers and the palm of your hand, press down very firmly, especially in the corners of the pan. Make the top as level as possible.

Bake 1½ hours until the cake is semi-firm to the touch, covering the top loosely with foil for the last half hour of baking. Remove from oven and cool in pan for 20 minutes. Cover with a rack and invert. Remove pan and aluminum foil. Cover with another rack and invert again to cool, right side up.

When cool, wrap airtight and refrigerate for at least several hours, or a day or two if you wish. Freeze for longer storage.

It is best to slice the cake in the kitchen, and arrange the slices on a tray, or wrap them individually in clear cellophane. Turn the cake upside down to slice it. Use a very sharp, thin knife. If you have any trouble, hold the knife under running, hot water before cutting each slice. Cut with a sawing motion. It is difficult to cut this cake into very thin slices; for smaller portions cut each slice in half.

NOTE: *Fruit cakes slice best if very cold; I think they also taste best when cold.*

Creole Christmas Cake

Almost 6 pounds of rich butter cake thick with raisins and nuts. This is traditionally served during the Christmas holidays, but please don't wait. I recommend it now—whenever it is.

16 PORTIONS

Finely grated rind of 2 large lemons

½ cup lemon juice

4 cups sifted all-purpose flour

2 teaspoons double-acting baking powder

3 cups (1 15-ounce box) seedless raisins
 (You may use all light raisins but I prefer
 2 cups of light and 1 cup of dark.)

1⅛ pounds (5 cups) pecans, coarsely cut

1 pound (2 cups) butter

2 cups sugar

6 eggs

Adjust rack one-third up from the bottom of the oven. Preheat oven to 325 degrees. Butter 10 × 4-inch tube pan. Line the bottom with paper. Butter the paper and dust all over lightly with fine, dry bread crumbs. Or, if you use a 10-inch nonstick tube pan, either line the bottom with baking pan liner paper (unbuttered) or line it with wax paper and butter the wax paper.

Mix the lemon rind and juice and set aside.

Sift together the flour and baking powder into a 6- to 8-quart mixing bowl. If you do not have a large enough bowl, use a saucepan, roasting pan, or a dishpan. Add the raisins and, with your fingers, stir and toss to separate and coat each raisin thoroughly. Stir in the nuts.

In the large bowl of an electric mixer cream the butter. Add the sugar and beat for about a minute or two. Add the eggs one at a time, scraping the bowl with a rubber spatula and beating after each until thoroughly incorporated. Remove from mixer and stir in the lemon rind and juice. Pour over the raisin-nut mixture and, with a heavy wooden spatula, stir until the flour is completely absorbed.

The batter will be stiff. Spoon it into the prepared pan and spread the top level. Let stand for 10 minutes and then place in preheated oven.

Bake for 1 hour and 50 to 55 minutes until the cake is well browned and a cake tester inserted all the way to the bottom comes out dry.

Remove from oven and let stand for 10 to 15 minutes. Cover with a rack and invert. Remove pan and paper. Cover with a rack and invert again to cool right side up.

When completely cool wrap in plastic wrap or aluminum foil and let stand for at least 10 to 12 hours or freeze for 1 to 2 hours before cutting. Cut in thin slices.

Toasted Almond Butter Cake

8 PORTIONS

A loaf cake that calls for almonds three ways: chopped, ground, and slivered.

⅓ cup blanched almonds, very finely chopped, not ground, for coating the pan (If the pieces are not small enough they won't stick to the pan.)

1⅓ cups sifted all-purpose flour

1 teaspoon double-acting baking powder

5⅓ ounces (⅔ cup) butter

½ teaspoon almond extract

1 cup sugar

3 eggs

3 ounces (generous ½ cup) blanched almonds, finely ground (See pages 10–12. For this recipe they do not have to be strained.)

⅓ cup slivered, blanched almonds (See Note.)

Adjust rack about one-third up from the bottom of the oven. Preheat oven to 350 degrees. Generously butter a loaf pan measuring 9 × 5 × 3 inches. Coat it all over with the finely chopped almonds.

Sift flour with baking powder and set aside. In small bowl of electric mixer cream the butter with the almond extract. Gradually add the sugar and beat at high speed for 5 minutes until very light. Scrape the bowl with a rubber spatula as necessary to keep the mixture smooth.

Add the eggs one at a time, beating well after each and beating for 2 minutes after the last one. On low speed add the ground almonds and then the sifted dry ingredients, scraping the bowl with the rubber spatula and beating only until the mixture is smooth.

Turn into prepared pan. Run batter up on sides of pan a bit, forming a slight trench down the middle.

Sprinkle generously with the slivered almonds, placing them heavily around the outer edges of the cake rather than at the center. Press them a little way into the batter.

Bake 1 hour and 10 minutes or until a cake tester comes out dry. Remove from oven. Cool in pan on a rack for about 15 minutes. Cut around sides to release cake.

To remove the cake from the pan without losing the topping, lay a piece of aluminum foil on top of the cake. Turn it down loosely around the sides. Place a pot holder or folded kitchen towel lightly over the foil. Turn the pan upside down into the palm of your right hand. With your left hand remove the pan and gently place a rack on the cake. Now invert it, right side up, to finish cooling on the rack.

OPTIONAL: *Top of cooled cake may be sprinkled with confectioners sugar through a fine strainer.*

NOTE: *Regarding "slivered" almonds: Almonds cut in thin slices are called "sliced." Those cut in fatter oblongs, or julienne style, are called "slivered." For this recipe the slivered almonds are preferable—sliced almonds would burn. They are available in packages in most supermarkets already cut.*

Danish Loaf Cake

2 LOAVES, EACH 6 TO 8 PORTIONS

3¾ ounces (¾ cup) blanched almonds, very finely chopped, not ground, for coating the pans (If the pieces are not small enough they won't stick to the pans.)

3 cups sifted all-purpose flour

1 tablespoon plus 1 teaspoon double-acting baking powder

½ teaspoon salt

2 cups heavy cream

2 teaspoons vanilla extract

½ teaspoon almond extract

2 cups sugar

4 eggs

3½ ounces (¾ cup) pignolias (pine nuts)

Adjust oven rack one-third up from the bottom of the oven. Preheat oven to 375 degrees. Heavily butter two 9 × 5 × 3-inch loaf pans. Coat the sides and bottoms of both pans with the finely chopped almonds.

Sift together flour, baking powder, and salt. Set aside. In large bowl of electric mixer, with bowl and beaters chilled, whip the cream with vanilla and almond extracts until it holds a shape. On medium speed quickly beat in the sugar all at once, and then the eggs, one at a time. (Adding the eggs will thin the cream a bit.) On lowest speed add the dry ingredients, scraping the bowl with a rubber spatula as necessary and beating only until smooth. Place about one-quarter of the batter in each pan. Spread to level a bit. Sprinkle about 2 tablespoons of the pignolias into each pan. Cover evenly with the remaining batter. Smooth the tops. Sprinkle with remaining pignolias, placing them more heavily around the outer edges than in the center.

Bake 1 hour or until the cakes test done. The tops of the cakes will crack the long way. They are done when the centers of the cracks feel firm and dry when lightly touched, and when a cake tester comes out dry. Place the cake pans on a rack and apply glaze immediately while cakes are still in pans.

GLAZE

⅓ cup kirsch
⅓ cup sugar

Stir kirsch and sugar together immediately before using. (They will not blend—that's O.K.) Brush on hot loaves. Let loaves cool in pans until they are tepid and can be handled comfortably.

With a small, sharp knife cut around the sides to loosen. Do not cut deeply—just around the upper edge.

To remove the cakes from the pans, lay a piece of aluminum foil on each cake and fold down loosely on the sides. Place a pot holder or folded kitchen towel lightly over the paper. Turn the pan upside down into the palm of your right hand. With your left hand remove the pan and gently place a rack on the cake. Now invert it, right side up, to finish cooling on the rack.

NOTE: *This recipe may be easily divided to make only one loaf, but the cake keeps very well for several days or, of course, it may be frozen.*

Coffee Walnut Loaf

3½ ounces (1 cup) walnuts, coarsely broken
1½ cups sifted all-purpose flour
2 teaspoons double-acting baking powder
¼ teaspoon salt
¼ pound (½ cup) butter
2 teaspoons vanilla extract
1 tablespoon plus 1 teaspoon instant coffee
1 cup sugar
2 eggs, separated
½ cup milk
½ ounce (½ square) semisweet chocolate,
   ground or very finely chopped

Adjust oven rack one-third up from bottom of oven. Preheat oven to 375 degrees. Butter a 9 × 5 × 3-inch loaf pan. Dust pan lightly with fine, dry bread crumbs.

Toss walnuts with 1 teaspoon of the flour and set aside. Sift remaining flour with baking powder and salt. Set aside.

In small bowl of electric mixer cream the butter. Add the vanilla, instant coffee, and sugar, and beat for about 2 minutes. Add the egg yolks and continue to beat for another minute or two. On lowest speed alternately add dry ingredients in three additions and milk in two additions, scraping the bowl with a rubber spatula as necessary and beating only until smooth after each addition. Remove from mixer. Stir in the nuts. Beat whites until stiff but not dry, and fold them into the batter.

Place about half of the batter in the pan. Spread it level. Sprinkle with the chocolate, and cover with remaining batter. Spread the top level.

Bake 55 minutes to 1 hour or until a cake tester comes out dry. Cool in the pan for 5 to 10 minutes. Cover with a rack and invert. Remove pan and cover with another rack. Invert again to cool.

Carrot Loaf

Moist and dark. You will not need an electric mixer.

1 LARGE LOAF

2½ cups sifted all-purpose flour
2 teaspoons double-acting baking powder
1 teaspoon baking soda
½ teaspoon salt
1 teaspoon cinnamon
5 ounces (1 cup) raisins
3–4 medium-size carrots
    (to make 1 cup grated and packed)
2½ ounces (¾ cup) walnuts, cut or
    broken into medium-size pieces
1 cup dark brown sugar, firmly packed
2 eggs
1 cup milk
2 ounces (¼ cup) melted butter

Adjust rack one-third up from bottom of oven. Preheat oven to 400 degrees. Butter an 8- to 10-cup capacity loaf pan. Dust it very lightly with fine, dry bread crumbs.

Sift together the flour, baking powder, baking soda, salt, and cinnamon and set aside.

Place the raisins in a large mixing bowl and with your fingers separate them thoroughly if stuck together.

Scrub the carrots to clean them—it is not necessary to peel them. Grate them finely on a grater. Pack down into a measuring cup to measure 1 cup, packed. Add carrots, walnuts, and brown sugar to the raisins and stir to mix.

Beat eggs lightly just to mix. Beat in the milk and the melted butter. Stir into the carrot mixture. Add sifted dry ingredients and stir with a rubber spatula, scraping the bowl and mixing only until thoroughly blended.

Turn into prepared loaf pan. Shake gently to level. Bake in preheated oven for 55 to 60 minutes or until a cake tester comes out dry.

Cool in pan on a rack for 5 minutes. Cover with a rack or a small cookie sheet. Invert and remove pan. Cover with a rack and invert again to cool, right side up.

Creole Apple- sauce Cake with Rum or Brandy

12 TO 18 PORTIONS

A *dark date-nut cake.*

5 ounces (1 cup) raisins
8 ounces (1 cup, packed) pitted soft dates
　　(each date cut into 3 or 4 pieces)
⅓ cup dark rum or brandy
2 cups sifted all-purpose flour
1 tablespoon cornstarch
2 teaspoons baking soda
1 teaspoon cinnamon
½ teaspoon mace or nutmeg
½ teaspoon salt
1 tablespoon powdered, unsweetened cocoa
¼ pound (½ cup) butter
1 cup sugar
2 eggs
15 ounces (1½ cups) applesauce
7 *ounces (2 cups) pecan halves or large pieces*
Optional: additional rum or brandy

Place raisins and dates in a 2-cup jar with a tight cover. Add rum or brandy. Let stand for several hours, or overnight or longer if you wish, turning jar occasionally from side to side and top to bottom.

Adjust rack to center of oven. Preheat oven to 375 degrees. Butter a 9 × 13 × 2-inch pan. Dust it with fine, dry bread crumbs and set aside.

Sift together the flour, cornstarch, baking soda, cinnamon, mace or nutmeg, salt, and cocoa. Set aside.

In large bowl of electric mixer cream the butter. Add the sugar and beat for a minute or two, scraping the bowl occasionally with a rubber spatula. Add eggs one at a time, beating after each until thoroughly incorporated.

On low speed mix in half of the dry ingredients, then the applesauce, and finally the remaining dry ingredients, scraping the bowl with the rubber spatula as necessary and beating only until incorporated after each addition.

Remove from mixer. Stir in raisins and dates with any remaining rum or brandy, and then add the nuts.

Turn the batter into the pan. Spread the top level. Bake 45 to 50 minutes or until top springs back firmly when lightly touched.

Cool in pan on a rack for 10 minutes. Invert onto a rack or cookie sheet. Remove pan and invert again onto a rack to finish cooling right side up. Additional rum or brandy may be sprinkled over the top of the still-warm cake.

Transfer to a cutting board. Cut, preferably with a long, serrated knife, into 12 oblongs. Or cut lengthwise and then across into 1-inch slices and arrange overlapping on a serving tray.

Serve as is or with a spoonful of Ginger Cream (page 396).

Date-Nut Cake Squares

9 TO 12 PORTIONS

8 ounces (1 cup, packed) pitted soft dates
    (each date cut into 3 or 4 pieces)
¼ pound (½ cup) butter,
    at room temperature
1 teaspoon baking soda
1 cup boiling water
1½ cups sifted all-purpose flour
1 teaspoon double-acting baking powder
1 egg
1 teaspoon vanilla extract
½ cup sugar
3½ ounces (1 cup) walnuts or pecans,
    coarsely chopped
optional: Confectioners sugar

Put dates, butter, and baking soda in a large bowl. Pour on boiling water. Stir until butter melts. Set aside to cool completely.

Adjust rack to center of oven. Preheat oven to 400 degrees. Butter a 9-inch square cake pan.

Sift together flour and baking powder. Set aside. In a small bowl, stir egg, vanilla, and sugar just to mix. When date mixture is cool, stir the egg mixture into it and then the flour mixture. Stir in the nuts. Turn into pan and tilt to level batter.

Bake 25 to 30 minutes or until top is well-browned and springs back firmly when lightly touched. Cool in the pan for 5 to 10 minutes. Cover with a rack and invert. Remove pan. Cover with another rack and invert again to cool right side up.

Cover top with confectioners sugar through a fine strainer or with the following caramel icing.

CARAMELIZED SUGAR ICING

⅓ cup heavy cream
3 ounces (6 tablespoons) butter
2 tablespoons granulated sugar
2 cups confectioners sugar
½ teaspoon vanilla extract
optional: 9–12 walnut or pecan halves

Heat cream and butter in a small saucepan and keep it warm over low heat.

Meanwhile, caramelize the granulated sugar in a medium-size heavy frying pan (9½ to 10 inches in diameter). Stir with a wooden spatula over moderate heat until it turns a rich, golden brown.

Pour hot cream all at once over caramelized granulated sugar. Be careful—it will bubble up hard. Keep stirring over heat until caramel melts and mixture is smooth.

Transfer to small bowl of electric mixer. Add confectioners sugar all at once, then vanilla, and beat only until smooth. If icing is too thick, thin it slightly with just a few drops of additional heavy cream. Use immediately. Pour it over the top of the cake. Quickly spread with a long, narrow metal spatula.

OPTIONAL: *Mark the top in 9 or 12 portions with a long knife, pressing down gently just to score the icing. Top each portion with half a walnut or pecan.*

Trinidad Torte

8 TO 10
PORTIONS

2 cups sifted all-purpose flour
1 teaspoon double-acting baking powder
1 teaspoon baking soda
4 ounces (1 generous cup) walnuts, ground
  (See page 11.)
½ pound (1 cup) butter
1 cup sugar
3 eggs, separated
¾ cup sour cream

Finely grated rind of 1 large orange
Finely grated rind of 2 lemons
⅛ teaspoon salt

Adjust rack one-third of the way up from the bottom of the oven and preheat oven to 350 degrees. Butter a 9 × 2½- or 3-inch spring-form pan and coat it lightly with fine, dry bread crumbs.

Sift together flour, baking powder, and baking soda. Stir a few spoonfuls of the sifted dry ingredients into the nuts. Set aside.

In small bowl of electric mixer cream the butter. Add the sugar and beat well. Beat in the egg yolks one at a time. On lowest speed, alternately add the sifted dry ingredients in three additions with the sour cream in two additions, scraping the bowl as necessary with a rubber spatula to keep mixture smooth, and beating only until incorporated after each addition.

Transfer to a large bowl. Stir in the nuts and grated rinds.

Beat the whites with the salt until they hold a shape, or are stiff but not dry. Fold them into the batter. Pour into pan and level top by shaking pan briskly back and forth.

Bake 1 hour or until a cake tester comes out dry. A few minutes before removing cake from oven prepare the following glaze:

GLAZE

¾ cup sugar
2 tablespoons orange juice
2 tablespoons lemon juice

Mix ingredients in a small saucepan. Bring to a boil, stirring occasionally to dissolve the sugar.

When cake is removed from the oven, place the cake pan on a rack, and quickly prick all over the top with a small, sharp knife. Gradually brush the hot glaze over the hot cake until it is all absorbed. Let the cake cool completely in the pan.

When completely cool, remove the sides of the spring form. Cover with a rack and invert to remove the bottom of the pan. If the bottom does not lift off easily, use a small knife or spatula to release a bit at one edge and then the bottom will slip off. Immediately cover with a cake plate and invert again.

Pumpkin Cake

10 TO 12 PORTIONS

3 cups sifted all-purpose flour
2 teaspoons baking soda
2 teaspoons double-acting baking powder
1 tablespoon cinnamon
½ teaspoon powdered ginger
¼ teaspoon powdered cloves
¼ teaspoon nutmeg
¼ teaspoon allspice
1 teaspoon salt
5 ounces (1 cup) raisins, dark, light, or mixed
3½ ounces (1 cup) walnuts,
    broken into medium-size pieces
1 1-pound can (2 cups) pumpkin
    (plain pumpkin, not pie filling)
2 cups sugar
1¼ cups safflower oil, corn oil,
    or other salad oil (not olive oil)
4 eggs
optional: Confectioners sugar

Adjust rack one-third up from the bottom of oven and preheat to 350 degrees. Butter a 10 × 4½-inch tube pan. Line the bottom with paper and butter the paper, or use a 10-inch nonstick tube pan and line the bottom with unbuttered baking pan liner paper or with wax paper and butter the wax paper.

Sift together the flour, baking soda, baking powder, cinnamon, ginger, cloves, nutmeg, allspice, and salt. Add a tablespoon of the sifted dry ingredients to the raisins in a small bowl. With your fingers, toss the raisins to separate them and coat each one with the dry ingredients. Stir in the nuts and set aside.

In large bowl of electric mixer, place the pumpkin, sugar, and oil. Beat at medium speed until smooth. Add the eggs individually, beating after each until incorporated.

On low speed add the sifted dry ingredients, scraping the bowl with a rubber spatula and beating only until smooth. Remove from mixer. Stir in raisins and nuts.

Turn into the prepared pan. Rotate pan briskly to level top.

Bake 1 hour and 5 minutes or until a cake tester comes out dry. Cool on a rack for about 10 minutes. The baked cake will only fill about three-quarters of the pan.

Cover cake pan with a rack and invert. Remove pan and paper. Cover with another rack and invert again. Cool right side up on the rack.

When cool, top may be sprinkled with confectioners sugar through a fine strainer.

Serve as is or with a generous spoonful of Ginger Cream (page 396).

NOTE: *Plain canned pumpkin is not always available. At Thanksgiving time, when it is easy to find, I suggest that you stock up on it for this cake, which is delicious all year.*

Blueberry Crumb Cake

9 TO 12 PORTIONS   *2 cups fresh blueberries*

Pick over and wash the blueberries in a large bowl of cold water. Drain in a sieve or colander. Turn them out onto a towel. Pat them lightly with towel to dry. Set aside in a single layer on the towel to dry completely.

TOPPING

⅓ cup sifted all-purpose flour
½ cup sugar
1 teaspoon cinnamon
2 ounces (¼ cup) butter

Adjust rack to the center of the oven. Preheat oven to 375 degrees. Butter a 9-inch square baking pan. Coat it well, bottom and sides, with fine, dry bread crumbs. Set aside.

Prepare the topping: In a small bowl mix flour, sugar, and cinnamon. With a pastry blender cut in the butter until the mixture resembles coarse crumbs. Set aside.

CAKE

2 cups sifted all-purpose flour
2 teaspoons double-acting baking powder
½ teaspoon salt
2 ounces (¼ cup) butter
1 teaspoon vanilla extract
¾ cup sugar
1 egg
½ cup milk
Finely grated rind of 1 lemon
½ cup walnuts, cut medium fine
optional: Confectioners sugar

Sift together the flour, baking powder, and salt. Place the dried blueberries in a large bowl. Sprinkle with about 1½ tablespoons of the sifted dry ingredients. Using a rubber spatula, toss and turn gently to flour the blueberries without crushing them. Set aside both the floured berries and also the remaining sifted dry ingredients.

In small bowl of electric mixer, cream the butter. Beat in vanilla and sugar and beat for 1 minute. Add the egg and beat for 1 minute more. On lowest speed alternately add remaining sifted dry ingredients in three additions and milk in two additions, scraping the bowl with a rubber spatula and beating only until smooth after each addition.

Remove from mixer. Stir in lemon rind. The batter will be stiff. Pour it over the floured blueberries. With a rubber spatula gently fold together until just mixed.

Turn batter into the prepared pan. Spread smoothly. Sprinkle walnuts over top, and then sprinkle reserved topping over the nuts.

Bake 50 minutes or until the top is well-browned. Cool in the pan for about ½ hour.

Cut around sides of pan to loosen cake.

Cover top of pan with a piece of aluminum foil large enough to fold down around the four sides (in order not to lose any of the topping when the cake is inverted). Over the aluminum foil place a cake rack or cookie sheet. Invert and remove pan. Place cake plate or board upside down on cake and invert again.

This may be served while still warm or at room temperature—it holds its heat for 1 to 1½ hours after being removed from pan. If you wish, before serving cover the top generously with confectioners sugar sifted through a fine strainer.

Prune-Pecan Cake

10 PORTIONS

Very moist, a bit spicy, and full of nuts.

1½ cups sifted all-purpose flour

½ teaspoon baking soda

¼ teaspoon salt

1½ teaspoons nutmeg

1¼ cups pitted, stewed prunes
(about 15 extra-large prunes)

Finely grated rind of 1 lemon

1½ tablespoons lemon juice

¼ pound (½ cup) butter

1½ cups sugar

2 eggs

⅔ cup buttermilk

½ pound (2¼ cups) pecans,
cut or broken into large pieces

optional: Confectioners sugar

Adjust rack one-third up from the bottom of the oven. Preheat oven to 400 degrees. Butter a 9 × 3½-inch tube pan and line the bottom with paper. Butter the paper. Dust all over lightly with fine, dry bread crumbs.

Sift together flour, baking soda, salt, and nutmeg. Set aside. Cut prunes in quarters. (If they are very small, just cut them in halves.) Spread out on paper toweling to drain. Mix lemon rind and juice and set aside.

In small bowl of electric mixer cream the butter. Add the sugar and beat well. Add eggs one at a time. Beat for 2 to 3 minutes. On lowest speed add about half of the dry ingredients, then all of the buttermilk, and finally the remaining half of the dry ingredients, scraping the bowl as necessary with a rubber spatula and beating only until smooth after each addition.

Remove from mixer. Turn into a large bowl. Stir in lemon rind and juice, then prunes and nuts. Turn batter into the prepared pan. Rotate pan briskly to level batter.

Bake 1 hour or until cake tester comes out dry and top springs back when lightly touched. Remove from oven and cool in pan on a rack for about 20 minutes. Cover with a rack and invert. Remove pan and paper. Finish cooling on rack, either side up—the top will be flat. Cooled cake may be covered with confectioners sugar through a fine strainer.

Banana-Nut Cake

10 TO 12 PORTIONS

7 ounces (2 cups) pecan halves or large pieces
2½ cups sifted all-purpose flour
1 teaspoon baking soda
¼ teaspoon salt
3 large or 4 small bananas
    (to make 1½–1¾ cups mashed)
¼ pound (½ cup) butter
1 teaspoon vanilla extract
1½ cups sugar
2 eggs
¼ cup buttermilk

Adjust rack one-third up from the bottom of the oven. Preheat oven to 375 degrees. Butter a 9 × 3½-inch tube pan and dust it all over lightly with fine, dry bread crumbs.

In a small bowl toss the nuts with about 1 tablespoon of the flour to coat them thoroughly. Set aside. Sift remainder of flour with baking soda and salt. Set aside.

In small bowl of electric mixer break up the bananas. Beat them at low speed only enough to mash. You should get 1½ to 1¾ cups. Set aside.

In large bowl of mixer (with same beaters) cream the butter. Add vanilla and sugar and beat for a few minutes, using a rubber spatula as necessary to keep mixture blended. Add the eggs and continue to beat for 1 to 2 minutes. On lowest speed add half of the dry ingredients, then the buttermilk, and then the remainder of the dry ingredients, continuing to scrape bowl with rubber spatula as necessary. Add mashed bananas, beating only enough to blend. Remove from mixer. Stir in nuts.

Turn batter into prepared pan. Level top by rotating pan briskly back and forth. Bake 1 to 1¼ hours or until cake tester comes out dry.

Cool in pan on a rack for about 10 minutes. Cover with a rack or a small cookie sheet. Invert and remove pan. Cover with a rack and invert again to cool, right side up.

Peaches-and-Cream Rum Cake

8 PORTIONS

RUM SYRUP

¾ cup boiling water
1 cup sugar
½ cup light rum

Stir water and sugar in a 2- to 3-cup saucepan over moderate heat to dissolve the sugar. Boil without stirring for 3 minutes. Remove from heat. Cool to room temperature. Stir in the rum and set aside.

CAKE

1 cup sifted all-purpose flour
1 teaspoon double-acting baking powder
¼ teaspoon salt
2 eggs
1 cup sugar
½ teaspoon vanilla extract
½ cup milk
1 tablespoon butter

Adjust rack to center of oven. Preheat oven to 350 degrees. Butter a 9-inch round layer-cake pan and dust it lightly with fine, dry bread crumbs. Set aside.

Sift together the flour, baking powder, and salt. Set aside.

In small bowl of electric mixer beat eggs at high speed for 3 minutes until foamy and light lemon-colored. Gradually add sugar and vanilla and continue to beat at high speed for 5 minutes more until very thick.

Meanwhile, heat milk and butter in a small saucepan, bringing them just to a boil. On lowest speed, very gradually pour the boiling hot milk into the eggs, scraping the bowl with a rubber spatula and beating only until smooth.

Gradually add the sifted dry ingredients, continuing to scrape the bowl with the rubber spatula and beating only until flour is blended.

Turn batter into the prepared pan. Bake ½ hour or until top springs back when lightly touched and cake comes away from sides of pan. Cool in the pan for about 2 minutes. Cover with a rack and invert. Remove pan. Immediately invert again onto a serving plate, which must have a slight rim to keep the rum syrup from running over.

Gradually pour rum syrup all over hot cake until it is absorbed. Set aside to cool completely.

TOPPING

¼ cup apricot preserves
1 tablespoon rum
5 large freestone peaches
¼ cup water
¼ cup sugar

Stir preserves and rum to mix, then spread this over top of cake.

Blanch peaches briefly in boiling water to cover until the skin may be peeled off easily. Peel (see directions on page 100), cut in half from top to bottom, remove pits, and slice each half into 8 lengthwise wedges.

In a large skillet bring water and sugar to a boil. Reduce heat to low. Add a single layer of peach slices. Cover and simmer gently for a few minutes. Carefully, with a large spatula, turn peaches. Cover and simmer again very briefly until barely tender.

Gently remove peaches to a towel to drain. Repeat with remaining peaches.

Arrange the peaches overlapping closely in a ring around the top edge of the cake. Fill in the center section with remaining peaches, which may be cut into dice for easier arrangement.

WHIPPED CREAM

1½ cups heavy cream
¼ cup plus 2 tablespoons confectioners sugar
1½ teaspoons vanilla extract
optional: 2 tablespoons chopped green
   pistachio nuts, or toasted, sliced almonds
   (See Note.)

In a chilled bowl with chilled beaters, whip the cream with sugar and vanilla until cream holds a shape.

Using a pastry bag and a large star tube, press cream into large swirls over center of cake, letting most of the outer ring of peaches show. Refrigerate. This is best when very fresh. It should be served the day it is made.

Before serving, sprinkle optional pistachio nuts or almonds over the whipped cream.

NOTE: *To toast almonds, place them in a shallow pan in a 350-degree oven and stir occasionally until golden brown.*

Walnut-Peach Kuchen

6 TO 8 PORTIONS

PASTRY

1¼ cups sifted all-purpose flour
¼ teaspoon double-acting baking powder
¼ teaspoon salt
¼ cup sugar
2 ounces (¼ cup) cold butter,
    cut in 3 or 4 pieces
1 egg
3 tablespoons walnuts, very finely chopped

Sift together flour, baking powder, salt, and sugar into a bowl. With a pastry blender cut in the butter until the mixture resembles coarse crumbs. Stir the egg lightly with a fork just to mix. With the fork stir it into the above mixture. Stir in the walnuts.

Turn dough out onto a large board or a smooth surface and knead briefly only until the dough is smooth and holds together. Flatten slightly and place in the center of a 9-inch square unbuttered metal cake pan.

If the dough is sticky, dip your fingertips in flour as necessary. Press the dough evenly all over the bottom and about 1¼ inches up on the sides of the pan. See that it isn't too thick in the corners. Cut down any parts that are too high—fill in low parts—but don't worry about getting the top edge exactly even.

Adjust rack one-third up from bottom of oven and preheat oven to 450 degrees.

FILLING

1 tablespoon all-purpose flour
1 teaspoon cinnamon
⅓ cup sugar
4 ounces (1 generous cup) walnuts,
    cut into medium-size pieces
8 medium-size, ripe freestone peaches
2 tablespoons butter (See Note 1.)

Sift together flour, cinnamon, and sugar and set aside. Sprinkle two-thirds of the walnuts over the dough in the pan, reserving the remaining nuts.

To peel the peaches, place them, a few at a time, in a large pot of rapidly boiling water to cover. They should remain in the water for only a few seconds (a bit longer if they are less ripe), until the skin may be easily peeled off. Have ready a large bowl of cold water. To test, with a slotted spoon transfer a peach to the cold water. Using your fingers and starting at the stem end, peel off the skin. When it comes off easily, transfer all the peaches to the cold water. If you've started to skin a peach and you find it's not ready, replace it in the boiling water, but do not overcook.

After peeling all the peaches, cut them in half from top to bottom, remove pits, and then cut each piece in half again, the long way. Drain on toweling.

Place the peach quarters over the walnuts in the pastry shell, alternating them one round side up, the next round side down, and fitting them into each other very tightly in even rows.

Sprinkle with reserved ⅓ cup of cut walnuts and then with reserved flour, cinnamon, and sugar mixture. Dot with butter. (See Note 1.) Cover with a piece of aluminum foil large enough to turn down loosely around the edge.

Bake in 450-degree oven for 30 minutes. Meanwhile, prepare topping.

TOPPING

2 egg yolks
¼ cup heavy cream
¼ teaspoon vanilla extract

Stir yolks lightly just to mix, and stir in heavy cream and vanilla.

After cake has baked for 30 minutes, remove the aluminum foil. Without removing pan completely from oven, pour the topping evenly over all the peaches. Reduce oven temperature to 400 degrees. Bake uncovered 25 minutes longer (total baking time: 55 minutes) or until the edge of the crust is well-browned.

Remove from oven. Let cool slightly or completely. Cut into portions and, with a wide metal spatula, transfer to a serving plate or individual dessert plates.

NOTES: 1. *The best way to "dot with butter" is to cut the required amount from frozen butter, cutting in thin slivers or small dice. Refreeze until ready to use.*

2. *Walnut-Peach Kuchen is best served warm and à la mode with vanilla ice cream. Warm or not, it is best when very fresh.*

Apple Kuchen

⅓ cup light or dark raisins, or currants
  (See page 12.)
1¼ cups sifted all-purpose flour
1½ teaspoons double-acting baking powder
½ teaspoon salt
¼ cup sugar
2 ounces (¼ cup) butter
1 egg
¼ cup milk
1 teaspoon vanilla extract
2½ ounces (¾ cup) walnuts,
  cut into medium-size pieces

Adjust rack to center of oven. Preheat oven to 400 degrees. Butter a 13 × 9 × 2-inch baking pan.

Place the raisins in a small strainer over a saucepan of shallow boiling water. Cover and let steam for 3 to 5 minutes. Remove from heat and set aside.

Sift together the flour, baking powder, salt, and sugar into a mixing bowl. With a pastry blender cut in the butter until the mixture resembles coarse crumbs.

In a cup or a small bowl, stir the egg just to mix and then stir in the milk.

Add the egg, milk, and vanilla to the flour mixture, stirring with a fork only until the dry ingredients are thoroughly moistened.

Spread the batter evenly in the prepared pan—it will be a thin layer. Sprinkle with the raisins and nuts and set aside.

FILLING

4 medium-large apples (When Rome Beauties
  are available, they're my first choice.
  I also like Delicious.)
2 ounces (¼ cup) butter
¼ cup sugar
1½ teaspoons cinnamon

Peel, quarter, and core the apples. Cut each quarter into about 6 very thin wedges. Place them, overlapping, in three rows down the length of the cake. If there is a space between the rows, it may be filled in with additional slices placed in the opposite direction. If the apples are small, use one or two more and make four rows of slices.

Melt the butter and brush it over the apples. Mix the sugar and cinnamon, and sprinkle them over the butter. Cover the pan loosely with a cookie sheet or a large piece of aluminum foil.

Bake for 35 minutes, removing cookie sheet or foil for the last 5 minutes. Prepare glaze.

APRICOT GLAZE

½ cup apricot preserves
2 tablespoons sugar

Strain the preserves and stir in the sugar. In a small saucepan over moderate heat bring the mixture to a boil, stirring constantly. Boil, stirring, for 3 minutes. Immediately brush over the apples.

Serve while still warm or at room temperature, but it is best while very fresh.

Cut cake into 8 to 10 portions. With a wide metal spatula, transfer portions to a cake platter.

Plain, Loaf, and Other Old-Fashioned Cakes

MILDRED KNOPF'S ORANGE
 PUFF CAKE

SPONGE CAKE

YOGURT CAKE

SOUR CREAM CAKE

AUSTRIAN BUTTER CAKE

BUTTERMILK SPICE CAKE

EAST 62ND STREET LEMON CAKE

CARAWAY SEED CAKE

ORANGE CAKE (*Texan*)

SPANISH ORANGE CAKE (*Valencian*)

INDIAN RIVER SWEET ORANGE
 BREAD

HONEY CAKE

MARBLE SPICE CAKE

MARBLE LOAF CAKE

CARDAMOM CURRANT CAKE
 (*Danish*)

RUMANIAN SOUR CREAM–RAISIN
 LOAF CAKE

MOOSEHEAD GINGERBREAD

JAVA CAKE

COPA CAKE

Mildred Knopf's Orange Puff Cake

In Mrs. Knopf's marvelous cookbook The Perfect Hostess, *there is a recipe for a sublime cake. For many years it was my father's favorite— I made it for him at least once a week. We called it Daddy Cake. Gabe ate a slice of it every day for years and it always brought forth a smiling "Ah, there's good news tonight."*

ORANGE PUFF CAKE

[Pre-heat oven to 325°]

1 over-running cup egg whites
   (approximately 10
   egg whites)
¼ teaspoon salt
1 teaspoon cream of tartar
1⅓ cups sugar

⅔ cup water
7 egg yolks
Grated rind 1 large,
   deep-colored orange
4 tablespoons orange juice
1 cup pastry flour

FIRST Beat with a flat wire whip 1 over-running cup of egg whites (approximately 10 egg whites) with ¼ teaspoon salt on a large platter or in a large, wide bowl. When the whites are foamy, add 1 teaspoon cream of tartar, sifting into whites through a small strainer. Continue to beat until the mixture looks moist and shiny and forms peaks when the whip is lifted up.

SECOND Boil 1⅓ cups sugar and ⅔ cup water until it forms a thread when dropped from a silver fork.

THIRD Pour the cooked sugar over the egg whites in a thin stream, holding the pan high enough so as not to scald or curdle the egg whites. This will happen if the sugar syrup is added to the whites too rapidly. Pour with one hand and blend with the other, using silver fork, not the wire whip.

FOURTH After all the sugar syrup has been added, set the platter or bowl in a pan of cold water. Continue beating with the flat wire whip until cool, always using a high, lifting stroke to achieve a light texture.

FIFTH Beat 7 egg yolks until lemon-colored. Add grated rind 1 large, deep-colored orange and 4 tablespoons orange juice. Mix well and fold gently into the meringue.

SIXTH Sift 1 cup pastry flour. Measure and resift 4 times. Sift gently into mixture and fold in with a light, folding motion. Pour the mixture into an angel-food cake pan that has been rinsed in cold water, handling as little as possible. Use a spatula to scrape the bowl clean, then cut through the mixture in the pan with a knife to clear away the air pockets. Bake at 325° for 1 hour. Remove from oven and invert, allowing cake to "hang" until cool. Do not place by open window or in drafts, as this causes the cake to shrink.

NOTES 1. Most angel-food pans are equipped with small feet that allow the cake to "hang" (the pan is inverted but the cake does not touch the surface of the table). However, in case your pan is an ordinary tube pan and not a specially built angel-food pan, do not be discouraged. Insert a Coca-Cola bottle into the tube and allow the pan to "hang" supported by the bottle until cool.

2. At first glance, this cake may seem like a lot of trouble, but, believe me, this is the sort of adventure in baking that makes a cook's reputation. Just follow each direction separately, one at a time, and you will have it done before you know it. It is a superb achievement, and I heartily recommend it as one of the finest cakes in the entire collection.

I follow Mrs. Knopf's above directions—however, I use "cake flour," and since I do not have a silver fork, I use a stainless steel one. I use a loose-bottomed aluminum (not Teflon) angel-food cake pan that measures 10 × 4 inches, and, although it does have small feet to raise it when inverted, I find it necessary to "hang" the cake over a bottle anyhow, as it has risen so high that the feet do not raise it enough. Incidentally, flat wire whips are generally available in specialty kitchen-equipment shops. (Some of my students tell me that they make this cake in a large bowl with a large balloon-type whisk. Others make it in an electric mixer.)

In the second direction, the temperature the sugar and water should reach is 234° on a candy thermometer.

Use a serrated bread knife to cut the cake and handle very gently so as not to squash this light-as-air creation.

Sponge Cake

8 TO 10 PORTIONS

6 eggs, separated
1 cup sugar
¼ cup lemon juice (*Before squeezing juice, grate and reserve the rind of 1 lemon to use below.*)
1 cup triple-sifted cake flour
⅛ teaspoon salt

Adjust rack one-third up from bottom of oven. Preheat oven to 350 degrees.

In small bowl of electric mixer beat yolks for 1 minute. On low speed gradually add sugar. Increase speed to high and beat for 5 minutes until very thick. Mix in the lemon juice. On lowest speed gradually add the flour, scraping the bowl with a rubber spatula and beating only until incorporated. Remove from mixer. Stir in grated lemon rind.

In large bowl of electric mixer beat the egg whites with the salt until they hold a point or are stiff but not dry. It is important not to overbeat. A safety precaution is to beat the whites with a mixer only until they hold a very soft shape and then finish the beating with a large wire whisk.

Fold one-quarter of the whites into the yolks—do not be too thorough. Fold in another quarter. Then fold the yolks into the remaining whites, handling as gently and as little as possible and folding only until the whites have barely disappeared.

Gently turn the batter into an ungreased, loose-bottomed 9 × 3½-inch tube pan. Spread top level.

Bake 50 minutes or until top springs back when lightly pressed with your fingertips. During last 15 minutes of baking it might be necessary to cover top loosely with aluminum foil to prevent overbrowning.

Remove from oven and very carefully invert pan over the neck of a small bottle. Let cake hang until completely cool.

To remove cake from pan, cut around the sides with a firm, sharp knife, pressing firmly against the pan. Do not cut with an up and down motion. An up and down motion marks the side of the cake, but cutting without going up and down, just around the side of the pan without raising and lowering the knife, leaves smooth, beautiful sides. Holding the center tube, lift the bottom of the pan and the cake. Now cut between the bottom of the pan and the cake, pressing the knife firmly against the pan. Cut around the center tube. Cover the cake with a rack and invert to release the cake completely. Cover with another rack and invert again, leaving cake right side up; however, this cake may be served either side up.

Serve as is or prepare the following icing:

CHOCOLATE ICING

8 ounces sweet chocolate
  (Baker's German's Sweet Chocolate or
  Hershey's Special Dark
  are both fine for this.)
3 egg yolks
2 ounces (4 tablespoons) butter, at room
  temperature
1 tablespoon milk

Break up the chocolate and place it in the top of a large double boiler over hot water on moderately low heat. Cook, stirring with a wooden spoon or spatula, until almost melted. Remove top of double boiler from heat and continue to stir until completely melted and smooth. Let stand for 1 minute and then, beating briskly with the wooden spoon or spatula, add the egg yolks one at a time. Then beat in the butter, 1 tablespoon at a time, and finally, beat in the milk.

Use immediately or, if too thin, let stand at room temperature to thicken slightly.

Place the cake on a plate protected with four strips of wax paper.

Pour the icing over the top of the cake, letting a bit run down on the sides. Leave it that way, or with a long, narrow metal spatula spread on the sides and then the top.

Remove wax paper strips by pulling each one out by a narrow end. (See page 18.)

Yogurt Cake

10 PORTIONS

3 cups sifted cake flour
2 teaspoons double-acting baking powder
¼ teaspoon salt
½ pound (1 cup) butter
2 cups sugar
5 eggs, separated
1 cup unflavored yogurt
Finely grated rind of 2 large,
    deep-colored oranges

Adjust rack one-third up from the bottom of the oven. Preheat oven to 375 degrees. Butter a 9 × 3½-inch tube pan. Line the bottom with paper. Butter the paper and dust all over lightly with fine, dry bread crumbs.

Sift together flour, baking powder, and salt and set aside. In small bowl of electric mixer cream the butter until it is very soft. Gradually add the sugar and continue to beat at medium-high speed for about 10 minutes until mixture is almost liquid. Add the yolks one at a time, beating well after each. Scrape the bowl with a rubber spatula as necessary to keep the mixture smooth. Beat in the yogurt. Transfer mixture to large bowl of mixer. On lowest speed gradually add the dry ingredients, scraping the bowl with the spatula and beating only until smooth. Remove from mixer. Stir in orange rind.

Beat the whites until they hold a point, or are stiff but not dry. In two additions fold them into the batter and turn into cake pan. Rotate the pan briskly several times to level the top.

Bake 1 hour and 5 or 10 minutes until a cake tester comes out dry.

If the top of the cake seems to be browning too much, cover it loosely with aluminum foil for the last 15 minutes of baking time.

Cool in pan on a rack for about 15 minutes. Cover with a rack and invert. Remove pan and paper. Again, cover with a rack and invert to cool right side up.

OPTIONAL: *As soon as the cake is removed from the oven it may be sprinkled lightly with a few spoonfuls of Grand Marnier.*

Sour Cream Cake

12 PORTIONS

3 cups sifted all-purpose flour
¼ teaspoon baking soda
½ teaspoon salt
½ pound (1 cup) butter
2 teaspoons vanilla extract
3 cups sugar
6 eggs
1 cup sour cream
Finely grated rind of 1 large lemon

Adjust oven rack one-third of the way up from the bottom of the oven. Preheat oven to 350 degrees. Butter a loose-bottomed tube pan that measures 9 inches across the top and 3½ inches deep. (See Notes.) Dust all over with fine, dry bread crumbs.

Sift together flour, baking soda, and salt. Set aside. In large bowl of electric mixer cream the butter. Add vanilla and gradually add the sugar. Beat for 2 to 3 minutes. Add eggs, two at a time, beating until thoroughly incorporated after each addition, and for 2 or 3 minutes after last addition, scraping the bowl with a rubber spatula as necessary to keep the ingredients well mixed. On the lowest speed add half of the dry ingredients, then all of the sour cream, and then the balance of the dry ingredients, scraping the bowl with the spatula and beating only until smooth after each addition. Remove from mixer. Stir in lemon rind.

Pour into pan. Level top by rotating pan briskly back and forth several times. Bake 1 hour and 30 to 40 minutes or until a cake tester comes out dry.

Cool cake in pan for 10 to 15 minutes. Then cover with a rack and invert. Remove pan (and paper, if it was used). Cover with another rack and invert again to finish cooling right side up.

NOTES: 1. *If the pan does not have a loose bottom, butter the pan, line the bottom with paper, butter the paper, and dust it all with fine, dry bread crumbs.*

2. *If the pan is less than 3½ inches high (if it is only 3¼ inches high), prepare an aluminum foil collar to extend about 1 inch above the sides—butter about 1 inch of the length before wrapping it around the pan, buttered side up and facing in. Fasten it with straight pins or tie it on.*

Austrian Butter Cake

10 TO 12 PORTIONS

2 cups sifted all-purpose flour
2 teaspoons double-acting baking powder
¼ cup cornstarch, unsifted
¼ cup potato starch, unsifted
¼ teaspoon salt
1 pound (2 cups) butter
1 tablespoon vanilla extract
1½ cups sugar
6 eggs
Finely grated rind of 1 large lemon
  (or 2 small)

Adjust rack one-third up from the bottom of the oven. Preheat oven to 375 degrees. Butter a 9 × 3½-inch tube pan and dust it with fine, dry bread crumbs.

Sift together flour, baking powder, cornstarch, potato starch, and salt. Set aside. In large bowl of electric mixer cream the butter. Add vanilla and sugar and beat for 2 to 3 minutes. Add eggs one at a time, beating well after each. Mixture will look curdled at this point—O.K. On lowest speed gradually add the dry ingredients, scraping the bowl with a rubber spatula as necessary to keep mixture smooth. Beat only until blended. With a spatula stir in lemon rind. Spoon batter into prepared cake pan. Spread top level.

Bake 1 hour or until a cake tester comes out dry. Cool in pan on a rack for about 10 to 15 minutes. Cover with a rack and invert. Remove pan. Cover with another rack and invert again to cool right side up.

When completely cool, wrap airtight and let stand overnight before serving.

Butter-milk Spice Cake

12 TO 16
PORTIONS

3 cups sifted cake flour
1½ teaspoons baking soda
1 teaspoon salt
1½ teaspoons cinnamon
¾ teaspoon nutmeg
¼ teaspoon powdered cloves
6 ounces (¾ cup) butter
1 teaspoon vanilla extract
1¼ cups light brown sugar, firmly packed
1 cup granulated sugar
3 eggs
1½ cups buttermilk
Finely grated rind of 1 lemon

Adjust rack one-third up from the bottom of the oven. Preheat oven to 350 degrees. Butter a 13 × 9 × 2-inch pan and dust it all lightly with fine, dry bread crumbs.

Sift together flour, baking soda, salt, cinnamon, nutmeg, and cloves. Set aside. In large bowl of electric mixer cream the butter. Add the vanilla and then, gradually, both sugars and beat for 1 to 2 minutes. Add the eggs individually, scraping the bowl as necessary with a rubber spatula and beating well after each. On lowest speed alternately add sifted dry ingredients in three additions and buttermilk in two additions, scraping the bowl with the spatula and beating only until smooth after each addition. Remove from mixer and stir in lemon rind.

Turn into pan and spread top level.

Bake 50 to 55 minutes or until the top springs back when lightly touched and cake begins to come away from sides of pan.

Let cake cool in the pan on a rack for about 15 minutes. Cut around sides to release. Cover with a rack or a cookie sheet and invert. Remove pan. Cover with a rack and invert again to finish cooling.

When completely cool, prepare the following:

BROWN SUGAR ICING

1 cup light brown sugar, firmly packed
⅓ cup heavy cream
2 tablespoons butter
Pinch of salt
½ teaspoon vanilla extract

In a medium-size saucepan, over moderately low heat, stir the sugar and cream to slowly dissolve the sugar, brushing down the sides occasionally with a wet brush to remove any sugar granules. Stirring constantly, slowly bring the syrup to a boil and let boil for exactly 1 minute. Transfer to small bowl of electric mixer. Add butter and stir to melt. Add salt and vanilla and beat until creamy and slightly thickened. It will still be warm. Immediately pour over the cake and, with a long, narrow metal spatula, spread to cover.

NOTE: *Do not freeze this cake after it has been iced—the icing will become wet when thawed.*

East 62nd Street Lemon Cake

10 PORTIONS

This cake, my daughter's creation, has become rather famous since the recipe was printed in The New York Times. *The list of hostesses who now have it on hand at all times reads like a* Who's Who.

3 cups sifted all-purpose flour
2 teaspoons double-acting baking powder
½ teaspoon salt
½ pound (1 cup) butter
2 cups sugar
4 eggs
1 cup milk
Finely grated rind of 2 lemons

Adjust rack one-third up from bottom of oven. Preheat oven to 350 degrees. Butter a 9 × 3½-inch tube pan and dust it lightly with fine, dry bread crumbs.

Sift together flour, baking powder, and salt and set aside. In large bowl of electric mixer cream the butter. Add the sugar and beat for 2 to 3 minutes. Beat in the eggs individually, scraping the bowl as necessary with a rubber spatula to keep mixture smooth. On lowest speed alternately add the dry ingredients in three additions and the milk in two additions, scraping the bowl with the rubber spatula as necessary and beating only until smooth after each addition. Stir in lemon rind. Turn the batter into prepared pan. Level top by rotating pan briskly back and forth.

Bake for 1 hour and 10 to 15 minutes until a cake tester comes out dry.

Let cake stand in the pan for about 3 minutes and then cover with a rack and invert. Remove pan, leaving the cake upside down. Place over a large piece of aluminum foil or wax paper and prepare glaze.

GLAZE

⅓ cup lemon juice
¾ cup sugar

The glaze must be used immediately after it is mixed.

Stir the lemon juice and sugar and brush all over the hot cake until absorbed.

Let cake cool completely. Use two wide metal pancake turners or a cookie sheet to transfer it to a cake plate.

Do not cut for at least several hours.

Caraway Seed Cake

An Irish recipe for an old-fashioned favorite.

10 PORTIONS

3 cups sifted all-purpose flour
2 teaspoons double-acting baking powder
½ teaspoon salt
¾ teaspoon nutmeg
½ pound (1 cup) butter
1 teaspoon vanilla extract
2 tablespoons caraway seeds
2½ cups confectioners sugar
2 eggs plus 3 egg yolks
1 cup milk
Finely grated rind of 2 large lemons

Adjust rack one-third up from bottom of oven. Preheat oven to 350 degrees. Butter a 9 x 3½-inch tube pan and dust it lightly with fine, dry bread crumbs.

Sift together the flour, baking powder, salt, and nutmeg and set aside. In large bowl of electric mixer cream the butter. Add the vanilla, caraway seeds, and sugar and beat well. Beat in the 2 eggs and then the yolks one at a time. On lowest speed alternately add the sifted dry ingredients in three additions and the milk in two additions, scraping the bowl with a rubber spatula as necessary and beating only until smooth. Stir in the lemon rind.

Turn into prepared pan. Level top by rotating pan briskly back and forth.

Bake for 1 hour and 5 to 10 minutes until a cake tester comes out dry.

Remove from oven and let cake stand in pan for 10 minutes. Then cover with a rack and invert. Remove pan. Cover with another rack. Invert again over a large piece of wax paper. Prepare glaze immediately.

GLAZE

1¼ cups strained confectioners sugar
1 tablespoon lemon juice
1 tablespoon boiling water

Place all ingredients in a small mixing bowl. Stir with a rubber spatula until smooth. Pour over top of hot cake, letting some run down unevenly on the sides.

NOTE: *This is best served in thin slices.*

Orange Cake
(Texan)

8 TO 10
PORTIONS

Made with yogurt.

3½ ounces (¾ cup) white raisins
2½ cups sifted all-purpose flour
1 teaspoon baking soda
¼ teaspoon salt
¼ pound (½ cup) butter
1 teaspoon vanilla extract
2 cups light brown sugar, firmly packed
3 eggs
1 cup unflavored yogurt
Finely grated rind of 2 large oranges

Adjust rack one-third up from bottom of oven. Preheat oven to 350 degrees. Butter a 9 × 3½-inch tube pan and dust it lightly with fine, dry bread crumbs.

Chop the raisins coarsely on a board, using a long, heavy knife. Place them in a small bowl and toss with about 1 tablespoon of the flour. Use your fingers to separate and thoroughly flour each piece. Set aside.

Sift together the remaining flour with the baking soda and salt and set aside. In the large bowl of an electric mixer cream the butter. Add vanilla and sugar and beat for 1 to 2 minutes. Add eggs one at a time, beating until thoroughly incorporated after each. On lowest speed alternately add sifted dry ingredients in three additions and yogurt in two additions, scraping the bowl as necessary with a rubber spatula and beating only until smooth after each addition. Stir in orange rind and raisins.

Turn the batter into the prepared pan. Rotate pan briskly back and forth several times to level the batter.

Bake 1 hour and 5 minutes or until top springs back when lightly touched and a cake tester comes out dry. Remove from oven and let stand for 5 minutes.

Place a rack over the cake and invert. Remove pan. Cover with another rack and invert again. Place over a large piece of aluminum foil or wax paper. Prepare glaze.

GLAZE

½ cup granulated sugar
½ cup orange juice, or ¼ cup orange juice
and ¼ cup light rum or bourbon

Mix sugar with orange juice, or orange juice and rum or bourbon, and immediately brush all over top and sides of warm cake. Let stand for at least 2 to 3 hours.

Using a small cookie sheet as a spatula, transfer cake to a cake plate.

Spanish Orange Cake
(Valencian)

10 PORTIONS

2½ cups sifted all-purpose flour
1 tablespoon plus 1 teaspoon double-acting
  baking powder
¼ teaspoon salt
½ pound (1 cup) butter
1½ cups sugar
2 eggs, separated, plus 3 egg yolks
⅔ cup orange juice (Before squeezing juice,
  grate and reserve rind of 2 oranges
  to use below.)

Adjust rack one-third up from the bottom of the oven. Preheat oven to 350 degrees. Butter a loose-bottomed 9 × 3½-inch tube pan and dust it with fine, dry bread crumbs.

Sift together flour, baking powder, and salt. Set aside. In large bowl of electric mixer cream the butter. Add the sugar and beat for 2 to 3 minutes. One at a time, beat in the 5 egg yolks, beating well after each, and scraping the bowl with a rubber spatula as necessary to keep mixture smooth. On lowest speed alternately add sifted dry ingredients in three additions and the orange juice in two additions, continuing to scrape the bowl with a rubber spatula as necessary and beating only until smooth after each addition. Remove from mixer. Stir in orange rind. Beat the 2 egg whites until they hold a firm shape and fold them into the batter. Turn the batter into cake pan and level top by turning pan briskly back and forth.

Bake 1 hour or until cake tester comes out dry. Cool cake in pan for about 20 minutes. Cover with a rack and invert. Remove pan, leaving cake upside down. Place over wax paper or aluminum foil.

Prepare the following glaze.

½ cup orange marmalade
2 tablespoons water

Mix marmalade and water in a small saucepan. Bring to a boil. Brush over top and sides of cake. Let stand several hours before transferring to a cake plate, which is easily done by using a cookie sheet as a spatula.

Indian River Sweet Orange Bread

2 LOAVES

Serve as a plain cake or, even better, toast it and serve with butter, cream cheese, or Honey Butter (page 407).

4 cups sifted all-purpose flour
1 tablespoon plus 1 teaspoon double-acting baking powder
½ teaspoon baking soda
1 teaspoon salt
3 large oranges, approximately (to yield 1⅓ cups juice)
1½ cups sugar
⅓ cup water
3 tablespoons butter
3 eggs
optional: Walnuts or pecans and/or currants or raisins (See Note.)

Adjust rack one-third up from bottom of oven and preheat oven to 350 degrees. Butter two loaf pans, 8½ × 4½ × 2½ inches, and coat them all over lightly with fine, dry bread crumbs.

Sift together flour, baking powder, baking soda, and salt into a large mixing bowl and set aside.

With a vegetable peeler, remove the very thin, bright-colored, outer rind of about 2½ oranges and reserve it. Squeeze the oranges. You will need 1⅓ cups of juice. Set it aside. Cut the rind into slivers. (See directions for paring the rind and cutting it into slivers, page 375.)

Place the rind, sugar, and water into a large, heavy saucepan. Stir over high heat until sugar is dissolved and mixture comes to a boil. Reduce heat to moderate and let mixture boil gently without stirring for 5 minutes.

Remove from heat. Add butter and stir to melt. Stir in the 1⅓ cups of orange juice. Beat the eggs lightly just to mix and stir them in. Pour this over the sifted dry ingredients and stir until dry ingredients are thoroughly moistened.

Turn into prepared pans. Shake gently to level batter. Bake 55 minutes to 1 hour or until a cake tester comes out dry.

Cool in pans for about 10 minutes before removing to racks to finish cooling.

NOTE: *The batter may be divided in half and ½ cup chopped walnuts or pecans stirred into one half and ½ cup currants or raisins into the other half to make 1 nut and 1 raisin loaf.*

Honey Cake

1 9-INCH
LOAF

2¼ cups sifted all-purpose flour

¾ teaspoon double-acting baking powder

¾ teaspoon baking soda

½ teaspoon salt

2 teaspoons cinnamon

3½ ounces (1 cup) walnuts,
    cut into medium-size pieces

optional: 2–3 tablespoons candied orange peel,
    finely cut

3 eggs

¾ cup dark brown sugar, firmly packed

3 tablespoons melted butter

¾ cup honey

¾ cup cold, very strong coffee
    (2 tablespoons instant coffee dissolved in
    ¾ cup hot water)

Finely grated rind of 2 large oranges

Adjust rack one-third up from the bottom of the oven. Preheat oven to 350 degrees. Butter a 9 × 5 × 3-inch loaf pan and dust it very lightly with fine, dry bread crumbs.

Sift together flour, baking powder, baking soda, salt, and cinnamon. In a small bowl toss a spoonful of the sifted dry ingredients with the walnuts and optional candied orange peel. Set aside remainder of dry ingredients and floured nuts.

In large bowl of electric mixer beat the eggs and sugar slightly only to mix. Add the butter and honey and beat only to mix. On lowest speed add half of the sifted dry ingredients, then gradually add all the coffee, and finally the remaining dry ingredients, scraping the bowl as necessary with a rubber spatula and beating only until smooth after each addition. Remove from mixer and stir in the grated orange rind, the floured walnuts, and the optional candied orange peel.

Pour the batter into the prepared pan. Pan will be filled almost to the top. Bake 1 hour and 20 to 30 minutes until the top springs back firmly when lightly touched. About 20 minutes before the baking time is up, check to see if the top is becoming too brown. If so, cover loosely with aluminum foil.

Cool in pan on a rack for 5 to 10 minutes before removing to a rack to cool completely. Let stand for several hours or overnight before slicing. This is best cut in very, very thin slices.

NOTE: *The quality of this cake depends on the honey—it will vary considerably with different honeys.*

Marble Spice Cake

An old-fashioned Southern loaf cake.

8 PORTIONS

2 cups sifted cake flour
2 teaspoons double-acting baking powder
¼ teaspoon salt
¼ pound (½ cup) butter
1 cup sugar
2 eggs
⅔ cup milk
1 teaspoon powdered, unsweetened cocoa
1 teaspoon instant coffee
1 teaspoon cinnamon
½ teaspoon nutmeg
½ teaspoon powdered cloves
2 tablespoons molasses, light or dark

Adjust rack one-third up from bottom of oven. Preheat oven to 375 degrees. Butter a 9 × 5 × 3-inch loaf pan and dust it all lightly with fine, dry bread crumbs.

Sift together the flour, baking powder, and salt and set aside.

In small bowl of electric mixer, cream the butter. Add the sugar and beat for a minute or two. Add eggs one at a time. Increase speed to high and beat for 1 to 2 minutes.

On lowest speed alternately add sifted dry ingredients in three additions and milk in two additions, scraping the bowl with a rubber spatula and beating only until smooth after each addition.

Remove about half of the batter and set aside.

To the remainder, add cocoa, instant coffee, cinnamon, nutmeg, powdered cloves, and molasses and beat only until smooth.

Alternately spoon or pour large tablespoonfuls of both batters into prepared pan.

Bake 1 hour and 5 minutes or until a cake tester comes out dry.

Let stand in pan for about 10 minutes. Cover with a rack, invert, remove pan, cover with another rack, and invert again to cool completely, right side up.

Marble Loaf Cake

8 TO 10
PORTIONS

1½ ounces (1½ squares) unsweetened chocolate
2½ cups sifted cake flour
½ teaspoon salt
1 tablespoon double-acting baking powder
¼ pound (½ cup) butter
1 teaspoon vanilla extract
¼ teaspoon almond extract
1½ cups sugar
3 eggs
¾ cup milk
1 tablespoon instant coffee

Adjust rack one-third up from bottom of oven and preheat to 375 degrees. Butter an 11 × 5 × 3-inch loaf pan (see Note) or similar shape with an 8- to 9-cup capacity. Dust all over lightly with fine, dry bread crumbs.

Melt the chocolate in a small, heatproof cup set in a pan of shallow hot water on moderately low heat. Set aside to cool.

Sift together the flour, salt, and baking powder and set aside. In large bowl of electric mixer cream the butter. Add the vanilla and almond extracts and then the sugar. Beat for a minute or two. Add eggs one at a time and beat at high speed for 2 minutes, scraping the bowl occasionally with a rubber spatula.

On lowest speed alternately add the sifted dry ingredients in three additions and the milk in two additions, scraping the bowl with the rubber spatula as necessary and beating only until smooth after each addition.

Remove from mixer. Transfer one-third of the batter to small bowl of electric mixer. Add the melted chocolate and instant coffee and, with the same beaters, on low speed, beat only until mixed. Remove from mixer.

Alternately place spoonfuls of both batters in the prepared pan. With a small metal spatula, or a knife, cut zigzag through the batter, cutting in one direction first and then the other—do not overdo it.

Bake 1 hour or until the top springs back when lightly touched and a cake tester comes out dry.

Cool in pan for 10 minutes. Cover with a rack, invert, and remove the pan. Cover with another rack and invert again to cool on the rack, right side up.

THICK CHOCOLATE GLAZE

6 ounces (1 cup) semisweet chocolate morsels,
  or 6 squares semisweet chocolate
1 tablespoon butter
3 tablespoons light corn syrup
2 tablespoons milk

In the top of a small double boiler over hot water on moderate heat, melt the chocolate and the butter. With a small wire whisk beat in the corn syrup and milk, beating until smooth.

Remove from heat. Cool slightly, stirring occasionally. Place a large piece of wax paper under the cake on the rack. While glaze is still warm, pour it thickly over the top of the cake. Smooth it over the top only. If a bit runs down the sides, just leave it. Transfer cake to a platter or cake board.

Let stand for a few hours to allow the glaze to set.

NOTE: *This recipe may also be made in two smaller pans, each 8 × 4 × 2½ inches (1-quart capacity). The baking time will then be reduced to 50 minutes.*

Cardamom Currant Cake

(Danish)

8 TO 10 PORTIONS

Raisins usually have a tendency to sink to the bottom. Not so in this lovely recipe.

5 ounces (1 cup) currants,
      or coarsely chopped raisins
1½ cups sifted all-purpose flour
1 teaspoon double-acting baking powder
3 teaspoons ground cardamom (See Note.)
½ pound (1 cup) butter
1 teaspoon vanilla extract
5 eggs, separated
¼ teaspoon salt
1½ cups confectioners sugar
Finely grated rind of 2 lemons

Adjust rack one-third up from bottom of oven. Preheat oven to 350 degrees. Butter a 9 × 5 × 3-inch loaf pan and dust it all over lightly with fine, dry bread crumbs.

See directions for preparing currants (page 12).

Place the currants, or chopped raisins, in a small bowl with 1 tablespoon of the flour. Toss with your fingers until thoroughly coated. Set aside.

Sift the remaining flour with the baking powder and cardamom.

In large bowl of electric mixer cream the butter. Beat in the vanilla. On low speed gradually add the sifted dry ingredients, scraping the bowl with a rubber spatula and beating only until thoroughly mixed. Remove from mixer.

In the small bowl of the mixer, with clean beaters, at medium speed beat the egg whites with the salt until they barely hold a soft shape. Then reduce the speed and, still beating, gradually add ¾ cup of the sugar. (Reserve remaining ¾ cup.) Increase speed to high and continue to beat until whites hold a definite shape, or are stiff but not dry—do not overbeat. Transfer beaten whites to a large bowl and set aside.

You may now use the egg white bowl and beaters without washing them to beat the yolks. Beat at high speed for a few minutes until they are pale lemon-colored. Gradually add the reserved ¾ cup sugar and continue to beat for about 3 minutes more until mixture is thick and very pale.

Return the butter mixture in the large bowl to the mixer. On low speed gradually beat in the egg yolk mixture, scraping the bowl with a rubber spatula and beating only until smooth. Remove from mixer and, with a rubber spatula, mix in the grated lemon rind and the floured currants or raisins. Fold in the beaten egg whites, one-fourth at a time, folding only until incorporated. Do not handle any more than necessary.

Turn the batter into the prepared pan—the pan will be almost full. Smooth the top and then spread the batter up on the sides a bit, leaving it slightly lower in the center.

Bake for 1 hour and 10 minutes or until a cake tester comes out dry.

Cool in the pan for 10 to 15 minutes. Place a folded towel or a pot holder over the cake and invert into the palm of your hand. Remove the pan, cover with a rack, and invert again to cool right side up.

NOTE: *The cardamom may be omitted, or you may substitute 1 teaspoon cinnamon and ½ teaspoon nutmeg.*

Rumanian Sour Cream– Raisin Loaf Cake

8 PORTIONS

This butterless cake has an unusual texture—moist, firm, not very sweet.

3 ounces (⅔ cup) raisins, light, dark, or mixed
2 cups sifted all-purpose flour
1 teaspoon baking powder
1 teaspoon baking soda
¼ teaspoon salt
3 eggs
1 teaspoon vanilla extract
1 cup sugar
1 cup sour cream

Adjust rack one-third of the way up from the bottom of the oven. Preheat oven to 350 degrees. Butter a 9 × 5 × 3-inch loaf pan. Dust it lightly with fine, dry bread crumbs.

Place raisins in a small strainer over a deep saucepan containing a small amount of boiling water. Cover and steam for 5 minutes to soften the raisins. Remove from heat and dry on paper toweling. Place on a board and chop coarsely with a long, heavy knife. Place in a small bowl and set aside.

Sift together flour, baking powder, baking soda, and salt. Add a small spoonful to the raisins and toss with your fingers to separate and thoroughly coat each piece. Set aside remaining dry ingredients.

In large bowl of electric mixer beat eggs until frothy. Add vanilla and sugar and beat at high speed for about 3 minutes until fluffy and very light in color. Beat in the sour cream. On low speed add the sifted dry ingredients, scraping the bowl with a rubber spatula and beating only until smooth. Remove from mixer. Stir in the raisins. Turn the batter into the prepared pan.

Bake 1 hour and 10 to 15 minutes or until a cake tester comes out dry. Cool in pan for about 5 minutes. Cover with a rack and invert. Remove pan. Cover with another rack and invert again to finish cooling right side up.

Serve in thin slices, 2 or 3 to a portion.

Moose-head Ginger-bread

This sharp and spicy gingerbread comes from an old-time fishing guide in Maine.

10 TO 12 PORTIONS

2½ cups sifted all-purpose flour
2 teaspoons baking soda
½ teaspoon salt
1 teaspoon cinnamon
1½ teaspoons powdered ginger
½ teaspoon powdered cloves
½ teaspoon dry mustard
½ teaspoon black pepper, finely ground
¼ pound (½ cup) butter
½ cup dark brown sugar, firmly packed
2 eggs
1 cup molasses, dark or light
1 rounded tablespoon instant coffee
1 cup boiling water

Adjust rack to center of oven. Preheat oven to 375 degrees. Butter a 9-inch square pan. Dust it lightly with fine, dry bread crumbs.

Sift together the flour, baking soda, salt, cinnamon, ginger, cloves, mustard, and black pepper. Set aside.

In large bowl of electric mixer cream the butter. Add the sugar and beat for 1 to 2 minutes. Beat in the eggs one at a time. Use a rubber spatula all through the beating to help mix ingredients. Add molasses. Beat until smooth. Dissolve the instant coffee in the boiling water. On low speed alternately add sifted dry ingredients in three additions and coffee, which will be hot, in two additions.

Beat only until smooth. Mixture will be very thin. Pour into prepared pan. Bake 35 minutes or until the top springs back when lightly touched. Cool in pan on a rack for about 10 minutes. Cover with a rack and invert. Remove pan and cover with another rack to invert again. Serve warm or let cool.

NOTE: *May be cut into squares or thin slices. Frequently served with applesauce or vanilla ice cream.*

Java Cake

8 TO 10 PORTIONS

A plain loaf cake strongly flavored with coffee. Although I have given a recipe for Java Icing, this lovely plain cake may be served with no icing or it may be iced with Thick Chocolate Glaze, page 125. Coffee and chocolate are such a great combination of tastes.

½ cup milk
⅓ cup instant coffee
2 cups sifted all-purpose flour
2 teaspoons double-acting baking powder
¼ teaspoon salt
½ pound (1 cup) butter
1 teaspoon vanilla extract
1½ cups sugar
4 eggs

Adjust rack one-third up from bottom of oven and preheat to 375 degrees. Butter a loaf pan (see Note) measuring 14 × 4½ × 3 inches (or similar shape with 2-quart capacity) and dust it all lightly with fine, dry bread crumbs.

In a small saucepan, heat the milk and stir in the instant coffee to dissolve. Set aside to cool to room temperature.

Sift flour with baking powder and salt and set aside. In large bowl of electric mixer, cream the butter. Add the vanilla and sugar and beat for 1 to 2 minutes. Add eggs one at a time, beating well after each and scraping the bowl with a rubber spatula to keep mixture smooth. Beat at high speed for 1 to 2 minutes after adding the last egg. The mixture may look curdled—O.K.

On low speed, alternately add the dry ingredients in three additions and the cooled coffee-milk in two additions, scraping the bowl with a rubber spatula as necessary and beating only until smooth.

Turn into prepared pan and, with the rubber spatula, spread level. Then run the batter up on the sides a bit, leaving it slightly lower in the center.

Bake 55 minutes or until a cake tester comes out dry and the top springs back firmly when lightly touched. Timing will depend on shape of pan—a long, narrow loaf pan will take less time than a short, wide one.

Cool in pan for about 10 to 15 minutes. Cover with a rack, invert, and remove pan. Let cake cool and ice it upside down.

Prepare following icing:

JAVA ICING

2 tablespoons butter, at room temperature

1½ cups confectioners sugar

1 tablespoon instant coffee

1 egg yolk

1½–2 tablespoons boiling water

optional: Chocolate-candy coffee beans

Place butter, sugar, instant coffee, egg yolk, and 1½ tablespoons of boiling water in small bowl of electric mixer. Beat at high speed, scraping the bowl with a rubber spatula. Continue to beat for several minutes until the mixture forms a thick, marshmallowlike paste. If too thick, add a bit more water; if too thin, add more sugar.

As soon as mixture is smooth and thick, immediately spread it over the top of the cake. If a bit runs down the sides, just leave it—don't spread the sides.

Place optional chocolate coffee beans in a row down the center of the cake before the icing hardens.

NOTE: *This recipe may also be made in two smaller pans, each 8 × 4 × 2½ inches (1-quart capacity). The baking time will then be reduced to about 40 minutes.*

Copa
Cake

8 TO 10
PORTIONS

An exotic-looking and fancy "plain" cake.

2½ cups sifted all-purpose flour
1 teaspoon baking soda
¼ teaspoon salt
1 cup sugar
¼ pound (½ cup) butter
2 eggs
1 cup sour cream
1 teaspoon vanilla extract
Finely grated rind of 1 lemon
1 cup thick fruit preserves
    (peach, pineapple, or apricot)
3½ ounces (1 cup) walnuts,
    coarsely cut or broken
3 tablespoons powdered, unsweetened cocoa
1 teaspoon instant coffee
½ teaspoon cinnamon
¼ teaspoon baking soda
3 tablespoons boiling water

Adjust oven rack to the center of the oven. Preheat oven to 375 degrees. Butter a 13 × 9 × 2-inch pan. Coat it lightly with fine, dry bread crumbs and place it in the freezer or refrigerator.

Sift flour, 1 teaspoon baking soda, and salt into a large mixing bowl. Stir in sugar. With a pastry blender cut in the butter until mixture resembles coarse crumbs. Add unbeaten eggs, sour cream, and vanilla. Stir (or beat in the mixer at low speed, scraping bowl with a rubber spatula) until mixture is thoroughly mixed. Remove 1 cup of this batter and set aside. Stir lemon rind into remaining batter.

Remove the pan from the freezer or refrigerator and spread the batter with the lemon rind in a thin layer over the bottom of the pan. (The chilled pan will make it easier to do this.)

Stir the preserves briefly just to soften and then place them by small spoonfuls evenly over the batter. With the back of the spoon, spread preserves smooth, leaving a ½-inch border around the edges. Sprinkle the nuts evenly over all.

In a small bowl, mix the cocoa, instant coffee, cinnamon, ¼ teaspoon baking soda, and boiling water to make a smooth paste. Add the cup of reserved batter and stir until smooth. Place this chocolate batter by tea-spoonfuls all over the nuts, placing it in separate mounds so that the nuts and batter show through between the mounds. *Do not* flatten or smooth the chocolate mounds.

Bake for 35 to 40 minutes, or until the white batter has colored lightly and the top feels firm to the touch. Cool in pan on rack for 10 to 15 minutes.

To remove cake from pan: If the preserves ran out to the edge of the pan anywhere, run a knife around that part of the pan to release. Place a cookie sheet (not a rack) over the cake pan. Holding the cookie sheet firmly against the pan, invert it. Remove the cake pan. Cover with a rack or another cookie sheet. Invert again, leaving the cake right side up to finish cooling.

Transfer to a board and use a long, thin, sharp knife to cut.

Pound Cakes

TONI'S POUND CAKE

KENTUCKY POUND CAKE
  (*with bourbon*)

BLACK-AND-WHITE POUND CAKE

CHOCOLATE POUND CAKE

WALNUT OR PECAN POUND CAKE

WHOLE-WHEAT POUND CAKE

PEPPER POUND CAKE

Pound cakes should be served in thin slices, two or three slices to a portion. It is best to let pound cakes stand overnight before slicing. When completely cool, wrap in plastic wrap or aluminum foil and let stand at room temperature.

Toni's Pound Cake

This is named after my daughter because it's her favorite cake of all.

16 PORTIONS

Finely grated rind of 2 lemons
3 tablespoons lemon juice
1 pound (2 cups) butter
1 tablespoon vanilla extract
3⅓ cups sugar
½ teaspoon mace
10 eggs
4 cups sifted all-purpose flour

Adjust rack one-third up from the bottom of the oven. Preheat oven to 350 degrees. Butter a 10 × 4-inch tube pan, line the bottom with paper, butter the paper, and dust it all lightly with fine, dry bread crumbs. Or use a nonstick tube pan, in which case either line the bottom of the pan with baking pan liner paper or butter the bottom, line it with wax paper, and butter the wax paper.

Mix lemon rind with juice and set aside. In large bowl of electric mixer cream the butter. Add vanilla. Gradually add the sugar and mace. Beat at moderately high speed for 2 to 3 minutes, scraping the bowl with a rubber spatula as necessary to keep ingredients well mixed. Add eggs, two at a time, beating until thoroughly incorporated after each addition. On lowest speed gradually add the flour, scraping the bowl with the rubber spatula and beating only until smooth.

Remove from mixer. Stir in the lemon rind and juice.

Turn the batter into prepared pan. Turn pan briskly back and forth to level top. Cover the top of the pan with a piece of aluminum foil large enough to fold down loosely around the sides of the pan.

Bake for 30 minutes. Open oven door just enough to reach in and remove the aluminum foil. Continue baking for an additional 1¼ hours. (Total baking time is 1¾ hours.) Cake is done when a cake tester comes out dry.

Cool in pan on a rack for 10 to 15 minutes. Cover with a rack and invert. Remove pan, and paper, if it was used. Cover with a rack and carefully invert again to finish cooling right side up.

Kentucky Pound Cake

(*with bourbon*)

12 GENEROUS
PORTIONS

3½ cups sifted all-purpose flour
1½ teaspoons double-acting baking powder
¾ pound (1½ cups) butter
1 tablespoon vanilla extract
½ teaspoon mace
1 pound plus 1 cup light brown sugar
    (this will be 3¼ cups total), firmly packed
5 eggs
¾ cup milk
¼ cup bourbon } may be measured into 1 cup

Adjust rack one-third up from bottom of oven. Preheat oven to 350 degrees. Butter a 10 × 4-inch tube pan, line the bottom with paper, butter the paper, and dust it all lightly with fine, dry bread crumbs. Or use a non-stick 10-inch tube pan and line the bottom with baking pan liner paper, or line the bottom with wax paper and butter it.

Sift flour with baking powder and set aside. In large bowl of electric mixer cream butter with vanilla and mace. On low speed gradually add the sugar. Increase speed to moderately high and beat for a few minutes, scraping the bowl as necessary with a rubber spatula. Add eggs one at a time, beating until thoroughly incorporated after each addition.

On lowest speed, alternately add the sifted dry ingredients in three additions and the milk and bourbon mixture in two additions, scraping the bowl with the rubber spatula and beating only until smooth after each addition.

Turn the batter into the prepared pan. Rotate pan briskly several times to level batter.

Bake 1 hour and 25 minutes or until a cake tester comes out dry and top springs back firmly when lightly touched. Remove from oven. Cool in pan for 10 to 15 minutes. Cover with a rack and invert. Remove pan and paper, leaving the cake upside down. Place cake on rack over a large piece of wax paper or aluminum foil. Prepare glaze.

GLAZE

⅓ cup granulated sugar
¼ cup bourbon

In a small saucepan stir the sugar and bourbon over heat only long enough to dissolve the sugar. Brush the warm glaze all over the warm cake. Let stand for several hours or overnight.

Black-and-White Pound Cake

16 PORTIONS

1 pound (2 cups) butter
1 tablespoon vanilla extract
3⅓ cups sugar
10 eggs
4 cups sifted all-purpose flour
½ teaspoon almond extract
¼ teaspoon baking soda
2 tablespoons instant coffee
¾ cup Hershey's chocolate-flavored syrup
(See Note 1.)

Adjust rack one-third up from bottom of oven. Preheat oven to 350 degrees. Butter a 10 × 4-inch tube pan, line the bottom with paper, butter the paper, and dust it all lightly with fine, dry bread crumbs. Or use a nonstick 10-inch tube pan, in which case either line the bottom with baking pan liner paper, or butter the bottom, line with wax paper, and butter the wax paper.

In large bowl of electric mixer cream the butter. Beat in vanilla and gradually add the sugar. Beat on moderate speed for 2 to 3 minutes, scraping the bowl with a rubber spatula as necessary.

Add the eggs, two at a time, beating after each addition until thoroughly incorporated. On lowest speed very gradually add the flour, continuing to scrape the bowl with the rubber spatula and beating only until the flour is incorporated.

Remove half (or about 5 cups) of the batter and set aside. Mix the almond extract into the remainder and turn it into the prepared pan. Level the top by rotating pan briskly back and forth.

Return the other half of the batter to the mixer bowl and add the baking soda, instant coffee, and chocolate syrup. Beat on low speed, scraping the bowl with a rubber spatula and beating only until smooth.

Pour evenly over top of white batter. Level by rotating pan briskly back and forth.

Cover the top of the pan with a piece of aluminum foil large enough to turn down loosely around the sides of the pan.

Bake for 30 minutes. Open oven door just enough to reach in and remove the aluminum foil. Continue baking for an additional 1 hour and 20 minutes. (Total baking time 1 hour and 50 minutes.) Cake is done when cake tester comes out dry. Remove from oven. Cool in pan for 10 to 15 minutes.

Cover with a rack and invert. Remove pan and paper. Cover with another rack and carefully invert again to finish cooling right side up.

NOTES: 1. *Stir the syrup before using—the heavy part settles to the bottom if it has been standing for a while.*

2. *Some pound cakes form a too-heavy top crust; covering the cake with foil for the first half-hour helps prevent this.*

Chocolate Pound Cake

12 TO 16 PORTIONS

3 cups sifted all-purpose flour
1 tablespoon double-acting baking powder
¼ teaspoon salt
½ pound (1 cup) butter
1 tablespoon vanilla extract
½ teaspoon almond extract
2 tablespoons instant coffee
3 cups sugar
3 eggs
1 cup strained, powdered, unsweetened cocoa (preferably Dutch process)
1¾ cups milk

Adjust oven rack one-third up from the bottom of the oven. Preheat oven to 350 degrees.

Butter a 10 × 4-inch tube pan, line the bottom with paper, butter the paper, and coat lightly with fine, dry bread crumbs. Or use a Teflon 10-inch tube pan and line the bottom of the pan with baking pan liner paper, or butter the bottom of the pan, line it with wax paper, and butter the wax paper.

Sift together flour, baking powder, and salt. Set aside.

In large bowl of electric mixer, cream the butter. Add the vanilla and almond extracts, the instant coffee, and gradually add the sugar. Scrape sides and bottom of bowl with a rubber spatula as necessary all during mixing. Beat in the eggs one at a time, beating after each until it is incorporated. On lowest speed gradually add cocoa. Alternately add milk and sifted dry ingredients each in three additions; in this case, start with the milk since the batter is rather heavy at this stage. Beat only until smooth after each addition. Finish as usual with dry ingredients. Turn into pan. Shake pan briskly several times to level top.

Bake 1½ hours or until the top springs back when lightly touched and a cake tester comes out dry. Let the cake cool in the pan on a rack for 10 to 15 minutes. Cover with a rack and invert. Remove pan and paper. Cover with another rack and invert again to finish cooling right side up. When completely cool, prepare the following:

ICING

9 ounces sweet, semisweet,
    or bittersweet chocolate (I like to use
    Tobler or Lindt Extra-Bittersweet.)
9 tablespoons (¼ pound plus 1 tablespoon)
    butter, at room temperature

Break up the chocolate and place it in the top of a small double boiler over hot water on medium heat. When it is almost completely melted, remove the top of the double boiler and stir with a small wire whisk until smooth. Add the butter, about 1 to 2 tablespoons at a time, stirring with the whisk until smooth after each addition. The icing will thicken with the first few additions of butter, but then it will thin out as the remainder is added.

When all the butter has been added and the mixture is smooth, place the top of the double boiler into ice-cold water. Stir very briefly with a rubber spatula until the icing thickens only slightly. Or let it stand at room temperature, stirring frequently for about 20 to 30 minutes. Do not allow the icing to thicken too much; it should be semifluid. (If it should harden, it may be softened by stirring over hot water.)

Place four strips of wax paper around the outer edges of a cake plate. Place the cake on it, upside down.

Pour the icing over the top, letting some run down on the sides. With a long, narrow metal spatula, quickly spread over the sides first, and then the top.

Remove wax paper strips by pulling each one out by a narrow end. (See page 18.)

Walnut or Pecan Pound Cake

1 pound (2 cups) butter
2 teaspoons vanilla extract
½ teaspoon almond extract
3⅓ cups sugar
10 eggs
4 cups sifted all-purpose flour
1 pound (4½ cups) walnuts or pecans, chopped medium fine

16 PORTIONS

Using above ingredients, follow directions for Toni's Pound Cake (see page 137) through the addition of the eggs.

In a very large bowl stir the flour and nuts to mix thoroughly. Add the batter and, with a large wooden spatula, fold and stir only until the flour is all moistened.

Turn into pan and follow remaining directions for Toni's Pound Cake.

Whole-Wheat Pound Cake

10 TO 12
PORTIONS

½ pound (1 cup) butter
1 teaspoon powdered ginger
1½ tablespoons instant coffee
¼ teaspoon salt
1 teaspoon vanilla extract
2 cups dark brown sugar, firmly packed
6 eggs
2 cups strained, all-purpose whole-wheat flour
    (See Note.)
¼ cup milk

Adjust rack one-third up from bottom of oven. Preheat oven to 350 degrees. Butter a 9 × 3½-inch tube pan. Line the bottom with paper. Butter the paper and dust all over, including the center tube, with fine, dry bread crumbs.

In large bowl of electric mixer cream the butter. Add the ginger, instant coffee, salt, vanilla, and brown sugar. Beat for 2 to 3 minutes. Add the eggs, one at a time, beating well after each. Mixture will look curdled—O.K.

On low speed, while scraping the bowl with a rubber spatula, mix in about half of the flour, then all the milk, and finally the remaining flour, beating only until smooth after each addition. It might *still* look curdled. Don't worry.

Turn the batter into the prepared pan. Rotate pan briskly to level batter. Bake 1 hour and 10 minutes or until a cake tester comes out dry and top springs back when lightly touched.

Cool in pan for 10 to 15 minutes. Cover with a rack and invert. Remove pan and paper. Cover with another rack and invert again to cool right side up.

NOTE: *Flour packs down when it is left standing. It should be aerated in order to measure correctly. Most all-purpose whole-wheat flour is too coarse to go through a sifter; it is generally easier to strain it. Any coarse parts that don't go through the strainer may then be turned back into the strained flour and stirred in just a bit to mix.*

Pepper Pound Cake

12 TO 16
PORTIONS

A fine-grained Jamaican pound cake made with cream cheese and butter.

3 ounces cream cheese
½ pound (1 cup) butter
¼ teaspoon salt
½ teaspoon allspice
¾ teaspoon black pepper, finely ground (freshly ground is best)
1 tablespoon vanilla extract
1 cup dark brown sugar, firmly packed
1 cup granulated white sugar
7 eggs
3 cups sifted cake flour

Adjust rack one-third up from bottom of oven. Preheat oven to 350 degrees. Butter a 9 × 3½-inch tube pan. Line the bottom with paper. Butter the paper and dust it all lightly with fine, dry bread crumbs.

In large bowl of electric mixer cream the cream cheese and butter with the salt, allspice, pepper, and vanilla. Add both sugars and beat for 2 to 3 minutes, scraping the bowl occasionally with a rubber spatula.

Increase speed to high and add the eggs one at a time, scraping the bowl with the spatula and beating until each is thoroughly incorporated. The mixture will look curdled. Reduce the speed to low and gradually add the flour, continuing to scrape the bowl with the spatula and beating only until smooth.

Turn batter into the prepared pan. Level batter by briskly rotating pan in opposite directions. Let stand for 10 minutes before baking.

Bake for 1 hour and 20 to 25 minutes or until a cake tester comes out dry. (The top of this cake frequently cracks deeply. It is to be expected and doesn't matter.) Remove from oven and let stand on a rack for 10 to 15 minutes. Cover with a rack or a cookie sheet. Invert. Remove pan and paper, cover with a rack, and invert again to cool right side up. Let stand 8 to 10 hours or overnight before serving.

Cookie-Jar Cookies

ASPEN ROCKS

OATMEAL COOKIES

NEW ORLEANS OATMEAL COOKIES

HEALTH-FOOD COOKIES

TEA CAKES

HUNGARIAN BUTTER BISCUITS
  (*Vajas Pogácsa*)

CURRANT COOKIES

BLACK PEPPER COOKIES

SESAME PENNIES

CARAWAY COOKIES (*English*)

CARAWAY SEED WAFERS (*Irish*)

ITALIAN PINE-NUT MACAROONS

OLD-FASHIONED PEANUT BUTTER
  COOKIES

CRATERS

MULATTOES

FRENCH CHOCOLATE WAFERS

CHOCOLATE CRACKS

The rule is TLC—tender loving care. Try to make cookies all the same size. Practice. If they are not even, redo them. Use a ruler for icebox cookies and cookies cut into bars. Do not just put cookies in the oven, set the timer, and walk away until the bell rings. You must watch them . . . and baby them. If they are not browning evenly, reverse the pan front to back. If the bottoms are burning (check one to see), be prepared to slide an extra cookie sheet underneath. If the tops are burning, check the oven temperature—it might be too hot. Or lower the rack a bit. If you bake more than one cookie sheet at a time (I seldom, if ever, do), rotate position of cookie sheets so that each one spends some time in each position.

When baking cookies on baking pan liner paper or aluminum foil, you may shape the whole batch on pieces of paper or foil. They may then be baked, one sheet at a time, by just sliding the cookie sheet under the paper. When recipes call for lining the cookie sheets with foil, it is necessary to do so in order to keep the cookies from sticking.

Be sure to have plenty of racks handy for cooling the cookies, or the bottoms will get soggy and the cookies will be limp instead of crisp.

If cookies are large and thick (such as Aspen Rocks, New Orleans Oatmeal Cookies, Health-Food Cookies, etc.), it is advisable to raise the rack to make more room for air to circulate underneath. Just place the rack on a cake pan or any right-side up bowl or baking dish. Otherwise the heat of the cookies causes steam to form on the counter or table top, and as the steam rises it makes the bottoms of the cookies moist. Incidentally, this holds true even if the rack has feet. They just don't leave enough room for large cookies.

Cookies must be completely cool before you store them—airtight. If you do not have enough airtight containers, use freezer bags, but wrap and handle gently in order not to crack the cookies. Or pack them in boxes and wrap the boxes in freezer paper or aluminum foil. Of course cookies freeze beautifully. Thaw before unwrapping.

Aspen Rocks

40 LARGE COOKIES

These are large, old-fashioned drop cookies.

2¾ cups sifted all-purpose flour

1 teaspoon baking soda

½ teaspoon salt

½ pound (1 cup) butter

1 teaspoon each: cinnamon, mace, allspice,
dry mustard

1 teaspoon vanilla extract

1 tablespoon instant coffee dissolved in
2 tablespoons boiling water

1¾ cups dark brown sugar,
firmly packed

3 eggs

5 ounces (1 cup) raisins (See page 12.)

8 ounces (1 generous cup) dates,
coarsely cut in quarters
(See page 12.)

8 ounces (2 generous cups) walnuts,
coarsely broken

Adjust racks high in the oven. Preheat oven to 375 degrees. Cut aluminum foil to fit cookie sheets.

Sift together flour, baking soda, and salt. Set aside. In large bowl of electric mixer cream the butter. Beat in the cinnamon, mace, allspice, dry mustard, vanilla, and coffee. Gradually add the sugar and beat well. Beat in the eggs one at a time, beating until smooth after each addition. Scrape the bowl frequently with a rubber spatula to keep mixture smooth. On lowest speed gradually add the sifted flour mixture, scraping the bowl with the rubber spatula and beating only until blended. Remove from mixer. Stir in raisins, dates, and nuts.

Drop by rounded tablespoonfuls (make these large) 2 to 3 inches apart onto the aluminum foil. Slide a cookie sheet under the foil. Bake 15 minutes or until cookies are well-browned and tops feel firm and spring back when lightly touched. Reverse position of pan during baking to insure even browning.

While the first sheet of cookies is baking, prepare the following glaze:

GLAZE

1½ cups confectioners sugar
2 tablespoons soft butter
2 tablespoons plus 2 teaspoons light cream
1 teaspoon vanilla extract
Pinch of salt

In a small bowl mix above ingredients until smooth. If necessary add a few more drops of cream—mixture should be the consistency of mayonnaise. Cover it when not in use.

Slide the foil off the cookie sheet. Immediately, with a pastry brush, brush a thin coating of the glaze on the hot cookies. The heat of the cookies will melt it to a shiny, creamy coating which will be dry to the touch in just a few minutes. With a wide metal spatula transfer cookies to racks to cool.

NOTE: *Do not put more than one sheet of cookies in the oven at one time. When they are about half baked, a second sheet may go in. In this way you will be able to glaze all the cookies while they are still hot.*

Oatmeal Cookies

Semi-soft cookies, best baked on double cookie sheets to protect the bottoms from burning.

54 COOKIES

7½ ounces (1½ cups) raisins
1 cup water
2 cups sifted all-purpose flour
¾ teaspoon baking soda
1 teaspoon salt
1½ teaspoons cinnamon
½ pound (1 cup) butter
1 teaspoon vanilla extract
1 cup dark brown sugar, firmly packed
2 eggs

1½ cups old-fashioned or quick-cooking
(not instant) oatmeal
8 ounces (2¼ cups) walnuts,
coarsely broken
6 ounces (1 cup) semisweet
chocolate morsels

Adjust rack about one-third down from top of oven. Preheat oven to 375 degrees.

In small, heavy saucepan over high heat, boil the raisins and water. Stir occasionally for about 5 minutes, until there is ¼ cup plus 1 tablespoon of water remaining. Drain the raisins in a strainer, reserving the water. If there is not enough water left, add water or coffee to make the required ¼ cup plus 1 tablespoon. Set aside.

Sift together the flour, baking soda, salt, and cinnamon. Set aside.

In large bowl of electric mixer, cream the butter. Add the vanilla and sugar and beat for a few minutes until light in color. Add eggs and, scraping the bowl with a rubber spatula, beat until smooth. Beat in raisin liquid. On low speed gradually add sifted dry ingredients, continuing to scrape the bowl with a rubber spatula. Then mix in oatmeal, raisins, and nuts. Mix in chocolate morsels.

Drop by heaping teaspoonfuls on unbuttered cookie sheet, forming rather large cookies and placing them about 2 inches apart.

Place filled cookie sheet on a second cookie sheet and bake 15 minutes or until well-browned. If necessary, reverse position of cookie sheet during baking to insure even browning.

With a wide metal spatula, remove cookies to a rack to cool. (See page 146.)

New Orleans Oatmeal Cookies

36 VERY LARGE
COOKIES

2¼ cups sifted all-purpose flour
1 teaspoon baking soda
1 teaspoon double-acting baking powder
1 teaspoon salt
1 tablespoon cinnamon
½ teaspoon nutmeg
½ teaspoon allspice
½ teaspoon powdered cloves
6 ounces (¾ cup) butter
½ cup apricot preserves
2 teaspoons instant coffee
1½ cups dark brown sugar, firmly packed
2 eggs
¾ cup milk
2¼ cups old-fashioned or quick-cooking
  (not instant) oatmeal
8 ounces (1½ generous cups) raisins
8 ounces (2 cups) whole salted peanuts
  (preferably the dry-roasted type)

Adjust rack to top position in oven. Preheat oven to 375 degrees. Cut aluminum foil to fit cookie sheets.

Sift flour with baking soda, baking powder, salt, cinnamon, nutmeg, allspice, and cloves. Set aside. In large bowl of electric mixer, cream the butter and apricot preserves. Add the instant coffee and sugar and beat until well-mixed. Beat in the eggs one at a time, scraping the bowl with a rubber spatula as necessary to keep the mixture smooth. On lowest speed, alternately add the sifted dry ingredients in three additions and the milk in two additions. Beat only until smooth after each addition. Beat in the oatmeal. Remove from mixer. Stir in the raisins and peanuts.

Using a heaping tablespoonful of batter for each cookie. Drop 2 inches apart on the aluminum foil. Slide a cookie sheet under the foil and bake 20 minutes or until lightly browned and semi-firm to the touch. Reverse sheet during baking to insure even browning.

With a wide metal spatula remove cookies to a rack to cool. (See page 146.)

NOTE: *These have a tendency to burn on the bottoms; if you bake more than one sheet at a time be sure to use double cookie sheets under the lower ones.*

Health-Food Cookies

36 COOKIES,
4 INCHES
IN DIAMETER

I created this recipe for a health-food store in Miami Beach, and then baked for them until the demand became more than I could handle.

1 cup unsifted all-purpose whole-wheat flour
1 teaspoon double-acting baking powder
¾ teaspoon salt
1 tablespoon cinnamon
¼ teaspoon powdered ginger
7½ ounces (1½ cups) currants or raisins
  (See page 12.)
4 ounces (1 generous cup) walnuts,
  coarsely broken or cut
4 ounces (1 generous cup) pecans,
  coarsely broken or cut
3 ounces (½ generous cup) pignolias
  (pine nuts)
4 ounces (1 cup) peanuts, may be salted or not
2½ ounces (½ cup) sunflower seeds
2½ ounces (½ cup) sesame seeds
½ cup wheat germ
1 cup rolled oats or quick-cooking
  (not instant) oatmeal
½ pound (1 cup) butter
½ cup peanut butter (See Note 1.)
1¼ cups dark brown sugar, firmly packed
2 eggs
¼ cup milk

Adjust rack to top position in the oven. Preheat oven to 350 degrees. Cut aluminum foil to fit cookie sheets.

Whole-wheat flour is too coarse for sifting. Use a strainer and strain the flour, baking powder, salt, cinnamon, and ginger into a very large bowl. Add the currants or raisins and, with your fingers, toss until they are separated and coated with the dry ingredients. Add the walnuts, pecans, pignolias, peanuts, sunflower seeds, sesame seeds, wheat germ, and rolled oats or oatmeal. Mix together and set aside.

Cream together the butter and peanut butter. Add the sugar and beat well. Beat in the eggs and then the milk, scraping the bowl with a rubber spatula as necessary.

Pour over the flour-nut mixture. Stir with a heavy wooden spoon or spatula, or mix with your bare hand, until the dry ingredients are completely absorbed.

Make these large. Place by heaping tablespoonfuls 2½ to 3 inches apart on the aluminum foil. With the back of a spoon flatten the cookies to about ¾-inch thickness. Slide a cookie sheet under the foil.

Bake 18 minutes or until cookies are lightly browned and semi-firm to the touch. If necessary, reverse position of cookie sheet during baking to insure even browning.

Use a wide metal spatula to transfer cookies to racks to cool.

NOTES: 1. *Any other nut butter—cashew, almond, etc.—may be substituted for peanut butter.*

2. *It is best to bake these one sheet at a time. If you bake more than one at a time, use double cookie sheets under the lower ones to keep the bottoms from burning.*

Tea Cakes

36 VERY
LARGE
COOKIES

The absence of salt and flavoring is typical of early American cookies, often called tea cakes.

½ teaspoon baking soda
5¼ cups sifted all-purpose flour
½ pound (1 cup) butter
3 cups sugar
3 eggs
1 cup heavy cream

Sift the baking soda with 1 cup of the flour (reserve remaining 4¼ cups) and set aside.

In the large bowl of an electric mixer, cream the butter until soft. On low speed, gradually add the sugar and beat for 1 to 2 minutes. Scrape the bowl with a rubber spatula as necessary all during the mixing. Add the eggs one at a time, beating after each until it is thoroughly incorporated.

On lowest speed beat in 1 cup flour sifted with the baking soda. Then add the reserved flour in five additions, alternating with the cream in four additions. Beat only until smooth after each addition.

Divide the dough roughly in quarters. Wrap each airtight and refrigerate overnight.

Adjust rack to the top position in the oven and preheat oven to 400 degrees. Cut aluminum foil to fit cookie sheets.

Work with one-quarter of the dough at a time, keeping the rest refrigerated. On a floured pastry cloth with a floured rolling pin, roll the dough ¼–⅓ inch thick. Work quickly before the dough softens.

Cut out the cookies with a 3½-inch round cookie cutter, dipping the cutter in flour as needed. Transfer the cookies onto the aluminum foil with a metal spatula, placing them 2 inches apart. Slide a cookie sheet under the foil.

Bake 13 to 15 minutes until cookies are very lightly colored. Reverse position of cookie sheet during baking to insure even browning. Slide the foil off the cookie sheet and, with a wide metal spatula, transfer cookies to racks to cool.

Repeat rolling, cutting, baking with remaining dough. Leftover pieces should be pressed together and rechilled before rolling.

NOTE: *Unrolled dough may be kept in the refrigerator for several days or it may be frozen. If it is frozen, it should be refrigerated for several hours or overnight before rolling.*

Hungarian Butter Biscuits

(Vajas Pogácsa)

18 COOKIES

A rich butter cookie, somewhat like shortbread. This recipe is from Paprikas Weiss, the Hungarian food shop in New York City, where Mrs. Renée Weiss, the mother of the proprietor, prepares them. Mr. Weiss says, "This biscuit is direct from the folk culture of Hungary. So much so that my pastry chef friends tell me it is not taught in the culinary schools of Hungary. You can sense some social class distinctions in this food—remember Hungary was a feudal society until the end of World War II—but everyone in Hungary eats Pogácsa in its several variations."

3 cups sifted all-purpose flour
½ pound (1 cup) butter
4 egg yolks
1 cup confectioners sugar
¼ teaspoon salt
1 egg (for egg glaze)

Place flour in a large bowl. With a pastry blender cut in the butter until the particles are the size of peas. Add the egg yolks, sugar, and salt. Stir briefly. Turn out onto a board or smooth surface and work the dough with your hands, squeezing it through your fingers and kneading it slightly only until the dough holds together and is smooth. Work quickly and do not handle any more than necessary. Form into a ball, flatten slightly. Wrap airtight and refrigerate for an hour or so until firm enough to be rolled.

Adjust rack to the top position in the oven. Preheat oven to 350 degrees.

Roll the dough between two pieces of wax paper until it is ½ inch thick (*no thinner!*). Remove top sheet of paper.

Score the top of the dough with a long, sharp knife, making shallow lines about ¼ to ½ inch apart first in one direction and then in the opposite direction (use the full length of the blade, not just the tip). Cut the scored dough with a round 2¼- to 2½-inch cutter. With a metal spatula transfer the cookies to an unbuttered cookie sheet, placing them about 1 inch apart. If the cookies are too sticky to be transferred, slide a cookie sheet under the wax paper and transfer to the freezer or refrigerator until firm. (Rechilled cookies may have to be cut again with the cookie cutter.)

Stir the egg lightly with a fork just to mix and, with a soft brush,

brush it carefully over the top of each cookie. Bake about 30 minutes, reversing position of cookie sheet if necessary during baking to insure even browning.

Bake until cookies are a rich golden brown all over. Transfer with a metal spatula to cool on a rack.

NOTE: *Mrs. Weiss rolls the dough 1 inch thick. I prefer ½ inch. In any event, cookies must be baked until dry and crisp all the way through. Do not underbake.*

Currant Cookies

42 COOKIES

3½ ounces (¾ cup) currants
½ pound (1 cup) butter
½ teaspoon mace
1 teaspoon vanilla extract
1 cup sugar
1 egg
2⅓ cups sifted all-purpose flour
Finely grated rind of 1 large lemon
   (or 2 small)

See directions for preparing currants (page 12).

In small bowl of electric mixer cream the butter. Add mace, vanilla, and sugar, and beat for a minute or two. Beat in the egg. On lowest speed gradually add the flour, scraping the bowl with a rubber spatula and beating only until smooth. Remove from mixer, stir in currants and lemon rind.

Wrap airtight and refrigerate for about 1 hour. Or place in freezer until firm enough to handle.

Adjust rack to top position in the oven. Preheat oven to 375 degrees. Line cookie sheets with aluminum foil.

Using 1 rounded teaspoonful of dough for each cookie, roll between your hands into 1-inch balls. Place 2 inches apart on lined cookie sheets.

Flatten tops with the back of a fork continually dipped in sugar. It is most efficient to press all the cookies first in one direction, and then crosshatch them in the opposite direction, flattening the cookies to ⅓- to ½-inch thickness.

Bake one sheet at a time about 15 minutes until lightly-colored, reversing position of cookie sheet if necessary during baking to insure even browning. Remove with a wide metal spatula to cool on a rack.

Black Pepper Cookies

50 TO 60
COOKIES

3 cups sifted all-purpose flour
2 teaspoons double-acting baking powder
½ pound (1 cup) butter
¾ teaspoon black pepper, finely ground
   (preferably freshly ground)
Generous pinch of cayenne pepper
½ teaspoon powdered cloves
2 teaspoons cinnamon
1 tablespoon powdered ginger
1½ cups sugar
1 egg

Adjust rack high in the oven. Preheat oven to 400 degrees.

Sift together flour and baking powder. Set aside. In large bowl of electric mixer cream the butter. Beat in the black pepper, cayenne pepper, cloves, cinnamon, and ginger. Scrape the bowl with a rubber spatula as necessary to keep mixture smooth while beating in the sugar, the egg, and, on lowest speed, the sifted dry ingredients. When completely blended, remove from mixer to a board or smooth surface. Knead lightly. Divide the dough into three pieces. Work with one piece at a time. Do not chill the dough before rolling.

On a lightly floured pastry cloth, with a lightly floured rolling pin, roll to ⅛- to ¼-inch thickness. Cut with a 2¾-inch round cutter. Scraps may be rerolled and cut. Transfer cookies with a metal spatula to an unbuttered cookie sheet, placing them about ¾ inch apart.

Reverse the position of the sheet during baking to insure even browning and bake 12 minutes or until cookies are lightly browned.

If you bake more than one sheet at a time, change positions of sheets during baking. With more than one cookie sheet in the oven at a time, they will take longer to bake.

As cookies are done, transfer them with a wide metal spatula to cool on racks.

Sesame Pennies

36 COOKIES,
2½ INCHES IN
DIAMETER

2½ ounces (½ cup) benne (sesame) seeds
2 tablespoons butter
1 cup light brown sugar, firmly packed
2 egg yolks
2 teaspoons vanilla extract
½ teaspoon salt
¼ cup plus 2 tablespoons
    sifted all-purpose flour

Adjust rack to top position in oven. Preheat oven to 350 degrees. Cut aluminum foil to fit two or more large cookie sheets. (These will not be baked at the same time. If you only have one large cookie sheet, that's O.K., but prepare two or more pieces of foil.)

In a heavy 8- to 10-inch frying pan, stir the seeds over moderate heat with a wooden spatula to toast to a golden brown. Remove from heat and set aside.

In a medium-size saucepan over low heat, melt the butter. Remove from heat and, with a wooden spatula, stir in the brown sugar, then the yolks, vanilla, and salt. Stir in the toasted seeds and then the flour.

Spread out a large piece of foil or wax paper. Divide dough into 36 mounds, using 1 teaspoonful of dough for each and placing them on the foil or wax paper.

Release the mounds with a spatula. With wet hands (keep your hands very wet), roll each piece into a ball and place them at least 2 inches apart on the aluminum foil. Slide a cookie sheet under the foil and place in oven to bake 12 minutes or until well-browned (including the centers of the cookies). While baking these will flatten by themselves into thin, even rounds. Slide foil off cookie sheet and repeat baking process, baking only one sheet at a time.

Let cool completely and then peel foil away from cookies. Store airtight. Serve bottom, or shiny side, up.

Caraway Cookies

(*English*)

36 TO 42 COOKIES

¼ pound (½ cup) butter
½ cup sugar
2 egg yolks
2 cups sifted all-purpose flour
½ teaspoon baking soda
⅓ cup sour cream
Caraway seeds

Adjust rack high in the oven. Preheat oven to 375 degrees.

In small bowl of electric mixer cream the butter. Add sugar and beat for a minute or two. Beat in the egg yolks. On lowest speed, add half of the flour. Stir baking soda into sour cream and add that to the dough. Add remaining flour. Scrape the bowl with a rubber spatula as necessary to keep ingredients blended and beat only until smooth.

Roll the dough between two sheets of wax paper until it is about ¼ inch thick. Place it, still between the sheets of wax paper, on a cookie sheet in the freezer for about 15 to 20 minutes, or longer in the refrigerator, until the wax paper can be pulled off neatly without pulling away any of the dough.

Remove top sheet of wax paper, just to release it, and then replace it. Invert dough and remove other sheet of wax paper. Do not replace it.

Cut cookies with a floured, 2-inch round cutter. If at any time dough sticks to bottom wax paper, simply invert it onto another piece of paper. If dough softens, rechill it.

Place cookies 1 inch apart (these spread only very slightly) on unbuttered cookie sheet. Sprinkle a pinch of caraway seeds over each cookie. With your fingertips, gently press the seeds lightly into the dough.

Bake 15 minutes or until light golden brown. With metal spatula transfer to a rack to cool.

Caraway Seed Wafers

(Irish)

30 TO 36 COOKIES

2 cups sifted all-purpose flour
1 teaspoon double-acting baking powder
¼ teaspoon baking soda
¼ teaspoon salt
¼ pound (½ cup) butter
1 cup sugar
1 egg
1 tablespoon caraway seeds

Sift together flour, baking powder, baking soda, and salt. Set aside. In small bowl of electric mixer, cream the butter. Add the sugar and beat well. Beat in the egg. On lowest speed gradually add the sifted dry ingredients. Turn out onto a board or smooth surface. Add the caraway seeds and knead lightly only until seeds are evenly distributed.

Wrap airtight. Freeze for about 15 minutes and then refrigerate for 1 hour or until the dough is firm enough to roll.

Adjust rack to center of oven. Preheat oven to 375 degrees.

Work with about one-third of the dough at a time. On a lightly floured pastry cloth with a lightly floured rolling pin, roll to $\frac{1}{16}$ to $\frac{1}{8}$ inch thickness. Cut with a round cookie cutter about 3¼ inches in diameter. (Scraps may be rerolled and cut.) With a metal spatula transfer to unbuttered cookie sheets, placing cookies about ½ inch apart.

Bake 13 to 15 minutes or until lightly browned all over, reversing position of cookie sheet during baking. With a wide metal spatula, transfer individually as they brown to a rack to cool. Store airtight.

Italian Pine-Nut Maca-roons

46 COOKIES

2 cups sugar
10 ounces (2 cups) blanched almonds,
    finely ground (See pages 10–12.)
Pinch of salt
4 egg whites
½ teaspoon vanilla extract
¼ teaspoon almond extract
1½ pounds (4–5 cups) pignolias (pine nuts)

Adjust rack one-third from top of oven. Preheat oven to 400 degrees. Cut aluminum foil to fit cookie sheets.

Add 1 cup of the sugar (reserve remaining cup) to the almonds and stir to mix thoroughly. Set aside.

In small bowl of electric mixer, add the salt to the egg whites and beat until whites increase in volume and hold a soft shape. While still beating, gradually add the reserved cup of sugar. Continue to beat at high speed until meringue holds a firm shape and is very stiff but not dry.

Remove from mixer. Fold in vanilla and almond extracts and then fold meringue into almonds.

Spread out the pignolias in a shallow tray or baking pan. Use two teaspoons to form the cookies, one to pick up the dough and one to push it off, using 1 heaping teaspoonful of dough for each cookie. Drop cookies, a few at a time, into the nuts. Using the fingers of both hands, gently turn and toss the cookies to coat them thoroughly with the nuts, pressing gently so that nuts are well imbedded in the dough.

Place them 2 inches apart on the aluminum foil. Slide a cookie sheet under the foil.

Bake about 15 minutes, reversing position of pan during baking to insure even browning, until nuts are toasted golden brown and cookies are lightly colored. With a metal spatula, remove cookies to racks to cool.

One sheet at a time, bake remaining cookies.

Old-Fashioned Peanut Butter Cookies

48 COOKIES

1½ cups sifted all-purpose flour
¾ teaspoon baking soda
¼ pound (½ cup) butter
½ teaspoon vanilla extract
½ cup granulated sugar
½ cup light brown sugar, firmly packed
1 egg
½ cup smooth peanut butter
3 ounces (¾ cup) salted peanuts,
    finely chopped, not ground
    (must be very fine)

Adjust rack to top position in oven. Preheat oven to 375 degrees.

Sift together flour and baking soda. Set aside. In small bowl of electric mixer cream the butter. Add vanilla and both sugars and beat for about 1 or 2 minutes. Beat in the egg. On lowest speed add about half of the sifted flour mixture, scraping bowl as necessary with a rubber spatula. Add peanut butter and beat until smooth. Beat in remaining flour mixture and then the peanuts.

The mixture will be very stiff. Remove it from the mixer. Turn it out onto a board and knead it slightly only until everything is blended.

On a large piece of wax paper divide the dough into 48 mounds, using a rounded teaspoonful for each. Roll them into balls about 1 inch in diameter. Place 2 inches apart on unbuttered cookie sheets. Press the tops with the back of a fork. It is most efficient to press the cookies first all in one direction and then crosshatch them in the opposite direction, flattening the cookies to about ½-inch thickness. It is best to bake only one sheet at a time.

Bake about 12 minutes or until cookies are lightly browned, reversing position of cookie sheet as necessary to insure even browning. Watch carefully—they burn easily. These will harden and crisp as they cool. Cool on racks.

Craters

The combination of chocolate, cloves, and cinnamon makes an unusual and delightful flavor.

36 COOKIES

8 ounces (2 generous cups) walnuts, ground
(See page 11. For this recipe they do not
have to be strained.)
3 ounces (3 squares) unsweetened chocolate
¼ cup fine, dry bread crumbs
2 tablespoons sifted all-purpose flour
2 eggs
½ teaspoon powdered cloves
½ teaspoon cinnamon
1 cup granulated sugar
1 cup (about) strained confectioners sugar

The nuts may be ground in a blender, about one-third at a time. If there are a few uneven pieces it is all right. Transfer them to a medium-size mixing bowl.

Chop the chocolate coarsely and grind it in the blender. Add it to the ground nuts. With a rubber spatula stir chocolate and nuts to mix, pressing against the sides of the bowl to break up any lumps. Stir in the bread crumbs and the flour until well mixed.

In the small bowl of an electric mixer beat the eggs with the cloves and cinnamon. Add the granulated sugar and beat on high speed for 2 to 3 minutes. On lowest speed, gradually beat in the walnut-chocolate mixture. Remove from mixer.

On a long piece of wax paper, drop the dough by rounded teaspoonfuls into about 36 mounds. Let them stand for an hour or so, turning them occasionally with two metal spatulas until they are dry enough to be handled.

Adjust rack one-third of the way down from the top of the oven. Preheat oven to 350 degrees. Cut aluminum foil to fit cookie sheets. Strain confectioners sugar onto another long piece of wax paper. Drop the mounds of dough, a few at a time, into the confectioners sugar. Turn them around to coat with sugar and then roll between your palms into balls. Place the cookies 1½ to 2 inches apart on the aluminum foil. Slide a cookie sheet under the foil.

Bake for 15 minutes, one sheet at a time, until tops feel semi-firm to the touch. The centers should still be soft. Do not overbake. With a metal spatula remove to a rack to cool.

Mulattoes

This calls for three kinds of chocolate. The cookies are mocha, bittersweet, chewy, and candylike.

36 COOKIES

2 ounces (2 squares) unsweetened chocolate
6 ounces (6 squares) semisweet chocolate
2 tablespoons butter
¼ cup sifted all-purpose flour
¼ teaspoon double-acting baking powder
⅛ teaspoon salt
2 eggs
¾ cup sugar
2 teaspoons instant coffee
½ teaspoon vanilla extract
6 ounces (1 cup) semisweet chocolate morsels
8 ounces (2¼ cups) walnuts or pecans,
broken into medium pieces

Adjust rack one-third down from top of oven. Preheat oven to 350 degrees. Cut aluminum foil to fit cookie sheets.

In the top of a small double boiler over hot water on moderate heat, melt the unsweetened and semisweet chocolates and the butter. Stir until smooth. Remove top of double boiler and set aside to cool completely.

Sift together the flour, baking powder, and salt. Set aside. In small bowl of electric mixer beat the eggs, sugar, coffee, and vanilla at high speed for a minute or two. On low speed add the cooled chocolate, and finally the sifted dry ingredients, scraping bowl with a rubber spatula as necessary to keep mixture smooth and beating only until blended.

Stir in the chocolate morsels and nuts.

Drop by heaping teaspoonfuls 1 inch apart (these barely spread at all) on the aluminum foil. Slide a cookie sheet under the foil.

Bake 10 to 12 minutes, reversing position of cookie sheet if necessary during baking to insure even browning. Tops will be dry and crisp. Centers should remain soft and chewy. Do not overbake. With a wide metal spatula remove cookies to cool on a rack.

It is best to let these stand, or chill them a bit, until the chocolate morsels reharden before serving.

French Chocolate Wafers

Thin and crisp.

36 COOKIES

1½ cups sifted all-purpose flour
1¼ teaspoons double-acting baking powder
⅛ teaspoon salt
6 ounces (¾ cup) butter
1¼ cups sugar
1 egg
1 tablespoon dark rum or ½ teaspoon
    vanilla extract
¾ cup strained, powdered, unsweetened cocoa
    (preferably Dutch process)
Milk

Sift together flour, baking powder, and salt. Set aside. In large bowl of electric mixer cream the butter. Gradually add the sugar and beat for 1 to 2 minutes. Beat in the egg and rum or vanilla. On lowest speed gradually add the cocoa, scraping bowl with a rubber spatula. Beat in the sifted flour mixture, continuing to scrape bowl with spatula and beating only until smooth.

Remove from mixer and wrap airtight. Flatten lightly. Refrigerate for at least 1 hour or until firm enough to roll.

Adjust rack to the top position in the oven. Preheat oven to 400 degrees. Cut aluminum foil to fit cookie sheets.

Work with about one-third of the dough at a time. Keep the rest refrigerated. Work quickly before the dough softens. Lightly flour a pastry cloth and rolling pin. Roll the dough to a scant ⅛-inch thickness, turning it a few times to keep it from sticking, but don't use any more flour than necessary. Cut with a round 3¼-inch cookie cutter. Place ½ inch apart on the aluminum foil. With a soft brush, brush the tops lightly with milk.

Slide a cookie sheet under the foil. Bake 8 to 10 minutes, reversing position of cookie sheets during baking to insure even baking. Watch carefully. Do not let the edges burn. With a wide metal spatula transfer cookies to a rack to cool. They will crisp as they cool.

Save all the scraps. Rechill, roll, and cut them all at once in order not to incorporate any more flour than necessary.

Chocolate Cracks

48 COOKIES

3 cups sifted all-purpose flour
1¼ teaspoons baking soda
½ teaspoon salt
1½ cups dark brown sugar, firmly packed
6 ounces (¾ cup) butter
2 tablespoons water
12 ounces (2 cups) semisweet
    chocolate morsels or 12 ounces (squares)
    semisweet chocolate, coarsely chopped
2 eggs

Sift together flour, baking soda, and salt. Set aside. In a large, heavy saucepan over moderate heat, cook the sugar, butter, and water, stirring until the butter is melted. Add the chocolate morsels and continue to stir over heat until they are partially melted. Remove from heat and stir until chocolate is completely melted. Transfer to large bowl of electric mixer and let stand for about 5 minutes to cool slightly.

On high speed, beat in the eggs one at a time. Reduce speed to low and gradually add the sifted dry ingredients, scraping bowl with a rubber spatula and beating only until dry ingredients are absorbed. Let dough stand for about 10 minutes or longer until it can be handled easily.

Adjust rack high in the oven. Preheat oven to 350 degrees. Cut aluminum foil to fit cookie sheets.

Using a heaping teaspoonful of dough for each cookie, roll between your hands into shiny and moist-looking balls. Place 2 inches apart on the aluminum foil. Slide a cookie sheet under the foil.

Bake 12 to 13 minutes, reversing position of pan during baking if necessary to insure even baking. Tops will feel dry but not firm. Do not overbake. Cookies will crisp as they cool. With a wide metal spatula transfer to racks to cool.

Bar Cookies and Rusks

BROWNIES

BROWNIE CRISPS

PECAN SQUARES AMERICANA

PECAN-COCONUT BARS

DATE-NUT BARS

SOYA DATE BARS

AFRICAN DATE BARS

PEANUT BARS

PECAN BUTTERCRUNCH

RUSKS, ITALIAN STYLE
  (*Biscotti all'anice*)

ALMOND OR HAZELNUT RUSKS

Brownies

24 OR 32 BROWNIES

These are the Brownies with which I started my reputation as a pastry chef when I was about ten years old. The recipe has been changed and revised continuously over the years. I will probably continue to change it. This is the cookie recipe I have been asked for most often.

5 ounces (5 squares) unsweetened chocolate
5⅓ ounces (⅔ cup) butter
1 tablespoon instant coffee
4 eggs
½ teaspoon salt
2 cups sugar
1 teaspoon vanilla extract
¼ teaspoon almond extract
1 cup sifted all-purpose flour
10 ounces (2½ generous cups) *walnut halves*

Adjust oven rack one-third of the way up from the bottom of the oven. Preheat oven to 450 degrees. Butter a 10½ × 15½ × 1-inch jelly-roll pan. Line the bottom and sides with one long piece of wax paper. Butter the paper. Dust all over lightly with flour, shaking off excess.

Melt chocolate and butter in top of a small double boiler over hot water on moderate heat. Stir with a small wire whisk to blend. When melted and smooth, add instant coffee and stir to dissolve. Remove top of double boiler from heat and set aside to cool.

Meanwhile, in small bowl of electric mixer beat eggs and salt until slightly fluffy. Gradually add sugar and continue to beat at medium-high speed for 15 minutes until very fluffy. Transfer to large mixer bowl.

Add vanilla and almond extracts to cooled chocolate mixture. On lowest speed add the chocolate to the eggs, scraping bowl with a rubber spatula and beating *only enough to blend*. Still using lowest speed and rubber spatula, add the flour, beating *only enough to blend*. Fold in the nuts, handling the mixture as little as possible.

Pour into prepared pan and spread very evenly. Place in oven. *Immediately reduce oven temperature to 400 degrees.* Bake 21 to 22 minutes. Test with a toothpick. It should just barely come out dry. Do not overbake. Brownies should be slightly moist inside.

Remove from oven. Immediately cover with a large rack or cookie sheet and invert. Remove pan and wax paper. Cover with a large rack and invert again. After 10 or 15 minutes invert once again only for a moment to make sure that the Brownies are not sticking to the rack.

Cool completely and then let stand several hours or overnight at room temperature, or chill for about 15 minutes in the freezer or a bit longer in the refrigerator. Transfer to a large cutting board.

To mark portions evenly, measure with a ruler and mark with toothpicks. Use a long, thin, very sharp knife, or one with a finely serrated edge. Cut with a sawing motion into squares. I prefer to wrap these individually in clear cellophane.

Brownie Crisps

Similar to Brownies in taste, but thin and crisp. Made without a mixer.

16 LARGE OR
32 SMALL
COOKIES

¼ pound (½ cup) butter
1 ounce (1 square) unsweetened chocolate
1 teaspoon instant coffee
½ cup sugar
1 egg
¼ teaspoon vanilla extract
¼ teaspoon salt
¼ cup sifted all-purpose flour
½ cup walnuts,
    cut in medium-size pieces

Adjust oven rack one-third up from bottom. Preheat oven to 375 degrees. Butter a 15½ × 10½ × 1-inch jelly-roll pan.

Melt the butter and chocolate over the lowest heat in a 1½ to 2-quart heavy saucepan. Stir with a rubber spatula until smooth. Add the instant coffee and stir to dissolve. Remove from heat and stir in the sugar, and then the egg and vanilla. Mix thoroughly. Add the salt and flour and mix until smooth.

Pour batter into the prepared pan and spread evenly. Sprinkle with the walnuts.

Bake exactly 15 minutes, reversing position of pan once during baking to insure even browning.

Remove from oven and, without waiting, cut carefully with a small, sharp knife. Immediately, before cookies cool and harden, remove them with a wide, metal spatula. Cool on a rack. Store airtight.

Pecan Squares Americana

These marvelous, candylike cookies are the recipe of executive pastry chef Jacques Kranzlin of the Americana Hotel in Bal Harbour, Florida. Chef Kranzlin brought the recipe with him from Zurich, Switzerland.

48 SMALL SQUARES

PASTRY SHELL

½ pound (1 cup) butter
½ cup sugar
1 egg
¼ teaspoon salt
Finely grated rind of 1 large lemon
3 cups sifted all-purpose flour

Adjust rack one-third up from bottom of oven and preheat to 375 degrees. Butter a 15½ × 10½ × 1-inch jelly-roll pan and place it in the freezer or refrigerator. (It is easier to spread this dough on a cold pan.)

In large bowl of electric mixer cream the butter and sugar, just to mix well. Beat in the egg, salt, and lemon rind. Gradually add the flour and beat only until mixture is smooth and holds together.

Place mixture by large spoonfuls all over the bottom of the cold pan. With floured fingertips press firmly all over the bottom and the sides. There must not be any holes or thin spots in the bottom. Prick the bottom at ¼-inch intervals with a fork. Chill in the freezer or refrigerator for about 10 minutes.

Bake 20 minutes until half baked and lightly colored around the edges. If dough puffs up while baking, reach in to prick it with a fork very slightly and gently. Remove from oven *but do not turn off oven heat.* Prepare topping.

PECAN TOPPING

½ pound (1 cup) butter, cut in pieces
½ cup honey
¼ cup granulated sugar
1 cup plus 2 tablespoons dark brown sugar,
    firmly packed
¼ cup heavy cream
20 ounces (5 cups) pecan halves or large pieces

In a heavy 3-quart saucepan over moderately high heat, cook the butter and honey until butter is melted. Add both sugars and stir to dissolve. Bring to a boil and let boil without stirring for exactly 2 minutes.

Without waiting remove from heat and stir in heavy cream and pecans. *Immediately* spread the hot mixture evenly over the half-baked crust, spreading with the back of a wooden spoon to make as even as possible.

Bake in 375-degree oven with rack in same position for 25 minutes. Remove from oven to cool completely. Cut around sides to release. Cover with a cookie sheet. Invert and remove pan. (If pan doesn't lift off easily, it is because some of the topping has run through to the bottom. If this has happened, bang the inverted pan sharply against the cookie sheet to release.)

Cover with a large rack or another cookie sheet and invert again right side up. Slide off onto a cutting board. With a long, heavy knife, cut into small squares, cutting down firmly with the full length of the blade, and wiping the blade frequently with a damp cloth.

Pecan-
Coconut
Bars

CRUST

24 BARS

¼ pound (½ cup) butter
½ cup sugar
1 cup sifted all-purpose flour

Adjust rack one-third up from bottom of oven. Preheat oven to 400 degrees. Butter a shallow 9 × 13-inch pan and line the bottom *only* with aluminum foil.

In small bowl of electric mixer cream the butter. Beat in the sugar and on low speed add the flour. Beat only until dough holds together. Transfer dough to prepared baking pan. With fingertips press it to cover the bottom of the pan evenly.

Bake 12 to 15 minutes until the crust is lightly colored. While the crust is baking, prepare the topping.

TOPPING

2 tablespoons sifted all-purpose flour
½ teaspoon double-acting baking powder
⅛ teaspoon salt
2 eggs
1 teaspoon vanilla extract
1½ cups dark brown sugar, firmly packed
3½ ounces (1⅓ cups) shredded coconut
3½ ounces (1 cup) pecans, coarsely cut
      or broken

Sift together flour, baking powder, and salt. Set aside. In small bowl of electric mixer, beat eggs slightly just to mix. Beat in vanilla and sugar. On low speed beat in sifted dry ingredients. Remove from mixer and stir in coconut and pecans.

When bottom crust is baked to a light golden color, remove it from the oven. Reduce oven temperature to 350 degrees and raise the rack to the center of the oven. Pour topping mixture over the hot crust. Spread evenly. Return to oven.

Bake 25 minutes. Remove from oven. Let cool in pan on a rack.

When completely cool, cut around edges to release. Cover with a cookie sheet and invert. Remove pan and aluminum foil. Cover with a rack and invert again. Prepare following icing:

ICING

1½ cups confectioners sugar
2½ tablespoons lemon juice

Mix sugar and lemon juice until very smooth. The icing should be quite thick, about the consistency of a heavy cream sauce. Adjust the consistency by adding more sugar or lemon juice as needed. Pour it over the cake and spread with a narrow metal spatula. Let cake stand for a few hours until icing is dry. Transfer cake to a board. Use a ruler and toothpicks to mark even pieces. Cut with a long, heavy knife, cutting down firmly with the full length of the blade.

Date-Nut Bars

24 BARS

1 cup sifted all-purpose flour
¼ teaspoon double-acting baking powder
⅛ teaspoon salt
¼ pound (½ cup) melted butter
1 cup sugar
2 eggs
16 ounces (2 cups) dates, coarsely cut
7 ounces (2 cups) walnut halves
    or coarse pieces
Confectioners sugar

Adjust rack to center of oven. Preheat oven to 350 degrees. Line a shallow 9 × 13-inch pan with one piece of aluminum foil long enough to cover bottom and sides. Press the foil with a pot holder or small towel to mold it into place without tearing it. Brush the bottom and sides with very soft or melted butter. Set aside.

Sift together flour, baking powder, and salt. Set aside. In large bowl of electric mixer beat the melted butter and sugar. Add the eggs and beat for a minute. On lowest speed add the sifted dry ingredients, beating only until incorporated. Mix in the dates and nuts.

174

Spread this thick batter as smoothly as possible in the prepared pan, pressing it into place with the back of a large spoon.

Bake 35 minutes or until the top is a light golden brown. Remove from oven. Let cool in cake pan on a rack for about 10 minutes. Place a cookie sheet over the top. Invert. Remove pan and foil. Cover with another cookie sheet or a rack and invert again to cool completely.

Transfer to a cutting board. Use a ruler and toothpicks to mark even pieces. Cut with a long, thin, very sharp or finely serrated knife into 24 bars. Strain confectioners sugar generously over the tops.

NOTE: *To make this without a mixer, melt the butter in a 2½- to 3-quart saucepan, remove from heat, and stir in the sugar. Beat the eggs and stir them in. Then add the sifted, dry ingredients and mix until smooth. With a heavy, wooden spoon or spatula, mix in the dates and then the nuts.*

Soya Date Bars

2 eggs, separated
1 cup dark brown sugar, firmly packed
¼ cup plus 1 tablespoon boiling water
1 teaspoon vanilla extract
1 cup sifted whole-wheat pastry flour
   (See Note 2.)
½ cup sifted soya flour
¼ teaspoon salt
8 ounces (1 cup) dates, coarsely cut
4 ounces (1 generous cup) walnuts,
   coarsely broken or cut

Adjust rack to center of oven. Preheat oven to 375 degrees. Butter a 9-inch square cake pan and dust it with fine, dry bread crumbs.

In small bowl of electric mixer beat the egg yolks, sugar, and boiling water at moderately high speed for 3 to 5 minutes until the mixture becomes very light in color. Beat in the vanilla and then, on lowest speed, add both flours and salt, beating only until blended. Add the dates and beat briefly. Remove from mixer. Stir in the nuts.

Beat the egg whites until they hold a point, or are stiff but not dry. With a wooden spatula stir about one-quarter of the whites into the batter and then fold in the balance.

Turn the batter into prepared pan. Smooth the top. Bake 30 to 35 minutes or until top springs back when lightly touched.

Remove from oven. Let stand for about 10 minutes. Cover with a rack and invert. Remove pan and cover with another rack. Invert again to cool right side up.

When completely cool, transfer to a board and cut with a long, thin, very sharp knife.

NOTES: 1. *Both whole-wheat pastry flour and soya flour are available at health-food stores.*

2. *Any particles of flour too coarse to go through the sifter should be added to the sifted flour.*

African Date Bars

16 TO 24
SQUARES
OR BARS

¾ cup sifted all-purpose flour
1 teaspoon double-acting baking powder
1 teaspoon cinnamon
Pinch of salt
1 cup sugar
8 ounces (1 cup) dates, coarsely cut
4 ounces (1 generous cup) walnuts,
    coarsely cut or broken
2 eggs
1 teaspoon vanilla extract

Adjust rack one-third up from bottom of oven and preheat oven to 375 degrees. Butter a 9-inch square cake pan and line it with aluminum foil as follows: Turn pan upside down. Place a 12-inch square of foil on the pan and fold down the sides. Remove foil and turn pan right side up. Place the foil in the pan and press gently into place, pressing with a pot holder or folded towel in order not to tear the foil. Brush or spread soft butter all over the foil and dust with flour. Shake out excess. Set pan aside.

Sift together flour, baking powder, cinnamon, salt, and sugar into a mixing bowl.

Add the dates and toss with your fingers to separate and thoroughly coat each piece. Add the nuts and toss again.

Beat the eggs and vanilla until very light and stir them in. Turn the dough into the prepared pan and spread evenly.

Bake for 30 minutes. Remove from oven and let stand for about 10 minutes. Cover with a rack or small cookie sheet and invert. Remove pan and aluminum foil. Cover with a rack, invert, and let cool right side up.

When completely cool, remove to a board and, with a long, heavy knife, cut into squares or bars.

Peanut Bars

Thin caramel cookie bars topped with peanuts. As irresistible as peanuts. Easily mixed in a saucepan.

32 COOKIES

¾ cup sifted all-purpose flour
1 teaspoon cinnamon
½ teaspoon powdered ginger
¼ pound (½ cup) butter
6 ounces (1 cup) butterscotch morsels
1½ teaspoons instant coffee
¼ cup sugar
1 egg
3 ounces (¾ cup) salted peanuts, coarsely
    chopped (preferably the dry-roasted type)

Adjust rack to center of oven. Preheat oven to 325 degrees. Line a 10½ × 15½ × 1-inch jelly-roll pan with aluminum foil as follows: Turn the pan upside down. Cover with a piece of foil large enough to fold down on all four sides and fold the edges just to shape them. Remove the foil. Invert the pan. Sprinkle a few drops of water in the pan to keep the foil in place. Place the foil in the pan. Use a folded towel or a pot holder to press the foil firmly against the pan. Brush the foil with soft or melted butter. Place in freezer or refrigerator. (Chilling the pan makes it easier to spread the thin layer of dough.)

Sift together the flour, cinnamon, and ginger and set aside.

Place the butter and butterscotch morsels in a 2½- to 3-quart saucepan over moderate heat. Stir occasionally until melted. Stir in the instant coffee. Remove from heat and stir with a wire whisk until smooth. With a rubber or wooden spatula stir in the sugar and sifted dry ingredients.

In a small bowl stir the egg briefly with a fork just to mix and add it to the batter. Stir until smooth.

Turn the batter into the chilled pan and, with the back of a large spoon, spread as evenly as possible. It will make a very thin layer. Sprinkle with the peanuts.

Bake for 25 minutes until top is golden colored and springs back when lightly touched. Remove from oven and cool in pan for only 3 minutes. Cover with a large cookie sheet. Invert and remove pan and foil. Cover cake with another large cookie sheet and invert again. With a long, sharp knife, cut the warm cake into bars, cutting down firmly with the full length of the blade. With a wide metal spatula, transfer bars to a rack to cool.

Pecan Butter-crunch

16 LARGE BARS
OR 32 SMALL
SQUARES

Easy.

¼ pound (½ cup) butter
1¼ cups graham cracker crumbs
3½ ounces (1–1⅓ cups) shredded coconut
6 ounces (1 cup) semisweet chocolate morsels
6 ounces (1 cup) butterscotch morsels
1 15-ounce can (1⅛–1¼ cups) sweetened
    condensed milk (See Note.)
7 ounces (2 cups) pecan halves

Adjust rack to center of oven. Preheat oven to 350 degrees. Line bottom and sides of 9 × 13 × 2-inch pan with one long piece of aluminum foil. It is important not to tear the foil. Pressing gently against the foil with a pot holder or towel will help to smooth it into corners and against sides with less chance of tearing than if you use your bare fingers.

Put butter in lined pan and place it in oven until melted. Tilt pan to spread butter all over the bottom and about halfway up on the sides. Sprinkle crumbs evenly over butter on the bottom of the pan. Sprinkle coconut evenly over crumbs. Sprinkle chocolate and butterscotch morsels evenly over coconut. Pour condensed milk evenly over top. Cover with pecan halves placed rounded side up and quite close to each other.

Bake for 5 to 10 minutes, then reach into oven with a wide metal spatula and press gently on the nuts so that they become firmly imbedded and won't fall off later on.

Bake 35 to 40 minutes altogether, or until the condensed milk that shows between the nuts has turned a light golden color all over. Remove from oven.

Cool to room temperature. Place a cookie sheet on top and invert. Remove the pan and peel off the foil. Place a rack on top and invert again so that cake is now right side up. *Let stand overnight or freeze about 1 hour* (or refrigerate a bit longer) before transferring to a board and before cutting with a long, sharp knife.

NOTE: *Condensed milk should not be stored for more than six months. It darkens and thickens if it has been standing on the shelf for a long time, and becomes too thick to pour easily or to run over the top of the cake. Use fresh condensed milk, which is about the consistency of heavy cream and almost white in color.*

Rusks, Italian Style

(*Biscotti all'anice*)

48 RUSKS

4 eggs, separated, plus 1 egg yolk
1 cup sugar
½ teaspoon vanilla extract
1 tablespoon whole anise seeds
1 cup sifted cake flour
Finely grated rind of 1 large orange
⅛ teaspoon salt

Adjust rack to center of oven and preheat to 375 degrees. Line the bottom *only* of a shallow 9 × 13-inch baking pan with unbuttered wax paper. (Do not line the sides.) Set aside.

In small bowl of electric mixer, beat the 5 yolks and the sugar at high speed for 5 minutes until very thick. Beat in the vanilla and anise seeds. On lowest speed gradually add the flour, scraping the bowl as necessary with a rubber spatula and beating only until incorporated. Remove from mixer and stir in the orange rind.

Beat the 4 egg whites with the salt until they hold a point. The egg yolk mixture will be *very* stiff. With a wooden spatula, stir about one-quarter of the whites into the yolk mixture. In about three additions fold in the balance.

Turn into prepared pan and spread level. Bake 25 to 30 minutes until top is well-browned and cake springs back firmly when lightly touched.

Cool for 5 minutes. With a small, sharp knife cut around sides to release. Invert onto a rack. Remove pan and peel off paper. Let stand until cool.

Preheat the oven to 250 degrees.

On a board, with a long, thin, sharp knife, cut the cooled cake down the center, the long way. Then cut each half into narrow slices, about ½ inch thick.

Place the slices, top side up with a bit of space between them, on a large cookie sheet.

Bake 45 minutes to 1 hour or longer, until very lightly colored around the edges. Cookies will be soft when removed from oven but will become crisp when cool. (If not, they need more baking.) The cookies on the outer edges of the cookie sheet will begin to color sooner than those in the center. Remove them individually when done.

Cool completely before storing.

Almond or Hazelnut Rusks

36 RUSKS

1¾ cups sifted all-purpose flour
1½ teaspoons double-acting baking powder
3 ounces (6 tablespoons) butter
1 teaspoon vanilla extract
½ teaspoon almond extract
¾ cup sugar
2 eggs
5 ounces (1 cup) whole blanched almonds
   or blanched hazelnuts (filberts)
   (See page 10.)

Adjust rack one-third down from top of oven. Preheat oven to 400 degrees. Line a 14 × 16-inch cookie sheet with wide aluminum foil.

Sift together the flour and baking powder. Set aside. In small bowl of electric mixer cream the butter. Add vanilla and almond extracts, and sugar. Beat for a minute or two. Beat in the eggs one at a time. On lowest speed gradually add sifted dry ingredients, scraping the bowl as necessary with a rubber spatula and beating only until smooth. Remove from mixer and stir in the nuts.

Using two teaspoons, place the batter, one teaspoonful at a time, to form three long, narrow strips across the width of the prepared cookie sheet. Each strip should be about 12 inches long and 1½ inches wide. Leave about 3 inches of space between the strips. It is not necessary to smooth the tops or sides, as the batter will run slightly in baking.

Bake 15 minutes or until strips are golden-colored and tops spring back when lightly touched. Remove from oven. Reduce oven temperature to 300 degrees. Using a small cookie sheet as a spatula, transfer baked strips to a large rack to cool.

Transfer cooled cakes to a cutting board. Use a finely serrated knife or a long, very sharp, thin knife to slice cakes on an angle into cookies about ¾ inch wide. Replace cut strips on cookie sheet, top side up, with a bit of space between them.

Bake at 300 degrees for 25 minutes. Turn off heat. Open oven door slightly. Let cookies dry in oven for about 10 minutes before removing. Cool on racks.

Icebox and Shortbread Cookies

SWEDISH ICEBOX COOKIES
FRENCH ICEBOX COOKIES
OLD-FASHIONED WALNUT ICEBOX
   COOKIES
MONTEGO BAY ICEBOX COOKIES
SCOTCH SHORTBREAD COOKIES
SCOTCH WALNUT SHORTBREAD
SHORTBREAD DOUGHNUT COOKIES
SHORT'NIN' BREAD

I have made all of the cookies in this section (and many others) without a mixer. Cream the butter by hand in a bowl, add extracts if called for, and the sugar. Work them together by hand and then, in the bowl or on a board or smooth surface, work in the remaining ingredients. Knead until smooth by following directions for "breaking" the dough, page 224.

Swedish Icebox Cookies

100 TO 150
COOKIES

Spicy almond-ginger cookies.

3½ cups sifted all-purpose flour
1 teaspoon baking soda
¼ teaspoon salt
1 tablespoon powdered ginger
¼ teaspoon nutmeg
2 teaspoons powdered cloves
2 teaspoons cinnamon
½ pound (1 cup) butter
1 cup sugar
½ cup molasses, light or dark
5 ounces (1 cup) whole, blanched almonds

Sift together flour, baking soda, salt, ginger, nutmeg, cloves, and cinnamon. Set aside. In large bowl of electric mixer cream the butter. Gradually add the sugar and beat well. Add the molasses and beat, scraping the bowl with a rubber spatula, until smooth. On lowest speed, very gradually add the sifted dry ingredients, continuing to use the rubber spatula as necessary.

Turn out onto a board or smooth surface. Knead slightly only until smooth. Add the almonds and knead until they are evenly distributed. Divide the dough in half and shape each half into an oblong. Place each half on a piece of wax paper about 15 inches long.

Holding the paper against the dough, smooth each oblong into an even shape about 3 inches by 1 inch and 10 inches long. Wrap in the wax paper. Slide a cookie sheet under the two oblongs. Freeze for 30 to 45 minutes or refrigerate overnight, or until firm enough to slice.

Adjust rack high in the oven. Preheat oven to 325 degrees.

Using a very sharp, thin knife, slice cookies ⅛ to a scant ¼ inch thick. Place on unbuttered cookie sheets 1 inch apart. Bake about 10 minutes, reversing position of cookie sheet as necessary to insure even browning. Bake until cookies color very slightly and tops are semi-firm to the touch. Do not overbake. These will crisp as they cool. With a metal spatula, transfer to a rack to cool.

NOTE: *These cookies are best if they are sliced very thin. It is easiest to get them thin if the dough is frozen before it is cut.*

French Icebox Cookies

60 COOKIES

½ pound (1 cup) butter
1½ teaspoons vanilla extract
¼ teaspoon almond extract
¼ teaspoon salt
1 cup sugar
2½ cups sifted all-purpose flour
1 tablespoon water

In large bowl of electric mixer cream the butter. Mix in the vanilla and almond extracts, salt, and sugar. Beat until thoroughly mixed. On lowest speed gradually add about half of the flour. Then add the 1 tablespoon water. Add remaining flour, scraping bowl with a rubber spatula and beating only until flour is incorporated and mixture holds together.

Turn the dough onto a piece of wax paper about 20 inches long. Holding the paper against the dough, shape it into a roll about 2 inches in diameter and 15 inches long, or into an oblong about 3 inches by ¾ inch and 15 inches long. Enclose it in the wax paper. Slide a cookie sheet under the roll and place it in the freezer for about ½ hour, or refrigerate it overnight, until the dough is firm enough to be sliced.

Adjust rack high in the oven. Preheat oven to 400 degrees.

Use a very thin, sharp knife to slice the cookies ⅛ to ¼ inch thick.

Place 1 inch apart on unbuttered cookie sheets. Bake 10 minutes, or until cookies are sandy-colored and lightly browned around the edges. Reverse position of pan during baking to insure an even color. Do not let them get too brown. With a wide metal spatula, transfer to racks to cool.

Old-Fashioned Walnut Icebox Cookies

48 COOKIES

1¾ cups sifted all-purpose flour
2 teaspoons double-acting baking powder
⅛ teaspoon salt
½ teaspoon cinnamon
¼ pound (½ cup) butter
1 teaspoon vanilla extract
1 cup sugar, granulated, light brown, or dark brown (See Note.)
1 egg, extra-large or jumbo
2½ ounces (¾ cup) walnuts, finely chopped or cut

Sift together flour, baking powder, salt, and cinnamon. Set aside. In small bowl of electric mixer, cream the butter. Add vanilla and sugar, and beat for about a minute or two. Beat in the egg and then the walnuts. On lowest speed gradually add sifted dry ingredients, scraping the bowl with a rubber spatula as necessary and beating only until the flour is incorporated and the mixture holds together.

Turn out onto a piece of wax paper 15 to 20 inches long. Holding the paper against the dough, shape it into a roll about 2 inches in diameter and 12 inches long; or shape it as an oblong about 1 inch by 3 inches and 14 inches long. Enclose in the wax paper.

Slide a cookie sheet under the roll. Place it in the freezer for about ½ hour, or refrigerate it overnight, until it is firm enough to be sliced evenly.

Adjust rack near the top of the oven. Preheat oven to 400 degrees.

Use a thin, sharp knife to slice the dough ¼ to ⅓ inch thick. Place on unbuttered cookie sheets 1 inch apart.

Bake 10 minutes or until cookies are lightly colored, reversing position of cookie sheet if necessary during baking to insure even browning. With a wide metal spatula transfer to racks to cool.

NOTE: *The flavor of the cookies will vary considerably depending on the sugar used. Brown sugar should be firmly packed.*

Montego Bay Icebox Cookies

2 cups sifted all-purpose flour
¼ teaspoon salt
2 teaspoons double-acting baking powder
1 teaspoon mace
½ pound (1 cup) butter
2 teaspoons vanilla extract
½ cup sugar
1 egg

40 COOKIES

Sift together flour, salt, baking powder, and mace. Set aside. In large bowl of electric mixer, cream the butter. Add vanilla and sugar and beat until thoroughly mixed. Beat in the egg. On lowest speed gradually add the sifted dry ingredients, scraping the bowl with a rubber spatula and beating only until dry ingredients are thoroughly incorporated.

Turn out onto a piece of wax paper about 15 inches long. Holding the paper against the dough, shape it into a roll about 10 to 12 inches long. The roll may be either round and 2 inches in diameter, or oblong, about 1 inch by 3 inches. Enclose it in the wax paper. Slide a cookie sheet under the roll and place in the freezer for 20 to 30 minutes, or refrigerate for several hours until firm enough to slice.

Adjust the rack high in the oven. Preheat oven to 400 degrees.

With a very sharp, thin knife, slice the dough about ¼ inch thick. Place cookies on unbuttered cookie sheets 1 inch apart.

Bake 10 minutes or until cookies are sandy-colored and light brown around the edges, reversing position of cookie sheet during baking to insure even browning.

With a wide metal spatula, gently transfer these very fragile cookies to racks to cool.

Scotch Short- bread Cookies

55 TO 60
COOKIES

½ pound (1 cup) butter
1 cup confectioners sugar
1½ cups sifted all-purpose flour
1½ cups sifted cornstarch

Adjust rack to center of oven. Preheat oven to 350 degrees.

In large bowl of electric mixer cream butter until soft. Add sugar and beat for a few minutes. On lowest speed gradually add flour and cornstarch, scraping the bowl with a rubber spatula and beating only until incorporated.

Turn mixture onto a board or smooth surface and knead lightly until smooth. Use about half of the dough at a time. Wrap the balance airtight.

On a very lightly floured pastry cloth with a lightly floured rolling pin, roll the dough to ⅓-inch thickness. Cut with a floured 1½-inch round cutter. Save scraps, knead them together briefly, and reroll them all together. Place cookies ½ inch apart on an unbuttered cookie sheet.

Pierce each cookie three times with a fork, going all the way through to the cookie sheet. If this is a sticky job, first chill the cookies briefly in the freezer or refrigerator. Bake about 22 minutes, reversing position of cookie sheet during baking, until cookies have barely colored. Do not overbake. Shortbread should not brown—it should only turn a pale sandy color around the edges.

Transfer with a metal spatula to a rack to cool.

Scotch Walnut Short-bread

54 COOKIES

2 cups sifted all-purpose flour
⅓ cup sifted cornstarch
½ cup granulated sugar
½ pound (1 cup) butter
½ teaspoon vanilla extract
3½ ounces (1 cup) walnuts, very finely chopped (They must be fine, but not ground.)

Adjust rack to center of oven. Preheat oven to 375 degrees.

Sift together flour, cornstarch, and sugar into a bowl. With a pastry blender cut in the butter and vanilla until mixture forms crumbs. Stir in the nuts. Turn out onto a board or smooth surface. Squeeze the mixture together between both hands several times. Form it into a ball. Work quickly and, with the heel of your hand, push off small amounts at a time, pressing it firmly against the board and working away from you. Form it into a ball again and push it off two or three times until it holds together and leaves the board clean.

Roll about half of the dough at a time on a lightly floured pastry cloth with a lightly floured rolling pin, to ⅓-inch thickness. Cut with a floured 1½-inch round cutter. Save scraps and reroll them all together.

Place ¾ inch apart on unbuttered cookie sheet. Pierce each cookie three times with a fork, going all the way through to the cookie sheet. If the dough is sticky, first chill the cookies briefly in the freezer or refrigerator.

Bake about 20 minutes until cookies are lightly colored, reversing position of cookie sheet during baking. Do not overbake. Cool on racks.

Short-bread Doughnut Cookies

24 LARGE
COOKIES

½ pound (1 cup) butter
1 cup confectioners sugar
2 cups sifted all-purpose flour

Adjust rack to center of oven. Preheat oven to 375 degrees.

In large bowl of electric mixer cream the butter. Add sugar and beat until blended. On lowest speed gradually add the flour, scraping bowl with a rubber spatula as necessary to keep mixture smooth.

(If necessary, chill the dough slightly only until it can be rolled. Do not let it get too firm. If it does, let it soften slightly at room temperature and then beat again.)

On a lightly floured cloth with a floured rolling pin, roll the dough to ¼-inch thickness. Cut with a floured 3-inch doughnut cutter. Save all the scraps and reroll and cut them together. Place ¾ inch apart on unbuttered cookie sheets.

Bake 13 minutes, reversing position of cookie sheet during baking, or until cookies are lightly colored on the edges and barely sandy-colored on top. These should not brown. Do not overbake.

Remove from oven and let cool briefly on cookie sheets. Transfer with wide metal spatula to cool on a rack.

Short'nin' Bread

The kind mammy's little baby loves.

20 COOKIES

2 cups sifted all-purpose flour
Generous pinch of salt
½ cup dark brown sugar, firmly packed
½ pound (1 cup) butter

Adjust rack one-third down from top of oven. Preheat oven to 375 degrees.

Place flour, salt, and sugar in a bowl. With a pastry blender cut in the butter until the mixture resembles coarse crumbs. Turn out onto a board or smooth surface. Briefly squeeze the mixture between your hands and then knead slightly only until the dough holds together smoothly. Do not handle any more than necessary. (If you handle the dough too much it must be chilled before rolling.)

On a lightly floured cloth with a lightly floured rolling pin, roll all of the dough at one time to ½-inch thickness. Cut with a floured 2-inch round cookie cutter. Reroll and cut scraps. Place cookies 1 inch apart on an unbuttered cookie sheet.

Pierce each cookie three times with a fork, going all the way through to the cookie sheet. If cookies are sticky, first chill them briefly in the freezer or refrigerator.

Bake 20 to 22 minutes, reversing position of cookie sheet during baking, until cookies are lightly colored. Do not overbake.

Remove with wide metal spatula to cool on rack.

Dainty Cookies

HUNGARIAN HAZELNUT CRESCENTS
MEXICAN WEDDING CAKES
VIENNESE ALMOND CRESCENTS
PLANTATION PECAN COOKIES
SWEDISH JELLY SLICES
SWEDISH JELLY COOKIES
SPRITZ COOKIES OR PRETZELS
CHOCOLATE RIBBONS
SWEDISH DREAM COOKIES
LADYFINGERS
MADELEINES

Hungarian Hazelnut Crescents

Very fragile; do not stack in a cookie jar or they will break. However, they may be frozen in a single layer on a tray and then stacked, or packed on top of each other, in a freezer container.

42 COOKIES

½ pound (1 cup) butter

⅓ cup sugar

1 teaspoon vanilla extract

¼ teaspoon almond extract

5 ounces (1 generous cup) hazelnuts, blanched and finely ground (See pages 10–12.)

2¼ cups sifted all-purpose flour

optional: Confectioners sugar or vanilla confectioners sugar

Adjust rack one-third down from top of oven. Preheat oven to 350 degrees.

In large bowl of electric mixer cream the butter. Add sugar and vanilla and almond extracts and beat for a minute or two. Mix in the nuts and, on lowest speed, gradually add the flour, scraping the bowl with a rubber spatula as necessary, and beating only until the flour is completely incorporated.

Place dough on a large piece of wax paper. Then, using approximately 1 slightly rounded tablespoonful of dough for each piece, divide into 42 pieces.

Roll each piece into an elongated oval, about 3½ inches long, with tapered ends. Place cookies 1 inch apart on unbuttered cookie sheet, turning the ends down to form crescents.

Bake 18 minutes, reversing position of pan during baking to insure even browning, until cookies are lightly colored.

Very carefully, with a wide metal spatula, remove to a rack to cool.

Crescents may be served as they are, or they may be topped with a light sprinkling of confectioners sugar or vanilla confectioners sugar (see Note) sprinkled on through a fine strainer.

Carefully, with a spatula, transfer cookies to serving platter.

NOTE: *For sprinkling over cakes or cookies, vanilla sugar (p. 10) is preferable to plain sugar because of its flavor.*

Mexican Wedding Cakes

24 SMALL COOKIES

¼ pound (½ cup) butter
2 tablespoons confectioners sugar
½ teaspoon vanilla extract
1 cup sifted all-purpose flour
2½ ounces (¾ cup) walnuts,
    very finely chopped (They must be
    chopped fine, but not ground.)
Confectioners sugar

Adjust rack one-third down from top of the oven. Preheat oven to 375 degrees.

In small bowl of electric mixer cream the butter. Add sugar and vanilla and beat for 1 to 2 minutes. On lowest speed add the flour and then the walnuts, beating only until thoroughly mixed.

Remove from mixer. Use a scant tablespoon of dough for each cookie. Roll into 1-inch balls. Place 1 inch apart on unbuttered cookie sheet. Bake about 15 minutes, reversing position of sheet during baking, until lightly colored.

With a metal spatula, transfer to a rack to cool. When completely cool, strain confectioners sugar generously over the tops.

Viennese Almond Crescents

30 TO 36 COOKIES

5 ounces (1¼ sticks) butter
½ teaspoon almond extract
⅓ cup sugar
2 ounces (scant ½ cup) almonds,
    blanched and finely ground (See
    pages 10–12.)
1½ cups sifted all-purpose flour
Confectioners sugar

Adjust rack high in the oven. Preheat oven to 350 degrees.

In small bowl of electric mixer cream the butter. Add almond extract and sugar and beat for 1 minute. Beat in ground almonds and then, on lowest speed, add the flour and beat until incorporated. Turn mixture onto a board or smooth surface and knead lightly just until smooth.

Break off small pieces of dough, each a well-rounded teaspoonful. Roll between your hands into small cigar shapes, each about 3½ inches long, with tapered ends. Place 1½ inches apart on unbuttered cookie sheet, turning down both ends to form a crescent.

Bake 15 minutes or until the cookies turn a very light golden color. Reverse position of cookie sheet during baking and, if you bake two sheets at the same time, exchange their positions during baking.

Use a wide metal spatula to transfer these delicate cookies gently to a rack to cool.

When completely cool, strain confectioners sugar generously over the tops.

Plantation Pecan Cookies

22 COOKIES

4 ounces (1 generous cup) pecans
¼ pound (½ cup) butter
½ teaspoon vanilla extract
¼ teaspoon salt
¼ cup sugar
1½ teaspoons prepared coffee, water, or brandy
1 cup sifted all-purpose flour
22 pecan halves

Grind the heaping cup of pecans in a blender or a nut grinder and set aside. They need not be strained.

In small bowl of electric mixer cream the butter. Beat in the vanilla, salt, and sugar. Continue to beat for a minute or two. Beat in the coffee, water, or brandy. On lowest speed gradually add the flour. Scrape the bowl with a rubber spatula and beat until smooth. Add the ground pecans and beat until incorporated.

Remove from mixer and place on aluminum foil or wax paper. Flatten slightly, wrap, and refrigerate or freeze briefly until firm enough to handle.

Adjust rack one-third down from top of oven. Preheat oven to 375 degrees.

Remove chilled dough from refrigerator or freezer and cut into 22 equal pieces.

Roll each piece between your palms into a ball. Place 1½ inches apart on an ungreased cookie sheet. Press a pecan half firmly into the top of each cookie, flattening the cookie slightly as you do so.

Bake in preheated oven for 18 to 20 minutes until golden, reversing position of cookie sheet if necessary to insure even browning.

With a metal spatula, transfer cookies to a rack to cool thoroughly.

Swedish Jelly Slices

42 TO 48 BARS

2¼ cups sifted all-purpose flour

½ teaspoon double-acting baking powder

¼ teaspoon salt

6 ounces (¾ cup) butter

2 teaspoons vanilla extract

⅔ cup sugar

1 egg

¾–1 cup apricot preserves (or any thick, tart jam or jelly)

2½ ounces (¾ cup) almonds, blanched and finely sliced

Adjust rack one-third down from top of oven. Preheat oven to 375 degrees.

Sift together flour, baking powder, and salt. Set aside. In large bowl of an electric mixer, cream the butter. Add vanilla and sugar and beat well. Beat in the egg. On lowest speed add the sifted dry ingredients, scraping the bowl with a rubber spatula and beating until the dry ingredients are thoroughly incorporated. Turn out onto a lightly floured board. Shape into a ball. Cut into four equal parts.

Working on the board, with your fingertips (flour them if dough sticks) work each piece into a roll about 12 inches long and 1 inch in diameter.

Place the rolls crossways on a large, unbuttered cookie sheet, about 14 × 16 inches, leaving 2 to 3 inches of space between them. The rolls will spread a bit as they bake.

Make a narrow, shallow trench down the length of each roll by pressing gently with a fingertip. Leaving a little space at the ends, work the full length in one direction, and then work in the opposite direction. The ends and the sides should be higher. Do not make the trench too deep or the cookies will not hold together after they are baked and sliced.

To fill the trench with the preserves, use a pastry bag without a tube; or, if the opening of the bag is too large, use a plain, round tube about ½ inch in diameter. Or use a very small spoon. The filling should be level with the sides or very slightly higher. If it is thick enough it will not run over the sides. With your fingertips, generously sprinkle the sliced almonds over the preserves.

Bake about 25 minutes until the cookies are sandy-colored on top and golden brown around the edges, reversing position of pan during baking to insure an even color.

Shortly before removing cookies from oven, mix the following glaze:

1¼ cups confectioners sugar
2 tablespoons boiling water (approximately)

Mix sugar and water until smooth, using enough water to make the consistency similar to heavy cream. Cover airtight when not in use.

Remove cookie sheet from oven and apply the glaze by pouring it or spooning it down the length of each roll, over the preserves and nuts.

Using a cookie sheet as a spatula, carefully slide the rolls onto a large rack to cool for about 5 minutes. Then carefully transfer them to a cutting board. With a very sharp, heavy knife, cut each warm roll on an angle into slices about 1 to 1¼ inches wide. Replace cookies on the rack to finish cooling.

Swedish Jelly Cookies

42 TO 48 COOKIES

½ pound (1 cup) butter
⅛ teaspoon salt
¼ teaspoon almond extract
½ cup sugar
1 egg yolk, extra-large or jumbo
2¾ cups sifted all-purpose flour
Thick apricot preserves, or currant jelly

Adjust oven rack to top position. Preheat oven to 375 degrees.

In large bowl of electric mixer cream butter, salt, and almond extract. Beat in the sugar and then the egg yolk. On lowest speed gradually add the flour, scraping the bowl with a rubber spatula, and beating only until mixture holds together.

Using about 1 tablespoon of dough for each cookie (or a bit less for daintier cookies), roll into even balls 1 inch or less in diameter. Place the cookies 1 inch apart on ungreased cookie sheets. After shaping the dough balls, make a shallow hole in the top of each, using a blunt instrument about ½ inch in diameter, e.g., the end of the handle of a wooden spoon or spatula. Form the depressions quickly before the cookies dry out, or they will crack.

After shaping and denting all the cookies, fill the hollows with preserves or jelly. This is best done with a small paper cone, in which case the preserves should be strained first. For making a paper cone see directions on page 408, but start with a 12-inch square of wax paper or baking pan liner paper. Alternatively, the preserves or jelly may be applied with the tip of a small knife, in which case they would not have to be strained. Either way, fill the hollows level.

Bake only one sheet of cookies at a time, reversing position of pan during baking to insure even browning. Bake for 15 to 17 minutes until cookies are golden-colored.

While cookies are baking, prepare the following glaze:

GLAZE

1 cup confectioners sugar
2 tablespoons boiling water (approximately)

Mix sugar and water until smooth, using enough water to make the consistency similar to heavy cream. The glaze should not be too thick; it should be thin enough to flow easily when brushed on. Cover airtight when not in use.

When cookie sheet is removed from the oven, immediately brush the glaze over each cookie, using a soft brush and brushing over both jelly and cookie. Glaze will set immediately and then cookies may be transferred with a metal spatula to a rack to cool.

NOTE: *To make these fancier, sprinkle a very little bit of coarsely chopped green pistachio nuts or chopped toasted almonds on cookies before glaze dries. It would be best if someone could help with this, since glaze must be applied while cookies are hot.*

Spritz Cookies or Pretzels

48 SMALL COOKIES, OR 8 TO 10 LARGE PRETZELS (5 INCHES IN DIAMETER, MADE WITH ½-INCH ROUND TUBE)

These are the same cookies, but Spritz Cookies are shaped with a cookie press and Pretzels are shaped with a pastry bag.

½ pound (1 cup) butter
1½ teaspoons vanilla extract
½ cup sugar
1 egg, extra-large or jumbo
2½ cups sifted all-purpose flour
optional toppings: nuts, glacéed fruit,
    chocolate morsels

Adjust rack to the center of the oven. Preheat oven to 400 degrees.

In large bowl of electric mixer cream the butter. Add vanilla and sugar and beat well. Beat in the egg. On lowest speed gradually add the flour, scraping the bowl with a rubber spatula and beating until smooth.

Press the dough through a cookie press onto unbuttered cookie sheets, placing the cookies 1 inch apart. Do not attempt to shape cookies through a press onto warm cookie sheets—they will pull away from the sheets. If necessary, chill the sheets in the freezer. Decorate cookies with optional toppings, pressing them in gently.

PRETZELS

Fit a large pastry bag with a plain, round tube ¼ to ½ inch in diameter. The dough will be stiff and it will take strength to force it through the pastry bag, but it will be easier if the bag is not too full. Use about one-third to half the dough at a time in a 12- to 15-inch pastry bag. Until you become experienced at shaping pretzels, you may draw the shape roughly with a pencil directly on the cookie sheet and then just follow the lines.

1 egg yolk
1 teaspoon water
Pearl sugar

Make a glaze by stirring 1 egg yolk with 1 teaspoon water. With a small, soft brush, brush it over the tops of the pretzels. With your fingertips, sprinkle pearl sugar (see Note, page 205) generously over the tops.

Bake 10 minutes, more or less, depending on the size of the cookies, until lightly colored. During baking reverse position of cookie sheet if necessary to insure even browning. With a metal spatula transfer to racks to cool.

Chocolate Ribbons

60 4-INCH
COOKIES

A chocolate variation on Spritz Cookies.

2 ounces (2 squares) unsweetened chocolate
¼ pound (½ cup) butter
1 teaspoon vanilla extract
¼ teaspoon salt
optional: 1 tablespoon powdered instant coffee
(See Note 1.)

1 cup sugar
1 egg
2 tablespoons milk
2 cups sifted all-purpose flour

Adjust rack to center of oven. Preheat oven to 350 degrees.

Melt the chocolate in the top of a small double boiler over hot water on moderate heat. Set aside to cool.

In the large bowl of an electric mixer cream the butter. Add vanilla, salt, optional powdered instant coffee, and the sugar. Beat until well mixed and then mix in the egg and the milk. Mix in the chocolate. On lowest speed gradually add the flour, scraping the bowl with a rubber spatula and beating only until smooth.

Fit a cookie press with the saw-toothed ribbon plate. Transfer some of the dough to the press. Use unbuttered cookie sheets. Hold the press at an angle, not upright, and press the dough into ribbons the full length of the cookie sheet, releasing the pressure as you near the end of each strip in order to stop the flow of dough. The ribbons may be placed close to each other—¼ to ½ inch apart.

Bake one sheet at a time for about 10 minutes. (See Note 2.) Reverse the position of the cookie sheet if necessary during baking to insure even baking.

Remove from oven and immediately, with a long, heavy knife, cutting across all the ribbons at once, cut into desired lengths—about 3 to 4 inches. Cut down firmly, using the full length of the blade. Immediately, before the cookies become crisp, loosen them from the sheet, using a wide metal spatula, a long, narrow one, or try using a small cookie sheet as a spatula. If you use a cookie sheet as a spatula, press down very firmly against the sheet that the cookies were baked on—you will be able to release them all and transfer them to a rack at the same time. Cool on racks.

NOTES: 1. *The coffee must be powdered instant, not the granules or chunks, which would clog the opening in the cookie press. If you only have granules or chunks, grind in a blender and strain.*

2. *When cool, these should be completely crisp. It is a good idea to bake a sample strip and adjust the timing accordingly.*

Swedish Dream Cookies

36 COOKIES

This classic Swedish recipe calls for ammonium carbonate, a leavening agent which gives the cookies a specific texture—light, crisp, flaky. Ammonium carbonate is available from drugstores in different forms. Buy the minimum amount available. If possible, buy it powdered; if you buy the granular, chip, or lump form, powder it using a mortar and pestle. It must be stored airtight in a dark place. Don't be concerned by the ammonia odor while cookies are baking—that will disappear completely.

2 cups sifted all-purpose flour
1 teaspoon powdered ammonium carbonate
½ pound (1 cup) butter
½ teaspoon vanilla extract
½ cup sugar
36 whole, blanched almonds
1 egg white
Pearl sugar (See Note.)

Sift flour with ammonium carbonate and set aside. In small bowl of electric mixer cream the butter. Add the vanilla and sugar and beat for a minute or two. On lowest speed gradually add the flour mixture, scraping the bowl as necessary with a rubber spatula and beating only until smooth.

Remove from mixer. Wrap airtight and chill in refrigerator or freezer only until dough is no longer sticky—do not chill it long enough for it to harden.

Meanwhile, adjust rack one-third down from top of oven. Preheat oven to 350 degrees.

Using a rounded teaspoonful of dough for each cookie, roll each between your palms into balls and place them about 2 inches apart on unbuttered cookie sheets.

Press an almond into the top of each, flattening the cookie very slightly as you do so.

Beat the egg white slightly only until foamy and, with a soft brush, brush it over each cookie.

Sprinkle cookies with the pearl sugar. Bake 20 to 23 minutes, reversing cookie sheet front to back once during baking to insure even browning.

When cookies are light golden brown, remove them with a wide metal spatula to cool on a rack.

NOTE: *Pearl sugar, also called crystal sugar (in German it is* Hagelzuker*), is coarser than granulated sugar. You may substitute crushed lump sugar, since crystal sugar is hard to find. In New York City it is available, under the name crystal sugar, at Paprikas Weiss, 1546 Second Avenue, 10028.*

Lady-fingers

24 TO 30 LARGE
LADYFINGERS

⅛ teaspoon salt
3 eggs, separated
2 tablespoons granulated sugar
1 teaspoon vanilla extract
1 cup confectioners sugar
¾ cup sifted all-purpose flour
Additional confectioners sugar
for dusting cookies

Adjust two racks to divide oven in thirds. Preheat to 350 degrees. Cut aluminum foil to fit two cookie sheets.

In small bowl of electric mixer beat the salt and the egg whites at high speed until they begin to thicken. Gradually add granulated sugar and continue to beat until they are firm and hold a definite point, or are stiff but not dry. Transfer to a large bowl. Set aside.

In same bowl with same beaters (not necessary to wash either) beat the yolks, then add vanilla and the cup of confectioners sugar and continue to beat at high speed for about 5 minutes, until the mixture becomes very thick and very light in color.

Fold the egg yolk mixture into the beaten whites. Do not be too thorough. Sift half of the flour over the egg mixture and fold it in gently. Repeat with the rest of the flour and fold only until the flour is all absorbed—do not try to blend too thoroughly.

Fit a large pastry bag with a plain, round tube measuring ⅝ inch in diameter. Put all of the batter in the bag and press Ladyfingers out onto the foil, shaping them about 4 to 4½ inches long and 1 inch wide, and placing them 1 inch apart. (Commercial ladyfingers are about 2½ inches long; I make them longer.)

Strain additional confectioners sugar lightly over them.

Slide cookie sheets under the foil and place in oven to bake. After 10 minutes, check Ladyfingers and, if they are not all browning evenly, reverse cookie sheets, top layer to bottom and front to back. Continue to bake until tops spring back when lightly touched and Ladyfingers are all evenly and lightly colored.

Slide aluminum foil off cookie sheets and, with a wide metal spatula, cut Ladyfingers from paper and place on racks to cool.

Madeleines

**12 MADELEINES
3 INCHES
LONG**

Plain, buttery, and spongy—traditionally baked in shell-shaped forms which are generally available in kitchen equipment shops that carry French utensils. This recipe is for one pan with twelve forms for cookies 3 inches long.

Madeleines became famous in French literature because it was the taste of a Madeleine dipped in a cup of tea which Marcel Proust used as the starting point of his literary journey into the past. They are delicious when just baked, but Proust's might well have been stale—when dry and stale they are great for dunking.

2 ounces (¼ cup) unsalted butter
1 egg plus 2 egg yolks, at room temperature
¼ cup sugar
½ teaspoon vanilla extract
½ cup sifted all-purpose flour
Finely grated rind of 1 large lemon

Adjust rack one-third up from bottom of oven. Preheat oven to 375 degrees. To prepare the pan: Bring about 1½ tablespoons of unsalted butter (this is in addition to that called for in recipe) to room temperature to soften. Do *not* use melted butter. With a pastry brush, brush the butter on the forms, brushing from the top to the bottom the long way and then reversing and brushing from the bottom to the top. Examine the forms carefully to make sure that you haven't missed any spots and also that the butter is not too thick anywhere. Now, over paper, sprinkle the forms with fine, dry bread crumbs. Tilt and shake the pan to coat the forms thoroughly. Invert the pan and tap it firmly, leaving a very light coating of crumbs.

Cut up the 2 ounces of butter and, in a small pan over low heat, melt it, stirring occasionally. Set aside to cool but do not let it harden.

In small bowl of an electric mixer beat the egg, egg yolks, sugar, and vanilla at high speed for about 15 minutes until mixture barely flows when beaters are lifted. On lowest speed gradually add the flour, scraping the bowl with a rubber spatula as necessary and beating *only* until the flour is incorporated—do not overbeat. Remove from mixer. (Use your fingertips to remove the batter from the beaters.)

Fold in the lemon rind and then, in four or five additions, the cooled butter, folding only until no butter shows. Bake immediately—do not let the batter stand.

Spoon the batter into the prepared forms. The batter will be mounded slightly above the tops of the forms. Do not smooth; the batter will level itself.

Bake 18 minutes or until the tops are golden brown and spring back firmly when lightly touched. If necessary, reverse the position of the pan for the last few minutes of baking to insure even browning.

Madeleines must be removed from the pan immediately. Quickly cover the pan with a rack or a cookie sheet and invert. Remove the pan. Cool the Madeleines on a rack.

NOTES: 1. *Never clean Madeleine pans with anything rough or anything other than soap and water—it might make the cookies stick.*

2. *This recipe may be doubled for two Madeleine pans if they will both fit on the same oven rack. The Madeleines must not be baked on two racks at one time or they will not brown properly. Therefore, to make a large number repeat the directions—the prepared batter should not stand.*

Rolled Wafers and Paper-Thin Cookies

FRENCH ALMOND WAFERS

OATMEAL WAFERS

BENNE SEED WAFERS

MORAVIAN GINGER THINS
  (*Pennsylvania Dutch*)

ROLLED CIGARETTES

French Almond Wafers

24 TO 30 WAFERS

Crisp, extremely delicate, and fragile lace wafers.

4 ounces (slightly generous ¾ cup)
    blanched almonds
½ cup sugar
¼ pound (½ cup) butter,
    at room temperature
1 tablespoon (must be exactly level)
    sifted all-purpose flour
2 tablespoons milk

Adjust rack one-third down from top of oven. Preheat oven to 350 degrees. Butter and lightly flour cookie sheets. (See Note 1.)

Grind the almonds finely in a nut grinder or blender. They need not be strained.

Place all ingredients in a 10- to 12-inch heavy frying pan. Using a wooden spatula, stir over low heat until butter melts and ingredients are thoroughly mixed. Remove from heat.

Drop by slightly rounded teaspoonfuls about 4 inches apart on prepared cookie sheets, placing only 4 or 5 cookies on a large sheet. Bake one sheet at a time for 8 to 10 minutes, reversing position of sheet if cookies are not browning evenly, until well-browned with no light spots left in the centers.

Remove sheet from oven and let cookies stand for a few seconds only, until they can be easily removed with a wide metal spatula.

Work quickly now—as you remove a cookie, immediately place it over a rolling pin (see Note 2) to shape (see Note 3). In a few minutes, as soon as they have set to hold their shape, they may be removed to make room for the remaining cookies.

Bake and shape remaining cookies.

As soon as cookies are thoroughly cool, place them in airtight containers. They will become limp if exposed to the air too long. If they are not to be served soon, they should be frozen. Package in a single layer, in a shallow, firm container.

NOTES: 1. *Baking pan liner paper may be used for these cookies, but if so, do not remove the paper from the cookie sheet until cookies have been removed, or they will cool too quickly to be shaped over the rolling pin.*

        2. *If you do not have two rolling pins to work with, use anything*

else of a similar shape—wine bottles, straight glasses, broom handles, etc.

3. If the cookies cool too quickly to shape, reheat in the oven long enough to soften.

4. Having said all of the above about shaping these cookies to curve them in the traditional manner, let me add that they are equally fine if left flat, and are much less fragile and therefore easier to wrap and store. If they are to be left flat, they may be baked on baking pan liner paper or unbuttered aluminum foil. When done, slide the paper or foil off the cookie sheet and let stand until cookies cool. Then just lift them off the paper or, very gently, peel the foil away.

Oatmeal Wafers

30 COOKIES

Spicy, crisp, extremely *fragile*.

¼ cup sifted all-purpose flour
½ teaspoon salt
⅛ teaspoon baking soda
½ teaspoon cinnamon
½ teaspoon powdered cloves
½ teaspoon allspice
½ teaspoon powdered ginger
½ teaspoon nutmeg
¼ pound (½ cup) butter
1 teaspoon vanilla extract
¼ cup granulated sugar
½ cup light brown sugar, firmly packed
1 egg
1 cup old-fashioned or quick-cooking (not instant) oatmeal
½ cup walnuts, thinly sliced or chopped medium-fine

Adjust rack one-third down from top of oven and preheat to 350 degrees. Cut aluminum foil to fit cookie sheets.

Sift flour with salt, baking soda, cinnamon, cloves, allspice, ginger, and nutmeg. Set aside.

In small bowl of electric mixer cream the butter. Add vanilla and both sugars and beat for a minute or two. Beat in the egg and then the oatmeal. On lowest speed add the sifted dry ingredients and then the nuts, scraping the bowl with a rubber spatula and beating until well-mixed.

Drop the batter on the aluminum foil by slightly rounded teaspoon-fuls, placing them far apart—about 3 inches—as they spread a lot. Slide a cookie sheet under the foil. With the back of a teaspoon dipped repeatedly in cold water, spread each cookie to flatten it. Make it thin, but don't worry about keeping the shape round.

Bake about 15 minutes until completely browned, reversing position of cookie sheet during baking to insure even browning.

Slide the aluminum foil off the cookie sheet. Allow cookies to cool completely on the foil and then peel the foil away from the backs of the cookies.

Handle with care! These are not cookie-jar cookies—they are too fragile. Place them on a platter or tray and cover airtight with plastic wrap. They must be stored airtight. They may be frozen.

Benne Seed Wafers

Dramatic wafers about 5 inches in diameter. Benne seed is the old Southern name for sesame seeds, and there is a legend that eating them brings good luck. Originally an old plantation recipe from Charleston, South Carolina, the wafers are traditionally made smaller.

25 WAFERS,
5 INCHES IN
DIAMETER

1 cup sesame seeds (benne seeds)
6 ounces (¾ cup) butter
½ cup sifted all-purpose flour
¼ teaspoon baking powder
¼ teaspoon salt
1 egg
1 teaspoon vanilla extract
1½ cups light brown sugar, firmly packed
3½ ounces (1 cup) pecans, chopped medium

Adjust rack to center of oven. Preheat oven to 350 degrees. Place sesame seeds in a shallow pan and bake for 15 to 20 minutes, shaking the pan frequently to toast the seeds an even, light-brown color. (Toasting brings out the nutlike flavor.) Remove from oven to cool.

Raise oven temperature to 400 degrees. Cut aluminum foil to fit cookie sheets.

Place the butter in a small pan over low heat to melt. Set aside to cool slightly.

Sift together flour, baking powder, and salt. In small bowl of electric mixer beat egg and vanilla just to mix. Beat in the sugar, sifted mixture, melted butter, toasted sesame seeds, and pecans, scraping bowl with a rubber spatula as necessary and beating until thoroughly mixed.

Drop by generous tablespoonfuls about 4 inches apart—they need a lot of room—on the aluminum foil. These need so much room that you will only be able to bake 2 or 3 cookies at a time on a medium-size cookie sheet. Slide a cookie sheet under the foil. Bake only one sheet at a time. Reverse position of pan during baking to insure even browning. Bake 7 minutes or until evenly browned.

Slide foil off cookie sheet and let stand until cookies are completely cool. Then peel the foil away from the cookies.

These must be stored airtight or they become sticky; they may be frozen.

Moravian Ginger Thins

(Pennsylvania Dutch)

48 COOKIES

1¼ cups sifted all-purpose flour
¼ teaspoon salt
¼ teaspoon nutmeg
¼ teaspoon allspice
¼ teaspoon powdered cloves
¾ teaspoon cinnamon
½ teaspoon powdered ginger
Tiny pinch of cayenne pepper
3 tablespoons butter
2 tablespoons dark brown sugar, firmly packed
⅓ cup molasses, dark or light

Sift together flour, salt, nutmeg, allspice, cloves, cinnamon, ginger, and cayenne pepper. Set aside. In small bowl of electric mixer, cream the butter. Beat in the sugar and then the molasses. On lowest speed add the sifted dry ingredients, scraping the bowl with a rubber spatula as necessary to keep mixture smooth. Beat only until smooth.

Wrap airtight and refrigerate for 4 to 5 hours. (May be refrigerated for several days, if you wish.)

Adjust rack one-third down from top of oven. Preheat oven to 350 degrees. Line a cookie sheet with aluminum foil.

Work with one-quarter of the dough at a time. Keep the rest refrigerated. On a well-floured pastry cloth, with a well-floured rolling pin, roll the dough very slightly. Turn it over, roll slightly, and turn again to thoroughly flour both sides. Work quickly before the dough softens and becomes sticky. Roll it paper thin (1⁄16 inch thick). Cut with a 2¾-inch round cookie cutter. With a wide metal spatula transfer cookies to lined cookie sheet, placing them close together.

Bake 8 minutes, or until cookies darken slightly. With a wide metal spatula transfer to a rack to cool.

Repeat with remaining portions of dough. Reserve scraps, wrap, chill, and reroll.

These cookies must be stored airtight in order to remain crisp for any length of time.

Rolled Cigarettes

Crisp, fragile, rolled wafers.

24 COOKIES

2 ounces (¼ cup) butter
2 egg whites, jumbo or extra-large
Pinch of salt
½ cup sugar
½ teaspoon vanilla extract
1 tablespoon plus 2 teaspoons
    sifted all-purpose flour

Adjust rack to center of oven. Preheat oven to 350 degrees. Butter several cookie sheets (or only one, if you prefer, since these will be baked one sheet at a time) and dust them lightly with flour. Shake off excess and set aside.

Melt the butter and set aside to cool.

In a small bowl beat the whites and the salt with a small wire whisk or a fork, beating only until foamy. Add the sugar and beat until mixed. Add the vanilla, flour, and melted butter, beating or stirring only until smoothly mixed.

Bake one sample cookie. If you wish, this may be done on an inverted layer cake pan, buttered and floured.

Drop about 1 tablespoonful of the batter onto the sheet, and with the back of the spoon spread it as smoothly as possible into an oval about 4 to 4½ inches long. It will be very thin—almost sheer.

Bake 6 to 8 minutes until golden brown with barely any light spots remaining. Remove from oven and wait for just a second or two before removing cookie with a wide metal spatula. Working quickly, immediately place cookie upside down on smooth surface and *immediately* roll rather tightly on a pencil or the handle of a wooden spoon or spatula. (These are very hot. Some people wear gloves to roll them.) Slip cookie off and set aside to cool.

If sample cookie shows that batter needs adjusting, add 1 to 2 teaspoons of melted butter to make it more flexible; or if the cookie is sticky and difficult to remove from the cookie sheet, add about ½ teaspoon of flour to make it firmer.

Until you get the hang of baking and shaping these cookies, I suggest baking only two at a time. If necessary, reverse position of pan during baking to insure even browning. If one cookie browns sooner than the other, remove it when it is ready and then continue to bake the other until done. If cookies cool on cookie sheet too long and become brittle, replace in oven for a minute or so until soft. Or, if a cookie becomes crisp while you are rolling it, don't force it or it will break. Remove the pencil and replace the cookie, on the cookie sheet, in the oven to soften. Remove from oven and finish rolling without the pencil.

Each cookie sheet must be washed, dried, buttered, and floured before reusing. Stir batter occasionally to keep it mixed.

Making these Cigarettes is slow work (I mean "play"). You may quit whenever you want and place any remaining batter in a covered container in the refrigerator.

As soon as the shaped cookies cool, place them carefully in a covered airtight container. Do not expose these fragile wafers to humidity for any length of time or they will become sticky, but they will keep well if airtight or they may be frozen. If frozen, thaw covered.

Individual Pastries and Petits Fours

MUSHROOM MERINGUES

VICTORIAS

FRENCH ALMOND MACAROON
  CRESCENTS

IRISH ALMOND CAKES

CAPRI PASTRIES

CHOCOLATE CUPCAKES

ETHIOPIAN TRUFFLES

FRENCH SANDWICH COOKIES
  WITH CHOCOLATE FILLING

Mush-room Meringues

These charming petits fours are a work of art. They call for patience, talent with a pastry bag, and a dry atmosphere.

24 RATHER LARGE
OR 36 MEDIUM
MUSHROOMS

½ cup egg whites (about 3–3½ whites
    if eggs are jumbo or extra-large),
    at room temperature
Scant ¼ teaspoon salt
¼ teaspoon cream of tartar
1 cup sugar
1 teaspoon vanilla extract
Cocoa
Chocolate (See Note.)

Adjust two racks to divide the oven into thirds. Preheat oven to 225 degrees. Cut aluminum foil to fit two cookie sheets at least 12 × 15 inches.

In the small bowl of electric mixer at moderately slow speed, beat the whites for about half a minute or until they are just foamy. Add the salt and cream of tartar. Increase the speed to moderate and beat for almost a minute more until whites hold a soft shape. Continue to beat and start adding the sugar, 1 rounded tablespoonful at a time—beat about half a minute between additions. When half of the sugar has been added, add the vanilla and then continue adding the sugar as before. When all of the sugar has been added, increase the speed to high and beat for 7 to 8 minutes more or until the meringue is very stiff and the sugar is dissolved —test it by rubbing a bit between your fingers. (Total beating time from start to finish is about 15 to 18 minutes, but it depends on the power of your mixer.)

To hold the aluminum foil in place, put a dot of the meringue in each corner of the cookie sheets. Cover with the foil and press firmly on the corners.

Do not let the meringue stand. Fit a large pastry bag (preferably at least 15 to 16 inches long) with a plain, round tube ½ to ¾ inch in diameter. (I like to use one that is ⅝ inch.) Fold down the top of the bag to form a deep cuff on the outside. Support the bag by holding it under the cuff with one hand. Using a rubber spatula, with your other hand transfer all of the meringue into the bag. Lift the cuff up and twist the top closed.

On one piece of the prepared aluminum foil shape the mushroom stems first. Hold the bag at a right angle and close to the foil. Press the meringue out gently while slowly raising the bag straight up. The base of the stem should be a bit wider for support. Keep the stem as straight as possible. Hold the bag upright and steady with one hand while, with the other hand, use a small knife to cut the meringue away from the tube. Don't worry if a small point is left on top of the stem; it can be removed later on. The stems may be about 1 to 1¾ inches high (the taller they are, the more difficult), but they may vary as real mushroom stems do. They should be placed ½ to 1 inch apart on the foil. (Some of the stems may fall over on their sides, so it is a good idea to make a few extras to be sure you wind up with a stem for each cap.)

Strain cocoa through a fine strainer lightly over the stems to imitate soil and natural mushroom coloring. Place in the oven on the higher rack.

On the other piece of foil shape the mushroom caps. Holding the bag straight up and close to the foil, press out even rounds of the meringue. The caps should be placed about ½ inch apart. The caps may average about 1½ to 1¾ inches in width and ¾ inch in height, but they may also vary as real mushroom caps do. Sharply twist the bag away to avoid leaving a peak on the top. The top should be as smooth as possible.

Strain cocoa lightly over the caps. Bake on the lower rack.

The measurements I have given are approximate—don't worry about them. Smaller or larger mushrooms are equally attractive. Even mushroom meringues with crooked stems or with a slight point on the cap will look great when finished.

Bake for 1 hour, or a bit longer depending on size, until meringues may be lifted easily from the foil and the bottoms are firm to the touch. The longer they bake the drier they are—and the better—but they should not be allowed to color (it affects the taste). Turn the heat off, prop the oven door open a little, and let the meringues dry out even more in the turned-off oven until cool.

Remove meringues from the foil. They may be placed on a clean piece of foil, on wax paper, or on a tray. Immediately, while the meringues are very crisp, using a finely serrated knife or a sharp paring knife, gently saw any points off the tops of the stems cutting parallel with the base.

One ounce of chocolate will be needed for 5 mushroom caps if they measure 1¾ to 2 inches in diameter. Using this formula, figure how much chocolate you will need and cut it coarsely and place in the top of a small double boiler over warm water to melt slowly over low heat. When almost melted, remove from the heat and stir until completely melted and smooth.

Hold a mushroom cap upside down. With a demitasse spoon spread a layer of chocolate over the bottom of the cap, spreading it just to the edge. It should be thin but not too thin. Place a stem upside down on the chocolate.

Now the mushroom must stand in that position, upside down, until the chocolate hardens. There are several ways to do this. The inverted mushrooms will rest securely in small cordial glasses, small brandy snifters, small egg cups, or in an empty egg carton—it will depend on their size.

Carefully place the mushrooms in their cordial glasses or egg cups or whatever in the freezer or refrigerator *only* until the chocolate is firm. Do not freeze or refrigerate any longer. (Do not freeze mushrooms after the chocolate has hardened—it will cause the finished mushrooms to come apart.) Remove and store at room temperature.

Do not cover the mushrooms airtight. I have kept them for weeks in an open straw basket in an air-conditioned room. They become drier, crisper, and better.

Serve the mushrooms either standing upright on a platter, or tumbled in a basket like real mushrooms, which these will resemble to an unbelievable degree. (Try a napkin-lined basketful as a centerpiece—at dessert time pass it around.) These may be eaten any way, but I suggest upside down, stem first.

The number of mushrooms this recipe yields will depend on their size—approximately 24 rather large or 36 medium. If you want more, prepare and bake one batch, and then repeat; meringue should not stand any longer than necessary before baking.

NOTE: *Almost any chocolate may be used for this recipe. My first choice is any commercial coating chocolate (see page 5) because it will never discolor and the mushrooms may be kept for weeks or even months. (Commercial coating chocolate will harden quickly and it will not be necessary to chill the mushrooms in order to set the chocolate.) Other chocolates are liable to discolor after a day or two. However, if the meringues are to be served rather soon, I have had good results with Baker's Semisweet, Baker's German's Sweet, and Hershey's Special Dark Chocolate.*

Victorias

These shells are made of classic French pastry dough called Pâte Brisée, which means "broken pastry." When you follow the directions for "pushing off" or "breaking off" the dough, you will understand its name. It is a joy—no problem to make and delicious. It may be refrigerated for several days, or frozen. It may also be baked in any size form and used with any filling.

When I discovered these chocolate tartlets at Angelina's (previously Rumpelmayer's) on the Rue de Rivoli in Paris, I fell madly in love with them. I tried desperately to get the recipe but it was impossible. The recipe was a secret and was not to be had. After returning home, I wrote to Angelina's requesting that they mail some Victorias to me. They answered saying that Victorias should be eaten while still fresh, and therefore they were enclosing the recipe so that I could make them myself and have them whenever I wanted them. I think there's a lesson somewhere in this but I don't know what it is.

PASTRY SHELLS

2½ cups sifted all-purpose flour
½ teaspoon salt
½ cup sugar
5 ounces (1¼ sticks) butter,
    cut in ½-inch pieces
1 egg plus 2 egg yolks

Place the flour on a large board, marble, or other smooth work surface. Make a large well in the center and add all the remaining ingredients. With your right-hand fingertips, work the center ingredients together. Gradually incorporate the flour, using a dough scraper or a wide spatula in your left hand to help move it in toward the center. When all the flour has been absorbed, knead briefly until the dough holds together and then finish by "breaking" the pastry as follows.

Form it into a ball. Start at the further end of the dough and, using the heel of your hand, push off small pieces (about 2 tablespoons), pushing it against the work surface and away from you. Continue until all the dough has been pushed off. Re-form the dough and push it or "break" it off again. Re-form the dough.

Adjust rack one-third up from bottom of oven. Preheat oven to 400 degrees.

Work with half of the dough at a time. On a floured pastry cloth, with a floured rolling pin, roll evenly to ⅛-inch thickness. Reverse the dough occasionally to keep both sides lightly floured. With a 4-inch round cookie cutter cut 18 rounds. Scraps of dough may be reserved and then rerolled together. (You will have a bit more dough than you need—extra shells may be frozen before or after baking, or extra dough may be frozen unrolled.)

As the pastry circles are cut, transfer them with a metal spatula and fit them into tartlet pans. (See Note 1; if you don't have enough tartlet pans to use the 18 rounds all at once, place the extras on wax paper and cover them with wax paper or plastic wrap until you are ready for them.) Do not stretch the dough. Press it gently into place. Place the lined pans on a jelly-roll pan or cookie sheet and freeze or refrigerate until firm.

Tear aluminum foil (against a ruler or table edge) into 4-inch squares. Line each frozen or refrigerated shell with foil, pressing it firmly against the bottom and sides. Fill with small, dried beans or uncooked rice, to keep the pastry from puffing up. Replace on pan or cookie sheet and bake 10 minutes until pastry is set. Then remove from oven and lift off the foil and beans or rice by carefully lifting opposite corners of the foil. (See Note 2.) Return to the oven to continue baking for 6 to 9 minutes until bottoms begin to color slightly and edges are golden.

As shells are baked, remove the pans from the oven individually with a wide metal spatula. With your fingertips, carefully remove the shells from the pans to cool on a rack. When cool, transfer to trays that will fit in the refrigerator. Prepare filling.

CHOCOLATE FILLING

8 ounces Maillard's Eagle Sweet Chocolate,
    broken into pieces (See Note 3.)
½ cup sugar
2 cups heavy cream

In the top of a large double boiler over hot water on moderate heat, melt the chocolate. Stir in the sugar. Beating with a small wire whisk, very gradually add the cream.

Cook uncovered over moderate heat for 15 minutes, scraping sides and bottom occasionally with a rubber spatula. Remove from heat and place top of double boiler in ice water. Stir continuously and gently with a rubber spatula, scraping the sides and bottom in order not to let the chocolate start to set. Test the temperature frequently on the inside of your wrist. As soon as it is cold, pour it into a pitcher.

Pour into pastry shells, pouring carefully just to the tops of the shells. They should be as full as possible, but be very careful not to let any run over in spots where the shells are lower. Carefully transfer to refrigerator. Refrigerate at least 5 to 6 hours, or overnight, until firm.

Victorias may be served very simply as they are at Angelina's, with just a light sprinkling of chopped green pistachio nuts right in the center, put on when the chocolate is partially set. Or they may be very elaborate, with whipped cream swirled on through a pastry bag and a star tube and then topped with candied roses or violet petals, or coarsely grated chocolate.

Serve very cold, directly from refrigerator, on individual dessert plates.

NOTES: 1. *You will need individual tartlet pans 3½ inches in diameter and ½ inch in depth, and a 4-inch round cookie cutter. Both are available at specialty kitchen equipment stores, including the Bridge Company, 212 E. 52nd Street, New York, New York 10022. The pans should be plain—not fluted.*

2. *Beans or rice should be stored in the freezer to be reused for the same purpose.*

3. *Other chocolate may be used—sweet, semisweet, or bittersweet.*

4. *Victorias may be frozen, but if the wrapping touches the chocolate filling it leaves a mark. It is best to freeze them on a tray that is deep enough so that they can be covered without having the covering touch the filling. Thaw in the refrigerator.*

French Almond Macaroon Crescents

12 LARGE
CRESCENTS

½ teaspoon vanilla extract
1 tablespoon strained apricot preserves
5 ounces (1 cup) almonds,
blanched and finely ground
(See pages 10–12.
For this recipe they do not have
to be strained.)
1½ cups confectioners sugar
1 egg white, extra-large
1 egg
8–10 ounces (2–2½ cups) thinly sliced
blanched almonds

Adjust rack to center of oven. Preheat oven to 350 degrees. Cut baking pan liner paper or aluminum foil to fit cookie sheets.

In a small cup stir the vanilla into the preserves. In the small bowl of an electric mixer, beat at lowest speed the ground almonds, sugar, egg white, and preserves, scraping the bowl with a rubber spatula until thoroughly mixed. The mixture will be very thick.

On a large piece of wax paper or aluminum foil, divide the dough into 12 even mounds. Lightly flour your hands and roll the mounds into cylinders about 6 inches long, with slightly tapered ends.

Beat the egg lightly just to mix and place it in a shallow, flat-bottomed dish. Place the sliced almonds on a large piece of wax paper or aluminum foil.

Roll the crescents, one at a time, first in the egg to coat thoroughly, and then in the sliced almonds, pressing on as many almonds as possible. Place on baking pan liner paper or aluminum foil 2 inches apart, curving the ends of each to form crescent shapes. Any remaining sliced almonds and egg may be mixed together and placed on top of the crescents.

Slide a cookie sheet under the paper or foil and place that on another cookie sheet to protect the bottoms from burning.

Bake one sheet at a time for 22 to 25 minutes or until golden brown. If necessary, reverse the position of the cookie sheet during baking to insure even browning.

If crescents have been baked on baking pan liner paper, they may be removed immediately with a wide metal spatula to cool on a rack. However, if you have used foil, remove the foil from the cookie sheet and allow the crescents to cool completely on the foil. Then, gently peel the foil away.

Irish Almond Cakes

8 PORTIONS
(16 LITTLE CAKES)

PASTRY

1½ cups sifted all-purpose flour
½ teaspoon double-acting baking powder
Generous pinch of salt
3 ounces (¾ stick) butter
¼ cup plus 1 tablespoon superfine sugar
1 egg

Sift together flour, baking powder, and salt into a bowl. With a pastry blender cut in the butter until the mixture resembles coarse crumbs. Stir in the sugar. Beat the egg lightly just to mix and add it to the mixture. Stir together a bit and then turn out onto a board or smooth surface. Squeeze the dough between your hands to work it together, and then knead it until it is smooth and the board is clean. Form into a roll about 8 inches long. Wrap airtight. Set aside at room temperature.

ALMOND PASTE

2½ ounces (½ cup) blanched almonds,
    finely ground (See pages 10–12.
    For this recipe they do not have
    to be strained.)
2 tablespoons superfine sugar
3 tablespoons confectioners sugar
1 egg
⅛ teaspoon almond extract
2 drops green food coloring

In a small bowl, with a rubber spatula, mix the ground almonds with both sugars, pressing against the sides and bottom of the bowl to mix the ingredients thoroughly. With a fork or small wire whisk, beat the egg lightly, just to mix. Reserve half of it (about 2 tablespoonfuls) to use later. To the remaining half, mix in the almond extract and food coloring. Add to the ground almond mixture and, still using the rubber spatula, work the egg mixture in to form a stiff, light green almond paste.

Using two teaspoons, one for picking up the almond paste and one for pushing it off, divide into 16 even mounds on a piece of wax paper.

Adjust the rack to the center of the oven. Preheat oven to 400 degrees. Cut aluminum foil to fit cookie sheets.

TOPPING

Granulated sugar
Reserved ½ egg
1¾ ounces (½ cup) finely sliced
    blanched almonds, coarsely broken
Confectioners sugar

Place some granulated sugar on a piece of wax paper. Roll each mound of almond paste in the sugar and then roll between the palms of your hands into a small ball. Set aside.

Cut the reserved pastry in half the long way and then across into eighths, forming 16 even pieces. Working with one piece at a time, flatten it quite thin between your hands, pressing with your fingers against the pastry in the palm of your other hand.

Enclose a ball of the almond paste in the flattened pastry. Bring up the edges of the pastry and pinch to seal. The almond paste should be completely enclosed. Roll into a smooth ball. Place 1½ to 2 inches apart on prepared aluminum foil.

Brush the tops and sides of the cakes with the reserved half egg. Sprinkle generously with the broken, sliced almonds.

Slide two or three cookie sheets under the paper to protect the bottoms of the cakes from burning. Bake 20 minutes or until pastry is lightly browned. With a metal spatula, transfer to a rack to cool.

Cover tops generously with confectioners sugar through a fine strainer.

NOTE: *These are finger food and should be eaten like cookies, not with a fork.*

Capri Pastries

Dramatic, extravagant.

ALMOND SPONGE ROLL

8 TO 10
PORTIONS

7 eggs, separated

¼ cup plus 2 tablespoons sugar

½ teaspoon vanilla extract

¼ teaspoon almond extract

¼ teaspoon salt

4 ounces (generous ¾ cup) almonds,
blanched and finely ground
(See pages 10–12.)

Adjust rack one-third up from bottom of oven. Preheat oven to 350 degrees. Butter a 10½ × 15½ × 1-inch jelly-roll pan. Line bottom and sides with one long piece of wax paper. Butter and flour the paper.

In small bowl of electric mixer beat egg yolks at high speed for 3 minutes until light. Reduce the speed while gradually adding ¼ cup of the sugar (reserving remaining 2 tablespoons) and the vanilla and almond extracts. Increase speed to high again and beat for an additional 5 minutes until very thick. Remove from mixer. (If you do not have an extra set of beaters for your mixer, wash and dry them thoroughly.)

In large bowl of electric mixer beat egg whites with salt until they hold a very soft shape. While beating, gradually add reserved 2 tablespoons sugar and continue to beat at high speed until whites hold a point and are stiff but not dry.

Fold one-third to one-half of the whites into the yolks. Then add the yolks and the almonds to the remaining whites and fold all together. Do not handle any more than necessary. Turn into prepared pan. Handling lightly, spread level with a spatula or the back of a spoon. Bake 40 minutes or until top springs back when lightly touched and cake begins to come away from sides of pan.

While cake is baking, wet and firmly wring out a kitchen towel (preferably smooth cotton, flour sacking, or linen). Spread it out smoothly on a flat surface.

Remove cake from oven. If it sticks to the sides of the pan, quickly cut around the edges with a small, sharp knife. Invert immediately onto the damp towel. Work quickly and carefully. Remove pan, peel off wax paper, and roll, rolling from a long side and rolling the cake and towel together. Be firm, but don't squash the cake. Place on rack to cool. Meanwhile, prepare the following Rum Syrup and Rum-Chocolate Filling:

RUM SYRUP

2 tablespoons sugar
2 tablespoons boiling water
3 tablespoons dark rum

In a small pan stir the sugar into the boiling water. Boil for ½ minute. Remove from heat. Cool slightly and stir in the rum. Set aside.

RUM-CHOCOLATE FILLING

4 ounces (4 squares) semisweet chocolate
2 ounces (2 squares) unsweetened chocolate
5 ounces (1¼ stick) butter
⅔ cup confectioners sugar
4 egg yolks
3 tablespoons dark rum

In the top of a small double boiler over hot water on moderate heat melt both chocolates. Remove top of double boiler from heat and set aside to cool.

In small bowl of electric mixer cream the butter. Add sugar and continue to beat until creamy. Add the yolks individually and beat well. Beat in rum and cooled chocolate. Continue to beat until light in color and thick.

Place in freezer or refrigerator, or place bowl into a larger bowl of ice and water. Stir occasionally until partially thickened and almost set. Beat again until fluffy.

Unroll cake. Brush with Rum Syrup and cover with filling. Close the two long sides over the filling—there is so much filling that they will just meet. Transfer to a chocolate-roll board or platter, seam side down. Refrigerate.

You have now made a Rum-Chocolate Almond Roll. It may be served as is, with confectioners sugar strained over the top. However, to make these very fancy individual pastries, continue with the following directions.

When filling is firm, using a ruler and toothpicks, mark the cake into 8 to 10 slices. Cut carefully. Turn each slice cut side up on any tray or board—they will be transferred to a serving platter later. Prepare following Whipped Cream Topping:

WHIPPED CREAM TOPPING

1 teaspoon unflavored gelatin
2 tablespoons cold water
2 cups heavy cream
½ cup confectioners sugar
2 teaspoons vanilla extract

Sprinkle the gelatin over the cold water in a small heatproof cup. Let stand for a few minutes and then place cup in a small pan of hot water on moderate heat until gelatin is dissolved. Remove from heat.

Chill the small bowl and the beaters of an electric mixer. In the chilled bowl, mix all but 1 to 2 large spoonfuls of the cream with the confectioners sugar and vanilla, and beat until cream barely begins to thicken. Stir the reserved 1 to 2 spoonfuls of cream into the dissolved gelatin and beat into the cream. Beat until mixture holds a shape.

Fit a large pastry bag with a large star tube. Place whipped cream in bag and form a large, high, pointed rosette on each slice of cake. The rosette should be wide enough to cover the chocolate filling completely and part of the cake roll; there should be only a small border of cake showing on the sides of the whipped cream.

Refrigerate for an hour or more until completely set.

Prepare following Chocolate Glaze:

CHOCOLATE GLAZE

1 teaspoon instant coffee
½ cup boiling water
1 tablespoon vegetable shortening
⅓ cup sugar
1 ounce (1 square) unsweetened chocolate
4½ ounces (4½ squares) semisweet chocolate

In a small saucepan on high heat, stir the coffee into the boiling water. Add vegetable shortening and sugar and stir to dissolve. Reduce heat to moderate. Add both chocolates. Stir occasionally until melted. Transfer to small bowl of electric mixer and stir or beat occasionally until cooled to room temperature. When cool, beat for 2 to 3 minutes until smooth and barely thickened.

Place cake slices on a rack over wax paper.

Transfer the chocolate glaze to a small pitcher and pour it over each slice, pouring unevenly so that a bit of the whipped cream shows through in places and the chocolate runs down unevenly in just a few places on the sides of the cake.

As soon as chocolate has set enough, use a wide metal spatula to transfer pastries to a serving tray and refrigerate.

Chocolate Cupcakes

24 CUPCAKES

2 cups sifted all-purpose flour
1 teaspoon baking soda
¼ teaspoon salt
½ cup powdered, unsweetened cocoa
    (preferably Dutch process)
5⅓ ounces (⅔ cup) butter
1 teaspoon vanilla extract
1½ cups sugar
3 eggs
1 cup milk

Adjust two racks to divide oven in thirds. Preheat oven to 350 degrees. Butter two pans of cupcake forms, each pan with twelve forms and each form measuring about 2¾ inches in diameter. Sift a bit of flour over them and shake out the excess. Or line twenty-four forms with cupcake liner papers. (See Note 2.) Set aside.

Sift together flour, baking soda, salt, and cocoa. Set aside. In large bowl of electric mixer cream the butter. Beat in the vanilla and sugar. Add eggs one at a time, beating until smooth after each and scraping the bowl with a rubber spatula as necessary to keep mixture smooth. On lowest speed alternately add sifted dry ingredients in three additions and milk in two additions. Continue to scrape the bowl with the rubber spatula and beat only until smooth. Do not overbeat.

Spoon the batter into the prepared pans, filling the cups only two-thirds to three-quarters full. There is no need to smooth the tops—the batter will level itself.

Bake for 25 minutes or until tops spring back when lightly touched. Do not overbake. Cool in the pans for 2 to 3 minutes before removing to a rack to finish cooling. Ice with the following chocolate cupcake icing:

CHOCOLATE CUPCAKE ICING

6 ounces (6 squares) semisweet chocolate
⅓ cup heavy cream
1 tablespoon sugar
1½ tablespoons butter

Place all the ingredients into a small, heavy saucepan over moderate heat. Cook, stirring occasionally, until the chocolate is almost melted. Remove from heat. Continue to stir until the chocolate is completely melted and the mixture is smooth. Transfer to a very small, shallow bowl. Let stand, stirring occasionally, until icing reaches room temperature.

Hold cupcakes upside down and dip the tops into the icing. Twirl slightly and then hold upside down for a few seconds for excess to drip off. After dipping them all, dip each one a second time. If there is still some icing left, the cakes may be dipped a third time. When the icing gets low, transfer it to a custard cup, but don't try to use up the last bit—the cakes won't look as smooth.

NOTES: 1. *When baking cupcakes, if you have only one pan with twelve cups, reserve the remaining batter and bake additional cakes after the first panful. If baking only one pan at a time, bake in the center of the oven.*

2. *Lining the pans with papers is a convenience and a timesaver. The cakes take on a better shape and rise higher, and they stay fresh longer. If you do use the papers, and if the cakes are being served at the table, the papers should be removed before serving.*

3. *To freeze frosted cupcakes, let them stand until the icing is no longer sticky. Place them on a pan or tray in the freezer until frozen firm. Then place over them a large piece of plastic wrap, turning it down securely on the sides and under the bottom. Return to freezer. To thaw, remove from freezer but do not remove plastic wrap until cupcakes have thawed.*

Ethiopian Truffles

Chocolate truffles wrapped in a light, tender pastry.

PASTRY

½ pound (1 cup) butter
½ teaspoon vanilla extract
½ cup confectioners sugar
2 cups sifted all-purpose flour

In large bowl of electric mixer cream the butter. Add vanilla and sugar and mix until smooth. On low speed add the flour, scraping the bowl with a rubber spatula and beating until the mixture holds together.

Transfer to a piece of wax paper. Flatten slightly and shape into an oblong. Wrap airtight and refrigerate briefly while preparing the following:

BLACK TRUFFLES

8 ounces (1⅔ cups) almonds, blanched or not
8 ounces sweet chocolate
    (See page 4.)
2 egg whites, jumbo or extra-large

The almonds and chocolate must both be finely ground—they may be ground in a blender or a nut grinder. But for this recipe they need not be strained. (The chocolate should be coarsely cut before being ground in a blender.) Mix them together in a bowl and then mix in the unbeaten egg whites. Knead briefly in the bowl until the mixture holds together.

Divide into 40 pieces, using 1 tablespoonful for each, and placing them on wax paper or aluminum foil. Now roll each piece between your hands to form a round ball and replace on the wax paper or aluminum foil.

Adjust rack one-third down from top of oven. Preheat oven to 375 degrees.

Remove the pastry from the refrigerator; it should *not* be chilled until hard. Cut into 40 pieces. Flatten a piece in the palm of your hand and wrap it around a truffle to cover completely. Roll into a ball between your palms. (Dust your hands with confectioners sugar if the dough sticks.) Place on an ungreased cookie sheet. Continue to shape remainder, placing them 1 inch apart.

Bake for 18 to 20 minutes until very lightly colored, reversing position of cookie sheet if necessary during baking to insure even browning. Let cool on sheet for a minute or two and then, with a wide metal spatula, transfer to a rack to cool.

OPTIONAL: *Cooled cookies may be topped with a bit of confectioners sugar, sprinkled on through a fine strainer.*

French Sandwich Cookies with Chocolate Filling

12 TO 14 LARGE
SANDWICH
COOKIES

7 ounces (1¾ sticks) butter
¼ teaspoon salt
1 teaspoon vanilla extract
⅓ cup sugar
3 egg yolks
2 cups sifted all-purpose flour
Confectioners sugar for
    dusting cookies

In large bowl of electric mixer cream the butter. Add the salt, vanilla, and sugar, beating well. Add the egg yolks and beat until smooth. Gradually, on lowest speed, add the flour, scraping the bowl as necessary with a rubber spatula and beating until the mixture holds together. Remove from mixer. Wrap airtight and refrigerate for about half an hour.

Adjust rack to the center of the oven. Preheat oven to 350 degrees. Cut aluminum foil to fit cookie sheets.

Work with half of the dough at a time. On a lightly floured pastry cloth, with a floured rolling pin, roll the dough ⅛ to ¼ inch thick. Cut with a floured 2¾-inch round cookie cutter, and place cookies 1 inch apart on the aluminum foil. Save the scraps and reroll them all together in order not to incorporate any more flour than necessary.

Slide a cookie sheet under the foil and bake 15 to 17 minutes until lightly browned, reversing position of cookie sheet during baking to insure even browning. Transfer with a wide metal spatula to racks to cool. Prepare following filling:

CHOCOLATE GANACHE FILLING

*6 ounces bittersweet or semisweet chocolate
(I like Lindt Excellence or Tobler
Tradition.)
2 ounces (¼ cup) butter
¼ cup plus 1 tablespoon heavy cream*

In top of a small double boiler over hot water on moderate heat, melt the chocolate and butter. When partially melted, stir with a small wire whisk until completely melted. Remove top of double boiler from heat. Gradually add the cream, stirring with the whisk. Let stand at room temperature, stirring occasionally, for half an hour or longer until barely thickened. Do not let it begin to harden.

Place half the cookies on a large piece of wax paper, upside down. Divide the filling among the inverted cookies, placing about a tablespoonful on each. Quickly cover with the remaining cookies, right sides up, and, very gently, press down to spread the filling to the edges.

Let stand at room temperature or chill briefly until filling is set.

Arrange the sandwiched cookies in straight rows on wax paper. Place a long strip of wax paper, ½ inch wide, on each row covering the center strip of each cookie. Sprinkle generously with confectioners sugar through a fine strainer. Remove wax paper carefully, leaving an unsugared strip through the center of each cookie.

Fried Cookies and Pastries

SQUID

FRENCH-FRIED WAFERS

CHURROS

BEIGNETS SOUFFLES

Squid

4 SQUID,
SERVE 1
TO A PERSON

To make these exotic, crisp, fried cookies, it will be necessary to have an empty tin can, measuring about 4 × 4 inches (i.e., a 1-pound Crisco can or one the same approximate size). Remove both the top and the bottom of the can.

Oil or shortening for deep frying
⅓ cup sifted all-purpose flour
1 cup sifted cake flour
Pinch of salt
¼ teaspoon double-acting baking powder
1 egg, jumbo or extra-large
3 tablespoons granulated sugar
1 tablespoon melted butter
1 tablespoon dark rum
Confectioners sugar for dusting

Put the oil or shortening at least 3 inches deep in a deep, narrow saucepan. Insert a frying thermometer. Slowly bring it to 370 degrees while preparing the dough.

Sift together the all-purpose flour, cake flour, salt, and baking powder and set aside. In the small bowl of an electric mixer, beat egg at high speed until it is light lemon-colored. Gradually add sugar and continue to beat for about 5 minutes until mixture flows very slowly when beaters are lifted. On low speed, add the butter, rum, and then the sifted dry ingredients, scraping the bowl with a rubber spatula and beating only until mixture is smooth.

Turn out onto a well-floured board. Turn the dough to coat with flour. Cut into four pieces, turning each piece to flour all sides.

With a floured rolling pin, roll one piece of the dough, turning it over occasionally to keep it from sticking. Roll into any shape, a scant ⅛ inch thick. With a pastry wheel or a small sharp knife, starting ½ inch from the edge, cut slits ½ inch apart—do not cut through outer edge; leave a ½-inch border.

With tongs, place the empty can upright in the oil or shortening, which should be kept at a temperature of 370 degrees. Gather the cut pastry together loosely and casually place it in the can, letting it fold over on itself. Fry for 1 minute until the squid holds its shape and is golden brown on the bottom. With tongs, remove the can. With two slotted metal spoons or flat wire whisks, turn the pastry over and fry for another

½ minute or until evenly and lightly colored. Remove from saucepan to drain and cool on absorbent paper.

Repeat with three remaining pieces of dough. Strain confectioners sugar generously over the tops.

NOTE: *Squid should be served on individual plates. They are eaten with the fingers, by breaking off the crisp tentacles of pastry.*

French-Fried Wafers

Dramatic, gargantuan, paper-thin, and as crisp as potato chips. To fry these pastries it will be necessary to have a very wide, shallow saucepan or frying pan, 11 to 12 inches wide and 2½ to 3 inches deep. A large electric frying pan, although not quite this deep, may be used.

16 LARGE
WAFERS

4 cups sifted all-purpose flour
1 teaspoon double-acting baking powder
1 teaspoon salt
½ teaspoon mace
2 tablespoons granulated sugar
2 eggs, jumbo or extra-large
¾ cup milk
2 ounces (¼ cup) melted butter
Large quantity of oil or shortening
    for deep frying
Confectioners sugar

Sift together flour, baking powder, salt, mace, and sugar into large bowl of electric mixer. In a small bowl, beat the eggs. Add milk and butter and beat to mix. On low speed gradually add the egg mixture to the sifted dry ingredients, scraping the bowl with a rubber spatula. The mixture will be too stiff to blend it all in the bowl. Turn it out onto a lightly floured board and knead just until it is smooth.

With your hands, roll it into an even roll 2 to 3 inches thick. Cut into 8 even slices. Cut each slice in half across the diameter. Place the 16 pieces on a tray, cover airtight with plastic wrap, and let stand at room temperature for about 30 minutes, or longer, if you wish. Standing makes the dough easier to roll and helps it hold its shape better.

Meanwhile, heat the oil or shortening in a wide frying pan or saucepan until it reaches 370 degrees. Adjust heat to maintain that temperature.

On a lightly floured pastry cloth, with a lightly floured rolling pin, roll one piece of the dough until it is paper-thin, turning it over frequently. Don't worry about what shape the edges take. When it is evenly rolled to 10 inches or more in diameter, lift it gently and carefully lower it into the hot oil. (If you wish to roll out several at a time you may, but stack with wax paper between them.)

With two flat wire whisks or two slotted metal spatulas, immediately straighten any edges that have folded over. Fry for about 1½ minutes until the bottom is golden. Using the two whisks or spatulas, turn to brown the other side, pressing down lightly on any white spots, until it is all evenly browned and there are no white spots remaining. With the two whisks or spatulas, raise it vertically over the saucepan for a few seconds to drain.

Place on crumpled paper toweling to continue to drain and to cool. Repeat with remaining pieces of dough. Strain confectioners sugar generously over the tops.

Pile them on a very large tray. Serve individually on dinner plates.

NOTE: *This recipe may easily be divided in half. The milk measurement for half the recipe is ¼ cup plus 2 tablespoons.*

Churros

These Cuban doughnuts are similar to French crullers.

6 LARGE
CHURROS

Oil or shortening for deep frying

⅔ cup water

1½ tablespoons granulated sugar

⅛ teaspoon salt

2 ounces (¼ cup) butter, cut in small pieces

1 cup minus 2 tablespoons
    sifted all-purpose flour

2 eggs (For this recipe the eggs must be
    graded extra-large or jumbo.)

1 tablespoon dark rum

⅛ teaspoon mace

Confectioners sugar

Place oil or shortening 1½ to 2 inches deep in a wide, shallow saucepan, a wide, deep frying pan, or an electric frying pan. Slowly bring it to a temperature of 370 degrees while preparing batter.

Place water, sugar, salt, and butter in a 1½- to 2-quart heavy saucepan over high heat. Stir with a wooden spatula until butter is melted and mixture boils rapidly. Remove from heat and immediately add flour all at once. Stir vigorously with wooden spatula until mixture is smooth and comes away from sides of pan to form a ball.

Transfer to small bowl of electric mixer and beat in eggs, one at a time. Add rum and mace and beat at high speed for 1 minute until smooth and shiny. Transfer to a large pastry bag fitted with a large star tube (about ¾-inch opening).

Tear or cut six squares of wax paper about 6 inches in diameter. Lightly brush them with salad oil.

Press the Churros onto the oiled paper squares in thick rings about 3½ to 4 inches in diameter, cutting them away from the star tube with a small knife.

Holding the edges of the paper with both hands, invert the Churros, only one or two at a time, over the hot oil or shortening. They will slide easily off the paper. Fry until richly browned on one side. Turn with flat wire whisk or slotted metal spoon to brown the other side. Do not undercook.

Drain on absorbent paper. Cool. Strain confectioners sugar generously over the tops. These are at their best when very fresh.

NOTE: *During frying maintain the temperature at 370 degrees and fry Churros about 3 minutes on each side.*

Beignets Soufflés

24 BEIGNETS

Oil or shortening for deep frying
Pâte à Choux, see Cream Puffs (page 256)
Confectioners sugar

In a wide, shallow saucepan, heat oil or shortening about 2 inches deep for deep frying. The fat should be maintained at a temperature of 370 degrees. Meanwhile, prepare Pâte à Choux as in Cream Puff recipe.

Dip two teaspoons into the preheated oil or shortening. On one, scoop up a well-rounded teaspoonful of the paste, and with the other push it off into the oil. Continue forming more and putting them into the oil, but do not crowd them. They need room to swim around in the oil, and adding too many at once lowers the temperature. Continue to dip the spoons in the oil occasionally to keep the paste from sticking to them.

As the beignets fry, they will turn over by themselves, but they might need a nudge or a bit of help occasionally. (There are very few cooking experiences more fun than watching the Beignets roll around from one side to another as they puff up in size.) Fry for about 10 minutes until they are an even golden brown with no light spots left. Do not remove from the oil too soon or they will collapse.

Remove with a slotted spoon or a flat wire whisk. Drain on absorbent paper. Generously sprinkle through a strainer on all sides with confectioners sugar.

Beignets may be served immediately while still warm or after standing several hours at room temperature. Pile them on a platter in a pyramid. Serve as is, to be eaten with the fingers, or on dessert plates with cold Custard Sauce (page 389) or warm Apricot Sauce (page 391).

NOTE: *If you have vanilla sugar (see page 10), use it for sprinkling over the beignets.*

Crêpes, Blintzes, Popovers, Cream Puffs, Puff Pastry, and Chocolate Soufflé

CREPES

ENGLISH CREPES *(London Style)*
ENGLISH CREPES *(Buckingham Palace)*
CREPES SUZETTE

SAIDIE HEATTER'S BLINTZES

SAIDIE HEATTER'S POPOVERS

CREAM PUFFS

PROFITEROLES
see Beignets Soufflés (page 245)

COUNTERFEIT PUFF PASTE

PETITS PALMIERS
ALMOND TWISTS
SHOE SOLES

CHOCOLATE SOUFFLE

Blintzes, cream puffs, and popovers are all variations of what is essentially the same recipe, or at least the same ingredients. Crêpes generally are another variation, but mine are a little different. They are close—but mine don't contain butter.

Crêpes

24 TO 30
5-INCH
CRÊPES

3 eggs
1 cup milk
½ cup sifted all-purpose flour

Beat the eggs lightly just to mix. Gradually add the milk and mix together. Place the flour in a small bowl. With an electric mixer or an egg beater, gradually mix the egg-milk mixture into the flour, beating only until smooth. Cover and refrigerate for at least 2 hours (or overnight if you wish).

A standard crêpe pan is made of black iron, and has widely flared, shallow sides. An average small size will have a 5-inch bottom. A new pan should be seasoned before using. Fill it with vegetable oil; over very low heat, heat it slowly until very hot. Remove from heat and let stand until the oil is cold. Then pour out the oil and wipe the pan with paper towels. It should be used only for making crêpes and it should *never be washed*. Just wipe it with oil and dry it with paper towels after every use. In place of a crêpe pan, use a small Teflon frying pan, or any other small, heavy frying pan with about a 5-inch base. With a crêpe pan, it will probably only be necessary to butter the pan once, before making the first crêpe. With other pans, butter as necessary. If you have clarified butter, use it. If not, use regular unsalted butter. Crêpe pans are generally available in specialty kitchen equipment shops that carry French utensils.

Heat the pan over moderately high heat. Spread very lightly with butter, spreading it with crumpled wax paper. Stir the batter briefly and continue to stir occasionally as the heavy part settles to the bottom. For a 5-inch pan, turn 1 generous tablespoon of batter into the hot pan and quickly tilt and rotate the pan in all directions to spread the batter thinly and evenly. (I use a kitchen tablespoon, which holds a little more than a measured tablespoon.) Continue tilting and rotating the pan until the batter stops running.

If the temperature is correct, it should take about ½ minute for the bottom to brown lightly and for the top to dry. With a small metal spatula, loosen the edges and then, with your fingers, turn the crêpe over. (See Note 1.) Cook for about 15 seconds more. The other side should not brown—it should only dry and have a few brown spots. (Do not be disappointed if the first few crêpes do not come out perfectly; they seldom do. But don't be discouraged, they always behave better as you go along.)

Remove the finished crêpe by inverting the pan and letting the crêpe fall out upside down on a plate. If necessary, straighten the crêpe with your fingers.

Continue making crêpes, stirring the batter occasionally, and stacking them on top of each other.

Crêpes may be made ahead of time, and may be reserved piled on top of each other. They should be wrapped airtight for the refrigerator or freezer. If you freeze them and think you might want to use a few at a time, pack with plastic wrap between them in order to be able to remove them individually.

NOTES: *1. If you use an aluminum or Teflon pan, the sides will be deeper than those of a crêpe pan and it might be difficult to turn the crêpes with your fingers. If you have a problem, because of either the sides or the heat, use a rubber spatula to help turn. There will be less chance of tearing them than with a metal spatula.*

2. To warm crêpes: Remove plastic wrap if you used it. Stack crêpes on top of each other. Wrap airtight in aluminum foil. Place in a moderate oven for 10 to 15 minutes until warm.

3. Serve 3 to 4 crêpes to a portion.

English Crêpes, London Style

Warm the crêpes and fold them in quarters, browned side out. Place them overlapping on warm dessert plates. Through a fine strainer, coat generously with confectioners sugar. Serve with lemon wedges and warm Apricot Sauce (see page 391).

English Crêpes, Buckingham Palace

Spread the browned side of the crêpes with slightly warmed Apricot Sauce (see page 391). Roll them loosely. Place them seam down in a lightly buttered, shallow, ovenproof serving dish. Sprinkle generously with granulated sugar. Place in a moderate oven for 5 to 10 minutes to warm—do not leave them in the oven longer than necessary or the edges will become dry. In a small, heatproof container, warm about ¼ to ⅓ cup Grand Marnier. At the table, pour the warm Grand Marnier over the warm crêpes and touch with a match to flambé. The Grand Marnier and the crêpes must both be warm in order to flame. After the flame dies down, serve with generous lemon wedges on warm plates.

Crêpes Suzette

6 to 8
PORTIONS

Crêpes
Suzette Sauce (See page 394.)
¼–⅓ cup brandy or Cognac

In a large chafing dish, at the table (or in a large shallow frying pan, in the kitchen) heat the sauce. Fold the crêpes in quarters and place them in the sauce to warm, gently turning them as necessary.

Immediately before serving, warm the brandy or Cognac in a small heatproof container. Pour it over the crêpes and quickly and carefully touch with a match to flambé. Spoon the flaming sauce over the crêpes. Serve when flame has died down.

Serve on warm plates, serving 3 or 4 crêpes to a portion and topping each with some of the julienne of orange rind and some of the sauce.

NOTE: *The sauce, crêpes, and brandy or Cognac must all be hot in order to flambé. But watch the brandy or Cognac—do not overheat or it will quickly boil away.*

Saidie Heatter's Blintzes

5 OR 6 PORTIONS

PANCAKES

3 eggs
1½ cups skimmed milk
1 cup minus 2 tablespoons
  sifted all-purpose flour
¼ teaspoon salt
3 tablespoons melted butter

In a small bowl, beat the eggs lightly just to mix. Gradually add the milk and mix together. Place the flour and salt in small bowl of electric mixer. On low speed, gradually add the egg-milk mixture, scraping the bowl with a rubber spatula, and beating only until smooth. Beat in the melted butter. Cover and refrigerate for 2 hours or more. (This may be refrigerated overnight if you wish.)

Cook the pancakes in a frying pan with about a 6-inch base. Use a large mixing spoon, one that holds a generous 2 tablespoonfuls, or one of the scoops that come in some cans of coffee, to measure the batter.

Heat the pan over moderately high heat. With crumpled wax paper, spread unsalted or clarified butter generously on the bottom and sides of the pan. The heat should not be so high that the butter burns. The heavy part of the batter will settle in the bowl, so stir it occasionally and always spoon from the bottom. Place 1 large measure (2 generous tablespoonfuls) of batter in the hot, buttered pan. Quickly tilt and rotate the pan in all directions to spread the batter evenly. Continue tilting and rotating the pan until the batter stops running.

Cook until top is dry. Bottom of pancake might not have browned, or it might be very lightly browned. If the heat is correct, it should take about 45 seconds to cook each pancake. Fry it on one side only. When top is completely dry and pancake is set, either jerk the frying pan quickly back and forth to loosen the pancake and then jerk it to one side to slide it out onto a plate, or, if jerking the pan tears the pancake, release and remove it with a rubber or metal spatula instead. (If pancakes have holes in them, the filling will run out. See Note.) Continue with the remaining batter, sliding each pancake out on top of the others. Rebutter the pan before making each pancake. This batter makes about 20 6-inch pancakes.

FILLING

1 pound farmer cheese
3 tablespoons sugar

2 eggs
Finely grated rind of 1 large,
bright-colored orange

In large bowl of electric mixer, beat the cheese just to soften it. Add sugar and eggs. Scrape the bowl with a rubber spatula and beat for a minute or two. Remove from mixer and stir in orange rind. (Mixture will not be smooth.) Transfer to a small bowl for ease in handling.

Spread out several long pieces of wax paper. Gently, in order not to tear them, lift off the pancakes and place them browned side (underside) up on the paper.

Divide the filling evenly over the pancakes. If you have made 20 pancakes, you will have enough filling for a heaping teaspoonful on each. Place it in the center of the pancake. Fold the edge of the side nearest you over the filling and roll the pancake loosely. Loosely turn under both ends to make an oblong package with the seam on the bottom. Place prepared blintzes on a tray covered with wax paper. Cover airtight with plastic wrap. Refrigerate for at least a few hours. (May be refrigerated overnight, or may be frozen.)

FINAL FRYING

In a large, heavy frying pan, over moderately low heat, melt enough unsalted or clarified butter to coat the bottom generously. Do not fry too many blintzes at once or it will be hard to turn them. They are delicate; handle with care. Fry them, seam down, until bottoms are browned. Very carefully, with two metal or rubber spatulas, turn to brown the tops. They should be golden brown. (Two panfuls may be fried at one time if you watch them both and do not let them burn.) To keep the blintzes from sticking, shake the pan occasionally, or move them gently with a spatula. The heat must not be so high that the blintzes become too brown before they heat all the way through. But cooking them too slowly or too long will make the filling dry and heavy. At the correct temperature, the frying should take about 8 to 10 minutes.

Serve immediately on warm plates, 3 to a portion. (As a brunch or luncheon entrée, serve 4 to a portion.)

Serve with apricot preserves which have been stirred well to soften, and cold sour cream. It is best to pass the preserves and cream separately.

NOTE: *Small holes or tears in the pancakes may be patched. Cut the one with the worst holes into large pieces and use the pieces as patches. Just place a piece over a small hole or tear before filling the pancake.*

Saidie Heatter's Popovers

10 LARGE
POPOVERS,
OR 8 VERY LARGE

My mother was called the Popover Queen—she was also the Blintz Queen, the Blueberry Pie Queen, the Queen of the Barbecue, etc. My father bestowed a title on her at almost every meal. Her popovers were incredible. Here they are.

Popovers are not a dessert. However, if you are looking for something to serve with coffee between meals in place of coffee cake, these popovers are gorgeous.

Although the batter may be used immediately, it may also be kept overnight. If anything, it improves with standing. Therefore, you may prepare the entire recipe and then bake popovers one or more at a time. Or, if you prefer, you may divide the recipe and prepare only half.

Plan the timing so that the popovers will be served immediately after they come out of the oven.

They are baked in individual ovenproof china or pottery custard cups which are deep and narrow, not ovenproof glass cups which are wide and shallow and flare too much. The cups may be either the 4-ounce or 6-ounce size. Naturally, the popovers will be more dramatic if baked in 6-ounce cups. Six-ounce ovenproof custard cups may be hard to find. Try a restaurant supply store. In New York City they are available at the Bridge Company, 212 East 52nd Street.

> 2 cups sifted all-purpose flour
> 1 teaspoon salt
> 6 eggs, jumbo or extra-large
> 2 cups milk
> 3 ounces (6 tablespoons) butter, melted
>   and cooled

If you are going to bake the popovers immediately, adjust the oven rack one-third up from the bottom and preheat the oven to 375 degrees.

Butter the cups generously. For the full recipe use eight 6-ounce cups or ten 4-ounce cups. Arrange them on a jelly roll pan for ease in handling, spacing them as far apart as possible.

You may use an electric mixer, an egg beater, or a wire whisk. Whichever you use, beat as little as possible to blend the ingredients. (An electric mixer must be used at low speed.)

Place the flour and salt in a large bowl. Beat the eggs lightly only to mix. Mix in the milk and butter. Very gradually beat liquids into dry ingredients. Do not overbeat; the batter should not be foamy. If it is lumpy, strain it. If necessary, strain it again. Pour into a pitcher (or a covered jar if it is to be refrigerated). Pour into the prepared cups, filling them to about ½ inch from the tops.

Place in preheated oven. Bake 6-ounce cups for 1 hour; 4-ounce cups for 50 minutes. Do not open the oven door until the baking time is almost up. However, ovens vary, so check the popovers about 10 minutes before the time is up. They should bake until they are really well-browned. Unless they are dark enough they will be soggy and limp instead of crisp and crunchy. When done, without removing them from the oven, reach in and with a small, sharp knife quickly cut two or three slits in each popover to release steam. Continue to bake 5 minutes more.

Remove from oven and take the popovers out of the cups immediately. If necessary, use a small, sharp knife to release them from the cups.

Serve immediately in a napkin-lined basket, but do not cover with the napkin or they will steam and soften. Serve with butter or Honey Butter (see page 407) and, if you wish, jam, jelly, or marmalade, and cottage cheese.

NOTE: *If the batter has been refrigerated it will settle on standing and should be stirred gently until smooth before using.*

Cream Puffs

Bake on double cookie sheets in order to protect the bottoms from burning.

CREAM PUFF PASTRY
(*Pâte à Choux*)

¼ pound (½ cup) butter,
    at room temperature
1 cup boiling water
Generous pinch of salt
1 cup sifted all-purpose flour
4 eggs, large (not extra-large or jumbo)
Confectioners sugar

Adjust oven rack to center of oven. Preheat oven to 425 degrees. Cut aluminum foil to fit a 14 × 17-inch cookie sheet. (See Note.) Place the foil on double cookie sheets, one on top of the other. (A few drops of water on the cookie sheet will keep the foil in place.)

In a heavy 2- to 3-quart saucepan over high heat, stir the butter, boiling water, and salt with a wooden spatula. As you stir, also cut the butter into pieces. When the butter is melted and the mixture boils hard, remove it from the heat and immediately add the flour all at once, stirring vigorously until the mixture forms a ball and leaves the sides of the pan clean. If necessary, replace briefly over low heat.

Turn mixture into small bowl of electric mixer. On medium speed, beat in 1 egg at a time, beating only until incorporated before adding the next. After adding the final egg, beat for an additional 1 minute, scraping the bowl occasionally with a rubber spatula.

Drop on the aluminum foil by rounded tablespoonfuls into 10 mounds, shaping them high and placing them 2 to 3 inches apart. Try to avoid leaving sharp, uneven peaks. Peaks may be flattened with a wet fingertip.

Bake for 15 minutes. Reduce the oven temperature to 350 degrees and bake for an additional 35 minutes (total baking time 50 minutes). Do not open oven door during first half hour of baking. Five minutes before the baking time is up, without removing puffs from the oven, reach in and, with a small, sharp knife, cut two or three slits in the tops and sides of each puff in order to let the steam escape. Do not underbake puffs or they will collapse. It will not hurt to bake them longer—but do not let them burn. Remove from oven and cool on a rack.

(When completely cool, puffs may be frozen in a freezer bag for future use. To serve, thaw and then place on a cookie sheet in a 325-degree oven for about 5 minutes to regain crispness. Cool on a rack and then fill.)

Either immediately before serving, or 1 or 2 hours before, with a serrated knife cut the upper third off each puff. Remove any soft dough from the centers.

Prepare either plain whipped cream or Rum-Mocha Whipped Cream, using 2½ cups of heavy cream.

Plain whipped cream: To the unwhipped cream add ⅔ cup confectioners sugar, 2 teaspoons vanilla, and an optional few drops of almond extract. (In place of the vanilla and optional almond extract, you might use 3 tablespoons of Grand Marnier or rum.)

Rum-Mocha Whipped Cream: To the unwhipped cream add ⅔ cup confectioners sugar, 2 tablespoons instant coffee, 3 tablespoons unsweetened cocoa, and 2 tablespoons dark rum.

In a chilled bowl with chilled beaters, whip the cream until it holds a shape.

Spoon generously into the bottom halves of the puffs, mounding it very high. Place the top halves of the puffs on the cream, letting a bit of cream show on the sides.

Strain confectioners sugar generously over the tops. Place on a platter and refrigerate.

Serve with Old-Fashioned Walnut-Chocolate Sauce (see page 397), at room temperature. Serve with a knife and fork.

NOTE: *Puffs may be baked on a smaller cookie sheet in two separate batches, baking only one sheet at a time. Reserve the remaining batter covered, at room temperature.*

Profiteroles

8 PORTIONS
OF 3 PROFITEROLES
EACH

Adjust rack to center of oven and preheat oven to 400 degrees.

Follow recipe and directions for Cream Puffs, page 256, dropping the paste by the well-rounded teaspoonful about 2 inches apart to make 24 small puffs.

Bake 15 minutes. Reduce oven temperature to 350 degrees and bake 30 minutes longer (total baking time 45 minutes), cutting one or two small slits in each puff 5 minutes before the baking time is up.

When cool, with a serrated knife cut off upper third of each puff, remove soft dough from centers, fill generously with ice cream and replace top.

As soon as each one is filled, immediately place it in the freezer. When all are filled, wrap or package airtight.

To serve, pile on a platter in a pyramid and sprinkle with confectioners sugar.

Serve with Old-Fashioned Walnut-Chocolate Sauce (page 397), first pouring a bit over the pyramid and passing the rest separately.

NOTE: *If you wish, serve with Hot Fudge Sauce (page 399) in place of Old-Fashioned Walnut-Chocolate Sauce, but if so, do not pour any of it over the pyramid. The ice cream might harden the sauce and make serving difficult. Pass the sauce separately.*

Counterfeit Puff Paste

This incredibly delicious product has the crisp, flaky, buttery qualities of classic puff paste, but it is child's play to put it together. When used in the following recipes, it is almost indiscernible from that made by the classic method. Puff paste items are best when very fresh. If they are not to be served soon, freeze them.

PASTRY

1½ cups unsifted all-purpose flour
½ pound (1 cup) butter
½ cup sour cream

Place the unsifted flour in a bowl. Coarsely cut the butter over the flour. With a pastry blender, cut the butter into the flour until the mixture resembles coarse crumbs. Stir in the sour cream. Turn out onto a board or smooth surface and knead briefly only until the mixture holds together. Form into a ball, flatten slightly, place on wax paper and wrap airtight. Refrigerate for at least 2 hours, or overnight or longer. Or, if you wish, freeze it.

Voilà! Puff paste! That's it. The directions for using it from this stage on are classic.

If the dough has been frozen, allow it to thaw in the refrigerator for 12 to 24 hours, or at room temperature for a few hours.

Work with half of the dough at a time. Refrigerate the other half until you are ready to use it.

On a board, with a heavy rolling pin, pound the unfrozen but still firm dough to make it workable.

Petits Palmiers

48 SMALL PALMIERS

Cover a section of a large board or smooth work surface generously with granulated sugar. Place the dough on the sugar, turning it to coat all sides. Keeping the dough *well*-sugared, roll it into a square about ⅛ inch thick and 12 inches square. Trim the edges. (Scraps may be rolled and cut to make Shoe Soles; see page 261.)

Sprinkle top of dough generously with additional sugar. Determine the center of the dough. Mark it lightly with a ruler or the back of a knife. Fold each side in thirds toward the center, folding so that, rather than meeting in the center, there is a ½-inch space between the edges. Then close it along that space like a book, making a compact roll about 2 inches wide, ¾ to 1 inch thick, and 12 inches long. Wrap airtight. Refrigerate for 1 hour or more, or freeze for about ½ hour, until dough is firm enough to be sliced evenly.

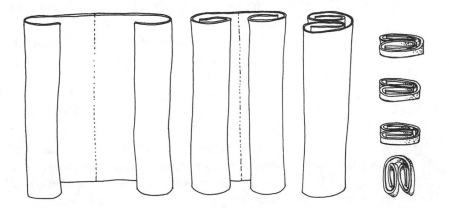

Adjust rack to center of oven. Preheat oven to 400 degrees. Line a cookie sheet with one large piece of aluminum foil.

With a very sharp, thin knife, slice the dough ½ inch thick. Dip both cut sides into sugar. Place cookies on their sides at least 2½ inches apart (they will spread considerably). Bake only one sheet at a time.

Bake 12 minutes or until the sugar on the bottom has melted and is well caramelized. (During baking reverse position of pan if necessary to insure even browning.) With two metal spatulas turn Palmiers over and continue to bake about 3 minutes longer until the sugar is lightly browned on the second side. Do not underbake; if Palmiers are underdone they will not be crisp as they should be.

Slide the aluminum foil off the cookie sheet. Let stand until Palmiers may be easily lifted off. Finish cooling on a rack.

Repeat with remaining half of the dough. Store airtight. If the Palmiers are not to be served rather soon, they should be frozen.

Almond Twists

24 TO 48 TWISTS

Adjust rack one-third down from the top of the oven. Preheat oven to 400 degrees. Line a large cookie sheet with aluminum foil. (A few drops of water on the sheet will keep the foil from slipping.) You may have to use two cookie sheets, but bake only one sheet at a time.

Prepare a glaze by mixing 1 egg with 1 teaspoon of water and set it aside. Prepare topping: Mix 5 ounces (one cup) of very finely chopped almonds with ⅓ cup sugar and set aside.

Roll the dough out on a well-sugared board, turning it frequently to sugar both sides. Roll ⅛ inch thick to a rectangle 8 × 12 inches. Trim the edges.

Brush the top heavily with some of the egg glaze. Sprinkle generously with half of the almond-sugar mixture. With the rolling pin gently press the almond-sugar into the dough.

Cut the dough into strips 8 inches long—they may be from ½ to 1 inch wide but they must all be the same size; use a ruler. With a long, heavy knife cut down firmly, using the full length of the blade.

Using both hands, pick up each strip by the ends and twist each end two or three times in opposite directions to make a corkscrew twist. Then place the strips on the cookie sheet with both ends sugar-nut side down. Place them 1 inch apart. After they are all in place, press down gently near the ends to keep the spirals from unwinding. Do not press directly on the ends. (It would flatten the ends and they would burn before the rest of the spiral had baked.)

Bake only one sheet at a time for 15 to 18 minutes, depending on the width of the strips. If necessary, reverse position of pan during baking to insure even browning. Do not underbake. These must be thoroughly dry and crisp.

Slide the foil off the cookie sheet and let stand briefly until the twists can be lifted off easily. Transfer to racks to finish cooling.

Excess sugar that runs out on the sides of the twists may be removed when twists are completely cool.

Repeat with the other half of the dough and remaining almond-sugar mixture.

These are best when very fresh. Store airtight or freeze.

Shoe Soles

20 LARGE WAFERS

Adjust rack one-third down from top of oven, so that the bottoms of the cookies will not burn before the tops brown. Preheat oven to 400 degrees. Line a cookie sheet with one large piece of aluminum foil.

Roll the dough out on a generously sugared board, turning often to coat both sides heavily with sugar. Also sprinkle the top frequently with additional sugar. Roll to ¼-inch thickness. Cut with a 3-inch round cutter. (Remaining scraps may be pressed together and rerolled.)

Sprinkle the tops with additional sugar and roll each round into an oval about 5 inches long, continuing to keep both sides heavily sugared. With a small, sharp knife cut a slit about 3 inches long along the length of each cookie. Do not cut all the way to the ends. (This cut is not traditional, but it will help the bottoms brown evenly.)

Place the cookies on the aluminum foil 1 inch apart. Bake only one sheet at a time. Bake about 14 minutes until tops are golden brown and the sugar on the bottoms has caramelized. Do not underbake—these must be crisp and the bottoms must be well-caramelized. Slide the foil off the sheet and let stand until completely cool.

Repeat with remaining half of the dough. Store airtight or freeze.

Chocolate Soufflé

Mrs. David Evins is a fabulous hostess. A meal at her table is memorable. She claims that the secret of her super soufflés is that she uses cornstarch rather than flour. This recipe is based on Mrs. Evins' formula.

5 OR 6 PORTIONS

1 tablespoon cornstarch
5 tablespoons sugar
Salt
⅔ cup milk
2 teaspoons instant coffee
1 tablespoon butter
2½ ounces (2½ squares) chocolate, sweet,
    semisweet, bittersweet, or extra-bittersweet,
    coarsely chopped
1 tablespoon Grand Marnier,
    or other orange liqueur
½ teaspoon vanilla extract
5 eggs, separated, plus 1 egg white

Adjust rack to the lowest position in the oven. Preheat oven to 400 degrees. Butter a 2-quart soufflé dish. Prepare a collar. Tear off a length of aluminum foil long enough to wrap around the dish and overlap slightly and fold it in half the long way. Butter the top half of one side of the folded length. Wrap it around the dish, buttered side up and facing in. Tie or fasten it with straight pins to make a tight fit. Place a few large spoonfuls of sugar in the dish. Tilt, tap, and turn to coat the dish and the foil completely with the sugar. Shake out excess.

In the top of a small double boiler off the heat, mix the cornstarch, 3 tablespoons of the sugar (reserving remaining 2 tablespoons), and a pinch of salt. Gradually at first, mix in the milk to make a smooth mixture.

Place over hot water on moderate heat. Cook, stirring very gently with a rubber spatula (do not beat), for about 6 minutes until the mixture thickens. Continue to cook, stirring gently for 1 minute more.

Remove top of double boiler from heat. Immediately add coffee, butter, and chocolate, continuing to stir gently until smooth. Mix in the Grand Marnier or other liqueur and the vanilla. Set aside to cool briefly for 5 minutes.

Meanwhile, in the small bowl of an electric mixer, beat the egg yolks at high speed for 4 to 5 minutes until pale lemon-colored. On low speed gradually beat in the chocolate mixture, scraping the bowl with the rubber spatula and beating only until smooth.

The soufflé may be completed now or the chocolate mixture may be covered and set aside at room temperature to be completed a few hours later.

If you have a large copper bowl and a large balloon-type whisk for beating egg whites, this is the time you should use it. If not, use any large bowl of an electric mixer. Add a pinch of salt to the 6 egg whites and beat at high speed until they increase in volume and begin to thicken. While beating, gradually add remaining 2 tablespoons of sugar and continue to beat until whites hold a firm shape or are stiff but not dry.

The chocolate mixture is thin. It must be added to the whites gradually. A little bit at a time at first, fold the chocolate into the whites, folding gently with the rubber spatula only until both mixtures are blended. Do not handle any more than necessary.

Gently turn the batter into the soufflé dish. Immediately place it in the oven, being careful not to hold the oven door open longer than necessary. Bake for 2 to 3 minutes and then reduce oven temperature to 375 degrees. Total baking time is 40 minutes.

Ovens vary, so test the soufflé about 5 minutes before the time is up. (Do not open the oven door before then.) Open the door only enough to be able to reach in and gently touch the top. Wiggle it a bit. It should move slightly, indicating that it is firm enough to hold its shape for a few minutes but still very light and only barely set.

Remove from oven. Quickly remove foil collar and serve immediately —I mean *now!*—on slightly warm dessert plates. Serve with any one of the custard sauces (pages 389–91), or with the following:

CREME CHANTILLY

> 1 cup heavy cream
> ¼ cup confectioners sugar
> 1 scant teaspoon vanilla extract, or
>   1–2 tablespoons Grand Marnier
>   or other orange liqueur

In a chilled bowl with chilled beaters, whip above ingredients only until the cream thickens slightly and barely holds a soft shape. Do not whip until firm; this is a sauce.

If the cream is prepared ahead of time, refrigerate it and, immediately before serving, stir briefly to mix. Serve cold.

Icebox Cakes and Cake Rolls

LEMON CHIFFON ICEBOX CAKE

    LEMON CHIFFON PIE

    COLD LEMON SOUFFLE

KENTUCKY CHOCOLATE ICEBOX
CAKE WITH BOURBON

CHOCOLATE RUM ICEBOX CAKE

CHOCOLATE ICEBOX CAKE,
COUNTRY STYLE

CHARLOTTE RUSSE

BLACK VELVET

CHOCOLATE ROLL

CREAM ROLL

see Almond Sponge Roll (page 230)

Lemon Chiffon Icebox Cake

ICEBOX CAKE,
PIE, OR
COLD SOUFFLÉ—
EACH SERVES
6 TO 8

48 single ladyfingers,
 or a jelly roll cut in thin slices
1 tablespoon (1 envelope) unflavored gelatin
¼ cup cold water
4 eggs, jumbo or extra-large
 (or 5 smaller), separated
Finely grated rind of 1 large lemon
½ cup lemon juice
1 cup sugar
1 cup heavy cream
Generous pinch of salt

Prepare a loaf pan with 2½- to 3-quart capacity. Cut two strips of aluminum foil to line the pan, one for the length and one for the width. Put them into place carefully. Place ladyfingers, curved side against the pan, close together on bottom and sides. (See Note.) Or line pan with thin slices of jelly roll.

Sprinkle gelatin over cold water and set aside. Place egg yolks in top of small double boiler off the heat, and stir lightly just to mix. Add the grated lemon rind and then gradually stir in the lemon juice and ½ cup of the sugar (reserve remaining ½ cup). Place over hot water on moderate heat and cook, scraping the sides and bottom continuously with a rubber spatula until mixture thickens slightly "to coat a metal spoon"—about 180 degrees on a candy thermometer. Remove top from heat. Add gelatin and stir to dissolve. Let stand, stirring occasionally, until completely cool.

When lemon mixture is cool, in a chilled bowl with chilled beaters whip the cream until it holds a soft shape.

In small bowl of electric mixer beat the salt and the egg whites until whites have increased in volume and started to thicken. While beating, gradually add reserved ½ cup sugar and continue to beat at moderately high speed until whites stand in peaks—do not overbeat; meringue must not be dry.

Gradually, in several additions, fold the lemon mixture into the whites and then, in a large bowl, fold together the lemon mixture and the whipped cream.

Turn into pan lined with ladyfingers or sliced jelly roll. Cover the top with a layer of ladyfingers or slices of jelly roll. Refrigerate for 5 or 6 hours. Cover with a serving dish and invert. Remove pan and aluminum foil.

TOPPING

optional: Tart jam or preserves
   (sour cherry, currant, raspberry, apricot)
1 cup heavy cream
¼ cup confectioners sugar
1 scant teaspoon vanilla extract
optional: Green pistachio nuts, chopped, or
   semisweet chocolate, coarsely grated

Stir 2 to 3 tablespoons of the preserves, if used, to soften and then spread over the top of the cake, or just place on at random by small spoonfuls.

In a chilled bowl with chilled beaters, whip the cream with the sugar and vanilla until it holds a definite shape. Either smooth it over the top, or apply it with a pastry bag and a large star tube, making heavy, rippled lines.

If you wish, sprinkle with chopped pistachio nuts or grated chocolate. Refrigerate.

NOTE: *When lining the pan with ladyfingers, cut them as necessary to fit into place. If they won't stand up on the sides, dot the aluminum foil lightly with a bit of soft butter wherever necessary to hold them up. If the ladyfingers are too long for the sides of the pan, cut one end and place them cut side up.*

Lemon Chiffon Pie

Use the same lemon chiffon mixture to fill a 9-inch graham cracker crumb crust (page 285), or Chocolate Cookie Crust (page 289). Refrigerate several hours until set. Cover with above topping, drizzling the optional preserves over the filling and spreading the whipped cream on top.

Cold Lemon Soufflé

The same lemon chiffon mixture may be used for a cold soufflé. Prepare a 3-inch collar for a 5-to 6-cup soufflé dish. Use a piece of aluminum foil long enough to wrap around the dish and overlap a few inches. Fold it in half lengthwise. Brush tasteless salad oil on the top half of one side.

Wrap it around the dish, oiled side up and facing in. Fasten tightly with string or straight pins. Pour in the lemon chiffon mixture. Refrigerate 5 to 6 hours. Remove collar and cover with above topping.

Kentucky Chocolate Icebox Cake with Bourbon

1 ounce (1 square) unsweetened chocolate
3 ounces (3 squares) semisweet chocolate
¼ pound (½ cup) butter
1 cup sugar
2 egg yolks
½ cup light cream
1 teaspoon vanilla extract
36 double or 72 single ladyfingers
¼–⅓ cup bourbon (See Note.)

6 TO 8 PORTIONS

In the top of a large double boiler over hot water, melt both chocolates and butter. Stir in the sugar. Mix the yolks, cream, and vanilla and, with a wire whisk, stir them into the chocolate. Cook over moderate heat, stirring occasionally, for about 15 minutes.

Remove top of double boiler and set aside to cool slightly, stirring occasionally; or stir very briefly over ice water.

Meanwhile, line a 9 × 5 × 3-inch loaf pan. Cut two strips of aluminum foil to line the pan, one for the length and one for the width. Put them into place carefully.

Line the bottom of the pan (not the sides) with a solid layer of single ladyfingers, placing them curved side against the pan and cutting them as necessary for a snug fit. Brush or sprinkle lightly with 1 tablespoon of the bourbon. Cover with one-third of the chocolate in a thin layer. Tilt pan to level chocolate. Continue making layers: four of ladyfingers and bourbon, three of chocolate.

After brushing or sprinkling the bourbon on the top layer of ladyfingers, cover that with another layer of ladyfingers without bourbon. Cover airtight and refrigerate 5 to 6 hours, or for a day or two, or freeze it. Although this is an icebox cake generally served from the refrigerator, I think it is also delicious served frozen.

To serve if you have frozen the cake, unmold it and either decorate with whipped cream immediately before serving, or serve the whipped cream separately.

To serve if you have refrigerated the cake, unmold and decorate with whipped cream whenever convenient before serving.

WHIPPED CREAM

1 cup heavy cream
¼ cup confectioners sugar
1 scant teaspoon vanilla extract

Whip above-ingredients in a chilled bowl with chilled beaters until barely stiff.

Spread over cake (top only), or apply over top using a pastry bag with a medium star tube to form three heavy rippled lines down the length of the top—first one on each side and then one in the center. Use the remaining cream to form two more long lines between the first three—or form six to eight heavy rippled lines going across the width of the cake.

NOTE: *The bourbon may be increased or decreased according to taste, or it may be eliminated entirely, or you may substitute light rum or brandy.*

Chocolate Rum Icebox Cake

8 PORTIONS

2 ounces (2 squares) unsweetened chocolate
2 ounces (2 squares) semisweet chocolate
½ cup light rum
2½–3 dozen double ladyfingers (See Note.)
½ pound (1 cup) butter
¼ cup strong prepared coffee
    (You can use 1 tablespoon instant coffee
    dissolved in ¼ cup water.)
1½ cups confectioners sugar
5 eggs, separated
⅛ teaspoon salt

Use a loaf pan that has a 10-cup capacity, preferably long and narrow instead of short and wide (about 14 × 4½ × 3 inches). Cut two strips of aluminum foil to line the pan, one for the length and one for the width. Put them into place carefully.

Melt both chocolates in the top of a small double boiler over hot water on moderate heat. Stir until smooth. Set aside to cool.

Brush or sprinkle some of the rum on the flat side of the ladyfingers and line the pan with them, placing them with the curved sides against the pan. Line the bottom of the pan first and then the sides.

In the small bowl of an electric mixer cream the butter. Gradually beat in the prepared coffee and then the sugar. Beat until very smooth. Add the yolks one at a time, beating well after each, and continue to beat for 2 to 3 minutes until very creamy. Beat in the chocolate, scraping the bowl with a rubber spatula as necessary to keep mixture smooth. Transfer to a large mixing bowl.

Add the salt to the egg whites and beat until they hold a point and are stiff but not dry. Fold about half of the whites into the chocolate. Then fold the chocolate into the remaining whites. Pour about half of the chocolate filling into the ladyfinger-lined pan. Cover with a layer of lady-fingers, brushing or sprinkling them with some of the rum.

Cover the ladyfingers with balance of chocolate filling. Spread the filling smooth. Again, make a layer of ladyfingers with rum. Any remaining rum may be sprinkled over the top. If you wish, cover with another layer of ladyfingers without rum.

If the ladyfingers on the sides of the pan extend too high, they should be cut level with scissors. Cover tightly with plastic wrap or aluminum foil. Press down very gently to make a compact loaf. Refrigerate overnight. (This may be frozen.)

Remove plastic wrap or foil topping. Place a serving plate on top and invert pan and plate. Remove pan and foil lining.

Cover with the following:

TOPPING

1 cup heavy cream
¼ cup strained confectioners sugar
1 teaspoon vanilla extract
optional: Chocolate, grated; pistachio
nuts, chopped; or almonds,
toasted and sliced

In a chilled bowl with chilled beaters, beat above ingredients until cream holds a shape. Spread thickly over top of cake or apply with pastry bag and large star tube. (If you use the pastry bag, make three long, rippled lines going down the length, first on one edge, then the other, and finally in the center. They should be heavy enough so that they touch each other and completely cover the top of the cake.) Do not put whipped cream on the sides.

Cake may be left as is or dusted lightly with grated chocolate, chopped pistachio nuts, or toasted, sliced almonds. Refrigerate.

NOTE: *The ladyfingers should be separated so that they are not double; however, they may be left in one piece, side by side, and cut to length as needed.*

Chocolate Icebox Cake, Country Style

8 PORTIONS

Must be made 12 to 24 hours ahead.

1 cup sugar
1 tablespoon (1 envelope) unflavored gelatin
1⅓ cups milk
5 ounces (5 squares) unsweetened chocolate
5 eggs, separated
Ladyfingers
Pinch of salt
1 cup heavy cream
1½ teaspoons vanilla extract
⅓ cup walnuts, coarsely broken or cut

Reserve 3 tablespoons of the sugar. In an 8- to 10-cup heavy saucepan, mix the remaining sugar and gelatin. Stir in the milk and then add the chocolate. Cook over moderate heat, stirring constantly, until the mixture is smooth and comes to a boil. Simmer for 1 minute. Beat with a wire whisk until smooth. Remove from heat.

In a bowl stir the egg yolks briefly just to mix. Gradually stir in a few spoonfuls of the chocolate mixture and then, stirring constantly, add the egg yolks to the remaining chocolate mixture.

Stir over low heat for a minute or two until mixture thickens slightly. Remove from heat. Transfer to a large mixing bowl and stir occasionally until cool.

Meanwhile, prepare a 10-cup serving bowl. This is most attractive in a straight-sided clear glass bowl or soufflé dish. Line the bottom and sides with ladyfingers. (For the sides, separate the double strips of ladyfingers, but do not separate each individual finger. Stand whole strips of them upright on the sides of the bowl, curved sides against the bowl.)

When the chocolate mixture has cooled, add the salt to the egg whites in the small bowl of an electric mixer. Beat until mixture has increased in volume and thickened slightly. While beating, gradually add the reserved 3 tablespoons of sugar and beat until mixture has the consistency of thick marshmallow sauce and holds its shape, but do not overbeat. It must not be dry.

In a chilled bowl with chilled beaters, whip the cream until it just holds a shape—not too stiff.

Stir the vanilla into the chocolate mixture.

Gradually fold a cup of the chocolate mixture into the beaten whites, and then fold the whites into the remaining chocolate mixture.

Now gradually fold a cup of the chocolate mixture into the whipped cream, and then fold the whipped cream into the remaining chocolate mixture. Handle lightly. If necessary, pour gently from one bowl to another to insure thorough blending.

Pour into ladyfinger-lined bowl. If the tops of the ladyfingers do not reach the top of the bowl, after pouring in most of the chocolate mixture, use a fork to gently raise the ladyfingers and then pour in the remaining chocolate.

Refrigerate for 10 minutes and then sprinkle top with walnuts. Return to refrigerator. When the top is firm enough, cover airtight with plastic wrap and refrigerate for 12 to 24 hours before serving.

Serve with a side dish of Soft Whipped Cream.

SOFT WHIPPED CREAM

1 cup heavy cream
¼ cup confectioners sugar
1 teaspoon vanilla extract

In a chilled bowl with chilled beaters, whip the above ingredients only until they thicken to the consistency of a sauce, semi-firm.

Charlotte Russe

This brings back memories of days when charlotte russes were sold from pushcarts on the streets of New York. How did an elaborate and classic French dessert wind up on pushcarts on the Lower East Side? And how did they make them so good?

18 double ladyfingers
optional: Light rum, framboise, or kirsch

This is beautiful if prepared individually in 8-ounce old-fashioned cocktail glasses, or other straight-sided glasses no deeper than the length of the ladyfingers.

Separate ladyfingers and cut them into individual fingers.

Pour 3 to 4 tablespoons of optional rum, or framboise or kirsch, into a small dish. With a pastry brush, brush the flat side of each ladyfinger very briefly with a bit of the rum and place fingers touching each other, rounded side against the glass, around the sides of six or seven straight-sided wide and shallow glasses.

FILLING

Prepare Vanilla Filling (see Vanilla Cream Pie, page 289), adding a scant ¼ teaspoon of almond extract along with the vanilla.

Spoon the filling (or pour from a wide pitcher) into the prepared glasses, mounding them high. Refrigerate 2 to 3 hours.

TOPPING

optional: Tart, dark red jam or jelly
1 cup heavy cream
¼ cup confectioners sugar
1 teaspoon vanilla extract

Top each dessert with a small spoonful of the optional jam or jelly. In a chilled bowl with chilled beaters, whip the cream with the sugar and vanilla until it holds a shape. With a pastry bag and a large star tube, pipe a heavy ring of the cream around the outer edge of the dessert, letting the jam or jelly show through in the middle. Refrigerate.

OPTIONAL: *Before serving decorate with candied violets or rose petals, a bit of grated chocolate, a piece of glacéed fruit, a few toasted, sliced almonds, and/or . . .*

Black Velvet

16 TO 24
PORTIONS

This is a big job, but well worth it. The ultimate chocolate icebox cake, adapted from the famous Chocolate Velvet, one of the most popular desserts served at Restaurant Associates' Four Seasons restaurant in New York City. Dense and rich—portions should be small.

Prepare two sponge sheets from the following recipe, making one after the other instead of doubling the recipe.

SPONGE SHEET

(This classic recipe will make a thin, rather solid but flexible sheet.)

> 5 eggs, separated
> ¼ cup sugar
> 1 teaspoon vanilla extract
> 3 tablespoons sifted all-purpose flour
> ⅛ teaspoon salt

Adjust rack one-third up from bottom of oven. Preheat oven to 375 degrees. Butter a 10½ × 15½ × 1-inch jelly-roll pan. Line bottom and sides with one long piece of wax paper. Butter the paper and dust it lightly with flour.

In small bowl of electric mixer, at high speed beat the yolks for about 3 to 4 minutes until thick and light lemon-colored. Add 2 tablespoons of the sugar (reserve remaining 2 tablespoons) and the vanilla. Continue to beat at high speed for 3 to 4 minutes more until mixture is very thick and falls very slowly from beaters when they are lifted.

Reduce speed to lowest and add the flour, scraping bowl with a rubber spatula and beating only until flour is incorporated.

In large bowl of electric mixer, with clean beaters, at high speed beat the whites with the salt until the mixture thickens enough to hold a very soft shape. Gradually add the reserved 2 tablespoons of sugar and continue to beat at high speed until mixture holds a firm shape and is stiff but not dry.

In three additions, fold one-half of the whites into the yolks—don't be too thorough—then fold the yolks back into the remaining whites only until no whites show. Handle as little as possible.

Turn batter into the prepared pan. Handle lightly. With a rubber spatula spread as smooth as possible; there should be no thin spots. (The batter will not run; it will stay where you put it.)

Bake for 15 to 18 minutes or until top is golden brown and springs back when lightly touched in the center, and cake comes away from sides of pan.

While cake is baking, spread out a dry kitchen towel (preferably smooth cotton, flour sacking, or linen).

Remove baked cake from oven. Invert immediately onto the towel. Remove pan and wax paper. Let cool on the towel.

Repeat to make second sponge sheet.

TO ASSEMBLE

Line the bottom of a 9 × 3-inch spring-form pan (sides *must* be 3 inches high) with wax paper, unbuttered.

At one short end of a sponge sheet, right up against the end, touching the edge trace around the spring form with a small, sharp knife just to indicate the circle. Remove spring form and, with scissors, cut out the circle of cake. Repeat with second sponge sheet, making second circle of cake. Place one of the cake rounds in the pan.

With a ruler and toothpicks, carefully mark remaining pieces of cakes into even slices 2¾ inches wide (two from one piece of cake and one from the other) marking from short end of sponge sheet, so they are 9½ inches long. (Even though the pan is 10½ inches on its shorter side, the sponge sheets will shrink to about 9½ inches.) Cut with a small, sharp knife, cutting against the ruler. That will give you three slices, each one 2¾ by 9½ inches.

Cut 1 inch off one of the long strips, making it 8½ inches long. Place it and the other two longer strips standing up around the sides of the pan, the top side of the cake against the pan. Fit the strips together tightly, pushing them into each other to make a tight fit.

Reserve remaining round of cake. You will not need the cut ends and pieces.

Prepare following Chocolate Filling:

CHOCOLATE FILLING

1½ pounds (24 squares) semisweet chocolate
1½ tablespoons instant coffee
½ cup boiling water
½ cup Grand Marnier

3 egg yolks

1 cup egg whites (See page 8.)

⅛ teaspoon salt

¼ cup sugar

1 cup heavy cream

Place chocolate in top of a large double boiler over hot water on moderate heat. Cover until partially melted, then uncover and stir occasionally until melted. Turn it into small bowl of electric mixer and let stand, stirring occasionally, until cooled to room temperature.

Meanwhile, dissolve instant coffee in boiling water and set aside.

When chocolate has completely cooled, on lowest speed very gradually beat in the prepared coffee and the Grand Marnier and then the egg yolks, scraping the bowl with a rubber spatula as necessary to keep mixture smooth. Beat only until smooth. Set aside.

In large bowl of electric mixer at high speed, beat the egg whites with the salt until they hold a very soft shape. Gradually beat in the sugar and continue to beat until whites hold a definite point, or are stiff but not dry.

Fold one large spoonful of the beaten whites into the chocolate mixture. Fold in another large spoonful. Gradually, in several additions, fold in half of the remaining whites—don't be too thorough. Then fold the chocolate into the remaining whites, folding completely until no whites show.

In a chilled bowl with chilled beaters, whip the cream until it holds a soft shape but is not stiff. Fold the cream into the chocolate mixture.

Pour the filling into the cake-lined pan. If it reaches to the top of the cake on the sides, cover with remaining circle of cake.

If the filling does not quite reach to the top of the cake (if it is ⅓ to ½ inch below), cut around the remaining circle of cake with scissors, cutting in ¼ inch from the edge to make the circle small enough to fit down inside the cake on the sides. Place it over the filling.

Cover with clear wrap or aluminum foil and a light weight. (I use a cake pan or a small cookie sheet with something not too heavy placed on the center of it.) Refrigerate for 5 hours or more (or freeze, if you wish).

Remove sides of spring form. Place dessert platter over dessert. *Very carefully* invert. Remove bottom of pan and paper.

Cut six strips of wax paper, each 1½ to 2 inches wide and 6 to 8 inches long. With a wide metal spatula or pancake turner, very gently raise a small section of the cake and slide a strip of wax paper under it to protect the plate when icing the cake. Continue all around the cake.

Cover with the following icing:

ICING

6 ounces semisweet
   or extra-bittersweet chocolate
      (I use Tobler Extra-Bittersweet.)
½ cup boiling water

Break or cut chocolate into pieces and place them in a small, heavy-bottomed saucepan. Add boiling water and place over low heat. Stir with a small wire whisk until smooth. Remove from heat and let stand at room temperature to cool. Stir the icing well. Work quickly before the cold cake hardens the icing. Pour it over the cake, completely covering the top and letting very little run down on the sides. With a small, narrow metal spatula spread smoothly on the sides.

Remove wax paper strips immediately before icing sets, pulling each piece out by a narrow end of the paper. (If the icing hardens before the wax paper is removed, cut around the base of the cake with a small knife to release the paper before pulling it away. See page 18.) Refrigerate.

NOTES: 1. *Black Velvet may be refrigerated for a day or two, or it may be frozen before it is iced.*
2. *Dip the knife in hot water, or hold it under running hot water, before cutting each slice.*
3. *Black Velvet may be served as is or with Grand Marnier Custard Sauce (page 390) or with whipped cream sweetened with confectioners sugar and flavored with Grand Marnier.*

Chocolate Roll

8 PORTIONS

CAKE ROLL

6 eggs, separated
¾ cup granulated sugar
¼ cup plus 1 tablespoon powdered, unsweetened cocoa
¼ teaspoon salt
optional: Confectioners sugar for sprinkling

Adjust rack one-third up from bottom of oven. Preheat oven to 375 degrees. Butter a 10½ × 15½ × 1-inch jelly-roll pan. Line bottom and sides with one long piece of wax paper. Butter and flour the paper.

In small bowl of electric mixer at high speed beat yolks for 4 to 5 minutes until light lemon-colored. Add half of the sugar (reserve remaining half) and continue to beat at high speed for 5 minutes until very thick. On lowest speed add cocoa and beat only until smooth.

In large bowl of electric mixer, with clean beaters, beat the whites and the salt until they increase in volume and begin to thicken. Gradually add reserved sugar and continue to beat at high speed until they hold a shape and are stiff but not dry.

In a few additions, small at first, fold half of the whites into the chocolate mixture and then fold the chocolate mixture into the remaining whites.

Turn into prepared pan. Handling lightly, spread level and place in the oven.

While cake is baking, wet and wring out a kitchen towel (preferably smooth cotton, flour sacking, or linen). Spread it out on a flat surface.

Bake the cake 30 minutes or until the top springs back when lightly touched. Remove from oven. If cake is sticking to sides of pan, cut around it quickly with a small, sharp knife. Immediately invert onto the damp towel. Work quickly. Remove pan and carefully peel off the wax paper. Starting at a long side, roll the cake and towel together. Be firm, but don't squash the cake. Place roll on a rack to cool; it must be completely cool before filling.

After the cake has cooled, if it is not to be filled soon (or if it is to be frozen) it should be unrolled from the towel to prevent the towel from sticking to it, and rerolled with wax paper or plastic wrap.

MOCHA CREAM FILLING

¾ teaspoon unflavored gelatin
  (See Note.)
1½ tablespoons cold water
1½ cups heavy cream
1½ tablespoons instant coffee
⅓ cup confectioners sugar

Sprinkle gelatin over water in small heatproof cup. Let stand for 5 minutes. Place cup in shallow hot water over moderate heat until gelatin is dissolved. Remove from heat. In chilled bowl with chilled beaters, start to whip the cream, instant coffee, and sugar. When slightly thickened, stir one or two spoonfuls into the gelatin and, still beating, add the gelatin to the cream. Continue to beat until the cream holds a shape.

Unroll the cake. Spread it with the filling and reroll. Place on a chocolate-roll board or platter. (If you have trouble transferring the filled cake roll, use a cookie sheet as a spatula.) Refrigerate.

The top of the roll may be sprinkled with confectioners sugar through a fine strainer. Or, if you wish to make a pattern on top, cut wax paper strips ¼ inch wide (9 to 10 inches long). Place them diagonally over the top of the cake about 1 inch apart. Sprinkle generously with confectioners sugar through a fine strainer. Carefully remove wax paper strips. Brush excess sugar off board or platter.

OPTIONAL: *If you wish, pass chocolate sauce separately.*

NOTE: *If chocolate roll is to be served shortly after completion, the gelatin may be eliminated (the gelatin only makes the whipped cream hold up longer). Simply whip the cream, instant coffee, and sugar.*

Cream Roll

8 PORTIONS

SPONGE CAKE

6 eggs, separated
¼ cup plus 2 tablespoons granulated sugar
Finely grated rind of 1 large orange
¼ teaspoon salt
¼ cup plus 2 tablespoons
   sifted all-purpose flour
optional: Confectioners sugar for
   sprinkling

Adjust rack one-third up from bottom of oven. Preheat oven to 375 degrees. Butter a 15½ × 10½ × 1-inch jelly-roll pan. Line bottom and sides with one long piece of wax paper. Butter the paper and dust all over lightly with flour (additional to that called for in the recipe).

In small bowl of electric mixer at high speed, beat the egg yolks for 3 minutes until light lemon-colored. Gradually beat in the sugar and continue to beat at high speed for 5 minutes more, until the mixture is very thick. Remove from mixer. Fold in orange rind and transfer to a large bowl.

In large bowl of electric mixer, with clean beaters, beat the egg whites and the salt until they hold a definite shape, or are stiff but not dry. Place half of the whites on the yolks. Sift half of the flour on top. Gently fold together—do not be too thorough. Repeat with remaining whites and flour, folding gently only until completely blended.

Turn into prepared pan and spread gently with a rubber spatula to level.

Bake 20 to 25 minutes until top of cake springs back when lightly touched and sides come away from pan.

While the cake is baking, wet and thoroughly wring out a smooth towel (smooth cotton, flour sacking, or linen) and spread it out smoothly on a flat surface.

When cake is done, remove it from the oven. If it is stuck to the sides of the pan anywhere, quickly release it with a small, sharp knife. Immediately invert onto the damp towel. Remove pan and pull off wax paper and, starting from one long side, quickly, gently, roll cake and towel together. Place on a rack to cool.

CREAM FILLING

2 teaspoons unflavored gelatin
2 tablespoons water
1½ cups heavy cream
¼ cup confectioners sugar
⅓ cup Cointreau
½ cup orange marmalade

Sprinkle the gelatin over the water in a small heatproof cup and let stand for about 5 minutes. Place cup in a small saucepan of hot water about a third of the way up the sides of the cup on moderate heat until gelatin is dissolved. Remove from heat and set aside.

In a chilled bowl with chilled beaters, whip the cream, sugar, and ¼ cup of the Cointreau (reserve balance) until it starts to thicken. Quickly stir a large spoonful of the cream into the gelatin and immediately add the gelatin to the cream, continuing to beat until cream is firm and holds a definite shape. Fold in the marmalade. Set bowl into a larger bowl of ice and water and fold cream occasionally, until it is firm enough not to run out of the cake when it is rolled. (This might take 20 or 30 minutes in a small, narrow mixer bowl—it will take less time if transferred to a wider bowl.)

Meanwhile, unroll the sponge cake. Sprinkle or brush with reserved Cointreau. (Use a bit more than called for, if you wish.)

When whipped cream is firm enough to hold its shape, spread it on the cake, heavily along the long edge from which you started to roll and stopping about ½ to 1 inch from the opposite edge. With the help of the towel, reroll the cake the long way so that the two long sides just meet in the middle and do not overlap. It will look like a tube.

(If the roll is too soft to be transferred, slide a cookie sheet under the towel and place it all in the freezer or refrigerator until it is firm enough to be handled.) Then, using a cookie sheet as a spatula, place the cake on a chocolate-roll board or a long platter, seam side down. Refrigerate for 5 to 6 hours.

The top may be sprinkled with confectioners sugar through a fine strainer. If you wish to make a pattern on top, cut wax paper in strips ¼ inch wide (9 to 10 inches long). Place them diagonally over the top of the cake about 1 inch apart. Sprinkle generously with confectioners sugar through a fine strainer. Carefully remove wax paper strips. Brush excess sugar off board or platter.

OPTIONAL: *Serve with a side dish of sliced and sweetened strawberries (see page 308), to be spooned over or alongside each portion after it is placed on an individual dessert plate. And/or serve with Honey Chocolate Sauce, page 398.*

NOTE: *Cut with a sawing motion in order not to squash the cream.*

Crumb Crust Pies

RUM PIE

COFFEE BUTTERCRUNCH PIE

VANILLA CREAM PIE

BLACK BOTTOM PIE

BLACK BOTTOM PECAN CREAM PIE

PEACE AND PLENTY

see Lemon Chiffon Pie (page 268)

General Directions for Crumb Crust

*How to line a pie plate with aluminum foil, shape
and bake the crust, and then how to remove the
foil.*

Although the crumb mixture may be pressed into place directly in the pie
plate, I prefer to line the plate with foil first and then remove the foil
before filling the crust. This guarantees easy serving—the crust *can't* stick
to the plate. It's a bit more work (or play), but I think well worth it.

For a 9-inch pie plate, use a 12-inch square of foil. Center it evenly
over the plate. Place over it a large pot holder or a folded towel. Using the
pot holder or towel to push, press the foil firmly into place, making sure
that it is touching all parts of the plate. Fold the edges of the foil down
over the rim of the plate.

Turn the crumb crust mixture into the lined plate. Using your fingertips, distribute the mixture evenly and loosely over the sides first and then
over the bottom. Then press the crust firmly and evenly over the sides,
pushing it up from the bottom to form a rim slightly raised above the
edge of the plate. Be careful that the top edge of the crust is not too thin.
To shape a firm edge, use the fingertips of your right hand against the
inside and press down against it with the thumb of your left hand. After
firmly pressing the sides and the top edge, press the remaining crumbs
evenly and firmly over the bottom. There should be no loose crumbs.

Bake in the center of a preheated 375-degree oven for 8 minutes, or
until very lightly browned on the edges. Cool to room temperature.

Place in freezer for at least 1 hour, or more if possible. It must be
frozen solid.

Remove from freezer. Raise edges of foil. Carefully lift foil (with
crust) from plate. Gently peel away the foil by supporting the bottom of
the crust with your left hand and peeling the foil, a bit at a time, with
your right hand. As you do so, rotate the crust gently on your left hand.

Supporting the bottom of the crust with a small metal spatula or a
knife, ease it back into the plate very gently so as not to crack it. It will
not crack or break if it has been frozen sufficiently.

Rum Pie

8 PORTIONS

CRUST

1¼ cups graham cracker crumbs
¼ cup sugar
2 ounces (¼ cup) melted butter

Adjust rack to center of oven. Preheat oven to 375 degrees.

Mix the crumbs with the sugar and then add the melted butter. With a rubber spatula, stir and press firmly against the bowl until completely mixed. The mixture will look crumbly but will hold together when pressed into place.

Use a 9-inch pie plate and follow directions for crumb crust (page 284).

FILLING

1 tablespoon (1 envelope) unflavored gelatin
¼ cup cold water
5 egg yolks
¾ cup sugar
¾ cup dark rum
1 cup heavy cream

Sprinkle gelatin over cold water in a heatproof glass measuring cup or a small heatproof bowl. Let stand.

In small bowl of electric mixer at high speed, beat the yolks. Gradually add the sugar and beat for 5 minutes.

Meanwhile, stir ¼ cup of the rum (reserve remaining ½ cup) into the gelatin. Place the cup or bowl in a small pan of shallow hot water on moderate heat until the gelatin is dissolved. (Stir with a metal spoon so that you can see when the granules have dissolved.)

Beating on low speed, slowly add the warm gelatin mixture to the egg yolks, scraping bowl with a rubber spatula to keep mixture smooth. Beat in the reserved ½ cup rum.

In a chilled bowl with chilled beaters, whip the cream until it holds a soft shape, not stiff. Set aside.

Place the bowl of egg yolk mixture into a larger bowl of ice and water. Stir and scrape the bowl occasionally until mixture starts to thicken to the consistency of a medium cream sauce. This might take as long as 15 minutes in a small, narrow bowl. However, if you transfer it to a large, wide bowl, it will thicken in 5 to 7 minutes. In a large, wide bowl, stir and scrape the bowl almost constantly. Once it has thickened, fold one-quarter of the egg yolk mixture into the whipped cream. Fold in another quarter again and then fold the cream into the remaining egg yolk mixture. If necessary, gently pour back and forth from one bowl to another to insure thorough blending.

Fill the shell as full as possible without letting it run over. There will be some leftover filling. Let it stand at room temperature while you chill the filled shell (only about 7 to 8 minutes in the freezer, or a bit longer in the refrigerator) until filling is semi-set. Then pour on the remaining filling, mounding it higher in the center.

Refrigerate at least 5 to 6 hours or more. Prepare following whipped cream topping:

WHIPPED CREAM

1½ cups heavy cream
⅓ cup confectioners sugar
1½ teaspoons vanilla extract

In a chilled bowl with chilled beaters, whip above ingredients until firm enough to hold a shape. Place a spoonful at a time first around outer edge of filling, and then continuing toward the center. If the spoonfuls are even, leave the top as is. If not, it may be spread smooth or swirled with the back of a spoon.

OPTIONAL: *Sprinkle the outer rim of the whipped cream with finely chopped green pistachio nuts and/or place coarsely grated chocolate in the center.*

NOTE: *A variation of this pie may be made by substituting for the rum ½ cup whiskey and 2 tablespoons instant coffee dissolved in ¼ cup hot water.*

Coffee Butter-crunch Pie

This rich creation is the famous Coffee-Toffee Pie from Blum's in San Francisco. I never know what to answer when people tell me, as they often do, that this is better than sex.

8 PORTIONS

CRUST

(This may be doubled. The extra crust may be frozen.)

½ package pie crust mix
    (Measure the contents of a package
    into a measuring cup
    and use half.)
1 ounce (1 square) unsweetened
    chocolate
¼ cup light brown sugar,
    firmly packed (strained if lumpy)
2½ ounces (¾ cup) walnuts,
    very finely chopped
    (must be finely chopped—not ground)
1 teaspoon vanilla extract
1 tablespoon water

Place the pie crust mix in a mixing bowl.

Grind the chocolate in a nut grinder, a small Mouli grater, or cut it coarsely and grind it in a blender. Stir it into the pie crust mix. Stir in the sugar and nuts. Mix the vanilla and water and gradually drizzle it over the mixture—don't pour it all in one place—while using a fork to stir and toss. The mixture will be lumpy and crumbly. Do not try to make it smooth, stir it very briefly. It will hold together when you press it into place.

Adjust rack to center of oven and preheat to 375 degrees.

Use a 9-inch pie plate and follow directions for crumb crust (page 284). However, for this recipe *bake the crust for 15 minutes.*

Meanwhile, prepare the following filling:

FILLING

(This may be doubled if you have made
two crusts. The extra filled crust may be frozen.)

1 ounce (1 square) unsweetened chocolate
¼ pound (½ cup) butter
¾ cup light brown sugar, firmly packed
  (strained if lumpy)
2 teaspoons instant coffee
2 eggs

Melt chocolate over hot water and set aside to cool. In small bowl of electric mixer cream the butter. Gradually add the sugar and beat at moderately high speed for 2 to 3 minutes. Mix in the cooled, melted chocolate and the instant coffee. Add the eggs individually, beating for 5 minutes after each, and scraping the bowl occasionally with a rubber spatula.

Pour the filling into the prepared crust. Refrigerate for 5 to 6 hours or overnight. (Pie may be frozen now or it may be refrigerated for a day or so. If you freeze it, freeze until filling is firm before wrapping airtight. Frozen pie should be uncovered and thawed overnight in the refrigerator.)

Either shortly before serving, or a few hours before, prepare the following:

TOPPING

2 cups heavy cream
2 tablespoons instant coffee
½ cup confectioners sugar
optional: Chocolate, coarsely grated

In a chilled bowl with chilled beaters, whip the cream with the coffee and sugar until firm. Do not overbeat, but it must be firm enough so that it holds its shape when pie is served.

Spread smoothly over filling, or apply in fancy swirls with a pastry bag and a large star tube.

Sprinkle top with optional grated chocolate. Refrigerate.

Vanilla Cream Pie

6 TO 8 PORTIONS

Made with unbaked chocolate cookie crumb crust.

CHOCOLATE COOKIE CRUST

1½ cups of crumbs
    made from 6 ounces of chocolate wafers
    (Sometimes called icebox cookies.
    The crumbs may be made in a blender
    or by placing the cookies in a bag
    and crushing them with a rolling pin.)
optional: 1 teaspoon instant coffee
2⅔ ounces (⅓ cup) melted butter

With a rubber spatula, mix the crumbs and optional instant coffee with the butter, pressing against the sides of the bowl until completely mixed. Use a 9-inch pie plate and follow directions for crumb crust, page 284. However, this crust is not baked. After pressing the crumbs firmly into place, freeze the crust for at least 1 hour. Then follow directions for crumb crust to remove the foil.

VANILLA FILLING

3 eggs, separated
1¼ cups milk
1 tablespoon (1 envelope) unflavored gelatin
½ cup sugar
1 teaspoon vanilla extract
1 cup heavy cream
⅛ teaspoon salt

In the top of a small double boiler off the heat, stir the egg yolks just to mix. Gradually mix in the milk and then the powdered gelatin and ¼ cup of sugar (reserve remaining ¼ cup).

Place over hot water on moderate heat and stir until custard thickens enough to coat a spoon (175 to 180 degrees on a candy or sugar thermometer). Remove from heat and stir in vanilla.

Place the top of the double boiler into a bowl of ice water and stir until cool. Remove from ice water and set aside.

In a chilled bowl with chilled beaters, whip the cream until it holds a soft shape, not stiff. Set aside.

Add the salt to the egg whites and beat until they increase in volume and barely begin to thicken. Gradually add the reserved ¼ cup sugar and continue to beat only until whites hold a point, barely stiff. Set aside.

Replace the custard over the ice water and stir again until custard begins to thicken slightly. Gradually fold custard into whites and then gradually fold that into the cream.

Turn the filling into the prepared pie crust. There will probably be a little too much filling. Let the excess stand at room temperature while you chill the filled shell (about 10 minutes in the freezer or a bit longer in the refrigerator) until filling is almost set. Then pour on the remaining filling, mounding it higher in the center.

Refrigerate for a few hours. Prepare following whipped cream topping:

WHIPPED CREAM

1 cup heavy cream
¼ cup confectioners sugar
1 teaspoon vanilla extract

In a chilled bowl with chilled beaters, whip above ingredients until firm enough to hold a shape.

Place the whipped cream by heaping teaspoonfuls in a ring around the outer edge of the pie, very close to the crust. Leave the center of the pie uncovered. With the back of the teaspoon pull the cream up in peaks. Refrigerate.

Black Bottom Pie

8 PORTIONS

Marjorie Kinnan Rawlings, the Pulitzer Prize–winning author of The Yearling, also wrote a delightful cook book, Cross Creek Cookery (Charles Scribner's Sons, 1942), which is a mouth-watering account of the food served in her home in central Florida. In it, she says of her Black Bottom Pie, "I think this is the most delicious pie I have ever eaten . . . a pie so delicate, so luscious, that I hope to be propped up on my dying bed and fed a generous portion. Then I think that I should refuse outright to die, for life *would be too good to relinquish." My recipe is slightly different from Mrs. Rawlings', but my sentiments are the same.*

CRUST

1¼ cups graham cracker crumbs
1 tablespoon sugar
1 teaspoon powdered ginger
1 teaspoon cinnamon
2 ounces (¼ cup) melted butter

Adjust rack to center of oven. Preheat to 375 degrees.

In a bowl mix the crumbs with the sugar, ginger, and cinnamon, and then add the melted butter. Stir with a rubber spatula, pressing the mixture against the sides of the bowl until completely mixed. The mixture will look crumbly but will hold together when pressed into place.

Use a 9-inch pie plate and follow directions for crumb crust (page 284).

FILLING

2 ounces (2 squares) unsweetened chocolate
1 tablespoon (1 envelope) unflavored gelatin
¼ cup cold water
1 cup sugar
1 tablespoon cornstarch
Salt
4 eggs, separated
1¾ cups milk
2 tablespoons dark rum
1 teaspoon vanilla extract
⅛ teaspoon cream of tartar

Melt the chocolate in the top of a small double boiler over hot water on moderate heat. Remove from hot water and set aside.

Sprinkle the gelatin over the cold water and set aside.

In a small bowl mix ½ cup of the sugar (reserve remaining ½ cup) with the cornstarch and a pinch of salt. Set aside.

In the top of a large double boiler, stir the yolks lightly with a small wire whisk or a fork just to mix.

Scald the milk uncovered in a small, heavy saucepan over moderate heat until you can see small bubbles on the surface. Stir in the sugar-cornstarch mixture and pour very slowly, in a thin stream, into the yolks—stirring constantly. Place over, but not touching, hot water in the bottom of the double boiler on moderate heat. Cook, stirring gently and scraping the pot with a rubber spatula, for about 12 to 15 minutes, until the custard thickens to the consistency of a medium cream sauce. Lift top of double boiler off the hot water.

Remove 1 cup of the custard and set aside to cool for about 5 to 10 minutes until tepid, stirring occasionally.

Meanwhile, to the remainder of the custard in the top of the double boiler, immediately add the softened gelatin and stir until thoroughly dissolved. Stir in the rum and set aside.

Gradually add the 1 cup of reserved custard to the chocolate, stirring constantly with a small wire whisk. Mix thoroughly until smooth. Add the vanilla and turn the mixture into the prepared crust. Spread level and refrigerate.

In the small bowl of an electric mixer at moderately high speed, beat the whites with a pinch of salt and the cream of tartar until the mixture increases in volume and starts to thicken. While beating, gradually add the reserved ½ cup sugar and continue to beat until mixture holds a shape and is the consistency of thick marshmallow sauce.

Gradually fold the rum custard (which may still be warm) into the beaten whites. Pour gently from one bowl to another to insure thorough blending.

Pour over the chocolate layer, mounding it high in the center. (If there is too much filling and it might run over, reserve some at room temperature. Chill the pie in the freezer for about 10 to 15 minutes, or in the refrigerator for a bit longer, to partially set the filling. Then pour on the reserved portion and it will not run over.)

Refrigerate pie for 2 to 3 hours. Prepare whipped cream.

WHIPPED CREAM

1 cup heavy cream
¼ cup confectioners sugar
1 scant teaspoon vanilla extract

In a chilled bowl with chilled beaters, whip above ingredients until the cream holds a shape. Spread evenly over filling or use a pastry bag with a star tube and form a heavy, ruffled border of the cream.

OPTIONAL: *If the cream was spread over the pie, sprinkle it with coarsely grated chocolate; if it was put on to form a border, fill the center with grated chocolate.*

Black Bottom Pecan Cream Pie

6 TO 8
PORTIONS

CRUST

1¼ cups graham cracker crumbs
¼ cup sugar
2 ounces (¼ cup) melted butter
⅓ cup pecans, chopped or cut medium-fine

Adjust rack to center of oven and preheat oven to 375 degrees.

Mix the crumbs with sugar and then add the melted butter. Stir with a rubber spatula, pressing the mixture against the sides of the bowl until completely mixed. Stir in the nuts. The mixture will look crumbly but will hold together when pressed into place. Use a 9-inch pie plate and follow directions for crumb crust (page 284).

BLACK BOTTOM

1 cup light cream
8 ounces chocolate, sweet, semisweet,
    or bittersweet
1 tablespoon instant coffee
4 egg yolks

In a medium-size, heavy saucepan heat the cream. Break up the chocolate and add it, stirring frequently with a wire whisk until smooth. Add coffee and stir to dissolve. Remove from heat. With the wire whisk beat in the yolks one at a time. Let stand, stirring occasionally, until slightly cooled. Pour into shell and refrigerate for 2 to 3 hours until firm. Prepare topping.

CREAM TOPPING WITH NUTS

2 cups heavy cream
½ cup confectioners sugar
2 scant teaspoons vanilla extract
3½ ounces (1 cup) pecans, cut medium
optional: 6 or 8 large pecan halves

In a chilled bowl with chilled beaters, whip the cream with the sugar and vanilla until firm. Fold in the cut nuts.

Place one spoonful at a time on the chocolate, starting at the outer edge and working toward the center. Leave uneven or smooth with a metal spatula.

OPTIONAL: *Top with nut halves. Refrigerate.*

Peace and Plenty

From the Bahamas—cream cheese, sweet cream, sour cream, and fresh strawberries.

6 TO 8 PORTIONS

CRUST

Prepare Chocolate Cookie Crust as in recipe for Vanilla Cream Pie (page 289).

STRAWBERRIES FOR TOPPING

Use 1½ to 2 pints of berries. Rinse them briefly in a bowl of cold water, hull, and place on paper toweling to drain. Let stand until ready to use.

FILLING

1 tablespoon (1 envelope) unflavored gelatin
½ cup cold water
8 ounces cream cheese, at room temperature
Pinch of salt

1½ teaspoons vanilla extract
optional: 3 tablespoons Curaçao, Cointreau,
    Grand Marnier, or kirsch
½ cup sugar
½ cup sour cream
1 cup heavy cream

Sprinkle the gelatin over the water in a heatproof measuring cup. Let stand for a few minutes and then place cup in a small saucepan of shallow hot water over moderate heat until dissolved. Remove from heat and set aside.

In small bowl of electric mixer beat the cream cheese until soft and smooth. Beat in the salt, vanilla, optional liqueur, and sugar. Beat well, scraping the bowl with a rubber spatula. Beat in the sour cream. On low speed, very gradually beat in the dissolved gelatin (which may still be slightly warm), continuing to scrape the bowl occasionally with a rubber spatula.

In a chilled bowl with chilled beaters, whip the heavy cream until it holds a soft shape, not stiff. In several additions fold the cheese mixture into the whipped cream and then gently pour from one bowl to another to insure thorough blending.

Pour into prepared crumb crust. Immediately, before filling has a chance to set, start at the outer edge and form a ring of strawberries, placing them upright and touching each other. Continue with additional berries, placing them in concentric rings working toward the center until the top is completely covered. Refrigerate and prepare glaze.

GLAZE

¼ cup red currant jelly
1 tablespoon sugar

In your smallest frying pan or saucepan, on moderate heat, stir the jelly and sugar until melted and smooth. Bring to a boil and let the glaze bubble gently, stirring constantly, for 3 minutes. Use glaze immediately while very hot. With a soft brush, brush it over the strawberries. If glaze cools and thickens it may be remelted over low heat.

Refrigerate for several hours or more before serving.

Cheesecakes

CRAIG CLAIBORNE'S CHEESECAKE
  NUT CHEESECAKE
  BLACK-AND-WHITE CHEESECAKE
APRICOT CHEESECAKE SQUARES
FLORIDA CHIFFON CHEESECAKE
CREAM CHEESE PIE
PINEAPPLE CHEESE PIE
CREAM CHEESE AND YOGURT PIE
CHOCOLATE CREAM CHEESE PIE
COTTAGE CHEESE AND PINEAPPLE
  ICEBOX CAKE
COTTAGE CHEESE KUCHEN

Craig Claiborne's Cheesecake

This is my version of a cheesecake that Craig Claiborne, dean of the food establishment, made famous when he printed the recipe in The New York Times. *I made it daily for many years for my husband's restaurant—everyone loved it.*

Finely grated rind of 1 lemon

3 tablespoons lemon juice

2 pounds cream cheese,
    preferably at room temperature

1 teaspoon vanilla extract

1¾ cups sugar

4 eggs

⅓ cup graham cracker crumbs
    (to be used after cake is baked)

Adjust rack to lowest position in the oven. Preheat oven to 350 degrees.

Cheesecake pans can be bought in restaurant or bakery supply stores. (See Note 1.) They are deep and do not have removable bottoms. Do not use a spring form. Use a round, 8-inch cheesecake pan, 3 inches deep. Butter it lightly all the way up to the rim and the inside of the rim itself, or the cake will stick to the rim and will not rise evenly. Any unbuttered spots will prevent the finished cake from sliding out of the pan easily.

Mix the lemon rind and juice and set aside. In the large bowl of an electric mixer at medium-high speed, beat the cheese until it is absolutely smooth. All during the mixing continue to scrape the sides and bottom of the bowl with a rubber spatula in order to keep everything evenly mixed. When the cheese is smooth, beat in the vanilla and sugar. Beat well and then add the eggs one at a time. After adding eggs, do not beat any more than is necessary to mix ingredients thoroughly. With rubber spatula stir in the lemon rind and juice.

Turn the batter into the prepared pan. Level top by briskly rotating pan a bit, first in one direction then in the other. Place the cheesecake pan inside a larger pan. The larger pan must not touch the sides of the cake pan and must not be deeper than the cake pan. Pour hot water into the larger pan until it is about 1½ inches deep. (If the large pan is aluminum, adding about ½ teaspoon of cream of tartar to each quart of water will keep the pan from discoloring.)

Bake for 1½ hours. The top of the cake should be a rich golden brown and feel dry to the touch, but cake will still be soft inside.

Lift the cheesecake pan out of the water and place it on a rack for a few hours until it is completely cool. Do not cool the cake in the refrigerator or the butter will harden and the cake will stick to the pan.

When the bottom of the cake pan has reached room temperature, place a flat plate or a board on top and invert. Remove the cake pan. Sprinkle the bottom of the cake evenly with graham cracker crumbs. Gently place another flat plate or board on top of the crumbs. Very carefully and quickly invert so that the cake is right side up. Do this without pressing too hard or you will squash the cake, which will still be soft.

Refrigerate for at least 5 to 6 hours or overnight. Or freeze it—it freezes perfectly. Serve very cold.

When cutting the cake, always dip the knife into hot water, or hold it under running hot water, before each cut to prevent the cake somewhat from sticking to the knife. (It will stick a bit anyhow.)

The only way I have found to avoid the sticking is to cut the cake when it is frozen almost solid. Either freeze it until it is almost completely firm, or freeze it for as long as you wish and then let it stand (wrapped airtight) for about 30 minutes. Then unwrap and use a large heavy knife to cut the whole cake into portions at once. If the cake is too firm you won't be able to cut it, but when it is just right it will cut cleanly and beautifully. Cover the cake airtight with plastic wrap while it finishes thawing.

NOTES: 1. *Cheesecake pans are available at the Bridge Company, 212 East 52nd Street, New York, New York 10022.*

2. *The cheesecake will rise above the top of the pan while it is baking and will sink down below the top as it cools.*

Nut Cheesecake

Mr. Claiborne created a marvelous Nut Cheesecake based on the previous recipe.

Prepare 7½ ounces (1½ cups) of blanched almonds or hazelnuts as follows. Spread them in a shallow pan and bake in a 350-degree oven, stirring them occasionally, for about 15 minutes until lightly browned. Cool and then grind the nuts in a blender—it is all right if they are not evenly ground and if there are some pieces larger than others.

Mix the batter as in the previous recipe but eliminate the lemon rind and juice, add a scant ½ teaspoon almond extract along with the vanilla, and add the ground nuts to the batter after adding the eggs. Beat until evenly mixed. Continue with remaining directions.

Serve this rich cake in small portions.

Black-and-White Cheesecake

In the top of a small double boiler over hot water, melt 2 ounces (2 squares) of unsweetened chocolate. Remove from heat and let cool.

Prepare oven, cake pan, and batter for cheesecake as in recipe, page 299, omitting lemon juice and rind and adding ¼ teaspoon almond flavoring with the vanilla.

Place one third of the batter in the small bowl of an electric mixer. Add melted chocolate and mix until smooth.

Place alternate large spoonfuls of the white batter and small spoonfuls of the chocolate batter in the prepared pan, placing some of the chocolate directly against the rim of the pan so that it will show on the outside of the cake. Bake and finish as above.

Apricot Cheesecake Squares

A large, dense cake with a definite lemon flavor. Suitable for a buffet, since it is cut into portions ahead of time. Cake may be made a day ahead; topping should be put on the day it is to be served.

16 PORTIONS

Finely grated rind of 1 large lemon
¼ cup lemon juice
3½ pounds (7 8-ounce packages) cream cheese, preferably at room temperature
1¼ cups sugar
Pinch of salt
1 teaspoon vanilla extract
1 cup sour cream
6 eggs

Adjust rack to lowest position in oven. Preheat oven to 400 degrees. Butter a 13 × 9 × 2-inch pan.

Mix lemon rind and juice and set aside. In large bowl of electric mixer at low speed beat cream cheese until soft and smooth. All during beating scrape the bowl as necessary with a rubber spatula. Add sugar. Gradually increase speed to medium. Beat in salt, vanilla, and sour cream. Beat until smooth. Add the eggs one at a time and beat after each until smooth. Remove from mixer and stir in lemon rind and juice.

Turn the batter into the prepared pan. Shake gently to level or spread smooth with a rubber spatula. Place the cheesecake pan in a larger pan, which must not be deeper than the cake pan. Place pans in oven. Pour 1 inch of hot water into the larger pan. (If the larger pan is aluminum, adding ½ teaspoon of cream of tartar to each quart of water will keep the pan from discoloring.)

Bake about 45 minutes until top is golden. (During baking, if the back of the cake browns faster than the front, very carefully reverse position of pan.) The sides will have risen about ¾ inch above the pan. Remove cheesecake pan from hot water and place cake pan on rack to cool until only slightly warm. Do not chill before removing from pan. (The butter would harden and the cake could not be removed easily.) During cooling, cake will sink to the level of the pan.

Place a large board over the cake. It may be a board to be used for serving or, if you wish, use any kitchen board or a cookie sheet and later transfer the finished individual portions to a serving tray. Carefully invert. Remove pan leaving cake upside down. Refrigerate for a few hours or overnight.

The cake is cut into portions before the topping is put on. With a ruler and toothpicks mark the cake into 16 portions. Cut with a very long, sharp knife. Hold the knife under hot running water for a few seconds before each cut. Cut straight down with the full length of the blade. The portions must stay in place—do not move them. Prepare the topping.

TOPPING

16 canned apricot halves
1 cup apricot preserves
¼ cup sugar
optional: Green pistachio nuts, chopped

Drain the apricots and set them aside on toweling to dry.

Strain the preserves. In a saucepan mix the preserves and sugar. Stir over heat until the mixture comes to a boil. Let boil for 2 minutes.

Pour a little more than half the mixture over the cake and smooth with a brush. Place one apricot half, cut side down, on each portion. Brush remaining preserves over the apricots. If desired, top each apricot with a pinch of pistachio nuts. Refrigerate.

Before serving, hold the knife under hot water again and cut through the glaze.

NOTES: 1. *Canned cherry-pie filling may be used as a quick and easy alternate topping. Use 2 21-ounce cans. In a large strainer set over a bowl, drain most of the syrup. Arrange the cherries on the cake and then pour on part of the syrup—you probably will not need all of it. Or use blueberry pie filling. Either one of the pie fillings may be spooned generously over individual portions or passed separately.*

2. *The cake may also be served with no topping, with a help-your-self bowl of fresh strawberries, or with just-thawed and partially drained frozen strawberries.*

Florida Chiffon Cheesecake

8 PORTIONS

PECAN CRUST

4 ounces (1¼ cups) pecans, finely ground
  (See page 11. For this recipe they do
  not have to be strained.)
2 tablespoons sugar
2 ounces (¼ cup) melted butter

Adjust rack to center of oven. Preheat oven to 350 degrees. Remove sides of a 9 × 2½ or 3-inch spring-form pan and set aside.

In a bowl, stir the pecans with the sugar and butter. Mix well and turn mixture out onto the bottom of the spring form. With your fingertips (floured if necessary), press the mixture to cover the bottom of the pan evenly.

Bake for 12 to 15 minutes until slightly colored. With a wide metal spatula, remove from oven very carefully. Immediately, while crust is hot, attach the sides of the pan. Set aside to cool completely.

FILLING

1 tablespoon (1 envelope) unflavored gelatin
1 cup cold water
3 eggs, separated
¾ cup sugar
16 ounces cream cheese,
  preferably at room temperature
¼ cup lemon juice
Finely grated rind of 1 large orange
1 cup heavy cream
Pinch of salt

Sprinkle gelatin over ¼ cup of water (reserve remaining ¾ cup). Set aside.

In a 1-quart heavy saucepan stir the egg yolks lightly just to mix. Gradually mix in the reserved ¾ cup water and the sugar. Place over moderate heat and cook, stirring constantly, until mixture barely coats a spoon, or reaches 180 degrees on a candy thermometer. Add gelatin-water mixture and stir to dissolve. Remove from heat and set aside.

In large bowl of electric mixer beat the cream cheese very well until it is soft and completely smooth. Beat in the lemon juice and then, very gradually, beat in the warm egg yolk mixture, scraping the bowl with a rubber spatula to keep the mixture very smooth. Remove from mixer. Stir in the grated orange rind and set aside to cool completely.

In a chilled bowl with chilled beaters, whip the cream until it just holds a shape, but is not stiff, and set aside. Add the salt to the egg whites and beat until they just hold a shape, or are stiff but not dry.

Gradually fold part of the cheese mixture into the whites, then fold all of the whites into rest of the cheese mixture. Now gradually fold a bit of this into the whipped cream and then fold the whipped cream into the cheese mixture. If mixtures aren't completely blended, very gently pour from one container to another to insure thorough mixing.

Turn filling into spring-form pan over baked and cooled crust. Refrigerate for 7 to 8 hours or overnight.

Cut around sides of cake to release. Remove sides of pan. Do not remove cake from bottom of pan. Place on a folded napkin on a cake platter. (The napkin will keep the pan from sliding on the plate.)

NOTE: *Make this early in the day for that night and serve it very cold.*

Cream Cheese Pie

6 TO 8
PORTIONS

CRUST

1¼ cups graham cracker crumbs
1 tablespoon sugar
½ teaspoon cinnamon
¼ teaspoon powdered ginger
3 ounces (6 tablespoons) melted butter

Butter a 9-inch pie plate and set aside.

In a bowl stir the crumbs, sugar, cinnamon, and ginger to mix. Add the melted butter and stir until thoroughly mixed.

Turn the mixture into the pie plate.

First, with your fingertips, distribute it loosely and evenly all over the sides and bottom, working enough up on the sides to form a ridge slightly above the top of the pie plate. Then, with your fingertips, press it firmly into place, first pressing the sides and then the bottom. Refrigerate while preparing filling:

FILLING

12 ounces cream cheese,
*   preferably at room temperature*
1 teaspoon vanilla extract
½ cup sugar
2 eggs
⅓ cup heavy cream

Adjust rack one-third up from the bottom of the oven and preheat at 350 degrees.

In small bowl of electric mixer beat the cream cheese until completely smooth. Beat in the vanilla, sugar, and then the eggs one at a time. Beat at moderate speed, scraping the bowl with a rubber spatula, until smooth. Add the heavy cream and beat only until smooth. Turn filling into chilled crust.

Bake for exactly 25 minutes. Remove from oven and let stand at room temperature for 20 minutes.

Adjust oven temperature to 300 degrees and, when the 20 minutes are up, prepare the topping:

TOPPING

2 cups sour cream
¼ cup sugar

In a small bowl stir sour cream and sugar briefly just to mix. With a tablespoon, gently spoon it over the cheese filling, starting around the outer edge and then filling in toward the center. With a long, narrow metal spatula, smooth over the cheese, being careful not to let the topping run over the crust.

Bake at 300 degrees for exactly 5 minutes. Remove from oven. Cool to room temperature. Refrigerate for several hours or overnight before serving.

Pineapple Cheese Pie

6 TO 8 PORTIONS

Prepare crust and filling as for above Cream Cheese Pie. Bake for 25 minutes. Remove from oven and cool completely. Meanwhile, prepare Pineapple Topping:

PINEAPPLE TOPPING

1 can (1 pound, 4 ounces) crushed pineapple
1 tablespoon cornstarch
1 tablespoon sugar
Yellow food coloring
½ teaspoon vanilla extract

In a large strainer set over a bowl, thoroughly drain the pineapple. Reserve pineapple and 1 cup of the juice. (If necessary add water to make 1 cup.)

In a 1-quart saucepan stir together the cornstarch and sugar to mix and then gradually stir in the pineapple juice.

Place over moderate heat and cook, stirring gently, until mixture barely begins to boil. Reduce heat and simmer gently for 1 minute.

Remove from heat. Stir in about 3 drops of yellow food coloring and the vanilla. Add the drained pineapple and stir gently to mix. Set aside to cool.

Gently spoon the cooled topping over the cooled pie. Spread level. Refrigerate for 5 to 6 hours or overnight. Serve very cold.

Cream Cheese and Yogurt Pie

Must be made at least 24 hours ahead.

8 PORTIONS

Prepare graham cracker crumb crust as in recipe for Rum Pie (page 285).

FILLING

16 ounces cream cheese,
    preferably at room temperature
1 teaspoon vanilla extract
¼ cup honey
1 pint unflavored yogurt

In small bowl of electric mixer, cream the cheese until soft and smooth. Beat in the vanilla and honey. On low speed gradually add the yogurt, scraping the bowl with a rubber spatula and beating only until smooth.

Pour as much of the mixture as you can into the prepared crust. There will be a bit too much filling. Chill the filled crust for about 20 to 30 minutes in the freezer or a bit longer in the refrigerator, until semi-firm. (Do not freeze any longer or the filling will lose its super-creamy consistency.) Then you will be able to top with the remaining filling without having it run over.

Refrigerate for at least 24 hours or more. Serve very cold.

Serve as is, or accompany each portion with a generous spoonful of the following strawberries:

STRAWBERRIES

Using 1 pint of berries, dip them briefly into a bowl of cold water to wash, then hull and drain. Cut in thick slices, lengthwise. Place in a bowl and sprinkle with 3 tablespoons of sugar. Let stand, stirring occasionally, for half an hour or so. Cover and refrigerate.

Serve separately in a small bowl.

Chocolate Cream Cheese Pie

8 PORTIONS

Prepare Chocolate Cookie Crust as in recipe for Vanilla Cream Pie (page 289).

FILLING

6 ounces (6 squares) semisweet chocolate
8 ounces cream cheese,
    preferably at room temperature
1 teaspoon vanilla extract
½ cup sugar
2 eggs, separated
Pinch of salt
1 cup heavy cream

In the top of a small double boiler over hot water on moderate heat, melt the chocolate. Remove from heat and set aside.

Meanwhile, in small bowl of electric mixer, beat the cream cheese until smooth. Beat in the vanilla and ¼ cup of the sugar (reserve remaining ¼ cup sugar). Beat in the yolks one at a time, scraping the bowl with a rubber spatula as necessary to keep the mixture smooth. Beat in the melted chocolate, which may still be slightly warm.

Beat the whites with a pinch of salt until they increase in volume and begin to hold a soft shape. Gradually beat in the reserved ¼ cup of sugar and beat until firm but not dry.

In a chilled bowl with chilled beaters, whip the cream until it holds a semi-firm shape, not stiff.

Gradually fold the cream into the chocolate mixture and then fold the chocolate mixture and the whites together.

Turn the filling into the prepared crust, mounding it higher in the center. Refrigerate for 5 to 6 hours or overnight.

Prepare whipped cream topping:

WHIPPED CREAM TOPPING

1 cup heavy cream
1 teaspoon vanilla extract
¼ cup confectioners sugar

In a chilled bowl with chilled beaters, whip above ingredients until the cream holds a shape. Place 1 rounded teaspoonful at a time (each touching the next) around outer edge of the filling to form a ring. Then make one or two smaller circles of cream inside the first, leaving the center of the filling uncovered.

OPTIONAL: *Cover the center with coarsely grated chocolate.*

Cottage Cheese and Pineapple Icebox Cake

10 PORTIONS

CRUST

1 cup graham cracker crumbs
2 tablespoons sugar
½ teaspoon cinnamon
2 ounces (¼ cup) melted butter

Stir above ingredients until thoroughly mixed. Place in bottom of a 9 × 3-inch spring-form pan with sides attached. Press firmly and smoothly all over bottom of pan. Chill in freezer or refrigerator, or bake in a 375-degree oven for 8 minutes. Baking is not necessary, but it does make for a better flavor and firmer texture.

FILLING

2 tablespoons (2 envelopes) unflavored gelatin
¾ cup sugar
¼ teaspoon salt
3 eggs, separated
¾ cup milk

1 small can (8¼ ounces—about 1 cup)
    crushed pineapple with syrup
3 cups (1½ pounds)
    creamed, small-curd cottage cheese
Finely grated rind of 1 large lemon
3 tablespoons lemon juice
1 cup heavy cream

In top of large double boiler mix gelatin with sugar and salt. In a small bowl stir 3 egg yolks just to mix and gradually stir in the milk. Stir into sugar mixture. Add the pineapple and mix well.

Place over boiling water on moderate heat and cook, stirring almost constantly for 10 minutes until mixture thickens slightly. Remove from heat and turn the mixture into a large bowl. Set aside until cool.

Meanwhile, force cheese through a sieve or food mill. It should be as smooth as possible. Mix lemon rind and juice together. When pineapple mixture has cooled, stir in the cheese and lemon rind and juice.

In a chilled bowl with chilled beaters, whip the cream until it holds a soft shape. Beat the egg whites until they hold a soft point, not dry. Fold the whipped cream and beaten whites into the cheese mixture. Pour it over the crust in the spring-form pan. Rotate pan gently to level filling. Refrigerate for 4 to 5 hours or overnight. With a small, sharp knife, pressing firmly against the pan, cut around sides of pan to release and remove.

TOPPING

1 cup heavy sour cream
3 tablespoons toasted, sliced almonds
    (See Note.)

In a small bowl stir the cream briefly only until it is soft enough to spread. With a long, narrow metal spatula spread it evenly over the top of the filling. Crumble the almonds coarsely and sprinkle them over the sour cream. Refrigerate.

NOTE: *To toast the nuts, place them in a shallow pan and bake in a moderate oven, shaking pan occasionally until nuts are a rich golden brown.*

Cottage Cheese Kuchen

9 PORTIONS

A German recipe with a thin pastry crust; the German name for this type of pastry is Mürbteig.

PASTRY

1¼ cups sifted all-purpose flour
¼ teaspoon salt
¼ teaspoon double-acting baking powder
¼ cup sugar
2 ounces (¼ cup) butter
1 egg

Sift together flour, salt, baking powder, and sugar into a bowl. With a pastry blender, cut in the butter until the mixture resembles fine meal. Add the unbeaten egg and stir thoroughly with a fork. Then work the dough very briefly with your hand until the mixture holds together and forms a ball.

Place in a 9 × 1¾-inch square cake pan. Dipping your fingers in flour as necessary, press the dough over the bottom and about three-quarters of the way up on the sides. This will make a thin layer—patience. (Watch the corners—one has a tendency to make them too thick.) Trim the top edge even, using any trimmings to fill in empty or thin areas. Refrigerate the pastry shell while preparing the filling.

FILLING

Finely grated rind of 1 lemon
3 tablespoons lemon juice (See Note 1.)
12 ounces (1½ cups) creamed cottage cheese
    (either large or small curd)
½ cup sugar
1 teaspoon vanilla extract
⅛ teaspoon salt
1 tablespoon melted butter
2 eggs
½ cup sour cream
½ cup apricot preserves
⅓ cup raisins, light or dark (See Note 2.)

Adjust rack one-third up from bottom of oven and preheat to 450 degrees.

Mix lemon rind and juice and set aside. In small bowl of electric mixer beat the cheese until almost smooth. Beat in the sugar, vanilla, salt, melted butter, and then the eggs. Beat well, scraping the bowl as necessary with a rubber spatula. Add the sour cream and beat until completely blended. Remove from mixer and stir in lemon rind and juice.

Heat the apricot preserves to soften. Strain and then brush evenly over bottom and sides of pastry shell.

Pour the filling into the prepared shell. Spread the top smooth and shake pan gently to level. Sprinkle raisins evenly over the top, and with the back of a spoon tap them down gently into the filling so that they are just barely covered with filling.

Bake for 15 minutes. Reduce the oven temperature to 375 degrees and bake for an additional 15 minutes.

Remove the cake from the oven and turn off the heat but keep the oven door closed. Prepare the topping.

TOPPING

2 cups sour cream
¼ cup sugar
1 or 2 drops almond extract

Stir the sour cream with the sugar and almond extract just to mix. Spoon the topping all over the filling and then spread evenly. Return to oven with the heat off for 5 minutes.

Remove from oven and cool to room temperature. Serve at room temperature or refrigerate and serve cold.

If necessary, cut around sides to release from pan. Cut into squares and, with a wide metal spatula, transfer to a cake platter.

NOTES: 1. *This filling will be tart—if you prefer it blander, adjust or eliminate the lemon juice.*

2. *If raisins are dry and hard they should be softened, either by soaking in hot water for a few minutes or by steaming in a strainer, covered, over boiling water for a few minutes. Either way, then drain and dry.*

Pots de Crème, Custards, and Puddings

To test custard to see if it is cooked enough, gently insert a small, sharp knife into the top. As soon as the knife comes out clean, the custard is done. But as the knife will leave a scar, do not test any more than is necessary.

With practice you can learn how to time a custard without having to use a knife and leave scars. When you first bake a custard, keep an exact record of just how long it took, then, all things being equal, the knife test won't be necessary the next time you prepare the same recipe.

Also, before the custard is done, reach into the oven and with a knife gently tap the edge of the custard cup and watch how the unbaked custard shakes. You will be able to see that it is still liquid. Continue to tap the edge of the cup occasionally during the end of the cooking, and watch carefully as it becomes firm. You will be able to teach yourself to recognize when it is done without having to insert the knife. Or, until you are sure of yourself with this method, with only one knife test.

Always be on guard not to overbake custard or it will separate.

Pots de Crème à la Vanille

12 POTS DE CRÈME POTS, OR 7 OR 8 CUSTARD CUPS

3 cups heavy cream
6 egg yolks
¼ cup sugar
⅛ teaspoon salt
1½ teaspoons vanilla extract

Adjust rack to the center of the oven. Preheat the oven to 350 degrees.

Scald the cream over hot water in the top of a large, uncovered double boiler on moderate heat until tiny bubbles begin around the edge or a slight wrinkled skin forms on top.

Meanwhile, stir the egg yolks with a fork, or very briefly with a wire whisk just to mix them—do not beat any air into them.

When the cream is scalded, remove it from the heat, add the sugar and salt, and stir to dissolve. Stirring constantly, very gradually pour the hot cream into the yolks. Do not beat enough to make any foam. Stir in the vanilla and strain into a pitcher.

Pour into ovenproof cups, using either about a dozen pots de crème pots with lids, or seven or eight custard cups. Do not fill them too full. (If you use pots de crème pots, be sure to leave enough headroom so that the lids do not touch the custard.) With a small spoon remove any foam that might have formed.

Place in a baking pan, which must not be deeper than the cups. Pour in hot water to about halfway up the cups. Cover the crème pots with their covers; place a piece of aluminum foil or a cookie sheet over the tops of the custard cups.

Bake for 25 to 30 minutes or until a small, sharp knife inserted into the custard just barely comes out clean.

Remove from hot water and cool uncovered on a rack.

When completely cool, the pots de crème pots may be re-covered. Refrigerate covered.

OPTIONAL: *A spoonful of whipped cream on the top of these seems to cut their richness, unlikely as it sounds. (Either with or without the whipped cream, if you have candied violets or rose petals this is a good time to use them—just one on each.)*

Pots de Crème au Café

6 TO 8 PORTIONS, DEPENDING ON SIZE OF CUPS

¼ cup instant coffee
¾ cup boiling water
7 egg yolks
1½ cups heavy cream
1½ cups light cream
¼ cup sugar
Pinch of salt
½ teaspoon vanilla extract

Adjust rack to the center of the oven and preheat to 350 degrees.

Dissolve the instant coffee in boiling water and set aside.

In a large mixing bowl stir the yolks just to mix.

Scald both creams over boiling water in the top of an uncovered double boiler, or in a heavy saucepan. When the cream forms a wrinkled skin on top or tiny bubbles around the edge, remove it from the heat. Add the sugar, salt, and prepared coffee and stir to dissolve sugar. Very gradually at first, and stirring constantly, add the cream mixture to the yolks. Just stir; do not beat or whip. Strain into a pitcher and stir in vanilla. Pour into six to eight custard cups, leaving a bit of headroom on each. With a small spoon remove any foam from the tops.

Place the cups in a baking pan which must not be deeper than the cups. Pour hot water into the pan to about halfway up the sides of the custard cups. Cover cups with a cookie sheet or a large piece of aluminum foil.

Bake 30 minutes or until a small, sharp knife inserted into the custard comes out clean.

Remove from hot water. Cool uncovered to room temperature. Refrigerate covered.

NOTE: *This recipe may be made in twelve small pots de crème pots, in which case the baking time will be reduced slightly. Bake the cups covered, but remove the covers while the desserts are cooling or moisture will form in the covers and drip back onto the custards. When cool, the covers may be replaced.*

Pots de Crème au Chocolat

This small recipe may be multiplied by any number. This amount will fill four 3-ounce pots de crème pots or three 4-ounce custard cups, or individual soufflé dishes. This is not baked and is very easy to prepare.

3 OR 4 PORTIONS

4 ounces chocolate,
    sweet, semisweet, or bittersweet (I like
    Tobler Tradition or Lindt Excellence.)
1 cup light cream
3 egg yolks

Break up or coarsely chop the chocolate. Place it with the cream in a small, heavy saucepan on moderate heat. Stir frequently with a small wire whisk until the chocolate is melted and the mixture comes to a boil. Reduce heat and simmer, stirring, for about 3 minutes.

In a small bowl stir the yolks slightly just to mix. Very gradually, in a thin stream, stirring constantly with the wire whisk, add the hot chocolate mixture to the yolks.

Pour into a pitcher and then pour into cups. Cool and refrigerate covered.

If you have used pots de crème pots, the covers may be placed on when completely cool.

NOTE: *Pots de crème are classically served* au naturel; *however, they are very elegant, and if they have been prepared in individual soufflé dishes or custard cups, they may be topped with a small rosette of whipped cream and a bit of candied violet or rose petals, or a sprinkling of crumbled, glacéed chestnuts.*

Baked Vanilla Custard

5 or 6
PORTIONS,
DEPENDING ON
SIZE OF CUPS

2¼ cups milk
1 vanilla bean, or 1 teaspoon vanilla extract
¼ cup sugar
Pinch of salt
4 egg yolks plus 1 egg

Adjust rack to center of oven and preheat to 325 degrees.

Place the milk in a heavy saucepan. If you are using the vanilla bean, split it, scrape the seeds into the milk, and add the bean also. (If you are using vanilla extract, add it later.)

Cook over moderate heat until milk is scalded or almost boiling. Stir in the sugar and salt and remove from heat.

In a bowl large enough to hold the milk also, beat the yolks and egg slightly, just to mix. Stirring constantly, very gradually add the hot milk mixture to the eggs. Just stir; do not beat any air into the mixture. Strain into a pitcher. If you are using vanilla extract, stir it in now.

Pour into five or six custard cups, leaving a bit of headroom on each. If you have used a vanilla bean, stir the mixture occasionally while pouring, so that the seeds of the vanilla bean do not all settle into the bottom of the pitcher.

If there is any foam on the tops of the custards, spoon it off.

Place cups in a shallow baking pan, which must not be deeper than the cups. Pour hot water into the pan to about one-half the depth of the cups. Cover with a cookie sheet or aluminum foil.

Bake for 1 hour, or a few minutes longer, until a small, sharp knife inserted into the custard comes out clean.

Remove from hot water. Cool uncovered on a rack and then refrigerate covered.

NOTE: *Apricot Sauce (page 391) with vanilla custard is a natural.*

Crème au Cacao

6 PORTIONS

1 cup milk
1 cup light cream
½ cup sugar
Pinch of salt
¼ cup plus 1 tablespoon
    powdered, unsweetened cocoa
1 tablespoon instant coffee
2 eggs plus 4 egg yolks

Adjust rack to the center of the oven and preheat oven to 300 degrees.

In a heavy saucepan, stir the milk, cream, sugar, salt, cocoa, and coffee occasionally over moderate heat until the mixture comes to a boil. Reduce heat and simmer for about 3 minutes.

Stir eggs and yolks slightly just to mix. Gradually, in a slow, thin stream, while stirring constantly, add the hot milk mixture to the eggs.

Strain into a pitcher and pour into six custard cups, leaving a little headroom on each.

Place the cups in a baking pan which must not be deeper than the cups. Pour hot water into the pan to about halfway up the sides of the cups.

Place in oven and cover with a cookie sheet or a large piece of aluminum foil.

Bake 35 to 40 minutes or until a small, sharp knife inserted into the custard barely comes out clean.

Remove custards from hot water and cool uncovered to room temperature. Refrigerate covered.

OPTIONAL: *Before serving, pour a thin layer of heavy cream (not whipped) over the tops.*

Caramel Custard

Caramel all the way through.

4 OR 5 PORTIONS

1 cup milk
1 cup heavy cream
½ cup sugar
4 egg yolks
Pinch of salt
½ teaspoon vanilla extract

Adjust rack to the center of the oven. Preheat oven to 350 degrees.

In the top of a double boiler over hot water, or in a heavy saucepan over moderate heat, scald the milk and heavy cream until small bubbles appear around the edge or a wrinkled skin forms on top. Reduce heat to lowest and cover to keep warm.

Meanwhile, in a large, heavy frying pan (at least 12 inches in diameter) over moderate heat, melt the sugar. As soon as it starts to melt, stir constantly with a wooden spatula until it is smoothly melted and golden brown.

Very, very carefully, gradually pour the hot milk and cream, stirring continuously, into the caramelized sugar. It will bubble up furiously—that's why the pan must be large. Continue to cook and stir until the caramel has melted and the mixture is smooth. Remove from heat and pour into a pitcher.

In a bowl at least 6- to 8-cup size, stir the yolks gently only to mix them. Very gradually, just a bit at a time at first, stir in the hot milk mixture. Do not beat or whip—the mixture should not be foamy. Stir in the salt and vanilla and strain back into the pitcher.

Pour into four or five custard cups. Cups should not be too full—there should be at least ¼-inch headroom. If there is foam on top, spoon it off.

Place the cups in a baking pan which must not be deeper than the cups. Pour hot water into the pan to about halfway up the sides of the cups.

Cover the cups with a cookie sheet or a large piece of aluminum foil. Bake 1 hour or until a small, sharp knife inserted into the custard comes out clean.

Remove from oven and place cups uncovered on a rack to cool to room temperature. Refrigerate covered.

NOTES: 1. *This recipe may be doubled.*

2. *If you wish, these custards may be topped with a spoonful or rosette of whipped cream.*

Flan

6 TO 8
PORTIONS

This tropical custard, flavored with lime, is baked in one large caramelized dish. It has an exquisite flavor and texture. Best made a day ahead.

1⅓ cups sugar
4 cups light cream
Finely grated rind of 1 large lime
3 tablespoons lime juice
12 egg yolks
optional: 2 10-ounce packages
    frozen raspberries

Adjust rack to the center of the oven and preheat oven to 350 degrees.

Caramelize 1 cup of the sugar (reserve remaining ⅓ cup) by placing it in a heavy skillet over moderately high heat. Stir occasionally with a wooden spatula until the sugar starts to melt, and then stir constantly until it has all melted to a smooth caramel. It should be a rich brown but do not let it become too dark or it will have a bitter burnt taste. If it is not cooked long enough it will be tasteless.

Immediately pour the caramelized sugar into a 2-quart soufflé dish or other round ovenproof dish. Using potholders, quickly tilt and turn the dish to coat the bottom and almost all the way up on the sides. Continue to tilt and turn the dish until the caramel stops running. Set aside.

Scald the cream, uncovered, in a heavy saucepan or in the top of a large double boiler over boiling water. Meanwhile, mix the lime rind and juice together and set aside. In a large mixing bowl stir the yolks just to mix. When the cream forms tiny bubbles around the edge and a slight wrinkled skin on top, remove it from the heat. Add the remaining ⅓ cup of sugar and stir to dissolve. Very gradually, just a bit at a time at first, add it to the yolks, stirring constantly. Strain and then gradually stir in the lime rind and juice.

Pour into the caramelized dish. Place in a large pan which must not touch the sides of the dish and must not be deeper than the dish. Pour hot water into the large pan to about two-thirds of the way up the sides of the custard dish. Cover loosely with a cookie sheet or large piece of aluminum foil.

Bake for 1¼ hours, or until a small sharp knife inserted into the center comes out clean. Do not make any more knife tests than necessary. Do not insert the knife all the way to the bottom of the custard or it will spoil the appearance when inverted. Remove from hot water and place on a rack. Cool uncovered to room temperature. Refrigerate for 10 to 24 hours. *Do not stint on the chilling time.* (See Note 1.)

If necessary, cut around the upper edge of the custard to release. Choose a dessert platter with a flat bottom and enough rim to hold the caramel, which will have melted to a sauce. Place the platter upside down over the custard. Carefully invert. Remove dish. Refrigerate. Serve very cold.

OPTIONAL: *Serve with a side dish of thawed and partially drained frozen raspberries.*

NOTES: 1. *If flan is underbaked or if it is not refrigerated long enough, it will collapse when cut. It is best not to invert it too long before serving. The beautiful shiny coating will become dull as it stands.*

              2. *To remove hardened caramel from utensils, place them in the sink and let hot water run over them until the caramel disappears.*

Crème Brûlée

6 TO 8
PORTIONS

A rich baked custard covered with a thin, crisp, broiled sugar topping. The custard may be made a day ahead. The topping may be completed from 1 hour to about 6 or 8 hours before serving. Crème Brûlée is generally considered a French recipe and it is occasionally referred to as English, but it is found in very few French or English recipe books. It is, however, in almost all old New Orleans publications.

4 cups heavy cream
8 egg yolks
¼ cup plus 1 tablespoon sugar
2 teaspoons vanilla extract
Light brown sugar

Adjust rack to center of oven. Preheat oven to 325 degrees.

In the top of a large double boiler over hot water on moderate heat, or in a heavy saucepan over low heat, scald the cream, uncovered, until it forms a thin, wrinkled skin on top or tiny bubbles around the edge.

Meanwhile, in a large bowl stir the egg yolks briefly with a fork or a wire whisk just to mix.

When the cream is scalded, add the sugar to it and stir to dissolve. Very gradually, just a spoonful at a time at first and then in a slow stream, stir the hot cream into the yolks. Do not beat—the mixture should not be foamy. Mix in the vanilla.

The custard should be baked in a wide, shallow, ovenproof casserole with a 6-cup capacity. An 11-inch Pyrex pie plate about 1 inch deep is very successful. Pour the custard into the casserole or pie plate and place it into a large, shallow baking pan. Pour hot water into the baking pan to half-way up the sides of the custard plate.

Bake for about 30 minutes in the pie plate, or longer if the custard is deeper, until a small, sharp knife inserted into the center comes out clean.

Remove from hot water and place on a rack. (If the custard was baked in a shallow pie plate it might be difficult to remove from the hot water. If so, use a bulb baster to remove most of the hot water first.) Cool to room temperature. Refrigerate 6 to 8 hours or overnight.

Use a scant ¾ cup of light brown sugar for an 11-inch pie plate; less for one with a smaller diameter. With your fingertips force the sugar through a strainer held over the custard to make a very even layer about ⅛ to ¼ inch thick. There should not be thinner spots or thin edges—they will burn. Also, the sugar should not be too thick or the caramel will be coarse instead of delicate. Cover the sugar with a large piece of wax paper and, with your fingertips and the palm of your hand, pat gently to make a smooth, compact layer. Remove wax paper. Wipe the rim of the plate clean.

Preheat the broiler for a few minutes, then place the custard about 8 inches below the heat. Leave the door open slightly so that you can watch it. Do not take your eyes off the sugar. Broil until the sugar is completely melted. It will take only a few minutes. If a few spots start to burn, cover them with small pieces of aluminum foil. When completely melted remove from broiler immediately. Cool to room temperature and then refrigerate from 1 to 6 or 8 hours. (Cooled any longer than this, the caramel will start to melt; although it will not be as crisp, it is still delicious. Many people prefer it after standing about 12 hours when the caramel has partially melted.)

Crème Brûlée is best very cold. It should be placed in the freezer for about 15 to 20 minutes before serving on well-chilled plates. At the table, tap the caramel with the edge of a serving spoon to crack it..

NOTE: *Crème Brûlée is a magnificent dessert as is. However, in New*

Orleans it is frequently served with cold, drained, stewed pears. Or it may be served with one or more brandied fruits—black cherries, pears, peaches, greengage plums. You may make your own by draining the syrup from canned fruit and placing the fruit in a shallow bowl. Pour on some brandy or kirsch. Cover and refrigerate, turning the fruit occasionally, for 12 hours or more.

Pumpkin Custard

6 TO 8 PORTIONS

1½ cups light cream
⅛ teaspoon salt
1 teaspoon cinnamon
¼ teaspoon powdered ginger
Generous pinch of allspice
Generous pinch of powdered cloves
Generous pinch of nutmeg
2 tablespoons dark rum
3 eggs
½ cup sugar
1 cup canned solid-pack pumpkin
    (not pie filling)
Finely grated rind of 1 orange

Adjust rack to the center of the oven and preheat to 325 degrees.

On moderate heat scald the cream uncovered in a heavy saucepan or in the top of a double boiler over hot water until it forms a wrinkled skin on top or small bubbles around the edge.

Meanwhile, in a small cup mix salt, cinnamon, ginger, allspice, cloves, nutmeg, and rum. Set aside.

With a wire whisk or a fork, stir the eggs lightly just to mix. Add the mixed spices and rum, sugar, pumpkin, and grated orange rind, stirring until smooth. Very gradually at first, stir in the hot scalded cream, mixing until smooth.

Transfer to a pitcher and pour into six to eight large custard cups, leaving about ⅓ to ½ inch headroom at the top of each.

Place the cups in a baking pan which must not be deeper than the cups. Pour hot water into the pan to about halfway up the sides of the cups. Cover the cups with a cookie sheet or aluminum foil.

Bake for 40 or 45 minutes, or until a small, sharp knife inserted slightly into the top of the custard comes out clean.

Remove cups from hot water. Place on a rack to cool, uncovered, to room temperature. Refrigerate covered.

If you wish, top with Ginger Cream (page 396), or the following:

OPTIONAL WHIPPED CREAM

½ cup heavy cream
2 tablespoons confectioners sugar
½ teaspoon vanilla extract

In a chilled bowl with chilled beaters, whip above ingredients until the cream holds a soft shape, and spoon a bit on top of each custard.

Pineapple Custard Pudding

Individual baked puddings with cakelike tops, creamy custard bottoms—served upside down.

6 TO 8 PORTIONS

1 cup drained, diced, canned pineapple
    (If you use chunks, cut them in quarters.)
Finely grated rind of 1 lemon
2 tablespoons lemon juice
3 eggs, separated
½ cup sugar
2 tablespoons melted butter
¼ cup sifted all-purpose flour
¼ cup milk
⅔ cup pineapple juice,
    or syrup from canned pineapple
Pinch of salt

Adjust rack to center of oven. Preheat oven to 350 degrees. Butter six or more of your largest custard cups. The six-ounce cups (see popover recipe, page 254) are best for this.

Divide the pineapple among the buttered cups and set aside.

Mix the lemon rind and juice and set aside.

In the small bowl of an electric mixer beat the yolks and sugar until light lemon-colored. On low speed, add the butter and flour. Then, gradually add the milk and pineapple juice, scraping the bowl as necessary with a rubber spatula and beating only until smooth. Stir in the lemon rind and juice.

Beat the egg whites with the salt, only until the whites hold a definite shape—don't let them dry. Gradually, just a bit at a time at first, fold the yolk mixture into the whites. Pour into a pitcher and pour over the pineapple in the prepared cups. (The cups will be full.)

Place cups in a baking pan which must not be deeper than the cups. Pour hot water into the pan to about halfway up the sides of the cups.

If you have made six custards in large cups, bake for 30 minutes; in smaller cups 3 or 4 minutes less. Puddings will brown on top and they will rise above the tops of the cups.

Remove from hot water, cool to room temperature, and then refrigerate. Puddings will sink back to level with the tops of the cups.

Cut around sides to release and invert onto individual dessert plates or shallow bowls. With a rubber spatula scrape any remaining custard out of the cups.

French Custard Rice Pudding

6 TO 8 PORTIONS

4 cups milk
⅓ cup sugar
½ teaspoon salt
½ cup uncooked rice
 (not instant, and not washed—
 I use Uncle Ben's converted rice)
3½ ounces (¾ cup) raisins, light or dark
4 egg yolks
2 teaspoons vanilla extract
¼ teaspoon almond extract
1 teaspoon nutmeg (preferably freshly grated)

In the top of a large double boiler, mix 3 cups of the milk (reserve remaining 1 cup), sugar, salt, and rice. Cook over moderate direct heat, stirring occasionally until very hot. Place over hot water in bottom of double boiler. Cover. Cook over moderate heat, stirring occasionally, for 1¼ to 1½ hours, or until rice is very tender and milk is almost but not completely absorbed, replacing water in bottom of double boiler if necessary.

While the rice is cooking, pour boiling water over the raisins to cover. Let stand 5 minutes. Drain.

Adjust rack to center of oven. Preheat oven to 350 degrees. Butter a 6-cup shallow casserole or baking dish.

Stir yolks with a small wire whisk or fork just to mix them. Gradually stir in the remaining cup of milk and vanilla and almond extracts.

Gradually mix part of the cooked rice into the yolks, and then mix the yolks into the rest of the rice. Stir in the raisins. Turn into the prepared casserole. Sprinkle with nutmeg. Place in a larger pan, which must not be deeper than the casserole. Pour hot water into the larger pan to about halfway up the side of the casserole.

Bake 45 minutes or until a small, sharp knife inserted into the pudding comes out clean.

Remove pudding from hot water. Cool on a rack. Serve warm, at room temperature, or chilled.

NOTE: *Serve as is, or with Apricot, Raspberry, or Custard Sauce (page 391, 393, or 389).*

Icebox Rice Pudding

8 PORTIONS

With gelatin.

3½ ounces (¾ cup) raisins, light or dark
⅓ cup light rum
4 cups milk
⅓ cup sugar
¼ teaspoon salt
¾ cup uncooked rice
    (not instant, and not washed—
    I use Uncle Ben's converted rice)
1 tablespoon (1 envelope) unflavored gelatin
3 tablespoons cold water
2 teaspoons vanilla extract
1 cup heavy cream

In a small jar with a tight cover, soak the raisins in the rum for 1 hour, more or less, turning the jar occasionally.

In a heavy saucepan over moderate heat, cook the milk, sugar, salt, and rice, stirring occasionally until it comes to a boil.

Reduce heat to low, cover the saucepan, and let it simmer, stirring occasionally for about 45 minutes until the milk is almost, but not completely, absorbed. Watch it carefully toward the end of the cooking time. The mixture will thicken more as it cools and it should not be too dry.

About 5 minutes before the rice is done, sprinkle the gelatin over the cold water in a small cup. Let stand for a few minutes to soften and then stir into the rice to dissolve.

Remove rice from heat and turn into a large mixing bowl. Stirring occasionally and gently, let it cool. Stir in the vanilla, raisins, and rum.

When the rice is completely cool, whip the cream in a chilled bowl with chilled beaters until it holds a soft shape. Don't beat the cream stiff, or the pudding will be heavy.

Fold into the rice. Turn the pudding into a dessert bowl (about 8-cup capacity, preferably glass and wide rather than deep). Smooth the top.

This should be served with Apricot Sauce (page 391). Pour the sauce over the rice. Tilt dish very gently to run it all over the top.

Refrigerate for several hours.

NOTES: 1. *This may also be prepared individually; it is attractive in large wine glasses or straight-sided glasses meant for old-fashioneds. Or it may be prepared in a 2-quart bowl or mold, chilled until firm,* and then inverted and unmolded onto a dessert platter, in which case pour on the topping immediately before serving, or pass it separately.

2. If the pudding is unmolded as above, it may also be circled with fruit—either fresh, unhulled strawberries, or fresh stewed apricots, peaches, or pears, or a combination.

3. With a generous amount of fruit, the pudding will easily make 12 portions, in which case double the Apricot Sauce, pour a bit over the pudding just for looks, and serve the rest separately from a pitcher.

Pineapple Rice Pudding

6 TO 8 PORTIONS

1½ cups water
½ teaspoon salt
1 tablespoon butter
½ cup uncooked rice
    (not instant and not washed—
    I use Uncle Ben's converted rice)
2 8-ounce cans (or 1 20-ounce can)
    crushed pineapple
2 cups heavy cream
3 eggs
½ cup sugar
1½ teaspoons vanilla extract

In a 2½- to 3-quart heavy saucepan, bring the water to a boil. Stir in the salt, butter, and rice. Reduce the heat, cover, and let cook slowly for about 25 minutes or until the water is absorbed.

Meanwhile, drain the pineapple thoroughly in a strainer and set aside.

Adjust rack to center of oven. Preheat oven to 350 degrees. Butter a 6-cup shallow ovenproof casserole.

Add the cream to the rice. Stirring occasionally, bring to a boil. Remove from heat.

In a large bowl beat the eggs lightly just to mix. Very gradually stir in the hot rice and cream. Add the sugar, vanilla, and pineapple. Stir to mix thoroughly. Pour into prepared casserole.

Place casserole in a large pan, which should not be deeper than the casserole. Pour hot water into the large pan to one-half the depth of the casserole.

Bake for 40 to 45 minutes until a small, sharp knife inserted in the pudding barely comes out clean.

Remove pan and casserole from the oven, and take casserole out of the hot water. Cool to room temperature. Refrigerate for at least 2 to 3 hours. Serve very cold.

NOTE: *This rich, custardy pudding may be served as is, but it's even better with a generous amount of Strawberry Topping (page 392) or with just barely thawed and partially drained frozen strawberries.*

Plain Old-Fashioned Rice Pudding

3 TO 4 PORTIONS

Takes just a minute or two to prepare and three hours to bake.

4 cups milk
¾ cup sugar
Pinch of salt
2 tablespoons butter
3 tablespoons uncooked rice
    (not instant, and not washed—
        I use Uncle Ben's converted rice)
½ teaspoon vanilla extract
⅓ cup raisins or currants
    (See page 12.)
Cinnamon and/or nutmeg
    (preferably freshly grated)

Adjust rack to center of oven. Preheat oven to 300 degrees.

In a 5- to 6-cup ovenproof casserole, preferably shallow, mix milk, sugar, salt, butter, and the rice which must be measured carefully. (Just a bit too much will make the pudding dry.)

Bake uncovered for 2 hours, stirring occasionally—at least three or four times, or more, if you wish.

Add vanilla and raisins or currants. Stir well. Sprinkle a bit of cinnamon and/or nutmeg over the top. Bake 1 hour longer without stirring, in order to let a "skin" form on top.

Remove from oven. The pudding will sink slightly. Cut around the edge so that the "skin" will sink down with the pudding.

Serve while slightly warm, at room temperature, or chilled. Spoon into dessert bowls and pass a pitcher of very cold heavy cream.

Bread Pudding

10 TO 12
PORTIONS

2½ ounces (½ cup) raisins, light or dark
20 slices of firm white bread
    (1 1-pound, thin-sliced sandwich loaf)
3 ounces (¾ stick) soft butter
1 cup sugar
4 cups milk
1 cup light cream
6 eggs
2 teaspoons vanilla extract
Scant ½ teaspoon almond extract
⅛ teaspoon salt

Steam the raisins in a small strainer, covered, over boiling water for 5 minutes. Set aside.

Lightly butter the bread on one side. Stack in piles of five slices each. Cut the crusts from each stack. Cut each stack in thirds to make fingers.

Butter a shallow, oblong, 3-quart baking dish. Place a layer of the bread in the dish, buttered side up, leaving spaces between the fingers of bread. Sprinkle with 2 tablespoons of the sugar and some of the raisins. Continue stacking the fingers into layers, alternating the direction of the fingers, using ½ cup of the sugar (reserve remaining ½ cup) and all of the raisins. Do not use raisins over the top layer. There will probably be about four layers of bread, but that will depend on the size and shape of the baking dish.

In the top of a large double boiler over boiling water, or in a heavy saucepan over moderate heat, scald the milk and cream just until you see tiny bubbles around the edge or a wrinkled skin forming on top.

Meanwhile, in a large bowl mix the eggs lightly with a wire whisk or a fork. Do not beat them frothy. Continue to mix while gradually adding the hot milk, ¼ cup of the reserved sugar (reserve remaining ¼ cup), vanilla and almond extracts, and salt.

Transfer the mixture to a pitcher, then carefully pour it around the bread in the baking dish, pouring into the corners and along the sides. Do not pour over the top layer of bread. Let stand for at least 1 hour, pressing down occasionally with a wide metal spatula to help bread absorb custard from the bottom.

Adjust rack one-third down from the top of the oven. Preheat oven to 350 degrees.

Sprinkle reserved ¼ cup of sugar over the top of the pudding. Place baking dish in a large, shallow pan which must not be deeper than the baking dish. Pour hot water into the large pan to a 1-inch depth. (If the large pan is aluminum, adding ½ teaspoon of cream of tartar to each quart of water will keep the pan from discoloring.)

Bake 40 to 45 minutes until a knife inserted near the center just barely comes out clean. The sugar on top should have caramelized lightly to a golden color. If not, place it under the broiler for a very few minutes. Watch it carefully!

Remove from water. Serve warm (delicious!), at room temperature, or refrigerated.

NOTE: *Serve Bread Pudding as is, or with Custard, Apricot, or Raspberry Sauce (page 389, 391, or 393).*

Apple Pudding

Despite the name this dessert is not soft and custardy, but deliciously crisp.

6 TO 8 PORTIONS

TOPPING (In Germany this is called a *Streusel*—pronounced "shtroyzel.")

1 cup sifted all-purpose flour
½ cup dark brown sugar, firmly packed
1½ teaspoons cinnamon
¼ pound (½ cup) butter, cut up

Mix flour, sugar, and cinnamon in a bowl. With a pastry blender cut in the butter until mixture resembles coarse crumbs. Refrigerate.

APPLE MIXTURE

2½ ounces (½ cup) almonds,
    blanched, and slivered or sliced
3 pounds (6–8 medium) apples
3 tablespoons granulated sugar
Grated rind and juice of 1 small lemon
¼ cup raisins
⅓ cup apricot preserves

Place the almonds on a shallow pan in a 350-degree oven. Stir them occasionally until golden. Remove and set aside to cool.

Adjust rack one-third up from bottom of oven. Preheat oven to 400 degrees. Butter a shallow, ovenproof baking dish with a 2-quart capacity (about 8 × 10 × 2 inches).

Peel, quarter, and core the apples. Cut each quarter the long way into three or four slices. Mix them in a large bowl with the sugar, rind, juice, raisins, and almonds. Turn it all into the baking dish, scraping the bowl clean with a rubber spatula. Dot with small spoonfuls of apricot preserves.

Crumble the refrigerated topping loosely over the apple mixture to cover the apples completely.

Do not pack it down. Wipe the edges of the dish. Bake 30 to 45 minutes until apples are tender and top is lightly browned.

Remove from oven to cool. Serve warm or at room temperature, as is—or, even better, with vanilla ice cream or Old-Fashioned Lemon Sauce, page 396.

Mousses, Cold Soufflés, Bavarians, and Gelatin Desserts

CHOCOLATE MOUSSE HEATTER

MOUSSE AU CHOCOLAT

TURIN LOAF

DARK CHOCOLATE SPONGE

CHOCOLATE-MOCHA
  MOUSSE-SOUFFLE

COLD WALNUT-COFFEE SOUFFLE

COLD APRICOT SOUFFLE

STRAWBERRIES AND CREAM

ORANGE CREAM

TROPICAL MANGO CREAM

RASPBERRY-STRAWBERRY
  BAVARIAN

IRISH COFFEE JELLY

see Cold Lemon Soufflé (page 268)

Chocolate Mousse Heatter

6 PORTIONS

It has been said that chocolate is the sexiest of all flavors. If so, this is the sexiest of all desserts.

½ pound bittersweet chocolate
(I use Tobler Tradition or
Lindt Excellence.)
1 tablespoon instant coffee
⅓ cup boiling water
5 eggs, separated
Pinch of salt

Break up the chocolate into a small, heavy saucepan. Dissolve the coffee in the boiling water and pour it over the chocolate. Place over low heat and stir occasionally with a small wire whisk until mixture is smooth. Remove from heat and set aside to cool for about 5 minutes.

In the small bowl of an electric mixer at high speed, beat the egg yolks for 3 to 4 minutes until pale lemon-colored. Reduce the speed and gradually add the slightly warm chocolate mixture, scraping the bowl with a rubber spatula and beating only until smooth. Remove from mixer.

Add the salt to the whites and beat until they hold a definite shape but are not dry. (See Note 1.) Without being too thorough, gently fold about one-quarter of the beaten whites into the chocolate mixture, then fold in a second quarter, and finally fold the chocolate into the remaining whites, folding only until no whites show.

Gently transfer the mousse to a wide pitcher and pour it into six large dessert or wine glasses, each with about a 9-ounce capacity. Do not fill the glasses too full; leave generous headroom on each. (This mousse must be prepared in individual portions. It just won't work if it is all done in one large container.)

Cover with plastic wrap or aluminum foil and refrigerate 3 to 6 hours. (The mousse may stand longer—12 to 24 hours, if you wish. The texture will become more spongy and less creamy. Delicious both ways.)

Prepare the following:

MOCHA CREAM

1 cup heavy cream
¼ cup confectioners sugar
1 tablespoon instant coffee

In a chilled bowl with chilled beaters, beat the heavy cream only until it begins to thicken. Add sugar and coffee and beat until thickened to the consistency of a heavy custard sauce, not stiff. Pour or spoon onto desserts to completely cover the tops.

OPTIONAL: *Top with a light sprinkling of coarsely grated chocolate or place a few large Chocolate Slabs (page 410) standing upright in the cream.*

NOTES: 1. *I beat the whites with the salt in the large bowl of the mixer, beating at high speed only until the whites thicken or hold a very soft shape. Then I finish the beating with a large wire whisk so that there is less chance of overbeating.*

2. *This recipe may easily be doubled, if you wish.*

3. *Purely as a matter of interest, the chocolate mousse served at most of the fine hotels and restaurants is generally made with the addition of whipped cream folded into the chocolate mixture (see following recipe).*

Mousse au Chocolat

6 PORTIONS

As it is served at New York's Regency Hotel—a creamier and denser mousse than the previous.

6 ounces semisweet or sweet chocolate
    (You may use 1 cup of semisweet morsels
    or 6 squares of semisweet chocolate,
    or 1½ bars of Baker's
    German's Sweet Chocolate.)
4 eggs, separated
Pinch of salt
2 tablespoons confectioners sugar
½ cup heavy cream
½ teaspoon vanilla extract

Place chocolate in top of small double boiler over hot water on low heat. When it is partially melted, remove it from the heat and stir until completely melted and smooth. With a small wire whisk beat in the egg yolks, one at a time. Transfer to a larger bowl and set aside.

    Beat whites with salt until foamy. Gradually add sugar and continue to beat until whites hold a shape. Set aside.

In a chilled bowl with chilled beaters, whip the cream with the vanilla until it holds a soft shape.

Stir one-quarter of the egg whites into the chocolate mixture. Then fold in remaining whites and whipped cream, handling lightly and folding only until mixture is smooth. Pour into a serving bowl or six individual dessert bowls or glasses. Cover and refrigerate for at least 2 to 3 hours, or longer if you wish. It may stand overnight.

Serve as is or with whipped cream.

WHIPPED CREAM

1 cup heavy cream
¼ cup confectioners sugar
½ teaspoon vanilla extract

In a chilled bowl with chilled beaters, whip above ingredients until they barely hold a shape, not stiff. Think "sauce" instead of "whipped cream" in order not to overbeat.

Turin Loaf

This candylike chestnut-fudge loaf, or Pavé aux Marrons, is a creation of Henri-Paul Pellaprat, at one time head chef of the Cordon Bleu Cooking School in Paris. If this is not the richest of all desserts, you could have fooled me. A Hungarian pastry chef friend of mine insists on the addition of a few spoonfuls of dark rum. Note: This is a seasonal dessert and must be made with fresh chestnuts.

1 pound fresh chestnuts
¼ pound (½ cup) butter
5 ounces bittersweet chocolate
    (I use Tobler Tradition
    or Lindt Excellence.)
1 cup confectioners sugar
½ teaspoon vanilla extract

TO SHELL CHESTNUTS

With a strong, sharp, small knife, cut a cross in the flat end of the chestnuts, cutting through the hard outer shell. Don't worry if the cut goes down into the nut itself. In a large saucepan cover the chestnuts with boiling water and boil, covered, for about half an hour until tender. Test one through the cut in the shell with a small, sharp knife or a cake tester. Replace water as necessary to keep chestnuts covered. Remove from hot water only one or two at a time—they peel more easily while still hot. Remove shells and as much of the inner skin as possible. While the chestnuts are still warm, work them through a food mill or a strainer. (Yes, it is a slow job.)

Meanwhile, melt the butter and chocolate in the top of a small double boiler over hot water on moderate heat. Transfer to the small bowl of electric mixer. Add sugar and vanilla and beat only until smooth. Beat in the chestnuts.

Prepare a small loaf pan, 3- to 4-cup capacity, lining it with aluminum foil. Brush the foil lightly with tasteless salad oil. Press the mixture firmly into the mold—pack it down. Smooth the top. Cover and refrigerate for 4 hours or longer. (Overnight is O.K.)

Cover with a small platter and invert. Remove pan and foil. Refrigerate.

OPTIONAL: *Decorate with marrons glacés.*

NOTE: *This is traditionally served as is; however, it may be served with whipped cream: ⅓ cup heavy cream, 1 tablespoon confectioners sugar, and ¼ teaspoon vanilla. Apply with a pastry bag fitted with a star tube, or use more of each and whip only until thickened, not stiff, and serve separately as a sauce.*

Dark Chocolate Sponge

6 TO 8 PORTIONS

1 tablespoon (1 envelope)
  unflavored gelatin
¼ cup cold water
1 cup heavy cream
8 ounces (8 squares) semisweet chocolate
2 teaspoons instant coffee
4 eggs
⅓ cup sugar
1 teaspoon vanilla extract

Sprinkle the gelatin over the cold water and set aside.

In a small, heavy saucepan over low heat cook the cream and chocolate, stirring occasionally until chocolate is melted. Stir with a small wire whisk until smooth. Stir in the coffee and the gelatin to dissolve. Remove from heat and set aside

In the small bowl of an electric mixer beat the eggs and sugar at high speed for a few minutes. When eggs expand to reach top of bowl, transfer to large bowl of mixer and continue to beat for 5 minutes more.

Stir vanilla into chocolate mixture.

Fold a few spoonfuls of the eggs into the chocolate and then gently fold the chocolate into the remaining eggs, handling lightly. Pour gently from one bowl to another to insure thorough blending.

Rinse a 7- to 8-cup metal mold or loaf pan with ice water. Shake out but do not dry.

Turn chocolate cream into cold, wet mold. Refrigerate for 4 to 5 hours, depending on shape of mold, until thoroughly set. (As soon as the top of the chocolate is set, cover with plastic wrap or aluminum foil. If you wish, this may wait overnight before being unmolded.)

Very lightly brush dessert platter with a bit of tasteless salad oil in order to be able to move the unmolded dessert if necessary. Dip the mold briefly in very hot water. Place on towel. Quickly cover with inverted dessert platter. Invert mold and platter to unmold dessert. If necessary, dip again very briefly into hot water and/or tap mold carefully against platter to unmold. Refrigerate. Prepare whipped cream.

WHIPPED CREAM

1½ cups heavy cream
1 teaspoon vanilla extract
⅓ cup confectioners sugar

In a chilled bowl with chilled beaters, whip above ingredients until the cream holds a shape. Spread it over the top of the unmolded dessert, or use a pastry bag and a star tube to decorate the dessert with the whipped cream.

OPTIONAL: *If you wish, decorate with coarsely grated chocolate, or with finely chopped green pistachio nuts, or with chocolate cat's-tongue candies.*

Chocolate-Mocha Mousse-Soufflé

6 PORTIONS

2 ounces (2 squares) unsweetened chocolate
2 ounces (2 squares) semisweet chocolate
2 rounded tablespoons instant coffee
¼ cup boiling water
4 eggs plus 3 yolks
½ cup sugar
Pinch of salt
1 tablespoon (1 envelope) unflavored gelatin
¼ cup cold water
1 teaspoon vanilla extract
2 tablespoons dark rum
1 cup heavy cream

Prepare a 3-inch collar for a 5- to 6-cup soufflé dish. Use a piece of aluminum foil long enough to wrap around the dish and overlap a few inches. Fold it in half lengthwise. Brush tasteless salad oil on half of one side.

344

Wrap it tightly around the dish, oiled side facing up and in. Fasten with string or straight pins and set aside. (See Note.)

In the top of a small double boiler over hot water on moderate heat, melt both chocolates. Stir until smooth and remove from heat to cool.

Dissolve the coffee in the boiling water and set aside to cool.

In large bowl of electric mixer, at high speed beat the eggs, yolks, sugar, and salt for 15 minutes until very thick, fluffy, and pale lemon-colored.

Meanwhile, sprinkle the gelatin over the cold water in a small heat-proof cup. Let stand for about 5 minutes and then place cup in shallow hot water over moderate heat to dissolve. Remove from hot water and cool briefly.

Very gradually, mixing constantly with a small wire whisk, add the coffee to the chocolate. Mix until smooth, and then gradually stir in the gelatin, vanilla, and rum. Mix until smooth again.

Fold a few large spoonfuls of the beaten egg mixture into the chocolate, and then fold the chocolate into the remaining egg mixture.

In a chilled bowl with chilled beaters, whip the cream until it holds a soft shape. Gently fold the whipped cream into the chocolate.

Pour into prepared dish and smooth the top. Refrigerate for 6 to 10 hours.

Remove the foil collar and dry the outside of the soufflé dish. (Do not remove collar too far ahead of time—right before dinner is fine.)

OPTIONAL: *1. Before removing the foil collar sprinkle the top generously with finely grated chocolate, which may be grated on a regular grater or in a Mouli grater.*

2. This may be served as is but it is better with a sauce which may be passed separately—either sweetened and rum-flavored whipped cream, whipped only to the consistency of a sauce, Rum Cream Sauce (page 389), or Custard Sauce (page 389).

NOTE: *This does not have to be prepared as a soufflé. It can be made in any serving bowl, individual glasses, or individual soufflé dishes. But it is startling as a large soufflé in a clear glass soufflé dish (available at Bonnier's, 605 Madison Avenue, New York, New York 10022, or at the Bridge Company, 212 E. 52nd Street, New York, New York 10022).*

Cold Walnut-Coffee Soufflé

8 PORTIONS

4 eggs, separated
2½ cups milk
¼ cup dry instant coffee
1 cup sugar
2 tablespoons (2 envelopes)
    unflavored gelatin
½ cup cold water
1½ teaspoons vanilla extract
1 tablespoon dark rum,
    or Cognac
1 cup heavy cream
Pinch of salt
½ cup walnuts, finely sliced or cut

Prepare a 3-inch collar for a 5- to 6-cup soufflé dish: Use a piece of aluminum foil long enough to wrap around the dish and overlap a few inches. Fold it in half lengthwise. Brush tasteless salad oil on the upper half of one side. Wrap it tightly around the dish, oiled side facing up and in. Fasten with string or straight pins and set aside. (Or this may be prepared in a fancy mold that has been rinsed with cold water and not dried.)

In the top of a large double boiler off the heat, stir the yolks lightly just to mix. Gradually mix in the milk, instant coffee, and ½ cup of the sugar (reserve remaining ½ cup). Place over hot water on moderate heat. Cook, stirring frequently and scraping the sides and the bottom of the pan with a rubber spatula, for about 15 minutes or more until the mixture thickens slightly (about 180 degrees on a candy thermometer).

Meanwhile, sprinkle the gelatin over the cold water and let stand for 5 minutes. When the coffee mixture is done, remove the top of the double boiler. Add the softened gelatin and stir to dissolve.

Place the top of the double boiler in a bowl of ice and water and stir occasionally until completely cool. Stir in the vanilla and rum or Cognac. Remove from ice water temporarily and set aside.

In a chilled bowl with chilled beaters, whip the cream until it holds a soft shape. Set aside.

In the small bowl of an electric mixer, beat the whites with the salt until they barely hold a very soft shape. Gradually add the reserved ½ cup sugar and continue to beat only until whites achieve a thick marshmallowy consistency that holds its shape but is not stiff or dry. Set aside.

Replace upper section of double boiler in the ice water, adding more ice if necessary. Stir gently until mixture begins to thicken and is about the consistency of a thin cream sauce. Remove from ice water.

Gradually fold about half of the coffee mixture into the whites and then fold the whites into the remainder.

Fold 1 to 2 cups of the coffee mixture into the whipped cream. In a large bowl fold the remaining coffee mixture and the whipped cream together. If necessary, gently pour from one bowl to another to insure thorough blending.

Fold in the walnuts and pour into prepared soufflé dish.

Refrigerate 5 to 8 hours. Remove the foil collar. Wipe the soufflé dish.

WHIPPED CREAM

1 cup heavy cream
¼ cup confectioners sugar
1 scant teaspoon vanilla extract

In a chilled bowl with chilled beaters, whip the above ingredients only until the cream has thickened to hold a soft shape. Serve separately as a sauce.

NOTE: *If you wish, you may also serve Honey Chocolate Sauce (page 398). It goes beautifully with this soufflé.*

Cold Apricot Soufflé

8 PORTIONS

2 1-pound cans apricot halves

4 eggs plus 3 egg yolks

⅛ teaspoon salt

½ cup sugar

2 tablespoons (2 envelopes) unflavored gelatin

¼ cup cold water

¼ cup lemon juice

½ teaspoon vanilla extract

¼ teaspoon almond extract

2 tablespoons Cognac or rum

1 cup heavy cream

Prepare a 3-inch collar for a 5- to 6-cup soufflé dish: Use a piece of aluminum foil long enough to wrap around the dish and overlap a few inches. Fold it in half lengthwise. Brush tasteless salad oil on the upper half of one side. Wrap it around the dish, oiled side facing up and in. Fasten tightly with string or straight pins and set aside. (See Note.)

Drain the juice from the apricots and purée the halves in a food mill, or press through a strainer. Set aside.

In the large bowl of an electric mixer, at high speed beat the eggs, yolks, salt, and sugar for about 15 minutes until mixture is as thick as soft whipped cream.

Meanwhile, sprinkle the gelatin over the cold water and lemon juice in a heatproof cup or bowl. Let stand for a few minutes to soften and then place the cup in a shallow pan of hot water on moderate heat to dissolve the gelatin. (Stir occasionally with a metal spoon to see when the gelatin is dissolved.) Remove from hot water and set aside.

When egg mixture has been sufficiently beaten, add vanilla and almond extracts, and Cognac or rum. Still beating at high speed, beat in the dissolved gelatin. Reduce speed to low and mix in the puréed apricots. Remove from mixer.

In a chilled bowl with chilled beaters, whip the cream until it holds a soft shape. Fold 1 to 2 cups of the apricot mixture into the cream. Fold the cream into the remaining apricot mixture.

Pour into prepared soufflé dish. Refrigerate 4 to 5 hours. Remove foil collar. Wipe sides of dish.

Prepare topping.

WHIPPED CREAM TOPPING

1 cup heavy cream
¼ cup confectioners sugar
1 teaspoon vanilla extract,
     or 1 tablespoon Cognac or rum

In a chilled bowl with chilled beaters, whip the cream, sugar, vanilla, and Cognac or rum until mixture holds a shape. With a pastry bag fitted with a star tube, form a lattice or rosettes over the top.

NOTE: *This may also be prepared in a serving bowl or a ring mold (with 10-cup capacity) that has been rinsed with cold water but not dried. Or it may be poured into eight dessert bowls or wine glasses. In glasses, each portion may be topped with a drained apricot half, cut side down, and the whipped cream may be shaped in a ring around the apricot. Sprinkle with a bit of finely chopped green pistachio nuts or toasted, sliced almonds.*

Straw-berries and Cream

4 PORTIONS

CREAM

1½ teaspoons (½ envelope)
     unflavored gelatin
1 cup heavy cream
½ cup sugar
1 cup sour cream
1 teaspoon vanilla extract

Place the gelatin, heavy cream, and sugar in a small saucepan. Let stand for 2 to 3 minutes and then place over moderate heat. Stir with a rubber or wooden spatula until the gelatin and sugar are dissolved.

Place sour cream in small bowl of electric mixer. On lowest speed gradually add the hot cream and the vanilla, scraping bowl with a rubber spatula and beating only until smooth.

Rinse a 2½-cup metal mold with cold water. (A small, shallow mixing bowl may be used, or a small loaf pan, or a saucepan.) Shake out, but do not dry. Transfer cream mixture to wet mold. Refrigerate 4 to 5 hours or longer.

STRAWBERRIES

Wash 1 pint of strawberries quickly by dipping them briefly in cold water. Hull and drain on a towel. Slice them, cutting each berry lengthwise in 3 or 4 slices. Sprinkle with a few spoonfuls of sugar and, if you wish, a bit of optional kirsch. Turn into a bowl and let stand for about half an hour, turning occasionally. Then cover and refrigerate.

TO UNMOLD THE CREAM

Brush a serving platter very lightly with tasteless salad oil, in order to be able to move the unmolded dessert if necessary.

Cut around upper rim of mold to release it. Dip briefly in hot water. Place on a towel for just a second to dry. Cover with inverted serving platter and invert. If cream doesn't slip out easily, dip it again briefly in hot water.

Surround with the strawberries or pass them separately.

Serve a slice of the cream partially covered with a generous amount of the strawberries.

NOTES: 1. *This recipe may easily be doubled or tripled; however, the mold should not be too deep. For larger amounts, use a ring mold, a melon mold, a loaf pan, or a round cake pan.*

2. *This may be prepared a day ahead if you wish. If so, cover it airtight and leave it in the mold overnight.*

Orange Cream

8 GENEROUS PORTIONS

2 tablespoons (2 envelopes)
    unflavored gelatin
⅔ cup cold water
1 cup plus 3 tablespoons sugar
Finely grated rind of 2 deep-colored oranges
1 cup orange juice
¼ cup lemon juice
4 egg whites
Generous pinch of salt
1 cup heavy cream
Fresh oranges and strawberries
optional: Fresh mint, if available

In the top of a large double boiler off the heat, sprinkle the gelatin over the cold water. Let stand for about 5 minutes. Place over boiling water to dissolve. Stir in 1 cup of the sugar (reserve remaining 3 tablespoons). Stir to dissolve. Remove from heat and stir in the orange rind, orange juice, and lemon juice. Set aside to cool.

Meanwhile, in the small bowl of an electric mixer, beat the egg whites with the salt until foamy. Gradually add reserved 3 tablespoons of sugar and continue to beat until whites hold soft peaks, not stiff. Set aside.

In a chilled bowl with chilled beaters, whip the cream until it holds a soft shape, not stiff. Set aside.

Place the top of the double boiler into a bowl of ice water and stir continuously until the mixture barely begins to thicken to syrup consistency. (If it thickens a bit too much, whip briefly with a wire whisk; however, if it actually sets it will have to be melted again over hot water.) Gradually fold gelatin mixture into the beaten whites, and then gradually fold that into the whipped cream. Pour the mixture back and forth from one container to another to insure thorough blending. (If mixture separates, if the thinner part settles to the bottom, place over ice water and fold gently until it thickens enough so that it does not separate.)

Rinse a 6-cup ring mold or loaf pan with ice water. Shake it out but do not dry it. Pour in the Orange Cream and smooth the top.

Refrigerate until firm (about 2 to 3 hours in a ring mold).

Meanwhile, prepare fresh fruit. Peel oranges, removing every bit of white. Loosen sections by cutting down as close to the membrane as possible on both sides of each section. Rinse strawberries briefly, hull, and place on towel to drain.

To unmold the Orange Cream: Brush a serving platter lightly with tasteless salad oil in order to be able to move the unmolded dessert if necessary. With a small, sharp knife cut around the upper rim of the mold to loosen. Dip mold briefly in very hot water. Place it for a moment on a towel and invert the serving platter over it. Quickly and carefully invert. If the cream does not slip out easily, dip it again briefly in hot water. Remove mold and refrigerate cream.

Prepare whipped cream.

WHIPPED CREAM

1 cup heavy cream
3 tablespoons confectioners sugar
1 teaspoon vanilla extract

In a chilled bowl with chilled beaters, whip the cream with the sugar and vanilla only until it holds a soft shape. Don't let it get stiff.

If dessert has been prepared in a ring mold, place the whipped cream in the center and the fruit around the outside. If it has been prepared in a loaf pan, the fruit may be placed around the outside but the cream should be served separately.

If fresh mint is available, use washed and dried sprigs to decorate the platter.

NOTE: *If you wish, the orange cream may be flavored with 3 tablespoons of Grand Marnier or Cointreau in place of the lemon juice, and the sectioned oranges and strawberries may both be sprinkled with Grand Marnier or Cointreau and a bit of sugar. If so, prepare them a little ahead of time and let them stand, turning occasionally. The whipped cream may also be flavored with 1 to 2 tablespoons of Grand Marnier or Cointreau in place of the vanilla.*

Tropical Mango Cream

6 TO 8 PORTIONS

1 tablespoon (1 envelope) unflavored gelatin
⅓ cup cold water
3 mangoes, ripe and ready to eat,
    or even a bit overripe
      (to make 2 cups of pulp) (See Note 1.)
½ cup sugar
2 tablespoons lime juice
1 cup heavy cream
optional: Additional fresh fruit,
    including additional mangoes

Sprinkle the gelatin over the cold water in a small heatproof cup and set aside.

Peel 3 medium-size mangoes. Cut the meat away from the pits, scraping as much pulp from the pits as possible, and dice it coarsely. Work it through a food mill (or a coarse strainer, if necessary) to make 2 cups of pulp. Stir in the sugar and lime juice and set aside.

Place the cup of gelatin in a small pan of hot water to reach about halfway up the cup. Place over moderate heat until the gelatin is dissolved; stir it into the mango mixture.

In a chilled bowl with chilled beaters, whip the cream until it holds a soft shape, not stiff. Stir the mango mixture over ice until it barely begins to thicken. Gradually fold some of the mango mixture into the cream and then fold the cream into the remaining mango mixture. If necessary, pour back and forth from one container to another to insure complete blending.

Rinse a 5- to 6-cup metal ring mold with ice water. (See Note 2.) Shake it out; do not dry it. Pour the Mango Cream into the mold and chill for at least 3 to 4 hours until well set.

Brush a dessert platter very lightly with tasteless salad oil so the unmolded dessert may be moved if necessary. Cut around the upper edges of the mold with a small, sharp knife to release. Dip mold very briefly in hot water. Place on towel for a second to dry. Cover with inverted dessert platter.

Carefully invert to release dessert. If dessert does not slip out easily, dip it again very briefly. If necessary, tap it firmly on dessert platter. Remove mold and refrigerate the cream.

Fill the center of the mold with additional fruit, peeled and cut into large dice.

OPTIONAL: *If you wish, place a ring of additional fruit around the outer edge—strawberries go very well, as do peaches, orange sections, or sliced preserved kumquats.*

NOTES: 1. *The number of mangoes needed will depend on their size, and how much additional mango is to be served with the finished dessert.*

2. *Instead of serving this as a molded dessert, it may be poured into a dessert bowl or individual glasses. Serve as above with diced mango and/or other fresh fruit, or top with whipped cream and sprinkle generously with toasted coconut.*

3. *This soft, creamy dessert may be served as is, or with soft whipped cream: 1 cup heavy cream, ¼ cup confectioners sugar, with 1 scant teaspoon vanilla or 1 tablespoon of dark rum, whipped together only until the cream holds a soft shape.*

Rasp-berry-Straw-berry Bavarian

9 PORTIONS

This obviously is not an authentic Bavarian. It is, however, the most popular dessert I make. Most of my students have said that this is so easy that they feel like they're cheating when they make it.

6 ounces strawberry-flavored gelatin
2 cups boiling water
1 cup sour cream
1 pint strawberry ice cream
1 tablespoon lemon juice
2 10-ounce packages frozen raspberries
    (whole berries packed in syrup)
1 10-ounce package frozen, sliced strawberries
    (halves, packed in syrup)

Place gelatin in large bowl. Add boiling water and stir to dissolve. Add sour cream and beat with wire whisk or egg beater until smooth. Cut the frozen ice cream into the gelatin mixture, cutting it into about ten pieces. Stir until melted and smooth. Add lemon juice and frozen fruit. Use a fork to break up the frozen fruit a bit, then use your bare hands until there are no pieces larger than a single piece of fruit. It feels cold, but it does the best job. (Adding the fruit while it is frozen helps to set the gelatin mixture, so that by the time the fruit is broken up and separated, the Bavarian is firm enough to keep the fruit from sinking.)

Quickly pour mixture into a pitcher and pour into nine large glasses, each with about a 9-ounce capacity. (See Note 1.) Leave a generous amount of headroom on each. Refrigerate. Do not freeze. This will be ready to serve in an hour or two, or it may stand overnight.

Top with the following:

WHIPPED CREAM

2 cups heavy cream
1½ teaspoons vanilla extract
½ cup confectioners sugar

In a chilled bowl with chilled beaters, whip above ingredients until cream holds a shape. Place a large spoonful on each dessert. Decorate, if and as you wish. I use chopped green pistachio nuts, glacéed cherries, *and* chocolate leaves or slabs.

NOTES: 1. *I prepare this in heavy, stemmed beer glasses. This must be prepared for individual servings—it is too delicate to serve from one large bowl.*

2. *About ½ teaspoon each of strawberry and raspberry flavorings, added with the lemon juice, emphasizes the flavor and is a welcome addition. I use Flavor Mill brand flavorings, available at specialty stores.*

3. *If either frozen raspberries or frozen strawberries is not available, use 3 packages of whichever one you can get.*

Irish Coffee Jelly

4 PORTIONS

Clear coffee aspic which may take the place of both dessert and coffee for a light summer meal.

1 tablespoon (1 envelope)
    plus 1 teaspoon unflavored gelatin
½ cup cold water
2 tablespoons instant coffee
2½ cups boiling water
½ cup sugar
⅓ cup Irish whiskey, or brandy
¾ cup heavy cream

Sprinkle the gelatin over the cold water and let stand. Dissolve the instant coffee in the boiling water.

In a saucepan, mix the coffee, sugar, and softened gelatin. Place over high heat and cook, stirring with a metal spoon, until sugar and gelatin are dissolved. Remove from heat and set aside to cool.

Stir in the whiskey or brandy, and pour into four wine glasses, coffee cups, brandy snifters, or straight-sided old-fashioned cocktail glasses, leaving generous headroom. Refrigerate a few hours until set.

Top with a generous layer of unwhipped heavy cream.

Ice Creams and Frozen Desserts

JEAN HEWITT'S OLD-FASHIONED
  LEMON ICE CREAM

HONEY PARFAIT

   ALMOND PARFAIT

CREME COURVOISIER

GRAND MARNIER PARFAIT

MAPLE-PECAN PARFAIT

FROZEN HONEY MOUSSE

DEEP SOUTH CHOCOLATE
  ICE CREAM

WALNUT ICE CREAM

GIN ICE CREAM

   RUM RAISIN ICE CREAM

LIME SHERBET

APRICOT SHERBET

SPANISH LIME PIE

FRENCH ICE-CREAM CAKE

see Charlie Brown Sundae (page 401)

These ice creams and frozen desserts are all made in a home freezer or in the freezer section of a refrigerator without an ice-cream churn.

Before starting any of the following recipes, make room in the freezer, preferably on the bottom of the freezing compartment or on a shelf with a freezing coil, and adjust the control to coldest. When dessert is frozen, return the control to normal.

If ice cream has been frozen in an ice-cube tray or other shallow pan, it may be transferred after freezing. Pack it firmly in a deep, covered container.

For ease in serving, ice cream can be scooped ahead of time; place the scoops in a single layer in a shallow pan, cover, and store in the freezer.

One note of caution: In recipes in this section that call for whipped cream, be sure not to whip the cream stiff or the finished product will be heavy and buttery. Whip only until the cream holds a soft shape. Test it often.

Jean Hewitt's Old-Fashioned Lemon Ice Cream

ABOUT 3 CUPS

With this recipe, Jean Hewitt of The New York Times *started me on a beautiful and endless binge of ice creams and other frozen desserts made without an ice-cream churn. Mrs. Hewitt's recipes are infallible—this one is also miraculously easy.*

Finely grated rind of 1 large lemon
   (or 2 small)
3 tablespoons lemon juice
1 cup sugar
2 cups light cream
⅛ teaspoon salt

Combine lemon rind, juice, and sugar and stir to mix. Gradually stir in the cream and salt, mixing well. Pour into an ice-cube tray and freeze until solid around the outside and mushy in the middle. Stir well with a wooden spoon. Cover and continue to freeze until firm.

Honey Parfait

1 QUART

2 egg whites
Pinch of salt
⅓ cup honey
1 cup heavy cream
¼ teaspoon almond extract

In the small bowl of an electric mixer beat the whites and the salt until they hold a soft shape. While beating, gradually add the honey, pouring it slowly in a thin stream. Continue beating until meringue holds a point.

In a chilled bowl with chilled beaters, whip the cream and almond extract until it holds a soft shape.

Fold cream into beaten whites and turn into a large ice-cube tray, or a serving bowl, or, if you wish, freeze individually in large wine glasses, leaving a bit of headroom. Cover and freeze for about 4 to 5 hours (or longer) until firm.

NOTE: *Serve as is, or with a sprinkling of toasted, sliced almonds, and, if you wish, Honey Chocolate Sauce (page 398) may be passed separately.*

Almond Parfait

1 QUART

In a moderate oven, toast ½ cup coarsely chopped blanched almonds until golden brown.

Cool completely.

Prepare Honey Parfait. Reserve 2 tablespoons of the toasted almonds. Fold the remainder into the parfait along with 2 or 3 tablespoons of Cognac or rum. Spoon into about 6 glasses or individual soufflé dishes. Sprinkle with reserved almonds. Freeze for about 4 hours until firm, or longer, if you wish.

Crème Courvoisier

2 QUARTS

I am indebted to Arno B. Schmidt, executive chef of New York's Waldorf Astoria, for this great recipe. It is heavenly.

¾ cup water
1 cup sugar
8 egg yolks
⅓ cup Courvoisier
1 cup heavy cream

In a small saucepan (5- to 6-cup size) over high heat, stir the water and sugar to dissolve. Boil without stirring for 5 minutes. Meanwhile, in large bowl of electric mixer at high speed beat the yolks. Very gradually, still beating at high speed, add the hot syrup. Continue to beat until thick and completely cool. Gradually fold in the Courvoisier.

In a chilled bowl with chilled beaters, whip the cream only until it holds a soft shape, not stiff.

Lightly fold about half of the egg yolk mixture into the cream and then fold the cream into the remaining egg yolk mixture.

Pour into an icebox container or, if you wish, leave it in the bowl. Or pour into brandy snifters. Cover and freeze until firm (8 hours or more).

NOTE: *If you wish, you may make almost any substitution for the Cognac— rum, kirsch, Cointreau, bourbon, etc.—but I don't know if anything else can be as good; surely nothing can be better.*

Grand Marnier Parfait

2 GENEROUS QUARTS

6 egg yolks
⅓ cup water
1 cup sugar
Finely grated rind of 2 oranges
⅓ cup Grand Marnier
2 cups heavy cream

In the small bowl of an electric mixer beat the yolks on high speed until very thick and light-lemon colored.

Meanwhile, in a small saucepan over moderate heat cook the water, sugar, and orange rind, stirring continuously until the sugar dissolves. Raise the heat to high and let boil for a minute or two without stirring until the temperature reaches 220 degrees on a candy thermometer.

Pour the hot syrup in a thin stream onto the egg yolks, beating constantly. Continue to beat until completely cool. (If the mixture splashes, reduce the speed as necessary.) When cool, mix in the Grand Marnier and remove from mixer.

In a chilled bowl with chilled beaters, whip the cream only until it holds a soft shape, not stiff.

Gradually fold about half of the yolk mixture into the cream and then, in a larger bowl, fold the cream into the remaining yolk mixture.

Pour into any container, cover, and freeze until firm. (If you're in a hurry, freeze in a shallow metal pan or ice-cube trays—a deep container takes longer.)

Maple-Pecan Parfait

2 QUARTS

1½ teaspoons (½ envelope) unflavored gelatin
¼ cup cold water
4 eggs, separated
1 cup maple syrup
2 cups heavy cream
Pinch of salt
2 ounces (generous ½ cup) pecans, coarsely broken or cut

Sprinkle gelatin over cold water and let stand. Stir egg yolks slightly, just to mix, in top of small double boiler. Gradually mix in the maple syrup and place over boiling water on moderate heat. Cook, stirring constantly, until mixture thickens very slightly (about 180 degrees on a candy thermometer). Remove from heat. Stir in gelatin to dissolve. Transfer to a large bowl and set aside to cool completely. (May be stirred briefly over ice and water to hurry cooling.)

In a chilled bowl with chilled beaters, whip the cream until it holds a soft shape, not stiff. Beat the whites with the salt until they hold a soft shape, not stiff.

When maple syrup mixture is completely cool, very gradually fold it into the whites and then, gradually, fold that into the whipped cream.

Fold in the nuts and turn into any 2- to 2½-quart container or serving dish. Cover and freeze for several hours until firm.

About half an hour before serving take this out of the freezer and put it in the refrigerator so it will be soft enough to serve.

Frozen Honey Mousse

This is elegant and posh and, to me, completely irresistible. In spite of its "haute," the recipe, surprisingly, comes from a little roadside bee-raiser in Kansas.

9 CUPS OF
MOUSSE, OR
8 TO 10
PORTIONS

4 eggs, separated, plus 2 egg yolks
1 pound (1⅓–1½ cups) honey
2 cups heavy cream
Pinch of salt

In the top of a double boiler, off the heat, beat the 6 egg yolks briefly with a small wire whisk or an egg beater. Beat in the honey.

Cook over simmering water on moderate heat, stirring constantly with a rubber or wooden spatula for about 10 minutes, or until mixture reaches about 185 degrees on a candy thermometer.

Remove from heat and place top of double boiler into a bowl of ice and water. Keep stirring until it is cool. (Test on the inside of your wrist.) Remove from ice water and set aside.

In a chilled bowl with chilled beaters, whip the cream until it holds a soft shape.

Beat the 4 egg whites with a pinch of salt until they hold a definite shape, but are not dry.

Gradually fold about half of the honey mixture into the whites and then gradually fold the other half into the whipped cream. In a large bowl gently fold the two together.

Turn into any covered icebox container, or a 10- to 12-cup serving bowl, or 8 to 10 large wine glasses, leaving a bit of headroom. Cover with plastic wrap or aluminum foil and freeze until firm. (Freeze large container or bowlful for at least 12 hours; individual glasses for at least 4 to 6 hours.)

OPTIONAL: *The bee-raising gentleman responsible for this recipe folds chopped pecans in. I prepare it without the pecans, but with it, I serve Honey Chocolate Sauce, page 398.*

Deep South Chocolate Ice Cream

2 QUARTS

This recipe was given to me after I could not stop eating this extraordinary ice cream at a New Year's Eve buffet in a traditional Mississippi plantation mansion, where a bottle of Grand Marnier was passed around for pouring over the ice cream.

2 tablespoons instant coffee
½ cup boiling water
6 ounces (6 squares) semisweet chocolate
5 egg yolks
¼ cup water
½ cup sugar
¼ teaspoon cream of tartar
⅓ cup crème de cacao or Grand Marnier
3 cups heavy cream

Dissolve the coffee in the ½ cup boiling water. Place it with the chocolate in a small, heavy saucepan, or in the top of a small double boiler over hot water on moderate heat. Stir occasionally to melt the chocolate. Remove from heat and set aside to cool.

Beat the yolks in the small bowl of an electric mixer at high speed for several minutes until thick and light lemon-colored.

Meanwhile, in a small saucepan mix the ¼ cup water with the sugar and cream of tartar. With a small wooden spatula, stir over high heat until the sugar is dissolved and the mixture comes to a boil. Let boil without stirring for about 3 minutes until the syrup reaches 230 degrees on a candy thermometer (light-thread stage).

Gradually, in a thin stream, add the hot syrup to the egg yolks, still beating at high speed. Continue to beat for about 5 minutes more until the mixture is cool.

Stir the crème de cacao or Grand Marnier into the cooled chocolate mixture, and add that to the cooled egg yolk mixture, beating only until blended. Remove from mixer.

In the chilled large bowl of the electric mixer, with chilled beaters, beat the cream only until it holds a very soft shape. Fold 1 cup of the cream into the chocolate mixture and then fold the chocolate mixture into the remaining cream.

Pour into a shallow metal pan, measuring 13 x 9 x 2 inches (or several ice-cube trays) and freeze until firm around the edges (1½ to 2 hours in one large pan). Meanwhile, place large bowl and beaters of electric mixer in the freezer.

Beat the partially frozen cream in the chilled bowl until smooth. Return to pan or trays or any icebox container. Cover and freeze until firm (about 1½ hours in the one large pan).

Walnut Ice Cream

2 QUARTS

⅔ cup sugar
¼ cup plus 2 tablespoons water
6 egg yolks
2 cups heavy cream
2 tablespoons dark rum
2 teaspoons vanilla extract
2 teaspoons instant coffee
Generous pinch of salt
7 ounces (2 cups) walnuts, finely ground
   (See page 11.)
3½ ounces (1 cup) walnuts, coarsely cut

In a small saucepan over high heat, cook the sugar and water, stirring until the sugar dissolves. Bring to a boil and let boil without stirring for 2 minutes.

Meanwhile, in the small bowl of an electric mixer at high speed, beat the yolks. Very gradually, in a thin stream, add the hot sugar syrup to the yolks, beating constantly. Continue to beat at high speed until mixture is as thick as whipped cream and completely cool. (Test it on the inside of your wrist.)

Meanwhile, in a chilled bowl with chilled beaters, beat the cream, rum, vanilla, instant coffee, and salt until it barely holds a soft shape, but is not stiff.

Fold the cooled egg yolk mixture into the whipped cream mixture until completely blended and then fold in the ground nuts and the cut nuts.

Pour into 2 large ice-cube trays or any shallow container, cover, and freeze until firm.

NOTE: *This is great with any chocolate sauce.*

Gin
Ice Cream

If you taste the gin at all in this rich, vanilla ice cream, you will barely recognize it. But the ice cream has a lovely flavor and the alcohol keeps it from freezing too hard.

7 CUPS

1½ cups light cream
½ cup sugar
¼ teaspoon salt
4 egg yolks
2 teaspoons vanilla extract
½ cup plus 2 tablespoons
90- to 94-proof gin
2 cups heavy cream

See Note 2.

Scald the light cream in the top of a double boiler, uncovered, over hot water on moderate heat. When tiny bubbles begin to appear around the edge, or a slight skin forms on top, add the sugar and salt and stir to dissolve.

In a small bowl stir the egg yolks lightly with a fork just to mix. Very gradually, stirring with the fork, add about half of the hot cream to the yolks, and then add the yolks to the remaining cream in the top of the double boiler.

Replace over hot water on moderate heat and cook, stirring gently and scraping the pot with the rubber spatula, until custard thickens enough to coat a spoon (a scant 175 degrees on a candy thermometer).

Immediately transfer custard to a mixing bowl, or place top of double boiler in a bowl of ice and water to stop the cooking. Stir occasionally until custard is completely cool. Mix in the vanilla and gin.

In a chilled bowl with chilled beaters, whip the heavy cream only until it holds a soft shape, not stiff. Gradually, in several small additions, fold the cooled custard into the whipped cream. Gently pour back and forth from one bowl to another to insure thorough blending.

Pour into freezer trays, cover airtight, and freeze without stirring until it is firm.

NOTES: *1. Serve as you would vanilla ice cream. It is delicious as is, or with sliced and sugared fresh strawberries, or with any one of the chocolate sauces (pages 397–98).*

2. *Both Gin Ice Cream and Rum Raisin Ice Cream, which is a variation on it, are best made 6 to 12 hours before serving. If they stand longer than that there is a chance they might become granular and crystallized.*

Rum Raisin Ice Cream

See Note 2, above.

Soak ⅔ cup (3 ounces) dark raisins in ½ cup dark rum (80 proof) in a small, covered jar for several hours or overnight.

Follow above directions for Gin Ice Cream, omitting the gin. Substitute the raisins and rum and stir them into the cooled custard.

You will need three average-size, or one average- and one extra-large size ice-cube trays. When turning the mixture into the trays, spoon from the bottom to make sure that the raisins are equally distributed.

When the ice cream is slightly frozen—before it is actually firm—stir once gently, right in the tray, to keep the raisins evenly distributed.

Lime Sherbet

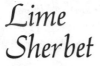

This recipe may be used for lemon sherbet, substituting lemon juice and yellow food coloring.

1 GENEROUS QUART

3 cups water
1¼ cups sugar
¾ cup light corn syrup
⅔ cup lime juice
optional: 3 drops green food coloring
2 egg whites
Pinch of salt

Combine water, 1 cup of the sugar (reserve remaining ¼ cup of sugar), and corn syrup in a saucepan. Stir over high heat to dissolve the sugar. Bring to a boil, reduce the heat to moderate, and let boil for 5 minutes without stirring. Remove from heat and let cool to room temperature. (May be hurried by setting saucepan in a bowl of ice and water.) Stir in lime juice and food coloring.

Pour into ice-cube trays or any shallow metal pan about 9 inches square. Place in freezer and freeze until firm throughout. Also freeze large bowl and beaters from electric mixer.

Remove lime mixture from freezer. Break up with a wooden spoon or spatula, and turn into frozen mixer bowl. With frozen beaters beat on low speed, scraping bowl with a rubber spatula and beating only until free from lumps. Work quickly and do not let the mixture start to melt. Immediately return to freezer right in the mixing bowl and refreeze until firm again. You may leave the beaters in the bowl, as they should be chilled, too, for the next beating.

When mixture is refrozen, beat the egg whites with the salt until slightly thickened. Gradually beat in reserved ¼ cup sugar and beat only until whites hold a definite shape, firm but not dry.

Remove lime mixture from freezer. Repeat breaking up and beating only until smoothly free from lumps. On lowest speed beat in beaten egg whites, beating very briefly only until whites are incorporated.

Immediately replace bowl of sherbet in the freezer, or return sherbet to ice-cube trays. Refreeze, folding gently two or three times during freezing, and folding all the way from the bottom up.

Serve when firm, or transfer to a deep covered container to store.

NOTE: *If you have made lemon sherbet, it is delicious with a little dark rum poured over each serving.*

Apricot Sherbet

2 QUARTS

2 cans, each 1 pound, 14 ounces,
    or 4 smaller cans, each 1 pound,
    1 ounce, apricot halves
¼ cup lemon juice
Scant ¼ teaspoon almond extract
1 cup sugar
4 egg whites
Pinch of salt

Drain the apricots, reserving the juice, and purée them in a food mill or press them through a strainer. Add enough of the juice to make 4 cups. Turn into a large bowl. Stir in the lemon juice, almond extract, and sugar.

Beat the whites with the salt until they hold a definite peak, but are not dry. Stir a cup of the apricot mixture into the whites and then stir and fold the whites into the remaining apricots.

Turn the sherbet into a large, shallow metal pan, or several ice-cube trays, and place in freezer. Also place large bowl of electric mixer and beaters in the freezer (or in the refrigerator, if there isn't room in the freezer).

When the sherbet has frozen solid around the edges and is mushy in the center, turn it into the cold bowl and beat it with the cold beaters until smooth and fluffy. Either return it to its original container or leave it in the mixing bowl. Freeze again until partly frozen. Beat again at high speed for 2 minutes. Turn it into a container or leave it in the bowl, cover, and freeze until firm.

NOTE: *About half an hour before serving remove the sherbet from the freezer and place it in the refrigerator so it can thaw a bit to the right consistency to serve.*

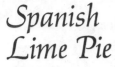

Spanish Lime Pie

8 PORTIONS

This is served frozen. If you wish, it may be made a few days ahead.

CRUST

1¼ cups graham cracker crumbs
1 tablespoon sugar
1 teaspoon cinnamon
3 ounces (¾ stick) melted butter

Adjust rack to center of oven and preheat to 375 degrees. Mix the graham cracker crumbs with the sugar and cinnamon. Add the melted butter. Stir with a rubber spatula, pressing the mixture against the sides of the bowl, until completely mixed. It will look crumbly but will hold together when pressed into place.

Use a 9-inch pie plate and follow crumb crust directions, page 284.

FILLING

Finely grated rind of 2 limes
1 cup lime juice
4 eggs, separated
2 15-ounce cans sweetened condensed milk
Pinch of salt

Mix the lime rind and juice. In a large mixing bowl, stir the yolks lightly with a small wire whisk or a fork just to mix. Gradually mix in the condensed milk. Very gradually add the rind and juice, stirring until smooth.

Add the salt to the whites and beat until they hold a point, or are stiff but not dry. In two or three additions, fold the whites into the yolk mixture.

The crust will not hold all of the filling. Pour in as much as the crust will hold without any running over. Reserve the balance at room temperature. Freeze the filled crust for about 20 minutes until semifirm. Then pour the balance of the filling on the top, mounding it high in the center. Return to freezer immediately. Freeze for 4 to 5 hours until firm. (May be frozen overnight or longer.) Let stand at room temperature 5 to 10 minutes before serving.

NOTE: *If a pie is to be kept frozen for any length of time: After it is frozen very firm, it may be covered with clear plastic wrap, but it must be com-*

pletely firm or the wrapping will stick and will spoil the looks. If that should happen, the top may be dusted lightly with a camouflage—grated chocolate, chopped nuts, or cookie crumbs.

French Ice-Cream Cake

In France, this is Biscuit Glacé au Grand Marnier. It may be made with bought ice cream, and is quite easy for such a fancy dessert. Must be made a day ahead.

8 PORTIONS

¾ cup candied orange peel, finely chopped
1 cup Grand Marnier
Ladyfingers, or sponge cake baked in a loaf pan
½ cup heavy cream
1 quart vanilla ice cream

In a small covered jar, marinate the orange peel in ½ cup of the Grand Marnier. (Reserve remaining ½ cup.) Let stand for an hour or so, or as much longer as you wish. Place large bowl and beaters from electric mixer in the freezer (or in the refrigerator if there isn't room in the freezer).

Line a loaf pan with a 2-quart capacity (11 × 5 × 3 inches) with one long piece of wax paper or aluminum foil to cover both long sides and the bottom and extend several inches above the top of the pan. It is not necessary to line the two short ends.

Line the long sides only with ladyfingers (round sides against the pan) or with ½-inch-thick slices of sponge cake, brushing both sides of each one with some of the reserved Grand Marnier before putting it in place. (Reserve some Grand Marnier for final layer of cake on top.) Do not place the cake or ladyfingers against the bottom or on the short ends of the pan.

In a chilled bowl with chilled beaters (not the ones in the freezer) whip the cream until it holds a soft shape.

Now, in the large chilled bowl, beat the ice cream briefly to soften slightly, beating only until smooth but not melted. Quickly, on lowest speed, mix in the whipped cream and the orange peel with its Grand Marnier marinade. Immediately pour into prepared pan and place in freezer.

Freeze for a few hours until slightly firm, and then cover top with a double or triple layer of ladyfingers, or sponge cake cut thicker than for the sides. Brush each layer generously with remaining Grand Marnier; use extra if you wish. Cover airtight and freeze overnight or longer.

To serve, cut around the two short ends to release, invert onto a chilled serving platter, remove pan and wax paper or aluminum foil, and replace in freezer.

OPTIONAL: *Shortly before serving, decorate the top with sweetened and flavored whipped cream, using a pastry bag and a star tube, or pass a bowl of whipped cream separately. Also, if you wish, serve with Honey Chocolate Sauce (page 398).*

Fresh Fruit, and Fruit and Ice-Cream Desserts

PREPARING ORANGES

FRESH FRUIT

APPLESAUCE

STEWED PEACHES

STEWED PEARS

POIRES HELENE

PECHES MELBA (*Maxim's*)

POIRES AU VIN ROUGE

BANANAS NIÇOISE

BANANAS CUBAINE

BAKED BANANAS

GLACEED STRAWBERRIES

BROOKFIELD CENTER
STRAWBERRIES

COUPE LONGCHAMPS

RASPBERRIES NIÇOISE

ORANGES IN RUM, CUBAN STYLE

ICE CREAM AMBROSIA

PINEAPPLE AND STRAWBERRIES
CREOLE

Preparing Oranges

Use large "in-season" oranges, preferably seedless—California navels or Florida temples.

To pare the rind: Use deep-colored oranges. Wash the fruit well. Use a vegetable peeler with a swivel blade to remove the colored, thin, outer rind. Do not press too hard or you will also be removing the white underskin, which is bitter. Try to make the pieces long instead of short.

To cut the rind in slivers: Use a long, heavy, sharp knife. Pile two or three long pieces of the rind on top of each other on a board. Hold the pieces in place with your left hand while cutting down firmly and sharply with your right, cutting into the thinnest and longest slivers possible. These are referred to as julienne.

To peel an orange (or grapefruit): Place it on a board on its side. With a very sharp, thin knife, cut off the top and the bottom. Turn the orange upright, resting on a flat end. Hold the orange with your left hand as you cut down toward the board with your right hand, curving around the orange and cutting away a strip of the peel—cut right to the orange itself in order not to leave any of the white underskin. Turn the orange a bit and cut away the next strip of peel. Continue all the way around the orange. After cutting all the way around, lift the orange and, holding it in the palm of your left hand, cut away any remaining white parts.

To section the orange (or grapefruit): Work over a bowl to catch the juice. With a small, thin, sharp knife, cut down against the inside of the membrane of one section on both sides, releasing the section and leaving the membrane.

After removing one or two sections, continue as follows: Cut against the membrane on one side of a section and then, without removing the knife, turn it up against the membrane on the other side of the section. The section will fall out clean. After removing all the sections, squeeze the leftover membrane in your hand for any juice. Carefully pick out any seeds in the sections; even seedless oranges frequently have them.

Fresh Fruit

As prepared at Le Cordon Bleu cooking school in Paris.

Use only ripe, in-season fruit—oranges, grapefruit, melons, apricots, peaches, pineapples, mangoes, berries, grapes, bananas—whichever are available. (See Note.)

Prepare the oranges and grapefruit according to the directions for sectioning oranges (page 375). Peel the peaches by dropping them very briefly in boiling water only until the skins can be peeled off with your fingers. Fifteen seconds is enough if the fruit is ripe. Cut up the large fruit in rather large pieces, but still only one bite—do not dice too small. Wash, hull if necessary, and drain the berries. If you are using bananas, don't peel or cut them until the last minute or they will darken. If the grapes have seeds, cut them in half the long way and pick out the seeds. Place all the fruit in a large bowl.

Prepare the following syrup:

SYRUP

(This is enough syrup for fruit
to serve 6 to 8 portions.)

1½ cups sugar
1 cup water
2–3 tablespoons kirsch

Stir the sugar and water in a small saucepan on moderate heat until it boils. Let it boil for 5 minutes. Remove from heat and cool slightly for just a few minutes. Stir the kirsch into the warm syrup. Pour the warm syrup over the fruit and stir gently to mix. Stir very carefully in order not to break up the fruit. Cover and refrigerate 1 to 2 hours or all day if you wish, stirring occasionally. Serve cold in chilled bowls or glasses.

At Le Cordon Bleu this fruit is prepared in scooped-out melon shells (from which the fruit is spooned out, cut up, and added to the other fruits). In Paris, very small melons are available so that each portion is served in an individual melon shell. Use chilled melons, cut off about one third from the top. Discard seeds. Remove fruit. Place the prepared fruit mixture in the shell and replace the top. Refrigerate. Serve with the melon tops on, on individual dessert plates, preferably placing the melons on large, flat, fresh green leaves.

The same procedure may be followed with larger melons (especially watermelon), serving the fruit at the table in chilled bowls or glasses.

If using watermelon, first find the flattest side for the bottom. Make sure it will stand firmly. Mark the upper third with a soft pencil and, with a very long, heavy, sharp knife, cut it off. Scoop out the fruit. If you wish, with a very sharp small knife cut the top edge in scallops or zigzag, first marking the pattern with a soft pencil. Cover the shell with a damp towel and then with plastic wrap. Refrigerate until serving time. Fill with prepared fruit immediately before serving. Place on a large platter and circle with fresh green leaves.

NOTE: *Preserved kumquats or Raffetto Old-Fashioned Cocktail Oranges are a nice addition to otherwise fresh fruit.*

Applesauce

6 CUPS APPLESAUCE

"Select fine-flavored apples" is a safe and common direction. The best way to accomplish this is to use apples when they are in season.

3 pounds apples (about 8 medium-large)
optional: 1 vanilla bean, 6–8 inches long
optional: 2 cinnamon sticks
Water
Sugar

Peel, quarter, and core the apples. Place them in a heavy saucepan. Slit the optional vanilla bean, scrape the seeds into the apples, and add the pod also. Add optional cinnamon sticks. Add about 2 cups of water, but the amount needed will depend on the apples. Additional water may be added later if needed, or excess water may be boiled down. Keep in mind that the applesauce thickens as it stands and is best if not too dry.

Cover and cook over moderate heat for 5 to 10 minutes until the apples begin to soften. Uncover and, with a heavy wooden spatula, stir and break up the apples. Leave some small chunky pieces. Continue to stir and mash, cooking only until tender but not completely mushy.

The amount of sugar needed will depend on the apples. Start with ¼ to ⅓ cup. Stir to dissolve. Taste and add more if necessary.

If you have not used the vanilla bean and cinnamon sticks, flavor with vanilla, powdered cinnamon, and/or nutmeg or mace, but with good apples go easy on the seasoning or you will hide the natural flavor.

If you have used vanilla bean and cinnamon sticks, do not remove them until serving time (they continue to give flavor), or, if the applesauce is being served from a glass bowl, they may be left in just for looks.

Stewed Peaches

6 large freestone peaches, ripe but firm
1½ cups water
1 cup sugar
1 vanilla bean, 6–8 inches long

6 PEACHES

To peel the peaches: Have ready a large bowl of ice-cold water, a slotted spoon, and a saucepan of boiling water deep enough to cover the peaches.

With the slotted spoon, place the peaches in the boiling water, two or three at a time. If the peaches are fully ripe they will need only about 15 seconds in the boiling water; if not quite ripe they will need more. With the slotted spoon, raise a peach from the boiling water and move your thumb firmly over the skin. If the skin has loosened enough it will wrinkle and feel loose from the fruit. At that point transfer to the ice water.

Peel with your fingers, starting at the stem end, and return the peeled fruit to the ice water. Partially peeled peaches may be returned to the boiling water for additional boiling if necessary. Continue blanching and peeling the remaining peaches.

In a saucepan large enough to hold the peaches in a single layer, place the water and sugar. Slit the vanilla bean and scrape the seeds into the water; add the pod also. Bring to a boil, stirring, and let boil about 5 minutes to make a syrup. With the slotted spoon, add the peaches and adjust the heat so that the syrup simmers gently. Cook covered, turning the peaches a few times with two rubber spatulas in order not to mar them. Baste occasionally with the syrup.

Test for doneness with a cake tester. Do not overcook. When just barely tender, transfer peaches gently with the slotted spoon to a large, wide bowl or casserole.

Raise the heat and boil the syrup rapidly for a few minutes to reduce slightly. Taste the syrup, and continue to boil until it tastes right—sweet enough and not watery. Pour the hot syrup over the peaches. Do not remove the vanilla bean. Set aside to cool, basting occasionally with the syrup.

Cover with plastic wrap or transfer to a covered icebox container. Refrigerate and serve very cold.

Serve in dessert bowls with a generous amount of the syrup.

Stewed Pears

Peel the pears as for Poires au Vin Rouge (page 380). Prepare the same syrup as for Stewed Peaches (page 378). Poach the pears, covered, until tender. Remove from syrup. Reduce the syrup as in the recipe for Stewed Peaches and pour over the pears. Cool and then chill, occasionally spooning the syrup over the pears.

Poires Hélène

On each chilled dessert plate, place a scoop of vanilla ice cream and a drained stewed pear. Separately, pass Plain Old-Fashioned Chocolate Sauce (page 397, Note), or any other chocolate sauce, either slightly warm or at room temperature.

Pêches Melba
(Maxim's)

Stewed Peaches (page 378)
Vanilla ice cream
Fresh Raspberry Sauce, Raspberry Sauce,
    or Sauce Melba (pages 392, 393)
Toasted, sliced almonds (page 35, Note)

The peaches should be stewed only until barely tender; they should remain slightly firm.

For each portion: On a chilled, flat dessert plate, place a scoop of vanilla ice cream and a drained, whole, stewed peach. Top with either Fresh Raspberry Sauce, Raspberry Sauce, or Sauce Melba, and sprinkle lightly with toasted, sliced almonds.

At Maxim's in Paris, this is served with whole, fresh raspberries, *not* a sauce. I prefer either of the above sauces, or thawed and partially drained frozen raspberries, or simply a purée of fresh raspberries. If you use frozen berries, plan it so that they have just barely thawed at serving time—they are much better than if they stand after thawing. Serve with a dessert spoon and a fork.

Poires au Vin Rouge

6 PEARS

3 cups water
Juice of 1 large lemon
6 large pears, firm but ripe
2 cups dry red wine
1 cup sugar
1 vanilla bean, 6–8 inches long

In a bowl large enough to hold the pears, place 3 cups of cold water and half of the lemon juice.

Use a vegetable peeler with a swivel blade to peel the pears, leaving the stems on. If necessary, slice a little off the bottoms so they can stand upright. As you peel them, place them in the cold, acidulated water.

In a saucepan large enough to hold the pears in a single layer, mix the wine, sugar, and remaining lemon juice. Slit the vanilla bean, scrape the seeds into the wine, and add the pod also. Bring to a boil and boil for about 5 minutes to make a syrup. Transfer pears from acidulated water to the syrup. Adjust the heat for the syrup just to simmer. Cook covered, occasionally turning the pears gently from side to side with two rubber spatulas in order not to bruise the pears. Baste occasionally with the syrup.

Test for doneness with a cake tester. They must be tender all the way to the core, but do not overcook. When done, with a slotted spoon carefully transfer the pears to a large, wide bowl or casserole, standing them upright.

Raise the heat and boil the syrup rapidly for a few minutes to reduce slightly. Pour the hot syrup over the pears. Do not remove the vanilla bean, as it continues to flavor the syrup—and it looks great. Set aside to cool, occasionally spooning the syrup over the pears. Cover with plastic wrap or gently transfer to a covered icebox container. Refrigerate and serve very cold. Serve individually in dessert bowls with a generous amount of the syrup.

NOTE: *If you wish, 2 to 3 tablespoons of Cognac or kirsch may be stirred into the cooled syrup.*

Bananas Niçoise

This lovely, simple dessert must be prepared immediately before serving, but it takes only a few minutes.

Use bananas that are fully ripe, but not overripe or mushy. Peel and slice into ½-inch-thick rounds. Place the slices in a wide, shallow bowl. For each small banana sprinkle on 2 teaspoons kirsch and 2 tablespoons heavy, sweet cream. If bananas are large, use a bit more kirsch and cream. Stir briefly and gently with a rubber spatula, coating each slice with the sauce. Let stand for just a few minutes and the cream will thicken slightly.

Serve immediately in shallow dessert bowls or flared glasses (champagne or double-martini glasses).

Plan on 1 to 1½ bananas per person.

Bananas Cubaine

Follow above directions, substituting dark rum for the kirsch. Fill an ice-cream scoop half full with coffee ice cream and the other half chocolate ice cream. (May be prepared ahead of time and frozen.) Place ice cream in chilled dessert bowls or large wide glasses and cover generously with prepared bananas.

Baked Bananas

6 PORTIONS

6 large, ripe but firm bananas
3–4 tablespoons lime juice
½ cup dark rum
½ cup brown sugar, strained if lumpy
2 tablespoons butter

Adjust oven rack high in the oven. Preheat oven to 400 degrees. Butter a shallow baking dish just large enough to hold the bananas; it should not be larger.

Peel the bananas. Cut each one into three pieces, cutting on a sharp angle. Arrange the pieces in the baking dish. Sprinkle with lime juice and ¼ cup rum. (Reserve remaining ¼ cup.) Sprinkle with sugar and dot with butter (most easily done with frozen butter).

Bake for 10 to 15 minutes, gently turning the bananas and basting them once or twice.

Heat the reserved rum in a small metal cup. Bring to the table immediately. Pour the rum over the bananas and immediately touch with a match to flambé.

As soon as the flame goes out, serve on warm dessert plates or with ice cream.

Glacéed Strawberries

Created by Chef Albert Stockli
for the Four Seasons restaurant in New York.

At the Four Seasons these are not served as a dessert, but they come with after-dinner coffee on silver pedestal platters. Although they represent the height of elegance, they are quite quick and easy to make.

The berries are coated with a paper-thin layer of clear, shiny glaze, as crisp and brittle as glass. They are eaten with the fingers, and biting through the crisp coating and the soft sweet berry together is an exquisite experience.

Make them only at the height of the strawberry season, when giant berries are available. They must be perfect berries with no soft spots. Ideally, the strawberries should have long stems, but since I am never able to get berries with long stems, and only occasionally with short stems, I use stemless berries.

Glacéed Strawberries must be made as close to serving time as possible. They should not wait for more than 1 hour or the glazed coating will start to melt. They should, if possible, be made on a dry day. You must use a candy thermometer.

1–2 dozen large strawberries
2 cups sugar
½ cup water
1 tablespoon light corn syrup
⅛ teaspoon cream of tartar
1 teaspoon water

Do not wash the berries but instead brush them gently with a soft, dry pastry brush. Pat and wipe them lightly with a soft towel. Place them on paper toweling on a tray in the refrigerator.

Also prepare another tray, this one covered with aluminum foil, for the berries after they have been glazed.

In a heavy 2-quart saucepan mix the sugar, ½ cup water, and corn syrup. Bring to a boil over moderate heat, stirring occasionally. Mix cream of tartar with 1 teaspoon water and stir into syrup. Raise the heat to high. Place a candy thermometer in the saucepan and let the syrup boil without stirring until the temperature reaches 290 degrees (the hard-crack stage). Immediately remove from heat. Work quickly. Holding a cold strawberry by the stem, or raising the leaves enough so that you can hold them, carefully dip the strawberry into the syrup to coat it thoroughly, except for the stem or leaves. Remove quickly and hold over the saucepan to let the excess syrup run off. (If this is not done carefully enough there will be too heavy a coating of the glaze around the base of the berry.) Place on its side on the aluminum foil. Repeat with remaining berries, refrigerating the glazed berries as quickly as possible.

Leave the thermometer in the saucepan while you are working. Reheat the syrup if necessary to maintain a temperature of 290 to 300 degrees. Work quickly before the syrup becomes dark—it affects the taste.

Keep the berries refrigerated until serving time, which should be just as soon as possible.

If you can do it, serve two or three berries per person. But these are such a rare treat that even one or two will be appreciated.

NOTE: *Incidentally, I do serve these as dessert, along with a light cake or some fancy cookies.*

Brook-field Center Straw-berries

Quickly wash fresh strawberries in cold water. Remove the green leaves, drain thoroughly, and slice each berry lengthwise into three or four slices. Refrigerate and serve very cold in individual bowls with a generous topping very cold Custard Sauce (page 389), or any of the custard sauces in the next section except chocolate. Pass the sauce separately. For more than three or four people, double the sauce recipe.

When strawberries are really good, this is one of the finest of all desserts.

Coupe Long-champs

This may be made with either of the raspberry sauces (page 392 or 393), or with Sauce Melba (page 393), or with bought Melba sauce. Stir a few spoonfuls of kirsch or maraschino into the sauce. In well-chilled parfait glasses, tulip champagne glasses, or large wine glasses alternate generous layers of coffee ice cream and raspberry sherbet with thin layers of the sauce. Freeze until serving time. Before serving decorate with whipped cream.

If you have candied violets or rose petals, place them sparingly on top.

Rasp-berries Niçoise

Fresh raspberries
Vanilla ice cream
Strawberry Topping (page 392)

It is not necessary to wash the raspberries.

In each chilled, individual dessert bowl, or in a large wine glass, place a scoop of ice cream. Circle with the raspberries and top generously with the Strawberry Topping.

Oranges in Rum, Cuban Style

4 TO 6 PORTIONS

6 large seedless oranges
2 tablespoons sugar
¼ cup dark rum
⅓ cup guava jelly, red currant jelly, or marmalade

Peel and section the oranges (page 375). Place the sections in a wide bowl. Sprinkle with the sugar and rum. Turn gently to mix and let stand for about 1 hour, turning occasionally. Drain the fruit and reserve the syrup.

Over moderate heat stir the jelly or marmalade to soften. When smooth, mix it with the reserved syrup and pour over the orange sections.

Cover and refrigerate, stirring occasionally.

Serve in large brandy snifters or wine glasses which have been in the freezer for about ½ hour. Serve quickly while glasses are still frosty.

NOTE: *In Havana each portion was topped with a few small pieces of guava paste.*

Ice Cream Ambrosia

Vanilla ice cream
Grated coconut (See Note.)
Oranges in Rum, Cuban Style (page 385)

In each chilled dessert bowl, large brandy snifter, or wine glass, place a scoop of vanilla ice cream. Top generously with grated coconut. Circle with the Oranges in Rum, Cuban Style.

NOTE: *This is best if made with fresh coconut, which is now frequently available in many frozen-food sections. If you use canned or packaged coconut, try to get that which is moist-pack, and preferably unsweetened.*

Pineapple and Straw- berries Creole

4 TO 6 GENEROUS
PORTIONS

1 ripe pineapple
3–4 tablespoons kirsch
Sugar
Strawberry Topping (page 392)

Peel the pineapple. Cut lengthwise into quarters and remove the core. Cut each quarter lengthwise into very thin slices. Place them on a large flat tray. Sprinkle with the kirsch and a bit of sugar, about 2 to 3 tablespoons depending on the sweetness of the pineapple. Cover and refrigerate.

On each chilled, flat dessert plate, place several overlapping slices of pineapple. Spoon a generous ribbon of the Strawberry Topping across the pineapple slices. Serve with a knife and fork.

Sauces

CUSTARD SAUCE
RUM CREAM SAUCE
GRAND MARNIER CUSTARD SAUCE
CHOCOLATE CUSTARD SAUCE
LEMON CUSTARD SAUCE

RICH CUSTARD SAUCE
RICH BOURBON OR RUM SAUCE

APRICOT SAUCE

STRAWBERRY TOPPING

FRESH RASPBERRY SAUCE

RASPBERRY SAUCE

SAUCE MELBA

SUZETTE SAUCE

FORTNUM AND MASON SAUCE

BOURBON-HONEY SAUCE
FROM MISSISSIPPI

BUTTERED RUM SAUCE
OLD-FASHIONED LEMON SAUCE

GINGER CREAM

OLD-FASHIONED
WALNUT-CHOCOLATE SAUCE

BITTERSWEET CHOCOLATE SAUCE

HONEY CHOCOLATE SAUCE

HOT FUDGE SAUCE

COFFEE SAUCE

PEANUT BUTTER SAUCE
CHARLIE BROWN SUNDAE

Many of the recipes in this book suggest which sauce to serve with them. But instead of saying after each sauce recipe "serve with fruit" or whatever—and as I don't really have any cut-and-dried rules about it—I suggest that you experiment and try your own combinations.

A jar or two of good sauce is a joy to have on hand. Served with ice cream or fruit, or both, you have a quick special dessert. Or try some of these with pound cake, or sponge cake, or un-iced chocolate cake squares. The combinations are endless and delicious.

Custard Sauce

1 cup milk
1 cup light cream
4 egg yolks
½ cup sugar
Pinch of salt
1 teaspoon vanilla extract

2⅔ CUPS
OF SAUCE

In a heavy saucepan over moderate heat, scald the milk and cream.

Meanwhile, in the top of a large double boiler off the heat, stir the yolks lightly with a small wire whisk just to mix. Gradually stir in the sugar and salt.

When you see steam rising from the milk and cream, a wrinkled skin forming on top, or tiny bubbles around the edge, remove it from the heat and very gradually stir it into the yolks.

Place over hot water, which must not touch the upper section of the double boiler and should be simmering gently, not boiling hard.

Stir the custard mixture constantly with a rubber spatula, scraping the sides and the bottom of the pot until the mixture thickens slightly or will coat a metal spoon. (This rather difficult moment to ascertain is easy with a candy thermometer: 180 degrees. It might take about 10 minutes.)

Remove from heat immediately to stop the cooking and strain into a bowl or container. Stir in the vanilla.

Cool uncovered, stirring occasionally. When cool, if sauce is not absolutely smooth, strain again through a fine strainer. Cover and refrigerate. Serve very cold. Stir briefly before serving.

NOTE: *To use a vanilla bean instead of the extract: Slit a 6- to 8-inch vanilla bean the long way. Scrape the seeds into the milk and cream and add the pod, also, before scalding. Leave it in until the sauce is strained.*

Rum Cream Sauce

Whip ½ cup of heavy cream. Gradually fold in 1 cup of cooled Custard Sauce (above) or Rich Custard Sauce (page 391) and 3 tablespoons of dark rum.*

* Other liquors or liqueurs may be substituted and you may use either more or less, to taste.

Grand Marnier Custard Sauce

Prepare the preceding recipe for Custard Sauce, substituting ¾ cup heavy cream for the 1 cup light cream. When cool, stir in 3 tablespoons Grand Marnier.*

Chocolate Custard Sauce

Prepare the preceding recipe for Custard Sauce with the following addition:

Before scalding the milk and cream, add 6 ounces of coarsely cut-up sweet or semisweet chocolate. Cook, stirring occasionally with a small wire whisk, until the chocolate is melted and the mixture is smooth. Continue to cook, stirring occasionally, until the mixture comes almost to a boil.

Continue with the rest of the recipe as is.

Chill 8 hours or overnight.

OPTIONAL: *Stir about 1 tablespoon (or a bit more to taste) dark rum into the cooled sauce.*

Lemon Custard Sauce

Prepare the preceding recipe for Custard Sauce but eliminate the vanilla. Cool the sauce to tepid, then stir in 3 tablespoons of lemon juice. Cool completely, cover, and refrigerate.

* Other liquors or liqueurs may be substituted and you may use either more or less, to taste.

Rich Custard Sauce

1½ CUPS
OF SAUCE

1 cup light cream
6 egg yolks
¼ cup sugar
Pinch of salt
1 teaspoon vanilla extract

Using above ingredients, follow the procedure and directions for previous Custard Sauce. However, due to the large amount of egg yolk in this recipe, it will thicken at a lower temperature, or at about 168 to 170 degrees.

This should be strained through a fine strainer, stirred frequently until cool, and then, if not absolutely smooth, it should be strained again through a fine strainer. Cover and refrigerate. Stir briefly before serving. Serve very cold.

Rich Bourbon or Rum Sauce

Stir 2 tablespoons of bourbon or dark rum into the above Rich Custard Sauce.

Apricot Sauce

1 GENEROUS CUP
OF SAUCE

1 cup apricot preserves
1 tablespoon water
¼ cup light or dark rum, or kirsch

In a small saucepan or skillet over moderate heat, stir the preserves and water until preserves are melted and come to a boil.

Remove from heat. Stir in the rum or kirsch and press through a strainer.

May be served warm or at room temperature. (This may also be kept refrigerated and warmed just slightly before serving.)

Strawberry Topping

2 CUPS OF SAUCE

1 pint strawberries
¼ cup sugar
2–3 tablespoons curaçao, kirsch, Cointreau,
    or Grand Marnier

Rinse the berries briefly in cold water. Pick off the stems and leaves and drain thoroughly on toweling. Slice each berry lengthwise in about three slices and place in a large bowl. Sprinkle with sugar and turn gently with a rubber spatula. Add liqueur to taste and mix gently. Cover and let stand at room temperature for 1 hour, stirring gently a few times. Refrigerate for at least 1 hour or more.

Serve generously over ice cream, custard, pudding, or sliced fresh peaches.

Fresh Raspberry Sauce

1½ CUPS
OF SAUCE

2 cups raspberries
2 tablespoons sugar
1 teaspoon lemon juice

Either mash and force the berries through a large strainer, or purée them in a food mill and then strain to remove seeds. Mix in sugar and lemon juice. Refrigerate. Serve cold.

NOTE: *This may either be a smooth sauce, as above, or you may reserve a few whole berries to stir in.*

Rasp- berry Sauce

2½ CUPS
OF SAUCE

2 packages (10 ounces each)
     frozen raspberries
¼ cup sugar
2 tablespoons cornstarch
Pinch of salt
¼ teaspoon almond extract

Thaw berries, drain them, and reserve the syrup. Add enough water to the syrup to make 1½ cups. In a medium-size saucepan mix sugar, cornstarch, and salt. Gradually add syrup and water mixture, stirring with a rubber spatula until smooth. Cook over medium heat, stirring slowly and constantly with the rubber spatula. Stir gently, do not beat. When the mixture thickens and begins to turn somewhat transparent and has just barely come to the boil, let it simmer gently for 1 or 2 minutes. Remove from the heat. (Overcooking or overbeating would thin the sauce.) Add almond extract and gently stir in the drained raspberries.

Refrigerate and serve cold.

Sauce Melba

Fresh raspberries
Red currant jelly

For every 2 cups of raspberries use about ⅓ cup of jelly.

Either mash and force the berries through a strainer, or purée in a food mill and then strain to remove seeds.

Stir the jelly over moderate heat to melt. When smooth, mix with the raspberry purée. Chill and serve cold.

Suzette Sauce

This will keep almost indefinitely in the refrigerator.

1¼ CUPS SAUCE

1 orange
½ lemon
3 tablespoons sugar
2 tablespoons butter
1 ounce (2 tablespoons) each kirsch,
    rum, marashino liqueur,
    curaçao

Pare and sliver the orange rind following directions on page 375. Place in saucepan. Squeeze the juice of the orange and the half lemon and add to saucepan. Add sugar and stir over moderate heat to bring to a boil. Simmer for about 10 minutes. Add butter and stir until butter is melted. Add kirsch, rum, maraschino, and curaçao. Bring to a boil and remove from heat immediately.

    Serve warm.

Fortnum and Mason Sauce

2 CUPS OF SAUCE

2 large, bright-colored oranges (See Note.)
12 ounces (1 cup) red currant jelly
1 tablespoon lemon juice
¼ teaspoon cinnamon
¼ cup curaçao or Grand Marnier
2 tablespoons dark rum

Use a vegetable peeler with a swivel blade to peel the very thin, orange-colored rind of the oranges—it must be thin. Squeeze the oranges to make ⅔ cup of juice and set aside. Cut the rind into slivers, following directions for paring the rind and cutting it into slivers (page 375). Place in a saucepan with the ⅔ cup of orange juice, currant jelly, lemon juice, and cinnamon.

Cook over moderate heat, stirring occasionally, until mixture comes to a boil. Adjust heat so that the sauce simmers slowly. Simmer uncovered without stirring for 15 minutes. Remove from heat and set aside to cool.

Stir in curaçao or Grand Marnier and rum. Refrigerate and serve cold.

Serve over vanilla ice cream, orange sections, or a combination of both.

NOTE: *The sauce will be bitter if the oranges are greenish, or if they are pared too deeply.*

Bourbon-Honey Sauce from Mississippi

Simply mix ¼ cup bourbon into ½ cup honey. Bourbon may be increased or decreased to your taste, but this is not meant to be a mildly flavored sauce. Make it strong or don't make it. (Rum may be used in place of bourbon.)

Try it over coffee ice cream with a sprinkling of toasted, sliced almonds.

Buttered Rum Sauce

1⅓ CUPS OF SAUCE

½ cup sugar
1 tablespoon plus 1 teaspoon cornstarch
⅛ teaspoon salt
1 cup hot water
2 tablespoons butter, at room temperature
2 tablespoons heavy cream
1 teaspoon vanilla extract
2 tablespoons dark rum

Mix the sugar, cornstarch, and salt in a rather small, heavy saucepan. Gradually stir in the water. Cook over moderate heat, stirring gently and constantly with a rubber spatula, for about 5 minutes until mixture is thick and clear. (Overbeating or overcooking would thin the sauce.)

Remove from heat. Add the butter and stir gently until it has melted. Stir in the cream, vanilla, and rum.

Serve warm, at room temperature, or refrigerated.

Old-Fashioned Lemon Sauce

Follow the preceding recipe for Buttered Rum Sauce with the following changes:

Eliminate the heavy cream, vanilla, and rum. In their places substitute the finely grated rind of 1 lemon and 2 tablespoons of lemon juice.

Ginger Cream

2 CUPS

1 cup heavy cream
2 tablespoons confectioners sugar
½ teaspoon vanilla extract
2 tablespoons Grand Marnier or curaçao
2 tablespoons crystallized ginger,
        very finely cut,
        or drained preserved ginger

In a chilled bowl with chilled beaters, whip the cream, sugar, vanilla, and Grand Marnier or curaçao only until the mixture holds a soft shape. Fold in the ginger.

Old-Fashioned Walnut-Chocolate Sauce

½ cup light cream
1 cup sugar
2 ounces (2 squares) unsweetened chocolate
2 ounces (2 squares) semisweet chocolate
¼ pound (½ cup) butter
2 egg yolks
1 teaspoon vanilla extract
3½ ounces (1 cup) walnuts, coarsely cut or broken

3 CUPS OF SAUCE

Place the cream and sugar in a heavy 1½- to 2-quart saucepan on moderate heat. Stir with a rubber spatula, scraping the sides of the pan, to dissolve the sugar and bring the mixture to a boil.

Add both chocolates and the butter. Cook, stirring with a small wire whisk, until very smooth. Remove from heat.

In a small bowl stir the egg yolks briefly just to mix. Gradually stir in a few spoonfuls of the chocolate mixture and then stir the egg yolks into remaining chocolate mixture.

Cook over low heat, stirring gently and scraping the saucepan with the rubber spatula, for 3 minutes. Remove from heat.

Stir in the vanilla and walnuts.

Serve slightly warm or at room temperature.

This sauce may be kept warm over warm (not hot) water, stirring occasionally. It may be refrigerated and then reheated over warm water.

NOTE: *To prepare Plain Old-Fashioned Chocolate Sauce follow above recipe, eliminating the walnuts. This will make 2 cups of sauce.*

Bitter-sweet Chocolate Sauce

1⅓ CUPS OF SAUCE

½ cup heavy cream
¼ cup sugar
4 ounces (4 squares) unsweetened chocolate
½ cup apricot preserves
2 tablespoons Grand Marnier, bourbon, or rum

Place cream, sugar, chocolate, and preserves in the top of a small double boiler. Place over hot water on low heat. Cook, stirring constantly, until everything is melted.

Remove top of double boiler. Stir in Grand Marnier, bourbon, or rum. Press through a fine strainer.

Serve hot or warm. This thick sauce will thicken even more as it cools.

NOTE: *The sweetness may be adjusted by substituting sweet or semisweet chocolate for all or part of the unsweetened chocolate. It is an equally lovely sauce either way.*

Honey Chocolate Sauce

1 CUP OF SAUCE

1 ounce (1 square) unsweetened chocolate
1 ounce (1 square) semisweet chocolate
¼ cup honey
½ cup heavy cream
Finely grated rind of ½ large orange
2 tablespoons rum, dark or light

In a small, heavy saucepan over moderate heat, bring both chocolates, honey, and cream to a boil, stirring occasionally with a small wire whisk. Reduce heat and, stirring constantly, simmer for 2 to 3 minutes. Stir in the orange rind.

Remove from heat. Cool to tepid and stir in the rum. Serve at room temperature.

NOTE: *This may be refrigerated or frozen. If it is frozen, it should be stirred briefly over hot water to soften.*

Hot Fudge Sauce

A note of warning before you serve this sauce to grandparents or dainty ladies: As soon as this sauce touches cold ice cream it turns to chewy, caramel-like fudge, most especially appreciated by teenagers or others with strong teeth.

1 CUP
OF SAUCE

2 ounces (2 squares) unsweetened chocolate
1 tablespoon butter
⅓ cup boiling water
2 tablespoons light corn syrup
1 cup sugar
1 teaspoon vanilla extract

Place the chocolate, butter, and boiling water in a 1½-quart saucepan. Cook over low heat, stirring until the chocolate is melted and the mixture is smooth. Mix in the corn syrup and sugar.

Raise heat to moderate and stir occasionally until it comes to a boil. *Stop stirring* and let boil moderately for *exactly* 8 minutes. Remove from heat and immediately place saucepan briefly in cold water in order to stop the boiling. Stir in the vanilla.

Use sauce while it is still warm, or let it cool and reheat over hot water. This may be refrigerated and then reheated. It must be served warm, as it hardens when it is cold.

Coffee Sauce

1⅔ CUPS
OF SAUCE

1⅓ cups sugar
⅛ teaspoon salt
1 tablespoon plus ½ teaspoon instant coffee
⅓ cup light corn syrup
⅔ cup boiling water
1 tablespoon butter
1 teaspoon vanilla extract

In a 2½- to 3-quart saucepan, mix the sugar, salt, and instant coffee. Gradually mix in the corn syrup and then the boiling water.

Cook, stirring, over high heat, until the mixture comes to a boil. Reduce the heat slightly and continue to boil without stirring for about 10 minutes, until slightly thickened (about 228 degrees on a candy thermometer). Mixture will boil up high; if necessary, adjust heat so that it doesn't boil over.

Remove from heat. Add butter and stir until dissolved. Place the bottom of the saucepan briefly in cold water to stop the cooking. Set aside and cool completely without stirring.

When cool, with a spoon remove the skin that will have formed on top. Stir in vanilla.

Serve warm or at room temperature. May be reheated.

Peanut Butter Sauce

1 ¼ CUPS
OF SAUCE

1 cup sugar
1 tablespoon light corn syrup
⅛ teaspoon salt
¾ cup milk
2 tablespoons butter
⅓ cup smooth peanut butter
½ teaspoon vanilla extract

In a 6- to 8-cup heavy saucepan, mix the sugar, corn syrup, salt, and milk. Stir over moderate heat until mixture comes to a boil. Insert a candy thermometer. Adjust heat so that the sauce boils gently, and let boil without stirring for 30 to 40 minutes or until the temperature registers 225 to 228 degrees. The sauce will have caramelized to a light golden color.

Remove from heat. Add butter and peanut butter. Stir briskly with a small wire whisk until smooth. Stir in the vanilla. Serve warm.

Sauce may be kept warm, or reheated, in the top of a small double boiler over hot water on moderate heat, stirring occasionally.

NOTE: *Over cold ice cream the sauce thickens to a hard caramel consistency.*

Charlie Brown Sundae

Serve warm Peanut Butter Sauce over vanilla ice cream and top generously with coarsely chopped salted peanuts.

Or, for a Charlie Brown Banana Split, place ice cream over a banana, split the long way. Top with whipped cream, chopped peanuts, and Peanut Butter Sauce.

Et Cetera

PEANUT BRITTLE

HOMEMADE APRICOT PRESERVES

HONEY BUTTER

CANDIED GRAPEFRUIT RIND

CHOCOLATE CONES

CHOCOLATE LEAVES

CHOCOLATE SLABS

GRATED CHOCOLATE AND
    CHOCOLATE CURLS

CHOCOLATE CIGARETTES

Peanut Brittle

This is not the usual peanut brittle. It is solid peanuts with barely enough brittle to hold them together. You will need a candy thermometer to make this.

2½ POUNDS
OF VERY
SOLID PEANUT
BRITTLE

1 pound (4 cups) dry-roasted, salted peanuts

1½ cups light brown sugar, firmly packed

1 cup light corn syrup

⅓ cup water

2 tablespoons butter, cut into 6 or 8 pieces

1 teaspoon vanilla extract

Adjust rack to center of oven. Preheat oven to 350 degrees. Butter a 14 × 17-inch cookie sheet and set it aside. Also butter the blade of a large wooden spatula or the back of a large, heavy wooden spoon and set aside.

Place the peanuts in a large shallow pan and bake for 5 minutes, stirring them once or twice. Turn off oven heat but let nuts remain in oven to keep warm.

In a 3-quart heavy saucepan over high heat, stir the sugar, corn syrup, and water until the sugar is dissolved. Place a candy thermometer in the syrup and continue to cook without stirring until the temperature reaches 275 degrees. Reduce the heat to moderate and continue to cook until the temperature reaches 290 degrees.

Immediately remove from heat. Work quickly. With a large wooden spoon or spatula (not the buttered one) stir in the butter, vanilla, and warm peanuts. Instantly turn out onto the buttered cookie sheet. Now use the buttered spatula or spoon to spread and flatten the candy. The mixture will be quite firm. It will take considerable pressure to flatten it. Press as hard as you can to press the peanuts into a single layer.

Let the peanut brittle cool to room temperature, then with a wide metal spatula remove it from the cookie sheet in one piece. Wipe the bottom with a paper towel to absorb the butter. Break the candy into large pieces. Immediately store airtight.

NOTE: *It is easy to remove the caramelized sugar from the utensils. Simply place them in the sink and let hot water run onto them until the sugar dissolves and washes away.*

Home-made Apricot Preserves

1 QUART

Marvelous as these preserves are, they should not be used for recipes calling for apricot preserves to be made into a glaze. This doesn't have enough pectin to set or dry firmly. Use a commercial brand.

1 pound dried apricots
2½ cups water
½ cup sugar

In a heavy saucepan with a tight cover, over high heat, bring the apricots and water to a boil. Reduce heat to low and let apricots simmer, covered, until they are very tender—about half an hour, depending on the apricots. The fruit should be very soft. The water should be partially but not completely absorbed.

Stir and mash vigorously with a wooden spatula, or press with a potato masher to break up the fruit somewhat, leaving some chunky pieces. Add the sugar and stir briefly to dissolve. Some apricots are more tart than others. Taste. If necessary add a bit more sugar, but this is best if it is not too sweet.

Remove from heat to cool. Pack in a covered container and refrigerate.

NOTES: 1. *Do not wash fruit unless necessary, in which case rinse quickly under cold running water.*

2. *Refrigerated this will keep indefinitely. If the preserves become too thick after a time in the refrigerator, just stir in a bit of water to correct consistency.*

Honey Butter

For each ¼ pound butter, use ⅓–½ cup honey, depending on your taste and the strength of the honey—some honeys have a stronger flavor than others. Cream the butter and gradually add the honey, beating until smooth. Pack in a crock, jar, or individual butter dishes. Refrigerate until firm. May be refrigerated for a week or so, or may be frozen.

Serve with toast, as you would serve butter, or with pancakes, waffles, or popovers.

Candied Grapefruit Rind

ABOUT 2½ POUNDS

3 large, thick-skinned grapefruits
(*The very thick-skinned fruit is best for candying, although it might mean a bit more work to get it dry enough.*)

Sugar

The grapefruit rind may be left over from serving half grapefruits. If so, remove all membranes but leave underskin on peel. Or, using whole grapefruit, cut through the skin and white underskin, cutting from top to bottom in large wedges. Peel off the rind and slice each wedge the long way into pieces about ½ inch wide at widest point.

Place the rind in a large saucepan. Pour boiling water over it to cover. Boil for 5 minutes. Drain and repeat three more times, using fresh boiling water each time (four waters, or blanchings, in all).

In a wide, deep frying pan, mix 2½ cups of sugar and 1½ cups of water. Place over high heat and stir until sugar dissolves. Let boil until syrup spins a thread (230 to 234 degrees on a candy thremometer). Add the drained peel. Stir well. Reduce heat so that syrup boils gently. Stir occasionally and let simmer, partially covered, for about 1 hour until peels are tender and have absorbed almost all of the syrup. Place peels in a single layer on a large piece of aluminum foil.

Place 2 to 3 cups of sugar in a shallow bowl or tray and roll each piece of warm peel in the sugar. Then place on cake racks and let stand overnight at room temperature to dry.

If peel is still a little too wet, let it stand longer until dry. But if it is still very wet, place the racks on cookie sheets in an oven set at the lowest temperature for 30 minutes to 1 hour, but no longer than necessary. This is best when still moist inside. Reroll in sugar and let stand again to cool.

Store airtight.

Chocolate Cones

Both these and the following Chocolate Leaves may be made in quantity and kept refrigerated or frozen—a fun way to spend a spare hour or so. Place them on a shallow tray, cover airtight, and place in a safe spot—they are very fragile.

Cut wax paper into squares measuring 4 to 5 inches. The smaller they are, the more elegant, and the more difficult to handle. Cut each square in half to form two triangles. Form each triangle into a cone by rolling two outer points, one after the other, to center point and double-folding to secure (see illustrations). The tip must be tightly closed or the chocolate will run out.

In the top of a small double boiler over hot water on low heat, melt a few squares (depending on the number of cones) of semisweet chocolate. Remove the chocolate from the heat before it is completely melted. Stir until completely smooth. With a small, pointed paring knife, spread the inside of a cone with the chocolate. Coat it completely, making sure not to leave any holes in the chocolate. (If the chocolate begins to harden while working with it, replace over warm water for a few minutes.) Place on a small plate and place in the freezer or refrigerator for a few minutes only until the chocolate is completely set and firm. Then gently, with a light touch, carefully peel off the wax paper, handling the cone as little as possible. The cones may then be frozen or refrigerated.

Chocolate Cones are used as a decoration. Generally, they are placed on a cake before the icing is dry—one cone to a portion. Place them on their sides with open ends pointing out and pointed ends toward the center. They may also be used on top of whipped cream on icebox cakes or other desserts. But do not use on nonrefrigerated desserts in a warm room or they might melt. They hold up perfectly in an air-conditioned room.

Resist the temptation to fill them with a squirt of whipped cream or buttercream; it would hide their thinness and delicacy.

Chocolate Cones are exquisite and make an elegant and exciting presentation. If you are handy, you will find them easy to make and great fun. The following chocolate leaves are an equally beautiful creation, considerably easier to make.

Chocolate
Leaves

You may use any fresh, green leaves, preferably gardenia, ivy, or rose leaves. In choosing leaves, try to pick those that are firm (if leaf is too thin and delicate it will tear while being peeled away from the chocolate) and have the most markedly raised veins on the back. Separate the leaves, keeping enough stem on each one to hold it by. Wash and dry thoroughly, patting both sides with a towel.

In a small double boiler over hot water on low heat, melt a few squares (depending on the number of leaves) of semisweet chocolate. Remove from heat before completely melted. Stir until completely smooth.

Hold a leaf in your left hand, upside down. With a small metal spatula spread a thin layer of the chocolate over the underside (or veined side) of the leaf. Be careful not to let the chocolate run onto the reverse side of the leaf. With a fingertip, wipe the edges of the reverse side to make sure there is no chocolate there. (If the chocolate begins to harden while working with it, replace it over warm water.) Place the leaf, chocolate side up, on a small plate in the freezer or refrigerator for a few minutes only until the chocolate is completely set and firm. Then, gently and carefully, peel away the green leaf, starting at the stem end and handling the chocolate leaf as little as possible. Immediately put the leaf on a plate or small tray. The chocolate leaves may be refrigerated or frozen.

If the green leaf has not torn it may be reused.

Chocolate leaves may be used to top any dessert, standing them on an angle or placing them flat on whipped cream, cake icing, or ice cream.

Chocolate
Slabs

Melt 2 or 3 squares of chocolate as directed in preceding recipe. While it is melting, cover a cookie sheet with wax paper. Stir the chocolate until smooth and then turn it out onto the wax paper. With a long, narrow metal spatula spread the chocolate very, very thin. Do not worry about making it perfectly smooth, and do not fuss with the edges. Work quickly, spreading the chocolate thin before it starts to harden. Place the sheet in the freezer (or in the refrigerator if there isn't room in the freezer).

When you are ready to use it, remove from freezer. Quickly bend the paper backward to break the chocolate into large, irregular slabs. Handling the chocolate as little as possible, let the slabs fall haphazardly directly on the dessert.

Chocolate slabs may be used on top of cake icing before it has hardened, and they are especially attractive on top of whipped cream.

Work quickly. These wafer-thin chocolates will melt quickly, which is all right after they have been placed on a dessert—but a mess if they melt in your hands.

Grated
Chocolate
and
Chocolate
Curls

Grated chocolate may be made with a coarse grater or with a swivel-bladed vegetable peeler. Very finely grated chocolate may be made in a small Mouli rotary grater. Use any chocolate you wish. Grate the chocolate over paper, then use a spoon to sprinkle it over the dessert. It may be stored in a container at room temperature.

Chocolate curls are very "iffy." If the chocolate is very fresh and if the room is not too cool and if you use just the right amount of pressure, they may possibly be formed with a swivel-bladed vegetable peeler. Use a square of semisweet chocolate. Work over paper or directly over the dessert. Cut downward firmly against a smooth side of the chocolate.

The beautiful, long, thin, cigarettelike chocolate curls, or the shiny little fat ones that one sees on elegant desserts in fine pastry shops and restaurants, or in titillating, mouth-watering photographs, are made with a commercial chocolate unhappily available only from bakery supply stores in 10-pound slabs. It generally contains a higher percentage of cocoa butter, so it is more flexible and behaves beautifully. I don't know any substitute. I can only suggest that you use chocolate leaves, cones, slabs, or grated chocolate, all of which can be made with easily available semisweet chocolate.

Chocolate Cigarettes

These are long, thin curls of chocolate that are used as a decoration. They are very professional.

To make chocolate cigarettes: coarsely chop about 8 ounces of Stollwerk's or Wilbur's Chocolate (see page 5). Melt it slowly over hot water. When partially melted, remove from hot water and stir until completely melted. Pour onto a marble work surface (or a large marble cheese board), forming a ribbon about 3 to 4 inches wide and 10 inches long. The chocolate will be about ¼ to ⅜ inch thick. Let cool at room temperature until it is no longer soft or sticky.

To make the curls use a long, heavy knife—I use a Sabatier cook's knife with a 12-inch blade. Hold it at a 45-degree angle across the width and right near the end of the chocolate. Cut down slowly and firmly. The chocolate will roll around itself as it is cut. Repeat, each time placing the blade very close to the cut end—the curls should be paper thin. Transfer them with a wide metal spatula to a shallow tray. Cover with plastic wrap and store either at room temperature if it is not too warm, or in the refrigerator or freezer.

NOTE: *If the room is too cold or if the chocolate stands too long it might not curl or it could crack when you form the cigarettes.*

Index

G

H

I

Icing(s)
  for Black Velvet, 278
  brown sugar, for Buttermilk Spice
    Cake, 114
  caramelized sugar, for Date-Nut
    Cake Squares, 90
  chocolate
    bittersweet, for Small Walnut
      Torte, 38
    for Rum Cream Layer Cake, 69
    for Sponge Cake, 110
  for Chocolate Cake Squares, 53, 55
  for Chocolate Cupcakes, 234
  for Chocolate Pound Cake, 141
  coffee buttercream, for Royal Vien-
    nese Walnut Torte, 43
  for Dobosh Torte, 27
  fluffy white, for Coconut Layer
    Cake, 72
  fudge, for Fudge Cake with Fudge,
    56
  Java, for Java Cake, 131
  for Mocha Pecan Torte, 45
  for Palm Beach Chocolate Layer
    Cake, 60
  for Palm Beach Chocolate Tube
    Cake, 61
  for Pecan-Chocolate Bars, 174
  for Queen Mother's Cake, 31
  rum chocolate buttercream, for
    Rum Chocolate Layer Cake,
    71
  seven-minute
    caramel coffee, for Montana
      Mountain Cake, 66
    for Devil's Food Cake, 64
  for Sour Cream Chocolate Layer
    Cake, 63
  for Truffles Torte, 33
  see also Glazes; Toppings
Indian River Sweet Orange Bread,
  120

Ingredients
  dry, to add alternately with liquid,
    19
  liquid, to add alternately with dry,
    19
  notes on, 3–12
  and procedures, note on, 19
Irish Almond Cakes, 228
Irish Coffee Jelly, 356
Italian Pine-Nut Macaroons, 160

J

Java Cake, 130
Jean Hewitt's Old-Fashioned Lemon
  Ice Cream, 359
Jelly Cookies, Swedish, 199
Jelly Slices, Swedish, 198

K

Kentucky Chocolate Icebox Cake
  with Bourbon, 269
Kentucky Pound Cake, 138
Kuchen
  Apple, 102
  Cottage Cheese, 312
  Walnut-Peach, 100
Kumquat(s)
  Chocolate Applesauce Torte with,
    36
  cream, for Chocolate Applesauce
    Torte with Kumquats, 37

L

Ladyfingers, 205
Lemon

A Note
About
the Author

Maida Heatter, daughter of Gabriel Heatter the radio commentator, has been cooking all her life. She studied fashion illustration at Pratt Institute and has done fashion illustrating and designing, made jewelry and painted, but her first love has remained cooking. For eight years she prepared all the desserts for Inside, a popular Miami Beach restaurant once owned by her husband, Ralph Daniels, and has also taught cooking classes in her home and given demonstrations in department stores.

Ms. Heatter has one daughter, Toni Evins, a painter and illustrator, who has done the drawings for Maida Heatter's Book of Great Desserts.

A Note on the Type

The text of this book was set in Electra, a type face designed by William Addison Dwiggins for the Mergenthaler Linotype Company and first made available in 1935. Electra cannot be classified as either "modern" or "old-style." It is not based on any historical model, and hence does not echo any particular period or style of type design. It avoids the extreme contrast between thick and thin elements that marks most modern faces, and is without eccentricities that catch the eye and interfere with reading. In general, Electra is a simple, readable typeface that attempts to give a feeling of fluidity, power, and speed.

W. A. Dwiggins (1880–1956) began an association with the Mergenthaler Linotype Company in 1929 and over the next twenty-seven years designed a number of book types which include the Metro series, Electra, Caledonia, Eldorado, and Falcon.

Composed by The Book Press, Brattleboro, Vt. Printed and bound by Haddon Craftsmen, Inc., Scranton, Pa. Typography and binding design by Virginia Tan. Cover photograph by Irwin Horowitz.